A Companion
to the
Alternative Service Book

A Companion to the Alternative Service Book

R. C. D. Jasper and Paul F. Bradshaw

First published in Great Britain 1986
SPCK
Holy Trinity Church
Marylebone Road
London NW1 4DU

British Library Cataloguing in Publication Data
Jasper, Ronald C.D.
A companion to The alternative service book.
1. Church of England. Alternative service book
2. Church of England—Liturgy
I. Title   II. Bradshaw, Paul F.
264'.03   BX5141

ISBN 0–281–04202–0

Photoset by Tradespools Ltd, Frome, Somerset
Printed in Great Britain at the
University Press, Cambridge

CONTENTS

INTRODUCTION

In November 1980 the services and other material in The Alternative Service Book were authorized for use in the first instance for ten years. Since then the General Synod of the Church of England has extended that use for a further decade. It is clear, however, that by the end of the present century all the contents of the book will have to be examined in the light of experience with a view either to improvement or to replacement. Inevitably there will be some change: and that is as it should be. Liturgy must be flexible. But come what may, the book now has a place in the liturgical history of the Church of England: and whatever form future services may take, they will be a continuation of, development from, or reaction against those which now exist. It therefore seems wise to attempt to give some account of the book and the way it came into being and to see where it stands in the light of previous Anglican Prayer Books, and of the earlier traditions of Christian worship.

When the ASB was due to appear, the Liturgical Commission was conscious of the immediate need of some guide or handbook to enable both clergy and laity—to quote the Archbishops of Canterbury and York—'to study the Service Book with care, and to enable them to use it profitably for their own spiritual well-being' (Foreword to ASB Commentary). It therefore produced a Commentary which, though admirable in many ways, was all too brief and was written with considerable speed. The present volume is now intended as a more comprehensive replacement, written rather less hurriedly, and making use of a great deal of valuable material which appeared over the years in a series of reports to the General Synod and its predecessors, some of which had a limited circulation and virtually all of which are now out of print. It attempts to fulfil for ASB a role similar to that served by Procter and Frere for 1662.

Obviously the volume is limited in scope, a limitation imposed to some extent by economic considerations. These are difficult days for publishing; and we are both amazed and grateful for the amount of space which SPCK has been able to allow us. But we have felt it wise, in the first place, to concentrate on what has happened in the Church of England, and not to attempt a wide-ranging comparative study, setting the ASB in a context of international liturgical development, both Anglican and non-Anglican. To have produced a book on those lines would have resulted in something massive and complicated: and in any case new service books still continue to appear. It has already taken Colin Buchanan three large volumes to examine Anglican Eucharistic Liturgies alone since 1958, for example. Studies such as this clearly merit separate treatment. But while we have not attempted a wide-ranging study, we have at least indicated the Church of England's indebtedness to the work of other Churches in a variety of fields.

Secondly, a great deal more could have been said on the way the ASB has evolved, particularly over the last quarter of a century, producing in far greater detail what the Preface to the Liturgical Commission's Commentary says so admirably and succinctly. But again this merits separate treatment; and hopefully a volume on this subject will appear in the not too distant future.

Thirdly, we have not discussed the question of liturgical language. This too merits a separate study—or indeed a whole series of studies; for work on the subject has hardly yet begun. In many respects the language of ASB is still quite conservative. Apart from addressing God as 'You' instead of 'Thou', there has been little fundamental change. The imagery employed has been traditional: collects and prayers still appear in the traditional form, with much of their traditional language and phraseology: and Professor David Frost has indicated that the ASB still conforms to the laws of classical rhetoric ('Liturgical Language from Cranmer to Series 3', in *The Eucharist Today*, ed. R. C. D. Jasper, 1974). Yet the fact has to be faced that the contemporary Church is placed in the situation of conducting public services in an age which lacks a public rhetoric to engage people in large numbers emotionally, intellectually, and spiritually. Is it enough simply to remain nostalgically with the familiar rhythms and rhetorical devices of a Prayer Book nearly 450 years old? Is it enough to remain with the imagery of such a book? Opinions are divided. Do we need to forge a new rhetoric within the tradition of Christian worship, yet open to the developments of the English language as a whole in the late twentieth century? If we do need this, we have hardly begun to consider the matter in any depth. A companion to the ASB is hardly the place to explore such a vast and complicated subject.

Nor again did we feel it right to provide a complete commentary on the Liturgical Psalter. This is another subject demanding separate detailed treatment. We have therefore confined ourselves to indicating only the more significant changes which have been made: and in this we are particularly grateful for the help and advice of the Rev. Andrew Macintosh.

Finally, we would like to thank all those who have helped us in any way with the production of this volume. To the publishers, for considerable patience and understanding; to those who have struggled with the typescript, particularly Mrs M. Carrington; to a number of friends who have given help and advice on points of detail; and to our long-suffering wives and families, who have endured the monopoly of our time with considerable forebearance.

ABBREVIATIONS

ARCIC   Anglican–Roman Catholic International Commission

ASB   The Alternative Service Book 1980

AV   The Authorized Version

CSI   The Church of South India

DBL   *Documents of the Baptismal Liturgy* (E. C. Whitaker, 1970)

ICET   International Consultation on English Texts

JB   The Jerusalem Bible

JEH   *Journal of Ecclesiastical History*

JLG   The Joint Liturgical Group

JTS   *Journal of Theological Studies*

LEW   *Liturgies Eastern and Western* (F. E. Brightman, 1896)

NEB   The New English Bible

PEER   *Prayers of the Eucharist: Early and Reformed* (R. C. D. Jasper and G. J. Cuming, 1975)

RP   The Revised Psalter

RSV   The Revised Standard Version

RV   The Revised Version

SJT   *Scottish Journal of Theology*

SL   *Studia Liturgica*

SP   *Studia Patristica*

TEV   Today's English Version

1
Services and Service Books:
An Historical Introduction

General Studies:
J. G. Davies, (ed.), *A Dictionary of Liturgy and Worship*. 1972, 2nd edn 1986.
Duncan Forrester, James McDonald, Gian Tellini, *Encounter with God*.
  Edinburgh 1983.
Cheslyn Jones, Geoffrey Wainwright, Edward Yarnold, (eds), *The Study of Liturgy*. 1978.
James F. White, *Introduction to Christian Worship*. Nashville 1980.

1 The Old Testament and Jewish Background

Jewish worship in New Testament times was still centred around the sacrificial cult of the Temple at Jerusalem, as it had been for centuries. There offerings were made for the nation every day, morning and evening, and additional sacrifices were offered on Sabbaths and festivals. For the majority of people, however, such worship was rather distant, and did not really impinge on them, except at the annual festivals when they might go up in pilgrimage to Jerusalem, or at other important points in their lives. For most Jews, therefore, worship centred around the home and the synagogue. In the home, prayers would be said at regular times during the day and before all meals, and special ceremonies were associated with the Sabbath and other festal occasions. The precise origins of the synagogue are uncertain, but it probably came into existence during or after the exile in Babylon in the sixth century BC, and it provided a place both for the study and proclamation of the Law (and eventually of the prophetic writings too), and also for regular acts of corporate worship.

At this period Jewish worship was still fluid in its nature: the broad outlines of its rituals and practices were established, but there were no written forms or service books, and different communities followed their own inherited traditions, often with quite significant liturgical variations from one another. Moreover, even within these conventions individuals were generally still free

1

to vary the wording of prayers and the details of ceremonial observances. Only in later centuries did a measure of uniformity emerge. There was therefore nothing particularly heretical or remarkable in groups of early Jewish Christians forming themselves into a distinct liturgical assembly or synagogue of their own, with their own distinctive pattern of worship. Other Jewish groups had already done something similar, most notably the Essenes, who regarded the worship of the Temple as corrupt and had withdrawn from all association with it, evolving instead their own system of worship and waiting for the coming of the Messiah. A large number of them lived a communal life at Qumran, and were responsible for the composition of the writings known to us as the Dead Sea Scrolls.

Studies:
Joseph Heinemann, *Prayer in the Talmud.* Berlin 1977.
H. H. Rowley, *Worship in Ancient Israel.* 1967.

2 *The New Testament*

Since both Jesus and the first Christian converts were themselves Jews, it is hardly surprising that one of the main influences on the shape of early Christian worship was the worship of Judaism, especially as the Christian faith was viewed by its adherents not as an alternative to the Jewish religion but as its proper fulfilment. We have no liturgical texts from this earliest period of Christian worship, not merely because none have survived but because the Christians apparently adhered to the Jewish custom of not writing down their prayers but of transmitting the tradition orally. We have to rely for our information, therefore, on our knowledge of Jewish practice of the time, which is itself limited, and on the brief references and allusions to worship in the New Testament. The result is that, although by this means we can learn something of what early Christian worship was like, we cannot reconstruct it as fully as we would like to be able to do. What does emerge from the New Testament, however, is the strongly eschatological character of primitive Christianity: it was a movement which expected the imminent return of Christ and the fulfilment of the kingdom of God, and hence its worship and ritual practices were all powerfully shaped by this fact. This is shown, for example, by the nature of the Lord's Prayer itself ('your kingdom come, your will be done').

Studies:
Roger T. Beckwith, 'The Daily and Weekly Worship of the Primitive Church in relation to its Jewish Antecedents' (*Evangelical Quarterly* 1984), pp. 64–80, 138–58.
G. Delling, *Worship in the New Testament*. 1962.
F. Hahn, *The Worship of the Early Church*. Philadelphia 1973.
R. P. Martin, *Worship in the Early Church*. Revised edn, 1974.
C. F. D. Moule, *Worship in the New Testament*. 1961, reissued 1978.

3 The Didache

In addition to the New Testament evidence, there is one source which may be able to shed some light on first-century Christian worship, and that is a document entitled the *Didache* or 'Teaching of the Twelve Apostles'. Written in Greek, it was rediscovered in 1873. In spite of the claim of its title, however, it is highly improbable that its contents are directly derived from the Apostles, and scholars are divided over its date and place of origin. There is also uncertainty as to whether it represents an authentic part of the development of mainstream Christianity or a more remote offshoot from the Christian movement. Some believe it does originate from the later part of the first century, but others would assign it to the second or even the third century. Some would judge that it comes from Egypt, others from Palestine or Syria. Thus it may only be used very cautiously as a witness to the early Christian tradition.

Text:
English translation in Maxwell Staniforth, *Early Christian Writings* (1968), pp. 225–37.

Studies:
F. E. Vokes, *The Riddle of the Didache*. 1938.
— 'The Didache still debated' (*Church Quarterly* 3, 1970), pp. 57–62.

4 The Second and Third Centuries

In this period information about Christian liturgical practice is more plentiful. There are descriptions and allusions in a number of Christian writings, notably those of Justin Martyr at Rome around AD 165, and Tertullian and Cyprian in North Africa in the third century. Even so, there are many details about which we lack certainty. The general impression which emerges, however, is that Christian worship did not develop as a single organized whole, but, as in Judaism, with a number of variant traditions in different geographical areas, and with considerable liberty of improvisation and adaptation being exercised. Earlier generations of scholars tended to search for an archetypal 'apostolic liturgy', believing that, behind the accretions of later centuries, there was a common nucleus which could be traced back to New Testament times. More recently scholars have recognized the existence of greater diversity in the practice of the early centuries, and have suggested that what was common was an archetypal shape or structure of the rites. Yet it is now emerging that even this cannot be accepted without some qualification: more variations in structure between different communities are beginning to be detected from the evidence, suggesting much more pluriformity in development from New Testament times.

5 The Apostolic Tradition of Hippolytus

Because of the relative paucity of other material, this document has come to be treated as a crucial source of information about the worship of the early Church. It consists of a collection of directions concerning the liturgical life of a community, including the text of many prayers, among them those for the Eucharist, for the Initiation rites, and for Ordination services. The original Greek version has not survived, and has to be reconstructed from an extant Latin translation, and from later Coptic, Arabic and Ethiopic versions, as well as from the use made of it by compilers of later liturgical documents. In the nineteenth century it was known as *The Egyptian Church Order*, but it was identified with the otherwise missing work of Hippolytus early in the twentieth century, and is now generally thought of as having originated in Rome around 215, though some scholars would still adhere to the view that it reflects the liturgical practice of Alexandria. Others have conjectured that the later translators may have deliberately emended the text so as to make it conform more closely with the practices of their own day and geographical location. Such uncertainties suggest that more caution is needed in using this as an historical source than has frequently been shown.

Texts and Studies:
'Classic' reconstruction by Gregory Dix, *The Treatise on the Apostolic Tradition of St Hippolytus of Rome* (1937; 2nd edn, with preface and corrections by Henry Chadwick, 1968); better version by Bernard Botte, *La Tradition Apostolique de Saint Hippolyte* (Munster 1963); English translation based on this edition by G. J. Cuming, *Hippolytus: A Text for Students* (1976); see also G. J. Cuming (ed.), *Essays on Hippolytus* (1978).

6 Worship in the post-Constantinian Era

After the conversion of the Roman Emperor Constantine to the Christian faith in 313, the situation of the Church changed quite dramatically. No longer merely a tolerated sect, constantly exposed to the risk of sporadic persecution, it now became the established religion of the Empire, and large numbers rushed to join the Church now that it was not only respectable but also possibly advantageous to be a Christian. This inevitably had a profound effect upon the nature of the Church's worship, though one must be careful not to overstate this, as has often been done in the past. Many of the developments which can be seen at this period have roots reaching back well into the third century, when in many places the Church was already quite comfortably settled in society and undergoing a transformation from its earlier outlook and practices. Hence in these respects the so-called Constantinian revolution served more to intensify an already existing trend than to initiate one. Nevertheless, it is in general true that a marked contrast can be observed between the worship of the pre-Constantinian and post-Constantinian periods.

There were, first of all, the consequences of the movement from private to public worship. Whereas the first Christians saw themselves as set over against the world, and were careful to avoid any compromise with paganism and its ways, stressing rather what distinguished Christianity from other religions, the Church now emerged as a public institution within the world, its liturgy functioning as a *cultus publicus*, seeking the divine favour to secure the well-being of the state. Thus paganism was no longer viewed as a threat; the old division between the 'public' and 'private' elements in the liturgy disappeared; and the Church was quite willing to absorb and Christianize pagan religious ideas and ritual practices, seeing itself as the fulfilment to which the earlier religions had dimly pointed. Thus, for example, one finds the introduction into Christian liturgy of the common language, style and imagery of contemporary religious prayers; the use of such things as blessed salt, and the burning of incense; and the taking over of sacred places as sites for Christian churches, and of pagan festivals as occasions for Christian feasts, with the inevitable dangers of syncretism which this brought.

Secondly, there were the effects of the growth in size of Christian communities, which meant that the relatively informal, intimate, quasi-domestic character of much pre-Nicene liturgy inevitably had to give way to much more formally structured services, taking place now in specially constructed church build-ings instead of the private houses more generally used in earlier centuries. As a result of this, elements of the ceremonial of the imperial court were assimilated into Christian worship, as it provided the natural model for a style of liturgical practice more appropriate for these larger assemblies. Because of the corporate understanding of worship inherited from the past, there was at first a considerable reluctance to divide the congregation into smaller units as it grew in size, and even when this became inevitable, attempts continued to be made in some places to link together the different congregations in some way. However, one of the more significant consequences of the expansion in the number of separate congregations was that the liturgy was no longer under the regular presidency of the bishop in most places.

Thirdly, there was a growing clericalization of the liturgy and a decline in lay participation. The catechetical system was unable to cope with the great increase in numbers, and so very many of those entering the Church in the wake of the Constantinian peace were only half-converted barbarians with little understanding of the true meaning of the Christian mysteries, who brought with them attitudes and behaviour inherited from their pagan past. This led to a widening gulf between the liturgical roles of the clergy and laity, and although the theory of liturgy as a corporate action survived for several centuries, as time went on less and less of an active or vocal part was left to the laity, and they began to be little more than spectators of the professionals who performed the liturgy on their behalf.

Studies:

J. G. Davies, 'The Introduction of the Numinous into the Liturgy: an Historical Note' (*SL* 8, 1970/71), pp. 216–23.
— *The Origin and Development of Early Christian Architecture.* 1952.
J. A. Jungmann, *The Early Liturgy to the time of Gregory the Great.* 1960.

7 *The Emergence of Liturgical Texts*

Not least as a consequence of the fear of the introduction of heretical teaching into liturgical formulations, the freedom of individual liturgical presidents and of local communities to extemporize prayer began to be curtailed to some extent by the regulations of provincial synods seeking to enforce conformity to alleged doctrinal and liturgical norms. Frequently it was insisted that any prayers used should be written down and subjected to the scrutiny of others. Although the composition of new prayers and formularies continued for several centuries under these conditions, it eventually declined virtually to the point of extinction, and ministers became expected to use traditional, agreed texts.

At first, the tendency seems to have been to write down single prayers—as for example the Eucharistic Prayer of the community—or collections of prayers for the presiding minister to use at various services and occasions, whilst allowing the remainder of the rite to continue to develop freely. The nearest thing at this time to the complete text of a service, including directions or 'rubrics' as they were later called as well as prayers, were the 'Church Orders' which flourished for a while in the East. These were similar to the *Apostolic Tradition* of Hippolytus, and usually drew upon that as a major source, and they include the so-called *Canons of Hippolytus* from Egypt and the *Apostolic Constitutions* from Syria, both fourth-century documents.

The emergence of written liturgical texts in turn encouraged a growing standardization of liturgy, not only within a particular geographical area but also to a considerable extent between different areas. Travellers and pilgrims visiting the hallowed sites of primitive Christianity were able to observe the diverse traditions of other Christian groups, and tended to adopt them in their own countries, so that there was thus a mutual interchange of liturgical practices, and this promoted a greater measure of uniformity. For example, Syria adopted the Western practice of post-baptismal anointing, while the West took over the Syrian baptismal formula; and the East added the Western feast of the Nativity to its liturgical year, while the West absorbed the Eastern feast of the Epiphany. Some differences between geographical areas still remained, however, and distinct 'families' of rites, each stemming from a particular region, can be discerned, but the variations between them are concerned with relatively superficial features rather than with fundamentals, and the more extensive pluriformity which seems to have existed in the preceding centuries disappeared.

8 Eastern Rites

In the East at least three main groups or families of liturgical rites may be distinguished. There is, first of all, the West Syrian type, which originated from the great liturgical centres of Jerusalem and Antioch. From this source are ultimately descended such contemporary Eastern rites as the Jacobite, Maronite, Armenian, and even the Byzantine rite itself, which is practised by the Greek and Russian Orthodox Churches. Although this last rite stems from Constantinople, or Byzantium as it was once called, yet because that city had no special ecclesiastical importance until the Council of Constantinople in 381 recognized it as the New Rome, it had no indigenous liturgical tradition and was thus dependent upon Antioch and to a lesser extent Cappadocia for the principal features of its worship. Later the prestige which it enjoyed enabled it to influence and finally supplant all other local rites of Orthodox churches in the East, just as the Roman rite did in the West. Secondly, there is the East Syrian family, which because of geographical and political factors developed in relative isolation from the West Syrian rites. To this type belong the Nestorian and Chaldean rites. Thirdly, there is the Egyptian or Alexandrian family, which includes the Coptic and Ethiopian rites.

Our knowledge of the historical development of Eastern liturgy is somewhat limited because of the fact that nearly all the liturgical texts which we possess are of a relatively late date when the various rites had already achieved what are substantially their present forms; and therefore attempts to reconstruct their earlier history and stages of evolution have to be rather tentative, and depend to a considerable extent on commentaries and other writings about liturgical practice from the earlier period. The oldest text of the Byzantine eucharistic rite, for example, dates from the end of the ·eighth century, and the texts of many other rites are much later than that.

In the course of their history, Eastern rites have accumulated much peripheral material, and frequently absorbed within a single service elements which were originally intended as alternative forms to one another, with the result that they are very long and repetitive, with a profusion of symbolic elaboration of what were formerly merely utilitarian actions. Because of the conservative nature of the tradition, however, they have often succeeded in preserving beneath the layers of later accretions many features of primitive Christian worship, even if only in a vestigial form, which have disappeared from Western rites. Moreover, unlike the West, the language of the liturgy has remained in the vernacular, even if in most places it has become archaic in the course of time and somewhat removed from the normal form of contemporary speech.

9 The Medieval West

Western rites may be divided into two main groups, the practice of Rome itself, which was followed throughout southern Italy, and the non-Roman family of rites. The latter may be further subdivided into the Ambrosian rite, stemming from Milan and practised throughout northern Italy; the Gallican rite, practised in France; the Mozarabic rite, practised in Spain; and the Celtic rite of the British Isles.

At first these various traditions evolved in relative independence. However, it was not long before they began to exercise a mutual influence upon one another. There was also a natural tendency for the churches of the West to turn to Rome as the ancient and apostolic centre of Christianity in that part of the world for authoritative guidance in matters of liturgical practice, and for missionaries from Rome to carry their own way of doing things into the countries to which they went. This was the way in which, for example, the Roman rite gradually supplanted the Celtic tradition in the British Isles. In the Franco-German empire rulers such as Pepin and his son Charlemagne in the eighth century tried to impose the Roman usage throughout their realm for both religious and political motives. In this process, however, a considerable element of intermingling took place between the imported Roman liturgical material and the indigenous Gallican tradition, so that what resulted was not the pure Roman rite but a form enriched and modified by Gallican elements. The ironical consequence of this was that at the end of the tenth century, when liturgical life at Rome had sunk to a very low ebb, it was revitalized by the importation of this Gallicanized version of its own rite. Thus what eventually spread throughout the West in the later part of the Middle Ages was this mixed form of the Roman liturgy, which supplanted native traditions but gathered to itself local variations and customs wherever it went, so that there was

substantial similarity everywhere but not total uniformity anywhere. In England, for example, in addition to the different
customs followed in each of the various monastic traditions
represented here, there were minor variations between different
diocesan centres, though the use of Sarum (Salisbury) was
particularly influential.

In the early Middle Ages the tendency was to provide separate
liturgical books for the different ministers involved in the celebration of a rite, each containing the parts of the service needed by
that person. Thus the bishop or priest presiding over a liturgical
rite would have had a *Sacramentary* containing the prayers he was
to say; those responsible for the readings at a service would have
had a *Lectionary*, which would have indicated the beginnings and
endings of the passages to be read; the singers would have had an
Antiphonary containing the musical parts of the service; and, at
Rome at any rate, the ceremonial directions for the rite were
contained in an *Ordo*. It was much later before it became general
practice for the whole of a service, texts and rubrics, to be
included in a single volume, and this came about largely as a result
of the decline of the corporate celebration of liturgy and the
growth of the practice of a single minister conducting the whole
rite. Ordinary lay people did not usually have a copy of the service
at all, partly because of the illiteracy of most people, partly
because of the high cost of copying out texts by hand, and partly
because liturgy had by now become something done by the clergy
on behalf of the people, who were expected to occupy themselves
meanwhile with their own private devotions. On the other hand,
books of suitable devotions, or 'Primers' as they were called, were
produced in the late Middle Ages for those lay people who were
able to read and to afford their cost.

10 The Reformation

The rejection of medieval doctrines by the Reformers necessarily
demanded a reformation in worship, for much of the teaching
which they regarded as a corruption of pure Christianity was
embodied and expressed in liturgical rites and practices. They
sought to return to the model of the worship of the New
Testament period, but because of the limitations of their scholarship and historical perspective, they were only able to do this to a
limited extent, and in some ways were as much victims and heirs
of medieval ways of thinking and acting as they were Reformers.

With regard to the ceremonial of worship, most Reformers tried to make a distinction between those things which they considered to be commanded by God in the New Testament, as for example the eating of bread and drinking of wine in the Eucharist or the pouring of water in the name of the Trinity in baptism, and those things which they regarded as merely human additions to the essential nucleus. They believed that the former had necessarily to be observed but the latter should be critically examined: if the practices were contrary to the gospel or encouraged superstition, then they should be abolished; but if they served a valuable purpose, then they might be kept (see for example 'Of ceremonies, why some be abolished and some retained' in the Book of Common Prayer). Some extreme Reformers, however, regarded anything which they judged was not explicitly commanded in Scripture to be inadmissible in Christian worship.

Fundamental features of Reformation worship were the use of the vernacular and the restoration of the ministry of the word to a prominent place, chiefly through the preaching and expounding of Scripture and through the inclusion within the services of the reading of long passages of doctrinal instruction and moral exhortation. With the exception of extreme Reformers, who believed that prayers which were read from a book were not real prayers at all, the majority were not opposed to set forms of liturgy. Indeed fixed orders of service and prescribed texts were valuable instruments in ensuring that what was said and done in each congregation really was 'pure' and did not contain objectionable features. Although, therefore, they did tend to allow some freedom to individual ministers in shaping worship, the Reformers continued to produce orders of service as models to be followed, and thus the recent invention of printing was an important factor in enabling the Reformation ideas to be disseminated effectively and the orthodoxy of its worship to be controlled.

Studies:

J. M. Barkley, *The Worship of the Reformed Church*. 1966.

H. G. Hageman, *Pulpit and Table: some chapters in the history of worship in the Reformed Church*. Richmond, Virginia 1962.

H. O. Old, *The Patristic Roots of Reformed Worship*. Zürich 1975.

Luther D. Reed, *The Lutheran Liturgy*. Philadelphia 1947.

V. Vajta, *Luther on Worship*. Philadelphia 1958.

11 The Church of England

Studies:
The standard textbook is by G. J. Cuming, *A History of Anglican Liturgy* (2nd edn 1982), which contains a comprehensive bibliography. See also G. J. Cuming, *The Godly Order* (1983). A shorter introduction is provided by D. E. W. Harrison and Michael C. Sansom, *Worship in the Church of England* (1982). Rich background material is offered in the substantial work by Horton Davies, *Worship and Theology in England* (5 vols, Princeton 1961–76). Older studies still having value include F. Procter and W. H. Frere, *A New History of the Book of Common Prayer* (1901), and W. K. Lowther Clarke (ed.), *Liturgy and Worship* (1932).

Reformation proceeded very slowly in England, for although Henry VIII had broken with Rome in 1532, he remained as solidly opposed to any major doctrinal or liturgical changes as he had been before. The first noticeable influence of the Protestant Reformation on worship, therefore, was in the use of the vernacular. Material for private devotions, including a number of Primers, appeared in English in the 1530s, and gradually elements of public worship also came to be translated. In 1537 Edward Lee, Archbishop of York, ordered the liturgical Gospels to be read in English in his diocese. In 1538 injunctions were issued which required an English Bible to be set up in every church in the land, so that it might be read outside services; incumbents were to recite the Creed, the Lord's Prayer, and the Ten Commandments in English to their people, so that they might learn them; and no one was to be admitted to communion until he/she could recite them. In 1543 the English Bible began to be used liturgically, when it was ordered that every Sunday and holy day one chapter of it was to be read aloud, without exposition, after the Te Deum at Mattins and after the Magnificat at Vespers. Then in 1544 an English form of the Litany appeared, from which the the invocation of the saints was almost entirely purged and many other changes made. By a Royal Injunction of October 1545 it was to be used every Sunday and holy day.

When Edward VI, then only nine years old, came to the throne in January 1547 after Henry's death, Thomas Cranmer, Archbishop of Canterbury, could at last begin to put into effect the doctrinal and liturgical reforms which he desired. In July 1547 a book of homilies was issued by royal authority, and in August of

the same year injunctions appeared which included the requirements that one of the homilies was to be read to the people every
Sunday; the Epistle and Gospel at the Eucharist were to be in
English; a chapter from the New Testament was to be read in
English at Mattins, and one from the Old Testament at Vespers,
the services being otherwise shortened to allow for this; Prime and
the lesser hours of the day were to be omitted when there was a
sermon, and when there was no sermon, the Creed, the Lord's
Prayer, and the Ten Commandments were to be recited in English
after the Gospel; images, pictures, and stained-glass windows
before which votive candles had been burnt were to be removed;
and only two candles could be left on the high altar. In January
1548 various traditional ceremonies associated with certain days of
the liturgical year were also forbidden.

12 The First English Prayer Book 1549

Various experiments with whole services in English began to take
place, and in December 1547 it was decreed that Holy Communion should be received in both kinds, bread and wine, an
order for this being produced in March 1548. This was followed
soon after by the first complete English Book of Common
Prayer, on which a committee of bishops and other divines had
begun work on 9 September 1548. Since the complete text was
delivered to the King some three weeks later, it is obvious
that a preliminary draft must have been prepared beforehand,
doubtless by Thomas Cranmer himself. The book was finally
approved by Parliament on 21 January 1549, and by an Act of
Uniformity was to be used throughout the country from Whitsunday of that year, 9 June. The ordination services were issued
later in 1550, as was a musical setting of parts of the Prayer Book
services by John Merbecke, under the title, *The Book of Common
Prayer Noted*.

As will be seen from the accounts given of the individual
services elsewhere in this commentary, this first English Prayer
Book was a quite conservative revision in comparison with much
of the material being produced on the Continent, and it retained a
considerable measure of the structure and some of the ceremonies
of the medieval rites which had preceded it. It was essentially a
compromise between the desires of the more extreme Reformers
and the need to try to carry along the more conservative members
of the Church, from bishops to ordinary lay people. Inevitably,

therefore, it satisfied no one completely: it was criticized by some for not going far enough, and opposed by others for going too far. Further annoyance was caused to the more radical Reformers by the fact that some conservative bishops and divines claimed that its eucharistic rite could be considered compatible with traditional Catholic teaching, and by the fact that others were celebrating it in a manner not very different from the old rite. Obviously, both doctrine and practice needed to be made more explicitly Reformed.

Texts in F. E. Brightman, *The English Rite* (2 vols, 1915, 2nd edn 1921); *The First and Second Prayer Books of Edward VI* (1910, (ed.) E. C. S. Gibson; 2nd edn 1949, (ed.) E. C. Ratcliffe; 3rd edn 1968, (ed.) D. E. W. Harrison); Colin Buchanan (ed.), *Background Documents to Liturgical Revision 1547–1549* (1983), and *Eucharistic Liturgies of Edward VI: A Text for Students* (1983).

13 *The 1552 Prayer Book*

Further changes were not long in appearing. Indeed some scholars believe that the first Prayer Book was only ever intended as an interim step and that the text of the second book was already envisaged when the first was being produced. Certainly by January 1551 the bishops had agreed to many changes being made, and in April 1552 a new Act of Uniformity ordered the replacement of the first Prayer Book by a second one from All Saints' Day onwards. As one would have expected, this was a thorough-going Protestant revision, with none of the ambiguity of doctrine or conservatism of practice of its immediate predecessor. This time the ordination services were bound up with the rest of the book. It was, however, short-lived, for in July 1553 Edward VI died, and the succession passed to the Catholic princess Mary, who immediately repealed all the Edwardine legislation and restored the traditional liturgical practices of the medieval rites. Only in Scotland did the 1552 book continue in use. A number of leading English bishops and divines fled into exile on the Continent, where they came into direct contact with Calvinism. This served to encourage many of them to pursue doctrinal and liturgical change even further in a Reformed direction than the 1552 book, and tensions and quarrels developed over this issue among the exiles, some wishing to adhere to the English book, some demanding a Calvinist form, and others seeking a compromise between the two positions.

Texts of 1552 book in Brightman, op. cit.; and *The First and Second Prayer Books of Edward VI*; eucharistic rite only in Buchanan (ed.), *Eucharistic Liturgies of Edward VI: A Text for Students*. For the practice of the exiles see Robin Leaver (ed.), *The Liturgy of the Frankfurt Exiles 1555* (1984); W. D. Maxwell (ed.), *The Liturgical Portions of the Genevan Service Book* (1931; 2nd edn 1965).

14 *The 1559 Prayer Book*

In November 1558 Elizabeth I came to the throne and began by restoring the liturgical situation to what it had been immediately prior to the death of her father, Henry VIII. The English litany was reinstated, as were the English versions of the Epistles and Gospels, the Creed, the Lord's Prayer, and the Ten Commandments. However, the return of the exiles created pressure for further reform. They rejected as unacceptable a suggested return to the 1549 book, and insisted on going further. Faced with the possibility that some might demand the wholesale introduction of Calvinist forms of service, as in fact did happen in Scotland, there seemed no alternative but to agree to the compromise of the adoption of the 1552 book.

In April 1559, therefore, an Act of Uniformity was passed restoring the 1552 book with a few small alterations, the most important of which related to the service of Holy Communion and permitted a somewhat broader interpretation of the meaning of the rite. Thus once again, as in 1549, no one really wanted the book they were given: the Queen and others would have preferred something less Protestant, and the returned exiles something closer to the practice of the continental Reformed churches, such as had been adopted in Scotland. Many of the latter were extremely unhappy with the compromise book, and found even its few ceremonial directions (such as the wearing of the surplice by ministers and the use of a ring in marriage) objectionable because they were without scriptural warrant. Known as 'Puritans', this group continued to struggle for further change throughout the rest of Elizabeth's reign, but without success.

Texts in J. E. Booty (ed.), *The Book of Common Prayer 1559* (Charlottesville 1976); W. K. Clay (ed.), *Liturgical Services of the Reign of Queen Elizabeth* (1847); H. Gee, *The Elizabethan Prayer-Book and Ornaments* (1902).

15 The 1604 Prayer Book

When James I succeeded to the throne in 1603 on the death of Elizabeth, hopes rose among the Puritan party that, as a result of his experience as ruler of Scotland, he might be more kindly disposed towards them, and a petition expressing their desired reforms was presented to him. James referred the matter to a conference between the Prayer Book and Puritan factions, which met at Hampton Court in January 1604. After three days' discussion a number of very small concessions to the Puritan conscience were agreed upon for incorporation into the Prayer Book. This was by no means sufficient to satisfy them, however, and their criticism of the Prayer Book continued in the years which followed. They received an even less sympathetic hearing than in the previous century. There was no longer the same political necessity for appeasing the extreme Protestants in order to present a united front against the papists which had marked the early years of Elizabeth's reign, and there was a growing element among the adherents of the Prayer Book who favoured a more Catholic theology and liturgical practice, usually known as 'Laudians', after William Laud, Archbishop of Canterbury from 1633 to 1645. Although they continued on the whole to retain the text of the Prayer Book intact in their worship, they did make changes in the manner in which the services were celebrated, especially in the adornment of church buildings and in the vesture of ministers. The minister wore a cope for the celebration of the Eucharist, and the holy table was kept in its old 'altar' position against the east wall of the church, from which it had been removed in 1552, with a fine covering over it and surrounded with rails.

16 The Scottish Prayer Book of 1637

After the accession of James I, bishops had been appointed in Scotland in place of the reformed Presbyterian system of church government which had previously obtained, and, not surprisingly, there was pressure from the Laudian party for Scotland also to come into line with the liturgical practice of England. Strong resistance was encountered to this. However, during the reign of Charles I (1625–49) work began on the preparation of a prayer book for Scotland which was not dissimilar to the 1549 book and in many ways reflected what the Laudians would have liked to have introduced in England. Unfortunately, when it was pub-lished in 1637, it gave rise to such violent opposition in Scotland that it had to be abandoned.

Meanwhile opposition to the Laudians had also been growing in England, and the Puritan party were in the ascendant, with the aim of total reform of the Church, including the abolition of both episcopacy and the Book of Common Prayer. No compromise was now possible, and in January 1645 Parliament declared the use of the Prayer Book illegal, its place being taken by the Presbyter-ian *Directory for the Public Worship of God*. Both Laud and Charles I were executed, and the episcopal party lay low or fled into exile.

Texts in G. Donaldson, *The Making of the Scottish Prayer Book of 1637* (1954); G. W. Sprott (ed.), *Scottish Liturgies of the Reign of James VI* (1901); Ian Breward (ed.), *The Westminster Directory* (1980).

17 *The 1662 Prayer Book*

In 1660 Charles II returned to England, episcopacy was restored once more, and the question immediately arose as to which form of the Prayer Book, if any, was to be imposed. There was, naturally enough, strong support for a return to the book which had been in use prior to 1645, though the Presbyterians hoped that some concessions might be made to them, and some second-generation Laudians, among them Matthew Wren, Bishop of Ely, and John Cosin, Bishop of Durham, were engaged in preparing a possible revision of the Prayer Book which would be more in accord with their theological position and include some of the features of the ill-fated Scottish book. Once again a conference was called to consider the different points of view. Known subsequently as the Savoy Conference, it met in 1661 and was composed of twelve bishops and an equal number of leading Presbyterian divines. The bishops were not disposed to accept any but the most insignificant of changes in the Prayer Book proposed by the Presbyterians, and the conference broke up after three months without achieving any agreement.

Meanwhile an Act of Uniformity imposing the Prayer Book of 1604 was already on its way through Parliament, a body which was equally unfavourable to changes in any direction. The Laudian party, therefore, arranged for Convocation to meet in November 1661 and to undertake the work of revising the Prayer Book. A committee of eight bishops was entrusted with the preparatory work for this, and they presented their recommendations to full sessions of Convocation meeting briefly each day. The whole process was completed very rapidly, in a total of only twenty-two days. The final form was approved on 21 December 1661, and subsequently annexed to the Act of Uniformity in Parliament, which received the Royal Assent on 19 May 1662, and came into effect on St Bartholomew's Day, 24 August. Much of the less controversial material from Cosin's and Wren's work was incorporated, and other minor changes made, including some small concessions to the Presbyterian objections, but both lack of time and, more significantly, the lack of sufficiently widespread support for a strongly Laudian version made the result something of a compromise. As Geoffrey Cuming has concluded, 'neither Laudians nor Presbyterians had achieved more than a small part of their desires; they had compelled an administration which would have preferred to reprint the 1604 text intact to make concessions to both sides; but in the end it is the same book that emerges with only minor alterations' (*History of Anglican Liturgy*, p. 127).

Texts in Brightman, op. cit.; and G. J. Cuming, *The Durham Book* (1961).

18 The Book of Common Prayer after 1662

The imposition of the book was regarded as intolerable by many Presbyterian and Puritan ministers, and more than a thousand of them were deprived of their benefices in 1662 for refusing to submit to episcopal ordination, which was now written into the ordination services as a requirement for ministry in the Church of England. Nevertheless, even after this efforts directed towards the 'comprehension' of dissenters within the Church of England still continued. An attempt was made to produce a revision of the Prayer Book which might be acceptable to all parties in 1689, but it had to be abandoned because of hostility to the idea in Convocation.

Text in T. J. Fawcett, *The Liturgy of Comprehension 1689* (1973).

Enthusiasm for such schemes subsequently declined, but the desire to revise the Prayer Book continued to surface among various groups of people from time to time in the following centuries. Generally, they were motivated by a wish to make the book conform more closely to their particular doctrinal position. Thus, for example, in the eighteenth century those with Unitarian leanings produced suggested versions which deleted overtly Trinitarian elements from the book. On the other hand, some scholars with knowledge of ancient liturgies, particularly among the Nonjurors, produced versions which tried to incorporate elements from these and so enrich the liturgical practice of the Church of England. All these attempts, however, eventually came to nothing, though the latter group did exert some influence on the Communion Service of the Episcopal Church in Scotland which appeared in 1764, and through that upon the revision of the Book of Common Prayer undertaken in the Episcopal Church in the United States of America in 1790.

Texts of eucharistic rites in W. J. Grisbrooke, *Anglican Liturgies of the Seventeenth and Eighteenth Centuries* (1958).

A new problem emerged in the course of the nineteenth century. At first the pressure for revision came from extreme Evangelicals, who wished to remove from the Prayer Book what they regarded as lingering traces of sacerdotalism and Romanism; but with the growth of the Anglo-Catholic movement in the Church of England there was a development in the opposite direction. The adherents of this party became increasingly dissatisfied with the provisions of the Book of Common Prayer and began to make additions to the worship of their churches, firstly by the introduction of furnishings which had not been seen for centuries (such as candles, crosses, credence tables, altar coverings, vestments and incense), and secondly by the incorporation of material from contemporary Roman Catholic sources into the text of their services. Feelings ran high against the 'ritualists', as they were called, and the bishops tried to settle the matter by appeal to law, to determine what might or might not legitimately be done in Anglican worship. Lawyers were divided as to the legality of a number of practices, and eventually a Royal Commission was appointed in 1867 to clarify, and if necessary amend, the directions of the Book of Common Prayer so as to secure uniformity of practice in what were deemed to be vital areas. Its final report, which appeared in 1870, failed to deal satisfactorily with the heart of the problem, much of it being taken up with controversy over the use of the Athanasian Creed, and the only real results of this protracted exercise were a revision of the lectionary in 1871 and the appearance of the Act of Uniformity Amendment Act (or 'Shortened Services Act' as it was generally called) in 1872. This mainly allowed Morning and Evening Prayer to be shortened on weekdays; additional services to be drawn up from material in the Prayer Book or the Bible for Sundays or other special occasions; and Morning Prayer, the Litany and Holy Communion to take place separately.

Since the problem of ritualism still remained, a Public Worship Regulation Act was passed in 1874. This was aimed at enforcing the law with regard to conformity to the Book of Common Prayer, and set up a special court with prescribed penalties. A series of prosecutions ensued, some resulting in the imprisonment of persistent offenders, which did nothing to lower the emotional temperature in the Church of England. Finally, in 1904 a Royal Commission on Ecclesiastical Discipline was appointed. This was to inquire into alleged breaches of the law with regard to worship and make recommendations for dealing with the situation. Its report appeared in 1906, and it concluded that the law was, 'in our belief, nowhere exactly observed'; it was 'too narrow for the religious life of the present generation'; it should be reformed to admit of reasonable elasticity, and then enforced. It recommended that Letters of Business should be issued to the Convocations to carry out the necessary work of amendment to the rubrics of the Book of Common Prayer. This was duly done, and official revision of the Prayer Book began once more.

Studies:
James Bentley, *Ritualism and Politics in Victorian Britain*. 1978.
R. C. D. Jasper, *Prayer Book Revision in England 1800–1900*. 1954.

19 The Proposed Prayer Book of 1927/8

Many wanted to make only the minimum change necessary, but others saw an opportunity to make significant alterations and improvements to the Prayer Book. Unfortunately, this common aspiration for revision did not tend in one uniform direction. Some were motivated by the desire to incorporate a broader doctrinal position, especially in a Catholic direction, others by a wish to provide more adequately for contemporary needs, and others by the hope of enriching current practice with the fruits of recent liturgical scholarship. This division of aims was to prove fatal for the project. For, though all these might have been agreed upon the need for revision, they were far from agreed upon the shape it should take.

The process dragged on tediously through the years until a final form was approved by the Church Assembly in July 1927, but, although it received overwhelming support in the Assembly (517 votes to 133, a majority of 79 per cent), it was not universally popular in the Church of England. Not only did Evangelicals remain resistant to any change at all in the Prayer Book, seeing it as a weakening of the Protestant position of the Church of England, but Anglo-Catholics too were dissatisfied with the final form which the book had taken, since it did not represent what they themselves would have wished to have. The difficulties mainly centred around the structure of the Eucharistic Prayer in the Service of Holy Communion and the provisions for the reservation of the consecrated bread and wine after the service, provisions which went too far for Evangelicals and not far enough for Anglo-Catholics. Because of this opposition, when the book was submitted to Parliament in December, it was passed in the Lords by 214 votes to 88 but defeated in the Commons by 238 to 205.

The bishops then decided to reintroduce the book with a number of minor changes which they hoped might pacify the opposition, but their efforts were in vain: they merely resulted in further loss of support among Anglo-Catholics without winning over Evangelicals. Reservation remained the bone of contention, and though the book was again approved by the Church Assembly in April 1928 (by 396 votes to 153, a majority of 72 per cent), it was rejected by the House of Commons by 266 votes to 220. Fortunately such a relationship between Church and Parliament did not exist in other parts of the Anglican Communion, and many provinces were able to carry through similar revisions of the Book of Common Prayer at around this period, some very conservative, others going beyond what had been proposed in England.

The bishops now found themselves in something of a quandary, with a Prayer Book which commanded the support of a substantial majority in the Church Assembly having been defeated twice in the House of Commons. They dealt with what was clearly a difficult situation in three ways. Firstly, they had the book published as it stood as a private venture, thus making it generally available to the Church. Since both in cost and appearance it was comparable with 1662, the man in the street could be excused for regarding it simply as 'a new Prayer Book', even though the bishops were careful to state on the introductory page that 'the publication of this Book does not directly or indirectly imply that it can be regarded as authorized for use in churches.'

Secondly, they issued a statement in 1929 in which they declared that 'in the present emergency and until other order be taken' they would not 'regard as inconsistent with loyalty to the principles of the Church of England the use of such additions or deviations as fall within the limits of these proposals.' Taken in conjunction with the publication of the book, it was a clear invitation to ignore the decision of Parliament, and an implicit claim that they themselves possessed authority to determine matters of liturgy, a claim which had no legal basis whatsoever, but which was generally unquestioned by subsequent generations of Anglican clergy. Hence many of the provisions of the 1928 book came into widespread, if strictly illegal, use in the Church of England.

Thirdly, they took the first steps in the search for some new method of dealing with liturgical revision which would avoid a repetition of the 1927–8 débâcle. This involved an examination of the relationships between Church and State with a view to constitutional change. Little did they realize that the exercise on which they were embarking would last for more than thirty years. However, in 1930 the Archbishops appointed a Commission under the chairmanship of Viscount Cecil of Chelwood to examine the relations between Church and State. Despite a unanimous report in 1935, little or nothing resulted from its recommendations, particularly that of a Round Table Conference to consider deviations from the Order of Holy Communion and the regulation of reservation. Nevertheless, it did raise the important issue of what was meant by 'lawful authority' and suggested greater autonomy for the Church.

Studies:
R. C. D. Jasper, *Walter Howard Frere: his Correspondence on Liturgical Revision and Construction*. 1954.

20 *The Liturgical Movement*

Meanwhile a movement had been growing in the Roman Catholic Church on the Continent since early in the nineteenth century which aimed at a recovery and revitalization of the Church's liturgical heritage. The Benedictine order was the main force in this, which came to be known as the Liturgical Movement. It was at first too medieval and archaeological in character and insufficiently concerned with the pastoral aspects of the liturgy, but in the twentieth century it did begin to have some impact on the Church's worship, and led to more frequent reception of Holy Communion, a desire for more lay participation in worship, and, among scholars, to greater research into the early history of Christian liturgy and the building of a sound theology of worship.

Similar stirrings can be detected in the Church of England in the early years of the twentieth century, but the process really started to get under way and the influence of the Continental movement began to be felt with the publication in 1935 of *Liturgy and Society* by A. G. Hebert SSM and two years later of a collection of essays, *The Parish Communion*, also edited by Hebert. From this was born 'the Parish Communion movement', which aimed at restoring the Eucharist as the central act of worship in a parish on a Sunday morning. At first those involved simply tried to present the eucharistic and initiatory rites of the Book of Common Prayer in a way which would best bring out their full meaning, but eventually it became clear that liturgical revision was necessary if a real renewal of worship was to happen.

21 *The Alternative Services Measure*

The movement towards liturgical revision was taken a stage further in another Archbishops' Commission appointed in 1939 under Archbishop Garbett of York to consider the revision and modification of the canon law. Its report in 1947 not only contained a proposed revised code of canons but a valuable memorandum by Mr Justice Vaisey on the meaning of 'lawful authority'. His conclusion that in fact it had no precise meaning in law encouraged the Commission not only to give it meaning in its proposed Canon 13 but also to indicate how it should be used in liturgical revision: 'deviations (whether by way of addition, alternative use, or otherwise) from the said form [i.e. the Book of Common Prayer] as the Convocations of the respective Provinces of Canterbury and York may respectively order, allow, or sanction within the said respective Provinces' would be deemed to be ordered by lawful authority.

This whole process was set out in much greater detail in the report of a further Archbishops' Commission on Church and State which sat under Sir Walter Moberly from 1949 to 1952. It proposed the redrafting of Canon 13 to include experimental services which would require approval by the Convocations, with agreement by the House of Laity. Such services, alternative to those in the Book of Common Prayer, should be sanctioned for optional and experimental use for a period of seven or ten years, with the option of renewal for further periods; and every sanction would require a two-thirds majority in each House. By this means of trial and error, it was hoped that an acceptable revision of the services in the Prayer Book might gradually be secured, after which they could be presented to Parliament by a Church Assembly Measure for statutory authorization. This was the basis of the proposals which were eventually embodied, after protracted negotiations, in the Prayer Book (Alternative and Other Services) Measure and passed by the Church Assembly in July 1964. On this occasion there was no objection from Parliament and the Measure received the Royal Assent in March 1965. It became operative on 1 May 1966. Under its terms, services alternative to those in the Prayer Book could be used experimentally for a period of seven years, with an option on a further period of seven years, provided that they secured two-thirds majorities in all five houses of the Convocations and the House of Laity. The Measure was, therefore, only operative until 1980.

22 The Liturgical Commission

Meanwhile, at the request of the Convocations, the Archbishops had already appointed a Liturgical Commission in 1955 to undertake the necessary preparatory work on new services. Its first major task was to prepare a report on the principles of Prayer Book revision, which was published in time for the consideration of the Lambeth Conference of 1958. In the following year it published its proposals for a revision of the services of Baptism and Confirmation, even though the legislation for authorizing their experimental use was still in the distant future. Their preliminary airing in the Convocations was decidedly unfortunate: they came in for considerable criticism, and it was not surprising that the whole project was put into cold storage while the Commission turned its attention to the less contentious services of Morning and Evening Prayer.

Its first task under the Alternative Services Measure was to secure the proper authorization of most of the services in the 1928 book, which had now been in unofficial use for over thirty years.

Since the Commission had not been involved in the drafting of this material, it was agreed that the House of Bishops should be responsible for this operation, with the help and advice of one or two members of the Commission. With few exceptions, these services—known as Series 1—were authorized for experimental use in 1966 for a period of seven years. Under this heading came Morning and Evening Prayer, Infant and Adult Baptism, Marriage, Burial, and Holy Communion. Confirmation failed to secure authorization by not receiving the necessary two-thirds majority in the House of Laity; Burial only narrowly secured authorization, owing to problems over prayer for the departed; and Holy Communion was an amended form of the 1928 rite. The 1928 Eucharistic Prayer had never been popular, and, unlike most of the book, was very rarely used. It was therefore replaced by a prayer which to all intents and purposes was that of the long-canvassed 'Interim Rite', and which could be used in a longer and a shorter form.

By this time the Liturgical Commission had already published the first set of its own proposals in *Alternative Services: Second Series* (1965), containing Morning and Evening Prayer, Intercessions and Thanksgivings, Thanksgiving after Childbirth, Burial, and an appendix. It was the appendix, containing an uncompleted draft of a new rite of Holy Communion, which created the greatest stir. Contrary to all expectations, it met with an enthusiastic reception from the Convocations and the House of Laity, all of which pleaded that it should be completed with all speed. This was done and, despite problems over prayer for the departed and the second half of the Eucharistic Prayer, it was authorized for use in 1967. Baptism and Confirmation, and Morning and Evening Prayer quickly followed suit in 1968. The proposed services for Burial and Thanksgiving after Childbirth failed to secure authorization, and no proposals for Marriage or Ordination were made. The Series 2 range of services was, therefore, strictly limited.

It was also becoming clear by the mid-1960s that they were in a sense 'interim rites', for by that time ecumenical co-operation in liturgical matters was becoming a reality and there was a general movement towards the use of contemporary English. Significant in this respect were the publication of the New Testament of the New English Bible in 1961 (and of the whole Bible in 1970) and of the Jerusalem Bible in 1966. The use of such versions in public worship was facilitated by the passing of the Versions of the Bible Measure in 1965, which enabled the authorization for use in public worship of any versions approved by the Church Assembly (later the General Synod). Under this measure the Revised Version, the Revised Standard Version, the New English Bible, the Jerusalem Bible, and the Revised Psalter were all authorized in addition to the Authorized Version of 1611. Subsequently The Bible in Today's English Version was also authorized in 1978, and the Liturgical Psalter in 1979.

In 1967 the Liturgical Commission, with help from the Poet Laureate, C. Day Lewis, published its *Modern Liturgical Texts*, containing versions of the Lord's Prayer, the creeds, and the canticles in contemporary English, together with modern versions of the Series 2 Baptism, Confirmation and Holy Communion rites. This document was published in time for consideration by the Liturgical Consultation of the Lambeth Conference of 1968, and undoubtedly helped to stimulate discussion throughout the Anglican Communion. Shortly afterwards the International Consultation on English Texts, representing all the major English-speaking churches throughout the world, came into being. Between 1968 and 1975 it produced three reports on *Prayers we have in common*; and its proposals on creeds and canticles ultimately secured general acceptance in English-speaking churches. Unfortunately it was less successful in its work on the Lord's Prayer; but even here only a single line (line 9: 'lead us not into temptation') really stood in the way of success.

Significant moves were also taking place on the ecumenical front at home. Largely owing to Anglican initiative, the Joint Liturgical Group, composed of official representatives of all the main churches in England and Scotland, came into being in 1963. In 1967–8 this group produced radical proposals for a revision of the Calendar, Lectionary and Daily Office, all of which were incorporated into the Church of England's programme of liturgical reform. They also had a profound influence on liturgical revision overseas, not least because of their timely publication before the Lambeth Conference of 1968.

Further constitutional change took place within the Church of England in 1970 with the advent of Synodical Government. This greatly simplified the procedure of liturgical revision, for instead of five Houses considering and voting on proposals, the three new Houses of Bishops, Clergy and Laity could now consider proposals together, although they still voted independently. A system was also devised whereby 'Provisional Approval' was first given to a service by a mere show of hands in the whole Synod; and this was followed by a revision stage, after which 'Final Approval' was required by two-thirds majorities in each House voting independently. One of the Synod's first major achievements was to secure freedom from parliamentary control in matters of worship and doctrine through the Church of England (Worship and Doctrine) Measure of 1974. Under its terms the General Synod was given power to produce and authorize forms of service as and when it was considered necessary, provided that the Book of Common Prayer remained available and unaltered. Thus it was only in matters concerning the 1662 Prayer Book that parliamentary approval was still required. Since it was now clear that 'lawful authority' lay with the General Synod, the Church was no longer faced with a possible repetition of the 1927–8 crisis. The Worship and Doctrine Measure also made the Alternative Services Measure of 1966 redundant, thereby releasing the Church of England from any obligation to work within a time limit of fourteen years for its new services.

In this transformed atmosphere of the 1970s, the Liturgical Commission proceeded to produce its Series 3 forms of service, all in contemporary English. The first to appear was Holy Communion in September 1971, and this included both the ICET texts and the JLG eucharistic lectionary. Despite its radical approach it was approved by overwhelming majorities in the General Synod in November 1972, and came into use on 1 February 1973. Further proposals then appeared in rapid succession and were duly authorized—Funerals, and Morning and Evening Prayer in 1975; Collects in 1976; Marriage in 1977, the Ordinal, and Calendar, Lectionary, and Rules to order the Service in 1978; and Initiation and the Liturgical Psalter in 1979.

It was not enough, however, simply to authorize services and other relevant material for experimental use for limited periods of time. Something with a greater degree of stability and permanence was required for the future. In 1973, therefore, a Working Party was appointed under Dr Habgood, Bishop of Durham, to consider future policy; and in February 1976 this group recommended that alternative services should be brought together into a single book. 1980 was fixed as the target date for publication, convenient not only as the original completion date of the old Alternative Services Measure but also because it was the latest possible date within the lifetime of the existing General Synod. It was agreed that all the contents were to be Series 3 services in contemporary English, with one exception—Holy Communion

Series 1 and 2 Revised, modern in structure and content, but traditional in language.

Apart from this rite, all the services underwent a process of revision and then adaptation, whereby they all conformed to a uniform style and format. The Synodical process was completed by November 1979, and *The Alternative Service Book 1980* was published in November 1980, being given authorization in the first instance for a period of ten years. It was produced in a variety of editions–with psalter, without psalter, case-bound, soft-back, and so on—but in every case pagination is identical, so that congregations can easily be directed to the right place by page reference. Finally, it should be noted that The Alternative Service Book is not an authorized book of services, but a book of authorized services: each service is there in its own right, having been independently authorized for use, and the General Synod can therefore extract, amend or replace individual services without involving the other contents.

Studies:

Colin Buchanan, *Recent Liturgical Revision in the Church of England.* 1973, plus supplements for 1973–4, 1974–6 and 1976–8.

— *Latest Liturgical Revision in the Church of England 1978–1984.* 1984.

2
Notes

The General Notes are simply guides to assist in the performance of services. Unlike the 1662 Book of Common Prayer and its predecessors, The Alternative Service Book makes no reference to such matters as the obligation of the clergy to recite the daily office, the vesture of ministers, or the arrangement of churches. These are regarded as matters which can be dealt with more appropriately in the canons.

3
Common Forms

A number of texts appear on several occasions. Rather than repeat information about them, they are brought together under the title 'Common Forms'.

The Lord's Prayer

General studies:
C. F. Evans, *The Lord's Prayer.* 1963.
ICET, *Prayers we have in common.* 2nd rev. edn 1975.
E. Lohmeyer, *The Lord's Prayer.* 1963.

The Lord's Prayer appears in two slightly different forms in the New Testament, Matthew 6.9–13 and Luke 11.2–4. The Matthean text has been consistently used in Christian liturgy. The doxology was added at a very early date: there is a doxology, although rather different, in the *Didache*, which could be as early as AD 60, and is certainly no later than 230. The present doxology dates from the fourth century. The prayer was evidently used as a Communion devotion: the early Fathers, both Latin and Greek, identified 'daily bread' with the bread of the Eucharist. Cyril of Jerusalem, for example, called it 'super-substantial' bread (cf. *Catechetical Lectures*, 23.11–18). By the fourth century it had found its place in the Eucharist, serving a similar purpose. In some liturgies it appeared before the fraction and in others after, but a position between the Eucharistic Prayer and communion was general. By the sixth century it had also established its place in the daily office, and it always had a place in the rites of initiation.

Vernacular texts in England go back to Anglo-Saxon times, the earliest dating from *c.* 700. In the Middle Ages these tended to vary in detail, but by an ordinance of Henry VIII in 1541 the Prayer Book text, following closely that in William Tyndale's New Testament, became the norm. The doxology did not appear until 1662, following its introduction in the Scottish Prayer Book of 1637. Cranmer clearly used it as a 'climactic' prayer: it was used immediately after communion, baptism, confirmation, matrimony and burial, and it introduced prayer which followed, as in the daily office. It was aptly described by J. H. Blunt as 'a royal Antiphon of Prayer'.

The prayer consists of an address and seven petitions. Its meaning is closely associated with its structure.

1 The Greek texts in the Gospels are themselves 'translations' from Hebrew or Aramaic.

2 The Greek text in Matthew has a well-defined, almost poetic, structure. After the address, there are three aspirations or petitions within an antithesis—'heaven–earth': these are expressed in rhyming syllables—the first word of each line ending in '*to*' and the lines ending in '—*a sou*'. This is followed by another three petitions, each with its own antithesis: today—tomorrow, debts—debtors, *not* temptation *but* deliverance; and here again the phrases are pointed with assonance or rhyme.

3 In all the lines except the one referring to bread, the verb stands first, taking the emphasis: and these verbs are in the aorist tense, expressing not continuous or repeated action, but a single definite act.

4 In the first and third petitions the verb is in the passive, and the second verb is intransitive: but the passive represents a Hebrew turn of speech which would not address God directly for reasons of reverence. So these petitions can be interpreted as asking God to undertake some precise action now. It represents an urgent seeking for the great eschatological deed of God to be executed and revealed.

5 Nevertheless, some scholars regard the first petition as doxological, parallel to such a Jewish acclamation as 'The Holy One, Blessed be He!': and they would argue that a case can be made, by reference to similar Jewish usage, for regarding the first three petitions as referring to human action—may men so act that God's name is hallowed, etc.

The retention of the traditional English pattern for the first three petitions allows for a breadth of interpretation—doxological or petitionary, and divine or human action. Except for the final petition, the text in ASB follows that of ICET.

Line 6. The petition for bread is unusual for two reasons:

31

1   The word order. It is the only line where the verb does not come first; and translated literally, it runs 'Our daily bread give us today'. 'Today' is therefore significant.

2   The Greek word for 'daily' is unusual: *epiousion*. It was not current Greek usage, and Origen claimed that the evangelists had invented it. Jerome provided an interesting clue, claiming that Aramaic-speaking Jewish Christians gave it the meaning 'of tomorrow'. If that be so, antithesis is evident here too: '*Tomorrow's* bread give us *today*'. This could mean not only the next day but the 'great tomorrow': it would be another eschatological reference, fitting the interpretation the early Fathers gave it of 'spiritual food'.

Here again, in view of the uncertainty, it is wise to keep to the familiar text, and let it bear both material and spiritual meanings: both are sound and indeed the one does not exclude the other.

Lines 9–10. The Greek word for 'temptation' does not mean what is meant by the word today. The reference is primarily eschatological. While accepting that fact, scholars have found no satisfactory way of expressing it. ICET used the phrase 'Save us from the time of trial', which expresses the right idea but is indeniably a paraphrase. Rather than create confusion, the General Synod opted for the traditional text. Admittedly it creates problems; but it does translate correctly what the Greek text of Matthew says.

Lines 11–12. The presence of the doxology in many Greek manuscripts, though they may not be early or very reliable, reflects the Jewish practice of concluding prayer with a doxology of praise. It has enjoyed a wide and long use, and it is liturgically appropriate.

Gloria Patri

General study:
ICET, *Prayers we have in common*. 2nd rev. edn 1975.

The Gloria Patri is of primitive origin, being referred to by Clement of Alexandria and Justin Martyr in the second century. According to Cassian it was used as a doxology to the psalms in Gaul in the fourth century. It has had various forms, and the present form was ordered by the fifth canon of the Second Council of Vaison in 529. The words 'as it was in the beginning' were then added as a safeguard against those who did not believe in the pre-existence of the Son. It has been described as a 'common antiphon' to the psalms in the office, encapsulating them in a Christian doxological frame. Its inclusion at the end of individual psalms and canticles likewise provides them with a Christian setting.

The translation in ASB is that provided by ICET with one small variation—'shall' is used instead of 'will'. The placing of both adverbs after their verbs in the response—'is *now*, and shall be *for ever*'—not only makes the parallelism clearer, but rightly places the emphatic words at the end of each phrase.

'This is the Word of the Lord'

General studies:

G. J. Cuming, 'This is the Word of the Lord', in G. J. Cuming, (ed.), *The Ministry of the Word*. 1979.

C. W. J. Bowles, 'The Ministry of the Word', in R. C. D. Jasper, (ed.), *The Eucharist Today*. 1974.

The versicle 'This is the word of the Lord' with the response 'Thanks be to God' have become the normal conclusion to readings of Scripture. This presents a problem for those people who find it difficult to relate every reading, and particularly some Old Testament passages to 'the word of the Lord'. For some it is clearly no problem: the whole Bible is inspired; others, again, are willing to demythologize. But for those who have a difficulty, it can be said that this versicle and response make no fundamentalist affirmation. It is a declaration of a thankful conviction that the Living Word speaks through the written and spoken word. To understand the full significance of any reading, its context in the Bible and in biblical history must be taken into account. The Revised Catechism expresses the position admirably: 'The Bible, in both the Old and the New Testaments, is the record of God's revelation of himself to mankind through his people Israel, and above all in his Son, Jesus Christ. We shall read the Bible with the desire and the prayer that through it God will speak to us by his Holy Spirit, and enable us to know him and to do his will.' Indeed, the word itself is grace-giving. (*The Revised Catechism*, 1962, secs. 28, 33, 35).

'The Lord be with you'/
'And also with you'

General studies:

W. C. van Unnik, 'Dominus Vobiscum, the Background of a Liturgical Formula', in A. B. J. Higgins, ed., *New Testament Essays: Studies in Memory of T. W. Manson*. 1959.

J. A. Jungmann, *The Mass of the Roman Rite* (1 vol.). 1959.

The versicle and response *Dominus vobiscum: et cum spiritu tuo* appears at various key points in services—usually at the beginning. It serves to focus the attention of the congregation on what is about to happen, and it is a reminder that the action is corporate, undertaken by both the minister and themselves.

Some scholars have argued that it is scriptural, based on the greeting of Boaz and the response of the reapers in Ruth 2.4— 'The Lord be with you' . . . 'The Lord bless you'. (cf. Judges 6.12) The fact remains, however, that this versicle and response cannot be found in its exact form anywhere in Scripture: and the earliest evidence of its existence is in the Sursum corda of the eucharistic rite in *The Apostolic Tradition* of Hippolytus. Nevertheless, its meaning is rooted in Scripture. Professor W. C. van Unnik has made a detailed study of all the references to the Lord 'being with people' in the Old and New Testaments: and he has argued cogently that the evidence consistently points to the fact that 'the Lord' refers to the Spirit, engaged in the dynamic activity of enabling either individuals or the community to do a particular task by protecting or helping them. The early Christians, for example, recognized that prayer acceptable to God needed the assistance of the Holy Spirit—it was a combined action of the divine and the human spirit. So St Paul could say, 'The Spirit helps us in our weakness; for we do not know how to pray . . . but the Spirit himself intercedes for us' (Rom. 8.26). The beginning of the Eucharistic Prayer is therefore a natural place for this versicle and response. A true Eucharist can only be celebrated when the Spirit of God is present to help.

Professor Jungmann has argued that *Dominus* could equally apply to Jesus Christ, e.g. Matthew 18.20, 'Where two or three are gathered together in my name, there am I in the midst of them': yet he also quotes two important passages from John Chrysostom which support van Unnik's theory. *In II Tim. nom. 10,3* speaks of the 'spirit' in the response *et cum spiritu tuo* as referring to the indwelling Holy Spirit; while his first sermon of Pentecost argues

34

that this response is a recognition on the part of the congregation of the fact that the bishop offers the sacrifice in the power of the Holy Spirit (quoted in J. Jungmann, *The Mass of the Roman Rite*, p. 242).

The versicle contains no verb. The question therefore arises as to whether it should be regarded as a wish or a statement of fact. Traditionally it has been regarded as the former—'The Lord be with you'. But on van Unnik's argument it is equally a statement of fact. It is an acknowledgement of the presence of the Spirit of God to help. 'The response of the congregation is very much to the point; when the minister assures them of the presence of the Spirit who "is with them", i.e. with their spirit as Christian folk, they in their turn assure him of the same divine assistance with his spirit.' (Higgins, p. 294)

In the Eucharist, therefore, ASB provides two forms of the versicle and response. There is a literal translation indicating a traditional approach—'The Lord be with you' 'And also with you'—the second 'you' being recognized as a Semitism—'your person' or 'you'. Secondly, there is a form which is admittedly a paraphrase, but may nevertheless be nearer to the true meaning— 'The Lord is here' 'His Spirit is with us'. Both versions are given equal weight. At the beginning of the Rite A, they appear in one order: in the Sursum corda they appear in the reverse order.

The Litany

General studies:
J. Dowden, *The Workmanship of the Prayer Book.* 1889.
W. J. Grisbrooke, 'Intercession at the Eucharist', in *SL* iv.3, 1965.
E. C. Ratcliff, 'The Choir Offices: the Litany', in W. K. Lowther Clarke, (ed.), *Liturgy and Worship*.

The Greek word *litania* simply meant 'prayer' or 'entreaty': but it came to mean a particular kind of prayer, in which people made fixed responses to biddings or petitions expressed by a minister. Nor was it an exclusively Christian form of prayer: evidence for it existed in pagan ritual, and it would appear that early Christians simply made use of a form which had been found acceptable in other religions. The earliest form of Christian litany, consisting of biddings with the response *Kyrie eleison*, is found in the Antiochene liturgy in the *Apostolic Constitutions* Book 8, *c.* 375. It was a form of prayer which spread through Syria to Constantinople, where it became a notable feature of the Byzantine rite, and ultimately it spread to the West.

Little is known of the beginnings of the Litany in Rome: but the earliest known form is the *Deprecatio Gelasii*—a litany which Pope Gelasius (492–6) translated from the Greek and appointed to be sung at Mass between the entrance rite and the collect of the day, replacing the older *orationes* after the readings and sermon. It should be noted that this litany is a *deprecatio*—an intercession pure and simple, and in the time of Pope Gregory the Great (590–604) it was reduced to its triple Kyrie eleison, except on special occasions. Later litanies differed considerably both in form and use, a change indicated by a change in designation: it was no longer a *deprecatio* but a *litania*, a title which could be applied to a penitential observance or to a procession or to both. This form of litany, which apparently grew out of a private form of devotion, could be used inside or outside church, and noteworthy examples were the Rogationtide litanies on the three days preceding Ascension Day and the *Litania Maior* in Rome on 25 April which replaced the *Robigalia*, the pagan festival for the protection of the crops. In style and form it had remarkable similarities to the pagan supplications of Roman soldiers as recorded in Lactantius and Eusebius—further evidence of the Church using commonly accepted forms of prayer and devotion.

This type of litany was introduced into Rome by the Greek-speaking Syrian Pope, Sergius I (687–701), so once again it was of Eastern provenance. It came to be known as the Litany of the Saints, and finally absorbed and supplanted the earlier forms in the West. In its developed form there were six constituent elements:

1 An introductory Kyrie followed by Invocations of the Trinity, with the response 'Have mercy on us'.

2 The Invocations of the Saints, from which the whole litany derived its title.

3 The Deprecations, or supplications for deliverance, with the response, 'Deliver us, Lord'.

4 The Obsecrations, or supplications through the various events of the life of Jesus Christ, with the response, 'Deliver us, Lord'.

5 The Intercessions—there was only a single intercession in the

original form—with the response, 'We beseech thee to hear us'.

6 Concluding devotions to the Cross and to Jesus Christ as the Son and as the Lamb of God.

Other prayers could follow, varying with the time and the place.

A very early form of this Litany is found in the Irish *Stowe Missal*, which dates from the early eighth century. While still undeveloped in form, all the essential elements of the structure are there: a threefold invocation of Christ, one deprecation, one obsecration—'By thy Cross deliver us, O Lord'—one intercession, and the final devotions to the Lamb of God—the Agnus Dei. This particular litany was still part of the priest's private preparation for Mass: but with the passage of time the processional litany became very popular in England. It came to be used on Rogation Days, 25 April, the Easter Vigil, Ordinations, the Visitation of the Sick, the Consecration of Churches, during Lent, and in places before the Mass on Sunday. Then, in times of emergency, it was used on Wednesdays and Fridays—as, for example, in August 1543, by royal command, when excessive rain damaged the crops. It therefore had two main uses—as a separate office of devotion, or as an introduction to the Mass. Texts were available, not only in the Sarum Processional, but also in English in the Primer after *c.* 1400.

It was therefore not surprising that, when Henry VIII was at war with Scotland and France, Cranmer should produce his Litany in 'our native English tongue'—the first public prayer set forth by authority in the vernacular. Based on the Sarum Litany of the Saints, it was supplemented by elements from other sources— Luther's Litany of 1529, the Deacon's Litany in the Liturgy of St John Chrysostom, the Sarum Litany for the Dying, the Sarum Supplication for use in time of War, a collect from the *Missa pro tribulatione*, the Unction of the Sick, and an antiphon to the Penitential Psalms. Despite the mixed ingredients, it formed a remarkably cohesive whole; and F. E. Brightman truly described it as 'one of the magnificencies of Christendom'. 'As the Litany is enough to prove, he [Cranmer] had an extraordinary power of absorbing and improving upon other people's work' (*The English Rite*, vol. 1, p. lxvii). As in Sarum, Cranmer began with Invocations of the Trinity, but with a difference. No longer are they in the form of versicles and responses, but each invocation is repeated by the congregation, while Kyrie eleison is expanded to 'Have mercy upon us, miserable sinners'. Subsequent use has perhaps indicated that Cranmer introduced a little too much of the penitential note. Kyrie eleison in the classic rites certainly did not carry this deeply penitential, almost tragic, mood conveyed by the constant repetition of 'miserable sinners'. The Invocations of the Saints were drastically reduced: whereas in some medieval forms there could be as many as two hundred, Cranmer reduced them to three, one to Mary, one to the angels, and one to the saints. The Deprecations were no longer introduced by a brief versicle and response, but by a long petition from an antiphon based on Tobit 3.3 and Joel 2.17 from the Sarum Breviary: here, as elsewhere in the Litany, Cranmer grouped congruous clauses into one suffrage, instead of using them singly in the old Latin form. In the Obsecrations he followed the fuller form of Luther's Litany. The Intercessions, like the Deprecations, were a combination of Sarum and Luther, and were grouped: they fell into three main classes— for the Church and State, for special needs, and for material and spiritual blessings: the response was expanded by the addition of 'Good Lord'. The final Petitions were composed of a twofold Agnus Dei, a sixfold Kyrie eleison, and the Lord's Prayer. A number of the suffrages found in medieval forms were omitted, and instead Cranmer followed Luther with a versicle and response and a medieval collect from the Mass for the troubled in heart. Then followed a set of suffrages from the Sarum Supplication for use in time of War, and six prayers.

Cranmer's Litany of 1544 was ordered to be used 'in the time of processions'; but this regulation was short-lived. In 1547 the Royal Injunctions forbade processions about the church or churchyard, so the Litany was to be sung or said kneeling, in the midst of the church immediately before High Mass, and no other was to be used. Clearly at this stage, despite losing its status as a procession, the Litany was regarded as a preliminary to the Mass; and so it remained in 1549. Here the Litany was printed immediately after the Communion rite, and a rubric indicated that it should be said or sung before the Communion service began, according to the Royal Injunctions, on Wednesdays and Fridays— an arrangement which Cranmer might well have borrowed from the German Church Orders. The 1549 rubric then went on to direct that if there were no communicants on these two days, then after the Litany the priest should vest in a plain alb or surplice with a cope and say the first part of the Communion Service 'until after the Offertory'. There were also some changes in the text: the invocations to Mary, the angels and the saints were eliminated, and only the first and last of the six final prayers were included. 1552 saw further significant changes, which tended to make the Litany an appendix to the Office rather than an introduction to the Eucharist. (It must be remembered that at this time it was customary to have an interval of two or three hours between the two services: and it was the Puritan Archbishop Grindal of York who in 1571 issued an injunction requiring Morning Prayer, Litany and Holy Communion to follow one another without intermission. Later as Archbishop of Canterbury he attempted to enforce this on the whole Church of England: though there is evidence that he was not completely successful.) The rubric at the end of the Communion Service directing the use of the Litany on Wednesdays and Fridays disappeared: the text was transferred to a place immediately after Morning and Evening Prayer: and a title was added, 'Here followeth the Litany, to be used on Sundays, Wednesdays and Fridays, and at other times, when it shall be commanded by the Ordinary'. Furthermore, the prayers for rain and fair weather, which in 1549 had been included at the end of the Communion service, were now appended to the end of the Litany together with four other new prayers—two for use in time of death or famine, one in time of war, and one in times of plague and sickness. In 1559 only one change was made—the petition for delivery 'from the tyranny of the Bishop of Rome and all his detestable enormities' was omitted. Then in 1662 there were a number of changes:

1   The occasion of its recitation was clearly stated in the title to be 'after Morning Prayer' on Sundays, Wednesdays and Fridays.

2   It was required to be 'sung or said' rather than simply 'used'.

3   The occasional prayers at the end were removed to a section by themselves.

4   Delivery from 'rebellion' and 'schism' were added to the Deprecations.

5   'Bishops, pastors, and ministers' became 'Bishops, priests, and deacons'.

In 1872 the Act of Uniformity Amendment Act stated quite clearly that Morning and Evening Prayer, the Litany and Holy

Communion could be used as separate entities. Not only did this spell the end of the long and wearisome single 'Morning Service', but people like W. H. Frere began to examine the possibility of using the Litany once again as a processional introduction to Holy Communion. 1928 attempted to deal with this situation in a number of ways, which resulted in a distinct improvement, although they were far from ideal:

1   Except for the Rogation Days and the occasions commanded by the Ordinary, the use of the Litany became entirely optional. It could therefore be normally omitted on a Sunday morning.

2   Abbreviation was permitted after the opening Invocations, by the omission of any of the Deprecations, Obsecrations and Intercessions, provided some of each group were retained.

3   The final section, following the Lord's Prayer, was printed separately as 'A Supplication', which could be said separately on Rogation Days, at penitential seasons, or in times of trouble: or it could be added to the Litany.

4   When Holy Communion was to follow immediately, everything following the Kyries could be omitted. If permission had also been given to omit everything in the Communion Service preceding the Collect of the Day, an even better result would have been achieved.

5   Permission was given to add any of the Occasional Prayers and Thanksgivings to the Litany.

6   Additional petitions for Embertide, for the Missionary Work of the Church, and for the Armed Forces were included; while footnotes permitted the inclusion of travellers by air, and the substitution of 'the High Court of Parliament and all the Ministers of the Crown' for 'the Lords of the Council, and all the Nobility'.

A further revision and modernization of the Litany was undertaken in connection with Morning and Evening Prayer Series 3 in 1975, and with one or two small changes, this is the form which now appears in ASB. Three provisions are made for its use:

1   In the Ordinal, relevant portions are set out as the form of intercession for the candidates and for the ministry of the

whole Church. This is the only occasion in ASB where its use is mandatory.

2   The rubric at the end of the Litany and Note 12 at Morning and Evening Prayer permit its use at either office as an alternative to the prayers following the Apostles' Creed. If this is done, it concludes with the Lord's Prayer, the collect of the day, and the Grace.

3   In the Appendix of Holy Communion Rite A, Sections 3, 4 and 5 are set out as an alternative form of Intercession. In this case it may be supplemented by biddings, either at the beginning or in each section.

Apart from these provisions, the Litany is available as a private or a public devotion, either by itself, or in conjunction with other services. It may be said or sung, kneeling or in procession. Nor need it always be used in its entirety. The introductory rubric indicates that provided Sections 1 and 6 are always used, a selection of suffrages from Sections 2–5 may be made. In this way it can be adapted to a particular theme or occasion, as in the Ordinal. Slightly shorter than in 1662 and 1928, the Litany is divided into its traditional elements.

Section 1: The Invocations

These have been abbreviated and restored to something approaching their original form—four simple invocations of Father, Son, Holy Spirit and the Trinity, without relative or subordinate clauses. Instead of the repetition of each invocation as a response, Kyrie eleison has been restored as the traditional response. Cranmer's addition of 'miserable sinners' has been omitted (cf. p. 38).

Section 2: The Deprecations and the Obsecrations

These two elements, both addressed to Christ, are combined in a single section. The first five are the Deprecations and the second four are the Obsecrations. Taken together, they pray for deliverance from our outward and inward enemies by Christ's mighty works. Cranmer's long introductory antiphon, with its rather excessive emphasis on the divine wrath and anger, has been omitted. The sins and evils from which we pray for deliverance are rearranged in a more logical order. Hardness of heart and contempt for the divine word and law, for example, come more appropriately with the spiritual shortcomings than with sedition, violence and murder. Other elements, not included in 1662, are also thought worthy of mention—sloth, worldliness and love of money. 'Sudden death' has been replaced by 'dying unprepared': there have been numerous criticisms ever since the Reformation against the phrase 'sudden death' as misleading. The Latin was *a subitanea et improvisa morte*, i.e. a death which is unexpected and for which we are not prepared. The final Obsecration in 1662—'In all time of our tribulation . . .'—is really a Deprecation and accordingly has been transferred, becoming 'In all times of sorrow; in all times of joy'.

The Obsecrations have been extended from two to four. To proceed from our Lord's baptism and temptation straight to the passion without any reference to his earthly ministry is to ignore an important element of his mighty works: hence the inclusion of 'By your ministry in word and work'. It was also considered an improvement to distinguish between the events of the passion, culminating in death and burial, and the events of Easter, Ascension and Pentecost: the single Obsecration of 1662 has therefore been extended to become two.

Section 3: Intercessions for the Church

In 1662 the petitions for the Church came in no logical order and were interspersed with petitions for the State and for those in need. They have now been brought together in a single section, and the unity and mission of the Church are included. 'Bishops, priests, and deacons' are replaced by 'ministers' in recognition of the fact that ministry is exercised by a great many people both ordained and unordained.

Section 4: Intercessions for the World

Here again the petitions for the world have been brought together and are clearly set in a world-wide context, beginning with 'the leaders of the nations' and ending with 'all your people'. 'The magistrates' is extended to cover all who administer the law, while commerce and industry are included in the penultimate petition, 'Teach us to use the fruits of the earth'.

Section 5: Intercessions for the Suffering and the Departed

An attempt has again been made to set out the petitions in a more logical order, avoiding, for example, the incongruous mixture in 1662 of 'all that travel by land or by water, all women labouring of child, all sick persons and young children, and to shew thy pity upon all prisoners and captives'; although admittedly this petition is remarkably similar to a grouping in the Liturgy of St John Chrysostom. It has also been considered appropriate to make specific reference to certain groups whose needs are very real today—the homeless, the hungry, the destitute, prisoners, and refugees. The final petition includes not only committed Christians, but those outside the Church.

Section 6: Conclusion

The conclusion is brief, and omits the 1662 Supplication in time of War. It takes the final 1662 petition, asking for true repentance, forgiveness and amendment of life, and then ends with the Trisagion, an Eastern form which appears for the first time; although Cranmer did use a paraphrase of it in the Committal at the Burial Service. Traditionally this was sung in the East at the Little Entrance, but it came to be used in the West both in the Gallican and Roman rites in the Reproaches on Good Friday. It also appeared in the Sarum Breviary within the Antiphon to the Nunc Dimittis at Compline in the second half of Lent. Luther also made a metrical translation which was suggested for use at burials in Hermann's *Consultation*. This may have inspired Cranmer to use it in his Burial rite. It forms a much better ending than simply Kyrie eleison, and balances the invocations at the beginning.

4

The Calendar

A

HISTORY

General studies:
M. Crum, 'Our approach to the Christian Year; chronological or eschatological' (*Worship* 51, 1977), pp. 24–32.
A. A. McArthur, *The Evolution of the Christian Year*. 1953.
R. Taft, 'Historicism Revisited' (*SL* 14, 1982), pp. 97–109.
—'The Liturgical Year: Studies, Prospects, Reflections' (*Worship* 55, 1981), pp. 2–23.
T. J. Talley, 'Liturgical Time in the Ancient Church: the State of Research' (*SL* 14, 1982), pp. 34–51.

1 The Week

Christians inherited the seven-day week from Judaism, where the seventh day, the Sabbath, formed the climax, commemorating both the completion of God's work of creation (see Exod. 20.8–11) and also the liberation of Israel from bondage in Egypt (Deut. 5.12–15). It was observed both by complete abstinence from work and also by special acts of worship—the doubling of the daily sacrifices in the Temple (Num. 28.9–10) and the reading of the Law and the Prophets in the synagogue. Certain other days of the week also came to be marked in a particular way: on Mondays and Thursdays, the old market days of Palestine when the country folk would congregate in the villages and towns and so might be expected to be able to attend worship, there were services of the word in the synagogue similar to that on the Sabbath. These days were also kept as times of voluntary fasting by the pious, and occasionally as public fasts.

Although Jesus is said to have deliberately infringed the regulations concerning the keeping of the Sabbath (see, for example, Mark 2.23ff.; 3.1ff.; Luke 13.10ff.; 14.1ff.) and not to have practised fasting (Matt. 9.14–15; 11.18–19), the Gospels record his continued attendance at synagogue services on the Sabbath (see, for example, Luke 4.16ff.), and his followers appear to have adhered to this custom after his resurrection (see, for example, Acts 13.5,14; 14.1). Gentile Christians, however, seem to have abandoned the observance of the Sabbath along with the other demands of the Jewish Law, and the only mark of respect for the day which remained later was that it was thought improper to fast then, with the sole exception of the Saturday immediately preceding Easter Day when fasting was a universal custom. On the other hand, from the fourth century onwards there was a growing tendency to hold a celebration of the Eucharist every Saturday and thus accord it a certain privileged position within the week.

From very early times it became the rule among Christians to meet every Sunday for a celebration of the Eucharist. Indeed for the first few centuries this was the only day upon which the Eucharist was regularly celebrated. Because it was a day of joy, kneeling for worship and fasting were both forbidden on this day. At first it was a normal working day, but it was made a civil day of rest in AD 321 by the Emperor Constantine.

In spite of the fact that Jesus himself had not practised fasting, the early Christians resumed the tradition of regular weekly fast-days, but adopted Wednesdays and Fridays for these instead of Mondays and Thursdays. Like the Jews, they held services of the word on these days, usually at 3 p.m., to commemorate the death of Christ and mark the end of the period of fasting that day. Later these services included a celebration of the Eucharist, though eventually in the West the Wednesday fast ceased to be observed.

Studies:
S. Bacciocchi, *From Sabbath to Sunday.* Rome 1977.
R. T. Beckwith and W. Stott, *This is the Day.* 1978.
D. A. Carson (ed.), *From Sabbath to Lord's Day.* 1982.
W. Rordorf, *Sunday.* 1968.

2 Easter

At first Easter was the only annual festival of the Christian Church, and commemorated in a single feast both the death and the resurrection of Christ. It is not clear, however, when its observance first began. Although some scholars would continue to assign its origin to apostolic times, others believe that it only became widespread in the course of the second century. Similarly, although some still adhere to the traditional view that it was from the outset kept on the Sunday following the Jewish Passover, and that the custom of celebrating it on the date of the Jewish Passover, which obtained in Asia in the second and third centuries, was a local deviation from the norm, others now believe that the latter practice was in fact the original tradition, and the transference to Sunday a later development.

In many churches, at least from the end of the second century onwards if not sooner, baptism was closely associated with Easter, and was usually the only occasion in the year when it was administered. Thus new converts were sacramentally incorporated into the death and resurrection of Christ within the Church's annual celebration of those redeeming events, and then participated in the Easter Eucharist.

At this period the Easter liturgy consisted of a vigil of readings and prayer throughout the Saturday night, with the celebration of baptism and the Eucharist at cockcrow on Easter Day. It was preceded, as we have already indicated, by a time of fasting on the Saturday, which the more pious would extend to two days or even more.

Studies:

R. T. Beckwith, 'The Origin of the Festivals Easter and Whitsun' (*SL* 13, 1979), pp. 1–20.

Roger Greenacre, *The Sacrament of Easter*. 1965.

T. J. Talley, 'History and Eschatology in the Primitive Pascha' (*Worship* 47, 1973), pp. 212–21.

3 Ascension Day, Pentecost and Trinity Sunday

At least from the end of the second century, if not sooner, the celebration of Easter was extended for a period of fifty days, corresponding to the Jewish feast of Pentecost, which were treated as a continuous succession of Sundays, neither kneeling nor fasting being allowed during this time. At first no special emphasis was laid on the fiftieth day itself, but in the course of the fourth century there was a growing tendency for the liturgical practice of the Church to accommodate itself to the chronology of Luke–Acts, and eventually this day came to be seen as a commemoration of the events recorded in Acts 2 and a celebration of the mission of the Holy Spirit. This tended, of course, to break up the older understanding of Easter and its fifty days as a unified celebration of the whole work of redemption, and this process was further increased when the practice of giving special stress to the first eight days of the Easter season—from Easter Day to the following Sunday—was extended to other feasts in the year. Thus the Day of Pentecost too came to be treated as a separate feast with its own 'octave' attached to it. It also quite naturally came to be thought of as a particularly appropriate occasion for the celebration of baptism, and that seems to be the origin of the later English name for this day—Whitsunday—being an allusion to the white robes which the newly baptized wore.

Ascension Day naturally emerged alongside the separation of Pentecost in the fourth century, although apparently at Jerusalem, and perhaps elsewhere, there was a tendency at first to celebrate the ascension of Jesus on the fiftieth day along with the coming of the Spirit. But an increasing preference for ending the period of rejoicing on the fortieth day after Easter and resuming normal fasting practices then 'when the bridegroom is taken away' (Matt. 9.14–15; Mark 2.18–20; Luke 5.33–5) eventually gave rise to a universal custom of ending the season of Easter with a festival of the Ascension on that day.

Trinity Sunday did not emerge until the tenth century, and was enjoined for universal observance in the West by Pope John XXII in 1334. The medieval Sarum calendar in England then numbered the succeeding Sundays as 'after Trinity' instead of 'after Pentecost'.

Studies:

John Gunstone, *The Feast of Pentecost.* 1967.

Patrick Ryan, 'The Fifty Days and the Fiftieth Day' (*Worship* 55, 1981), pp. 194–218.

4 *Holy Week*

The origins of Holy Week are also to be sought in the fourth century at Jerusalem, where a dramatic commemoration of the events of the last week of the earthly life of Christ developed, with the whole Christian community there visiting the sites of those events at the very hours when they were said to have taken place. Thus on the Saturday before what later came to be called in the West Palm Sunday there was a visit to Bethany, where the account of the raising of Lazarus was read. On Palm Sunday they went to the Mount of Olives and returned in procession to the city bearing branches of palm. There was an evening visit to the Mount of Olives on Tuesday in Holy Week, recalling Christ's nightly withdrawal there. On Maundy Thursday the Eucharist was celebrated in the afternoon, a vigil kept at the Mount of Olives, Gethsemane visited after midnight, and then the congregation returned to the city on the Friday morning for the reading of the account of the trial of Jesus. During the day there was an act of worship before a supposed relic of the cross of Christ, a long service in commemoration of the passion, and a visit at the end of the day to the site of the Holy Sepulchre where the account of the burial of Jesus was read.

A flood of pilgrims to the Holy Land at this period inevitably carried news of this moving innovation back to their own countries. Clearly, it had a profound effect upon all who took part. Equally clearly, it was impossible for all Christians to be physically present at the sacred sites to celebrate Holy Week and Easter each year, but it was possible for them to be spiritually present: they could dramatically relive in their own churches the events of the gospel. And so, with considerable variation in detail from place to place, and with ever-growing elaboration in the course of the Middle Ages, Holy Week came to be celebrated everywhere, though it did not always entirely displace older customs. Thus in the West on Palm Sunday, although there was a dramatic re-enactment of the triumphal entry into Jerusalem before the Eucharist, the theme of that service itself, following an older custom, was the passion of Christ, and the whole of the passion narrative from Matthew's Gospel was read then in preparation for the celebration of the death and resurrection of Christ on the following Sunday.

Maundy Thursday derives its name from the Latin word *mandatum*, 'command', referring to Jesus' command to his disciples in John 13 that they should love one another and demonstrate that love by washing each other's feet, just as he had washed theirs. The custom arose for all superiors, such as bishops, abbots and kings, to wash the feet of their subjects during the Eucharist on this day, and the present-day distribution of Maundy money by the English monarch is a modified version of this ancient practice. This was also commonly the day on which the oils for use in the initiation rites of the Easter liturgy would be blessed by the bishop, since it was the last occasion on which the Eucharist would be celebrated prior to that, there being by tradition no full celebration of the Eucharist on Good Friday or Holy Saturday.

> *Studies:*
> J. G. Davies, *Holy Week: a short history.* 1963.
> J. W. Tyrer, *Historical Survey of Holy Week.* 1932.

5 *Lent*

This season takes its origins from the final period of preparation, usually of six weeks' duration, for those who were to be baptized at the Easter liturgy. The same period also came to be used as a time of public penance for those who had committed grave sin. They were solemnly expelled from the eucharistic fellowship at the beginning of the season in a ceremony which customarily involved the imposition of ashes on their heads, a biblical symbol of mourning and penitence, and they remained thus, temporarily excommunicated and expressing their repentance through fasting and works of charity, until they were received back into communion just before Easter and so enabled to participate in that celebration of redemption and liberation from sin. When, later, both the formal catechumenate for baptism and an official order of penitents went into decline, it became the custom for the whole Church to undergo this period of penitence and fasting, eventually fixed at forty days in imitation of Christ's forty-day fast in the wilderness.

Study:
Patrick Ryan, 'The Three Days and the Forty Days' (*Worship* 54, 1980), pp. 2–18.

6 *Christmas and Epiphany*

Unlike Easter, these festivals did not emerge until about the fourth century, and it would seem that at first they were alternative versions of one another, 25 December being observed in the West and 6 January in the East. Both were celebrations of the incarnation of Christ, and encompassed his birth, his baptism and his manifestation to the world. Liturgical scholars have generally explained the choice of date as a conscious reaction by the Church to the pagan celebration of the winter solstice on those days, different calendrical calculations being used in East and West to determine when this fell. Recently, however, it has been suggested that an older theory about their origins warrants reconsideration. This proposed that the dates were arrived at through a complicated Christian computation intended to determine the actual date of Christ's birth by reference to the supposed date of his death, the difference between East and West again being explained by differences in calculating the date of Easter in early times. Nevertheless, whatever the reasons for the original choice of these dates, by the fifth century, through a process of assimilation, both dates were observed in both East and West, 25 December now coming to be restricted to a commemoration of the nativity of Christ, and 6 January concentrating on the themes of the visit of the Magi, the baptism of Christ, and his manifestation at the wedding at Cana.

Study:
John Gunstone, *Christmas and Epiphany.* 1967.

7 *Advent*

This seems to have originated in Gaul in the fifth or sixth century as a period of preparation, first for Epiphany, when baptisms were often administered, in imitation of Eastern practice, and later for Christmas. Its length tended to vary from three weeks to forty days or even more. Its observance spread elsewhere, and its duration was eventually fixed as the four Sundays before Christmas. Though obviously influenced by Lent, it was never accompanied by such strenuous fasting and penitence as that season. Even in the 1662 Book of Common Prayer it is still not included in the list of days of fasting and abstinence.

8 *Saints' Days*

These began to be kept as early as the second century, but were at first confined entirely to a celebration of local martyrs on the day of their deaths and in the very place where they had been buried. Only very slowly were others besides martyrs added to local calendars, and only gradually did saints come to be celebrated in other churches besides their own. Because of this, the biblical saints were relatively late additions to the annual cycle of feast days. In the course of the Middle Ages the number of saints' days steadily increased, until eventually most days in the year had one such commemoration attached to them, and sometimes more than one.

Studies:
Peter Brown, *The Cult of the Saints.* 1981.
Michael Perham, *The Communion of Saints.* 1980.
For biographies of individual saints, see such works as Donald Attwater, *A Dictionary of Saints* (1965); H. Thurston and Donald Attwater (eds), *Butler's Lives of the Saints* (4 vols, 1956); F. L. Cross (ed.), *The Oxford Dictionary of the Christian Church* (1957).

9 The Church of England

The Reformed Churches tended almost to abolish the liturgical year in its entirety, but in England simplification was instead the aim. The Prayer Book of 1549 retained the general pattern of seasons inherited from the Middle Ages and the arrangement of readings and collects for the Sundays of the year, but provided little other liturgical variation: all ceremonies connected with different occasions in the year were swept away, and proper prefaces in the Eucharistic Prayer were appointed for only five days in the whole year—Christmas Day, Easter Day, Ascension Day, Whitsunday and Trinity Sunday. Similarly, only a total of twenty-five Holy Days, mainly feasts of Our Lord and of New Testament saints, were recognized and given their own collect and readings.

In 1552 four other traditional saints' days were restored to the calendar of the Prayer Book, but their entries were printed in black instead of red like the other feasts, and they were not provided with any means of liturgical observance—no collect or readings. Fifty-nine further Black Letter saints' days were added to the calendar during the reign of Elizabeth I, and retained in the 1662 book. It is probable that their inclusion in the calendar was mainly done for the purpose of assisting the secular calculation of dates and not with the intention of their liturgical commemoration.

The general arrangement of the seasons and the major festivals and feast days of the year was again preserved in the proposed 1927/8 revision, with only minor adjustments and improvements. Thus provision was made for those years when there were two Sundays between Christmas Day and Epiphany, and the Feast of the Transfiguration (6 August) was elevated from Black Letter to Red Letter status and given its own collect, epistle and gospel. Additional proper prefaces were included in the service of Holy Communion—for Epiphany and the seven days after, for Maundy Thursday, for the feasts of the Purification and Annunciation, for the Transfiguration, for principal saints' days, for the consecration and feast of the dedication of a church, and for use on any Sunday—and the use of others extended from the octave to the whole of the relevant season—that for Christmas until Epiphany, that for Easter until Ascension Day, and that for the Ascension until Whitsunday.

Considerable changes were made with regard to saints' days. One Red Letter day was added—the feast of Mary Magdalen (22 July), and a better selection of Black Letter days offered, and these were given liturgical material for their celebration: a common collect, epistle and gospel were provided for each category—martyrs, bishops, confessors, and so on. Many of the saints listed in the 1662 calendar about whom little was known or who had no real relevance to England were now omitted, and new ones substituted. The revisers restricted themselves to formally canonized saints from the pre-Reformation period, however, and drew back from adding any Reformation or post-Reformation figures, though they did designate 8 November, the octave day of All Saints', as the feast of 'Saints, Martyrs, Missionaries, and Doctors of the Church of England.' Another, perhaps more controversial addition, was the designation of 2 November as 'The Commemoration of All Souls'. Although this was an ancient observance, dating back to the end of the tenth century, it had disappeared at the time of the Reformation, along with all prayer for the departed and the offering of the Eucharist for their benefit. Its re-emergence is an indication of the greater doctrinal breadth of Anglicanism at this period.

Since the more recent history of the calendar in the Church of England has been bound up with the lectionary, it will be considered further with that (see below, pp. 298–322).

B
COMMENTARY

The Temporale: The Seasons
(pp. 15–16)

In ASB the Church's year begins on the ninth Sunday before Christmas. The length of the pre-Christmas period has varied in the course of history and is still of varying length. Milan keeps five weeks, the Eastern churches longer; while the Church of South India, although maintaining an Advent season of four weeks, nevertheless clearly thinks in 'Advent terms' for the last five Sundays of Pentecost. There is therefore no historical precedent for a strict adherence to an Advent of four weeks. The proposal for a nine-week pre-Christmas period appeared in 1967 in the Joint Liturgical Group's report on *The Calendar and Lectionary*. This was accepted by the Liturgical Commission in 1969 and finally endorsed by the General Synod in 1978. These nine weeks are divided into two groups. The first five—the 9th to the 5th Sundays before Christmas—have subsidiary titles—the 5th to the 1st Sundays before Advent; while the second four are the four Sundays in Advent with subsidiary titles—the 4th to the 1st Sundays before Christmas. Despite the changing titles, these nine weeks constitute a single 'season', and the first five have broken their association with the season of Pentecost.

The Christmas cycle depends on a fixed date—25 December—but the Easter cycle has no such fixed point. It would be a boon to those responsible for creating Calendars and Lectionaries if the various churches could agree on a fixed day for Easter. But until such agreement is reached, flexibility must be allowed in the season of Epiphany and in the season of Pentecost. However, the Calendar in ASB has reached a greater degree of uniformity by matching the pre-Christmas season of nine weeks with a pre-Easter season of nine weeks, a proposal which again came from the Joint Liturgical Group's Report of 1967. To the six weeks of Lent are now added the three previous weeks, which have long been associated with the titles Septuagesima, Sexagesima and Quinquagesima. Despite their long history, they present problems. Quinquagesima is certainly the fiftieth day before Easter: but the other two are not the sixtieth and seventieth days before Easter. Again, Quinquagesima falls into further problems if consideration is given to a traditional title for the first Sunday in

Lent—Quadragesima. Attempts have been made to find some kind of rationalization by arguing that the forty days of Lent should not include Holy Week; or by suggesting that in some places, e.g. in Milan, Saturdays were not included in the forty days. But no really satisfactory rationale can be found for these three titles, despite the fact that they were in the lectionary of St Jerome and in the ancient Sacramentaries. Significantly they are not found in the Eastern Church. By replacing these three incomprehensible titles with the simple nomenclature—9th to the 7th Sundays before Easter—attention is immediately directed forward to Lent and Easter, and not backward to Epiphany and Christmas. This is made even clearer by their subsidiary titles— 3rd to the 1st Sundays before Lent.

A subsidiary title is also given to the Sunday after Ascension Day—the 6th Sunday after Easter—another proposal coming from the Joint Liturgical Group. This draws attention to the unity of the great 'Fifty Days' from Easter to Pentecost. Pentecost also becomes the title of the final season in the Church's year—a title which not only marks it as the fiftieth day from Easter, but which is also found in the New Testament (Acts 2.1). It is only in Northern Europe that the Sundays of this season were named 'after Trinity' instead of 'after Pentecost'. Trinity is itself a late feast, dating only from the fourteenth century, and exceptional as proclaiming a doctrine, whereas the titles of other seasons proclaim events. The restoration of the ancient title 'Pentecost', drawing attention to the fact of the Church living in the power of the Holy Spirit, is now widely accepted by Christian churches. Trinity Sunday itself retains its title, however; and all the Sundays after Pentecost are given subsidiary titles of Sundays after Trinity.

Principal Holy Days
(p. 17)

The Red Letter days or 'major feasts' of the 1549–1928 Prayer Books are now designated under one of two titles, either Principal Holy Days or Festivals and Greater Holy Days. The former—the Principal Holy Days—include all Sundays in the year; for in a very real sense every Sunday is a festival of our Lord. Obviously, as Sundays, Easter and Pentecost are included; and there are five weekdays in this list—Christmas Day, the Epiphany, Maundy Thursday, Good Friday and Ascension Day. 1662 contained a much longer list, including not only Sundays and all the major

Feasts but also all the Red Letter days: all these were designated as 'feasts that are to be observed in the Church of England'. It is now recognized that a general obligatory observance of such a long list is unrealistic. A wider approach is to concentrate on Sundays and a small handful of other major days to which the Church attaches the greatest possible importance. This relatively short list of Principal Holy Days is therefore the equivalent of the former 'days of obligation'. Indeed, if Canons B6(2) and B14 are taken together, they provide a list of specific days which should be observed by a celebration of the Eucharist—Christmas Day, the Epiphany, the Annunciation, Ash Wednesday, Easter Day, Ascension Day, Pentecost, Trinity Sunday, and All Saints' Day.

It should be noted that the Epiphany has lost its 1662 sub-title 'The Manifestation of Christ to the Gentiles'. This was only inserted in 1662 and has now been omitted because it imposes an unnecessary limitation on the meaning of the Epiphany.

Festivals and Greater Holy Days
(pp. 17–18)

These are the 1662 Red Letter days with some amendments and additions. Their observance is now optional: but all are provided with special collects and readings, both for the Eucharist and for the daily office. It should also be noted that some of these days are also included in the Sunday provision, thereby giving them an additional opportunity for observance. The Epiphany is included in the provision for Christmas 2; the Presentation of Christ in the Temple on Christmas 1; the Annunciation on Advent 4; and the Transfiguration on Lent 4. Since the Church's year no longer begins with the first Sunday in Advent, it has been thought wise to set out this list according to the civil calendar, beginning on 1 January.

January 1: The Naming of Jesus, or the Circumcision of Christ

The 1662 title has now become the alternative title and has been replaced by 'The Naming of Jesus'. The significance of the name of Jesus—Saviour—is now recognized as greater than the significance of his circumcision, while the Gospel of the day (cf. Luke 2.21) gives emphasis to the Name. This change has been accepted elsewhere in the Anglican Communion, e.g. South Africa, America, Australia, Ireland. In 1928 it was observed on 7 August. The feast of the Circumcision is of Gallican origin and was in existence before the Council of Tours (567) as a Christian counter to a pagan New Year's festival.

January 25: The Conversion of St Paul

Another feast which was celebrated in the Gallican rite by the sixth century.

February 2: The Presentation of Christ in the Temple

Originally celebrated in Jerusalem in the fourth century forty days after the Epiphany—14 February. When 25 December was accepted as the date of the Nativity, the Presentation was moved to 2 February. The Syrian Pope Sergius I (687–701) introduced the procession with candles to Rome. 1549 called it 'The Purification of St Mary the Virgin' but 1662 changed it to 'The Presentation of Christ in the Temple, commonly called, the Purification of Saint Mary the Virgin'.

March 19: St Joseph of Nazareth, Husband of the Blessed Virgin Mary

The observance of this day has had a long history in other parts of the Church. The Copts of Egypt observed it in the fourth century, and there is evidence for its observance in the West in the ninth and tenth centuries. The Roman calendar adopted it in the fifteenth century. The day is now widely observed in the Anglican Communion.

March 25: The Annunciation of our Lord to the Blessed Virgin Mary

The title has been slightly amended to make it agree with the facts of the New Testament. The Annunciation was not *of* the Blessed Virgin Mary, but of our Lord, and it was made *to* the BVM. The date has links with that of Christmas. Once the latter became established on 25 December, the Annunciation became established on 25 March. The feast was celebrated in the East by the fifth century, and was instituted in Rome by the Syrian Pope Sergius I.

April 25: St Mark the Evangelist

This feast was of fairly late origin, beginning in the twelfth century. This date had been observed in the Gregorian Sacramentary as the date of the *Robigalia* or Major Litany—a Rogationtide procession (see p. 65).

May 1: St Philip and St James, Apostles

The feast dates from the late sixth century, when the Basilica of the Apostles was dedicated in Rome during the pontificate of Pope John III (561–74). Tradition says that relics of the two apostles were buried there.

May 14: St Matthias the Apostle

The observance has been transferred from 24 February, where it was frequently obscured by the fast of Lent. The Church of England follows the Church of Rome in making the change. The feast dates from at least the eleventh century. If worshippers prefer to keep the earlier date of 24 February, they are free to do so.

June 11: St Barnabas the Apostle

This feast was celebrated in the East by the fifth century, but it did not reach Rome until after the eleventh.

June 24: The Birth of St John the Baptist

St John the Baptist was held in great veneration in the East, being regarded as only second to the Blessed Virgin Mary. In the Gallican rite there were feasts both of the nativity and the 'passion'. The nativity appears in all the early Western sacramentaries. The Sarum Missal also had propers for the beheading on 29 August, but these were omitted by Cranmer in 1549. 1928 reintroduced it as a Black Letter day, but it has been omitted in ASB, one Red Letter day for the saint being considered sufficient. The title has been amended from the 'Nativity' to the 'Birth'.

June 29: St Peter the Apostle: St Peter and St Paul, Apostles

In addition to the observance of St Peter, ASB makes additional provision for those who wish to follow the ancient custom of commemorating both St Peter and St Paul on this day. This is one of the oldest observances in the Church, dating from AD 258 during the Valerian persecution in Rome. The Leonine Sacramentary had twenty-eight sets of propers for this day, and the two apostles were commemorated jointly in the Sarum Missal. Cranmer abandoned this ancient practice, retaining 29 June for St Peter only, and commemorating the Conversion of St Paul on 25 January. In common with many parts of the Anglican Communion, the Church of England now provides for the ancient Roman practice of a joint commemoration on this day. It is optional, however; and the 1662 observances of 25 January and 29 June may be followed if so desired.

July 3: St Thomas the Apostle

His commemoration, which apparently originated in Syria, is found in the West by the time of the Gelasian Sacramentary. In common with the Church of Rome, the Church of England has transferred this feast from 21 December, where it tended to be obscured by Christmas. If worshippers prefer to observe the December date, they are free to do so.

July 22: St Mary Magdalen

This feast appears to be of late origin: there is evidence that it was made a day of obligation at the Council of Oxford in 1222. Cranmer took it from the Sarum Missal in 1549, observing it as a Red Letter day. It was deleted in 1552 and restored in 1662 as a Black Letter day. 1928 upgraded it again to a Red Letter day, and so it remains in ASB.

July 25: St James the Apostle

The date of his observance has varied. In the Eastern churches his feast was celebrated near Easter. In the Gallican rites he was commemorated with his brother John on 27 December. In the Gregorian Sacramentary his feast appears on 25 July, but the reason for this choice is obscure.

August 6: The Transfiguration of our Lord

Although this feast was observed in the Eastern Church by the late fourth century and in certain Western monastic communities by the tenth century, it was not until 1457 that Pope Callistus III declared it a universal feast in the Western Church. Despite its having a place in the Sarum Missal, Cranmer omitted it in 1549. By 1662 it had returned as a Black Letter day, and 1928 upgraded it to a Red Letter day. Its observance is now widespread in the Anglican Communion.

August 24: St Bartholomew the Apostle

In the East he was first commemorated on 11 June with St

Barnabas. In the West his feast appears as early as the Gregorian Sacramentary.

September 8: The Blessed Virgin Mary

The feast of the 'Falling Asleep' or Assumption of the Blessed Virgin Mary is ancient, appearing in the East by the fourth century, and in the West in the Gelasian Sacramentary. The date was 15 August. The Feast of the Nativity was also observed, appearing in the Sarum Missal: Cranmer omitted it, however, in 1549, and it only appeared in 1662 as a Black Letter day. 1928 retained the Visitation as a Black Letter day, but in common with previous Prayer Books did not include the Falling Asleep on 15 August. After considerable discussion the General Synod decided to accord the Blessed Virgin Mary Red Letter status, but opted for 8 September rather than 15 August, in case the latter date would be associated with certain doctrines about the Assumption which the Church of England is not prepared to accept.

September 21: St Matthew the Apostle

In the East his feast day is 16 November: but in the West the date was 21 September as early as the Gregorian Sacramentary.

September 29: St Michael and All Angels

In Rome a feast in honour of St Michael was observed in the fifth century, when a church was dedicated to him. The Leonine Sacramentary also included the feast of St Michael. It was Cranmer who added 'All Angels' in 1549.

October 18: St Luke the Evangelist

The observance of his feast on 18 October is of early origin in both East and West. It appears in the Gregorian Sacramentary.

October 28: St Simon and St Jude, Apostles

In the East they are commemorated on 1 July, the traditional date of their martyrdom, supposedly in Persia. In the West, however, they appear in the Gregorian Sacramentary on 28 October: and the date may commemorate a translation of their relics to St Peter's Basilica.

November 1: All Saints

The feast is ancient, but the date has varied. Some traditions trace it to as early as 270, when it was apparently celebrated as a feast of All Martyrs. Some Eastern churches observe the Sunday after Pentecost, a date mentioned by St John Chrysostom. The East Syrians observe the Friday in Easter week, a date going back to the fifth century. The first evidence in the West is in 835 in a letter from Pope Gregory IV to the Emperor Louis the Pious, urging him to adopt the feast in his realm. Some authorities claim that 1 November as the date of the feast began in Ireland, and from there spread to England and the Continent.

November 30: St Andrew the Apostle

His observance on this day is of long standing both in the East and in the West. In Rome his feast was observed by the late fifth century, and it appears in the sacramentaries.

December 26: St Stephen the first Martyr

Another feast of ancient origin. It probably originated in Jerusalem in the fourth century. It was certainly observed in Rome in the fifth century, when a church was dedicated to him.

December 27: St John the Evangelist

Another feast celebrated both in the East and in the West from the earliest times. His feast appears in the Leonine Sacramentary.

December 28: The Holy Innocents

This feast was celebrated in Rome and other parts of the West by the late fifth century. Apparently it was also commemorated in May in Bethlehem by the fourth century, according to some scholars.

Lesser Festivals and Commemorations
(pp. 18–21)

The approach to Lesser Festivals and Commemorations in ASB is very different from that in previous Prayer Books. Such days did not even appear in 1549 and 1552; and while 1662 included a number of them in the Calendar, no propers were provided and no guidance was given as to their observance. 1928 did something to remedy this, but the result was still far from satisfactory. The list of days was revised, although it still contained no one later than the thirteenth century; propers were appointed for nine of the days, commons were appointed for the rest; and provision was made for other occasions such as the forty days of Lent, Ember Days and Harvest Thanksgiving.

The revision of such a list was no easy matter: for neither the Church of England nor even the whole Anglican Communion has any machinery for canonization. Unlike the Church of Rome they cannot designate certain people to be 'saints'. Valuable guidance on this question was given by a Commission appointed by the Archbishop of Canterbury to prepare a document for consideration by the Lambeth Conference of 1958. Its Report, *The Commemoration of Saints and Heroes of the Faith in the Anglican Communion*, while recognizing the difficulties involved in producing a Calendar, was able to provide certain basic principles which have generally stood the Anglican Communion in good stead ever since. It accepted that individuals could not be designated 'saints': but it pointed out that throughout its history the Church has produced men and women whose martyrdom or sanctity merit recognition. Such people could be commemorated annually, normally on the day of their death, if that be known. With the passage of time such annual commemorations are 'welded in' to the devotional life of the Church. It also recognized that saintly people who are greatly revered in one part of the world may be quite unknown in another. Provinces, and indeed individual dioceses, should therefore be free to draw up their own Calendars. The Church of England now recognizes this provincial and diocesan freedom in Canon B6(5): 'It is lawful for the Convocations of Canterbury and York to approve Holy Days which may be observed provincially, and, subject to any directions of the Convocation of the province, for the Ordinary to approve Holy Days which may be observed locally'. Finally, there are the criteria for recognition. First of all, the individuals should be people whose life and history are well attested, and of whose sanctity there is no doubt. Secondly, they should be recognized for individual merit, and should not be chosen simply because they represent a particular area, or a particular period, or a particular movement. Thirdly, they should be men and women whose lives have excited other people to sanctity. The Report concluded: 'By such a quiet and natural procedure, the Anglican Communion could with a more settled consciousness and by a more clearly defined method, honour its saints and heroes of faith, learn from the light of Christ manifest in their lives and achievements, and deepen its sense of communion and community with the eternal world' (pp. 72–3). To these principles the Church of England added one more, which it borrowed from the Anglican Church in the United States: to avoid any danger of succumbing to some 'cult of the passing moment', people should not be considered for inclusion in the Calendar until they had been dead for at least fifty years.

Despite a careful application of such criteria, it has to be recognized that any Calendar is bound to have a degree of subjectivity about it. It is therefore open to revision from time to time, and its observance is optional. It has also been kept within manageable proportions. There are 85 Lesser Festivals and Commemorations in the ASB Calendar covering the whole history of the Christian Church, from Timothy and Titus in the New Testament to Edward King, Bishop of Lincoln, who died in 1910. A device to permit the commemoration of other saintly people whose names do not appear in the Calendar has been the inclusion of eight days for 'Group Commemorations'—for Africa, 21 February; the Americas, 8 April; Europe, 3 February; Australia and the Pacific, 20 September; Asia, 3 December; England, 8 November; and the Reformation, 31 October. All these days have particular local significance:

Africa: 21 February. The date in the South African Calendar for the Missionaries and Martyrs of Africa.

The Americas: 8 April. The date in the ECUSA Calendar for commemorating William Muhlenberg, priest, one of America's saintliest figures.

Europe: 3 February. Already in the 1928 Calendar as the date for commemorating Anskar, one of Europe's great missionary bishops.

Australia: 20 September. The death day of John Coleridge Patteson, Bishop of Melanesia and Martyr: already in many Anglican Calendars.

Asia: 3 December. The death day of Francis Xavier, one of the great priests and missionaries to the East: already in many Anglican and the Roman Calendars.

England: 8 November. The octave of All Saints, and already in the

1928 Calendar for 'Saints, Martyrs, Missionaries, and Doctors of the Church of England'.

Reformation: 31 October. Already observed in Lutheran Calendars as Reformation Day.

It has to be admitted that the one day in the list of Lesser Festivals which causes some misgiving is one which would produce consternation if it were omitted, namely, that of St George, the Patron Saint of England. He is a shadowy figure, and the circumstances surrounding his acceptance as patron saint are also obscure.

Details of each entry in this list of Lesser Festivals have not been included in the Commentary. These are available elsewhere. In 1982 the Alcuin Club published *The Cloud of Witnesses*, which was a companion to the Lesser Festivals and Holydays in ASB. This contains not only collects and readings, but brief biographical details. Most of the entries occur in:

D. H. Farmer, *The Oxford Dictionary of Saints*. 1978.
D. Attwater, *The Penguin Dictionary of Saints*. 1965.

According to the terms of Rule 6, if a Lesser Festival falls on a Principal Holy Day, a Festival or Greater Holy Day, Ash Wednesday, the days of Holy Week and Easter Week, or Ascension Day, the Lesser Festival lapses. On the other hand, if a Lesser Festival is observed as the Feast of the Patron Saint or Title of a church, it may be treated as a Festival or Greater Holy Day. But even when such a day lapses, there is no reason why commemoration may not be made in the intercessions at the Eucharist or in the prayers after the third collect at Morning or Evening Prayer. This is provided for in Rule 7. On the occasions when two individuals are commemorated on the same day, e.g. 20 March (Cuthbert and Thomas Ken), or 17 November (Hilda of Whitby and Hugh of Lincoln), either or both may be commemorated, at the discretion of the minister.

Special Days of Prayer and Thanksgiving
(pp. 21–2)

There are a number of days in the Church's year for which ASB makes special provision. They do not fall within one particular category, but for various reasons merit observance.

63

1 The Eves of Christmas and Easter

An eve is a whole day, and should not be confused with a 'first evensong'. Christmas and Easter are two key days in the Church's year, and spiritual preparation no less than material preparation for them is important. These two eves are the survivors in ASB of the Vigils in 1662. Both days are provided with collects and proper readings.

2 Ember Days

The name 'Ember' is thought to come from the Old English words *ymb*, 'about', and *ryne*, 'course', meaning literally 'periodical'. The observance of such days can be traced to pre-Christian times. Pagan Rome had three seasons of sacrifice connected with agriculture, corresponding to the winter sowing, the summer reaping and the autumn vintage. These were taken over by the Christian Church—according to tradition by Pope Callistus I (*c.* 220)—and subsequently expanded from three seasons to four —the Quattuor Tempora. They were known as the fasts of the first, fourth, seventh and tenth months, and were observed on the three days of the week already observed as fasts—Wednesday, Friday and Saturday. The intention changed from agriculture to ordination; and the entire observance was well established by the time of Leo I (440–61), spreading throughout Western Christendom, and fixed according to the ecclesiastical year on the three days following the first Sunday in Lent, the feast of Pentecost, 14 September (Holy Cross Day), and 13 December.

It was precisely in this form that they appeared in 1662, being called the 'Ember Days at the Four Seasons' and designated as days of fasting and abstinence. (They did not appear in 1549 and 1552.) 1662 also provided two collects for those to be admitted to Holy Orders, to be said every day during the Ember weeks. In 1928 there were changes: in addition to the collects six readings were provided, three for the lesson or epistle and three for the gospel; the days were designated 'Lesser Fast Days'; and the services provided were optional, not mandatory. Only the Ember prayers were to be used daily through the Ember weeks.

ASB reflects a changed situation, however. Ember seasons no longer control ordinations: ordinations tend to control Ember seasons, and ordinations themselves are often determined by the time-tables of academic institutions. So while Ember Days still remain as Wednesdays, Fridays and Saturdays, the seasons are set out as within the weeks before Advent 3, Lent 2, and the Sundays nearest to St Peter's Day and Michaelmas. Furthermore, the bishop may also direct other days to be observed as Ember Days if he thinks fit. Nor is prayer confined to those to be admitted to Holy Orders: it embraces all who serve the Church in its various ministries both clerical and lay, as well as those to be ordained or commissioned to those ministries.

3 Rogation Days

These days are said to derive from the processions with litanies ordered by Mamertus, Bishop of Vienne (c. 470), on the three days before Ascension Day when his diocese was troubled by earth-quakes and eruptions. The custom spread throughout the West and there is evidence of their existence in Rome by the time of the Gregorian Sacramentary. In England they were adopted in the eighth century by the Council of Cloveshoe. These were the Minor Rogations. But there was also the Major Rogation, celebrated in Rome on 25 April to replace the *Robigalia*, the pagan festival for the protection of crops from mildew.

Outdoor Rogationtide processions were suppressed in England in 1547, but were restored in 1559 under the Elizabethan Injunctions. There is therefore no reference to Rogation Days in either 1549 or 1552. 1662, however, designated the three days before Ascension Day as Rogation Days and these were to be days of fasting, or abstinence: but no liturgical provision was made for them. 1928 went one stage further by including three prayers—one for agriculture, one for fisheries, and one for industry.

ASB now provides three collects, together with a complete set of readings for use at the Eucharist on all three days.

4 The Thursday after Trinity Sunday

This day, traditionally known as the feast of Corpus Christi, had for long been a day of thanksgiving for the institution of Holy Communion. It was kept on a Thursday because the traditional day of the Last Supper was a Thursday; and this particular Thursday was the first free one outside of Eastertide. It is said to have been instituted as the result of a vision of Juliana of Liège c. 1230. Its observance in the West became official in 1264 under Pope Urban IV. St Thomas Aquinas produced the collect used on this day together with the two famous hymns, *Lauda Sion* and

Pange Lingua. The day received no mention in 1549, 1552 or 1662: but 1928 provided a collect, epistle and gospel, with the proper preface for Maundy Thursday. No date was mentioned, however; and the propers could be used at any time. ASB also provides a complete set of propers, which may be used on any occasion: but the entry here in the Calendar makes specific reference to the Thursday after Trinity Sunday, although it avoids the title 'Corpus Christi'.

5 Harvest Thanksgiving

ASB makes specific reference to this occasion as a Special Day of Prayer and Thanksgiving. As in 1928 a full provision of collects and readings is included. No special day is mentioned; for clearly the observance will depend on local conditions and can cover various kinds of 'harvest'. Rule 8 provides for its celebration on a Sunday: and the only occasions when it cannot take precedence are the feasts of St Matthew, Michaelmas, and St Luke.

6 The Eve of St Andrew's Day (29 November)

This is a special day of prayer, widely observed throughout the Anglican Communion as an occasion for intercession and thanksgiving for the missionary work of the Church. A special collect and readings are provided in ASB on pp. 906–9, following the provision in 1928.

Days of Discipline and Self-Denial
(p. 22)

ASB has replaced the 1662 Table of Vigils, Fasts, and Days of Abstinence with a Table of Days of Discipline and Self-Denial. The 1662 provision of days of fasting or abstinence was certainly generous if not excessive. It is unrealistic to imagine that such a large number of days were going to be observed: and in any case in common practice vigils and Ember and Rogation Days were rarely observed as fasts. The vigils of the various festivals and Red Letter days have now been omitted, for they were manifestly unsatisfactory: some feasts had vigils and some had not, and no clear and convincing reasons could be found for the distinction. Furthermore, these many fast days have frankly lost their cogency: and little good will ensue from attempting to maintain observances which have little or no chance of being kept.

ASB lays down no rules as to how discipline and self-denial are to be observed: this is left to the individual to work out. The list provided calls for only two comments:

1 It is made very clear that the Sundays in Lent are not included in the forty days of Lent.

2 From a very early date the Church observed Wednesdays and Fridays as fast days—Wednesday as the day of our Lord's betrayal and Friday as the day of his passion. These were a counterpart to the Jewish fast days of Monday and Thursday. Friday still remains as the weekly memorial of the passion: but when a Friday coincides with a festival, it seems reasonable to make it an exception.

5
Rules to order the Service

The Prayer Books of 1549, 1552, and 1662 provided no clear guidance on the correct procedure to follow when two festivals fell on the same day or on consecutive days. What was to be done, for example, if the Feast of St Philip and St James fell on Ascension Day, or if the Feast of the Annunciation fell on Good Friday? Which day took precedence? And by what principle could a festival be transferred? The Convocations attempted to provide a solution to such problems by drawing up a Table of Occurrences in 1880, and a similar attempt was made in 1928: but neither Table received authorization. In this respect, therefore, ASB breaks new ground in providing a clearly defined procedure for the first time.

Rule 1 lays down the general principle that Sundays and certain other Principal Holy Days and Festivals are so important that nothing is allowed to interfere with their proper celebration. There are, however, certain exceptions; for two of these days may fall on the same day. So:

1 When All Saints' Day falls on the Eighth Sunday before Christmas, the propers of All Saints' Day are to be used. This is why Genesis 3.1–15 is provided as an alternative Old Testament Reading on this day, so that there need be no undue disruption in the sequence of Old Testament readings which only began a week before on the Ninth Sunday before Christmas.

2 If the Patronal or Dedication Festival of a Church falls on a Sunday, in certain seasons it may take precedence over the Sunday, i.e. on the Ninth to the Fifth Sundays before Christmas, on Christmas 1 and 2, and on every Sunday after Easter except Easter 1. Even when Baptisms, Confirmations, Ordinations and Marriages are held on days for which this Rule provides, the collect and readings appointed for the day must still be used, unless the bishop decrees otherwise.

Rule 2 indicates how these Sundays and Principal Holy Days are to be observed. Morning and Evening Prayer are of obligation: Holy Communion may be celebrated, but is not of obligation.

Rule 3 deals with Transferences. If a Festival or Greater Holy Day falls on a day referred to in Rule 1, it is transferred to the next free day. If it falls on a Sunday, therefore, it would normally be transferred to the Monday; or if it falls on Ascension Day, it would be transferred to the Friday. Only in two cases—the Feasts of St Joseph (19 March) and the Annunciation (25 March)—is the transference back to the preceding Saturday. This is because either of these two feasts could fall on Palm Sunday; and not only would it be undesirable to transfer to the Monday in Holy Week, but Rule 1 would also forbid it. If, however, these two feasts actually fall within Holy Week or Easter Week, they must be transferred to the week after Easter 1, the Annunciation coming first on the Monday, and St Joseph following on the Tuesday.

Rule 4 deals with Festivals or Greater Holy Days which fall on Sundays not referred to in Rule 1, i.e. the Sundays after Epiphany or Pentecost. In these two seasons the Festivals or Greater Holy Days take precedence, and the propers for the Sundays are simply omitted in that year.

All the Transferences involved in Rules 1, 3 and 4 are summarized on the Table on p. 29 of ASB.

Rule 5 gives guidance on the celebration of Evening Prayer on Festivals and Greater Holy Days. This question was discussed in detail by the late Professor E. C. Ratcliff in an Appendix to a Report to the Lambeth Conference of 1958 on *The Commemoration of Saints and Heroes of the Faith in the Anglican Communion* (pp. 81–3). According to Western practice, where a day runs from midnight to midnight, Evensong would be the last liturgical observance of the day: but according to Jewish practice, where a day runs from dusk to dusk, Evensong would be the first liturgical observance of the day. Over the centuries these two concepts came to be confused, resulting in a system of First and Second Evensongs. This can cause considerable confusion, particularly on the Festivals immediately following Christmas. Rule 5 now makes it clear that the normal practice is for Evensong to be celebrated on the evening of the day itself. Only if pastoral considerations make it necessary should it be celebrated on the previous evening. But it certainly cannot be both. These Festivals are *not* provided with two Evensongs: and where special provision is required for the previous evening, ASB makes that special provision, i.e. on the eves of Christmas, Epiphany, Easter, Ascension, Pentecost and All Saints' Day.

Rules 6 and 7 legislate for Lesser Festivals and Commemorations, the general principle being that when such days fall on a Principal Holy Day or a Festival or Greater Holy Day, they lapse and are not observed in that year, unless the Lesser Festival happens to be a Patronal Festival. In that case it may be treated as a Festival or Greater Holy Day. Lesser Festivals and Commemorations may also take precedence over Ember Days and Rogation Days. Prayers for Embertide and Rogationtide can in any case be included in intercessions at Holy Communion or after the third collect at Morning and Evening Prayer.

Rule 8 permits Harvest Thanksgiving to replace the celebration of a particular day except on the Feasts of St Matthew, St Michael and All Angels, and St Luke.

Rule 9 gives guidance on the use of collects. While it does not forbid the use of more than one collect at any one service, it nevertheless argues that they should be kept to a minimum; and unless there is urgent reason the norm should be a single collect. If a number of collects on unrelated matters follow one another, the unity of a service is impaired. Furthermore, the maintenance of a single collect system avoids the need to frame further rules on the minutiae of precedence. Rule 9 makes no provision, as there is in 1662, for anticipating a Sunday by using its collect at Evensong on the Saturday: and where there is an Eve, i.e. at Christmas and at Easter, the Eve is given its own provision. The rule also makes clear what the collect provision should be on the weekdays following Christmas Day, the Epiphany, Ash Wednesday and Ascension. According to 1662 arrangements, for example, if Christmas Day were to fall on a Monday, once St Stephen, St John and Holy Innocents had been observed on the Tuesday, Wednesday and Thursday, the collect for the Friday and Saturday would be Advent 4. This should be avoided: and the weekdays following these four Holy Days use the collects of those Holy Days. No mention is made in this Rule of the 1662 custom of repeating the collects for Advent Sunday and Ash Wednesday daily throughout the respective seasons of Advent and Lent.

Rule 10 deals with the Proper Prefaces of Advent, Christmas, Epiphany, Lent, Easter, Ascension Day and Pentecost. The older idea of octaves has been abandoned, and the Proper Prefaces may now be used for much longer periods than 1662 or 1928 provided for. Special provision is also made for every day in the weeks following Easter Day and Pentecost, although in differing degrees. While special provision is made for both Holy Communion and Daily Office in the former, it is confined to the Daily Office in the latter. Guidance on the use of Proper Prefaces is also given with the collects and readings.

6
Liturgical Colours

For many centuries there seems to have been little or no significance in the colour of hangings and vestments, except perhaps a preference for white—a colour associated with purity and referred to in Scripture, e.g. Revelation 3.4–5. Not until the twelfth century was there any evidence of an attempt to lay down an order of colours for particular seasons. The first sequence was then found in the use of the Augustinian Canons of the Latin Church at Jerusalem. They prescribed a sequence of colours even for a single festival: at Christmas black vestments were to be used at the first mass, red at the second, and white at the third, while the best frontal was to be hung over the altar, irrespective of its colour. Such sequences were at first local and informal; but what evidence there is suggests that it was customary to use simply the best at great festivals. In the East there were no definite rules about colours, although white appears to have been general for festivals, and more sombre colours for penitential seasons.

Colour sequences gradually emerged in the medieval West. Innocent III (1198–1216) drew up one sequence, proposing white for festivals, red for martyrs, black for penitential seasons, and green for ferial occasions. But these sequences still tended to be local. In England, for example, places like York, Westminster, Salisbury and Lincoln all made different arrangements. In Rome, Pius V formally laid down a general sequence in 1570:

Violet/Blue/Black: Advent, Septuagesima to Ash Wednesday, Funerals.

White/Gold: Christmas to Epiphany, Easter, Trinity, the Blessed Virgin Mary, Saints who are not Martyrs, Baptism, Confirmation, Ordination, Marriage, Dedication.

Green: Sundays after Epiphany, Sundays after Trinity, ordinary weekdays.

Red/Rose: Passion Sunday to Easter Eve.

Red: Pentecost, Apostles, Evangelists, Martyrs.

Colours veiled: Lent.

But even with this formal sequence, regional variation still tended to continue.

The Reformed Churches generally rejected colour as an adjunct to worship; but where colours were introduced—among Lutherans and Anglicans, for example—more often than not the 1570 Roman sequence was followed. Anglican colour requirements were certainly minimal. In 1549 the priest was ordered to wear at the Eucharist 'a white alb plain, with a vestment or cope', and in the Canons of 1603 Canon 24 ordered the celebrant at cathedrals and collegiate churches to wear a coloured cope over a plain alb: but specific colours were not mentioned. The Laudians in the seventeenth and early eighteenth centuries certainly wore coloured copes and the Nonjurors wore coloured vestments; most clergy, however, were content to follow Canon 58, which prescribed the surplice, an academic hood and a black tippet as the vestments to be worn at divine service and at the administration of the sacraments. From the middle of the nineteenth century liturgical colours were increasingly used in the Church of England, although Evangelicals regarded them as a sign of Popery. With the Liturgical Movement a new approach to colours began to be adopted, basing them on mood rather than on conformity to a rigid pattern. There was an inclination, for example, to use drab colours for penitential seasons, white and gold for festivals, red for martyrs, and green and yellow for growth and renewal. The Roman *Ordo Missae* of 1969 generally reaffirmed these principles, but made them a little more detailed. Thus red was used for Passion and Palm Sunday, Good Friday, Pentecost, the Passion of Christ, and Martyrs; and rose was used for Advent 3 (*Gaudete* Sunday) and Lent 4 (*Laetare* Sunday); while the old principle was reaffirmed of special occasions being marked by the best, irrespective of colour.

The fact that ASB has provided guidance on liturgical colours, including it with the collects and readings and the tables, is a new departure in official Anglican documents. Nevertheless, they are not to be regarded as mandatory. They simply provide guide-lines; and where other local or traditional uses are established, they may be followed. Here are the general principles on which these guide-lines have been established:

White or gold are the Church's festival colours.
Violet is an approximate colour and may vary from blue to

purple. It is the colour for Advent and Lent. But unbleached linen may also be used for Lent.

Black and white are alternatives to violet for funerals and All Souls' Day.

For the rest the 1969 Roman order is generally followed.

7
Morning and Evening Prayer

A
HISTORY

General studies:

Paul F. Bradshaw, *Daily Prayer in the Early Church*. 1981.

J. D. Crichton, *Christian Celebration: The Prayer of the Church*. 1976.

David Cutts and Harold Miller, *Whose Office? Daily Prayer for the People of God*. 1982.

C. W. Dugmore, *The Influence of the Synagogue upon the Divine Office*. 2nd edn, 1964.

W. J. Grisbrooke, 'A Contemporary Liturgical Problem: The Divine Office and Public Worship' (*SL* 8, 1971/2), pp. 129–68; (*SL* 9, 1973), pp. 3–18, 81–106.

J. A. Jungmann, *Christian Prayer through the Centuries*. New York 1978.

1 The Jewish Background

Alongside the sacrificial cult of the Temple, stretching back into Old Testament times, other regular acts of worship also existed in first-century Judaism, although their precise form and the antiquity of their origins are not altogether clear. Thus there is evidence for the recitation of the *Shema'* (a sort of creed, consisting of Deut. 6.4–9; 11.13–21; Num. 15.37–41) every morning and evening. There was also the observance of regular times of prayer each day, though there may have been some diversity with regard to these: many certainly prayed three times a day, in the morning, at the ninth hour (about 3 p.m.), and in the evening (the first two of these corresponding with the times of the daily sacrifices in the Temple); but some may have observed the morning, noon, and the evening, and some possibly only two prayer-times each day, morning and evening.

It has been argued by C. W. Dugmore that, at least in some larger towns and cities, the daily prayers would not simply have been recited individually wherever people happened to be, but would have been observed corporately in the synagogues. This may be true, but there is no real evidence to suggest that the practice was widespread. On the other hand, there were certainly services in the synagogue on some days of the week—the Sabbath, Monday, and Thursday, the last two also being the customary days on which the pious would fast. The services on these days consisted not only of the recitation of the *Shema'* and the prayers, but also of a reading from the Law, and at the Sabbath morning service a reading from the Prophets too, usually followed by an exposition or sermon. Although outline prayer-forms had already become established in many communities, the content of the prayers was not definitively fixed or uniform at this period, and the individual praying alone or the member of the congregation called upon to lead the prayers in the synagogue was free to use other words, provided that the main traditional themes of prayer were respected.

2 *The New Testament*

Jesus and his followers appear to have maintained the practice of attendance at the synagogue, and also, one may presume, of regular daily prayer, for which the Lord's Prayer seems to have been intended to provide a pattern. Thus we are told that one Sabbath Jesus went to the synagogue 'as his custom was', and was invited to read the lesson from the Prophets and to expound its meaning (Luke 4.16–30).

After the resurrection, his followers continued to attend synagogue services, at least on occasions in order to preach the good news (see, for example, Acts 13.5) even if not regularly in order to worship. At the same time, they are said to have 'persevered together in prayer' (Acts 1.14), and St Paul exhorts his readers to 'pray without ceasing' (1 Thess. 5.17). This injunction was linked with the strong expectation of the imminent return of Christ, which would bring with it the consummation of God's Kingdom. The New Testament writings are insistent that Christians must be constantly on the alert, ready and watchful for this event, lest it should catch them unawares, and prayer is regarded as the proper mode of eschatological vigilance: 'watch and pray that you may not enter into temptation' (Mark 14.38); 'persevere in prayer, being watchful in it with thanksgiving' (Col. 4.2).

But how could it be possible to pray without ceasing? Like

everyone else, the early Christians had to work, to eat, and to sleep. How then could they pray without ceasing? The answer which seems to be implied in the New Testament is that every action and every deed could—and should—become a prayer. As St Paul himself says, 'whether you eat or drink or do any other thing, do all to the glory of God' (1 Cor. 10.31). In this way the whole of life could be transformed to become, as it were, an act of worship, a sacrifice offered to God: 'I appeal to you therefore, brethren, by the mercies of God to present your bodies as a living sacrifice, holy and acceptable to God, which is your spiritual worship' (Rom. 12.1). Similarly, the Epistle to the Hebrews instructs its readers: 'do not neglect to do good and to share what you have, for such sacrifices are pleasing to God' (Heb. 13.16).

We do not know whether such 'perseverance in prayer' involved the continued observance of regular times of daily worship or not. It seems likely, and there are scattered references in the Acts of the Apostles to individual occasions of prayer, but none of them constitute proof of the regular observance of those hours: Peter and John go up to the Temple to pray at the ninth hour (Acts 3.1); Peter prays at the sixth hour (Acts 10.9); the Jerusalem church prays at night for the imprisoned Paul (Acts 12.5,12); and Paul and Silas pray at midnight while in prison (Acts 16.25).

There is also some uncertainty over the use of the canonical psalms in early Christian worship, and indeed there is some doubt as to whether they had any regular place in first-century Jewish synagogue services. Although the Christians of New Testament times valued the Book of Psalms very highly—it is cited more often in the New Testament than any other Old Testament book—it appears to have been more as a prophetic work—or rather as *the* prophetic work *par excellence* of the Old Testament—rather than as a treasury of devotion. They believed the psalms to have been written by David under the inspiration of the Holy Spirit and to have been speaking of the Christ who was to come later. There are allusions in some New Testament books to the singing of psalms and hymns (1 Cor. 14.26; Eph. 5.19; Col. 3.16; Jas. 5.13), but it is not clear whether the canonical psalms are meant to be included in this designation or whether the references are simply to hymnic material composed by the early Christians themselves, of which there seem to be examples in parts of the New Testament. The limited evidence available suggests that such compositions may chiefly have found a place in communal gatherings, and in particular at the community meals of the early Christian congregations, where individuals sang them to the rest, 'teaching and admonishing one another' (Col. 3.16).

3 The Second and Third Centuries

The New Testament understanding of ceaseless prayer was taken up by Christians in the succeeding centuries. Clement of Alexandria, for example, writing at the end of the second century, claims to be citing a scriptural quotation to this effect, though it cannot be identified: 'good works are an acceptable prayer to the Lord' (*Paed.* 3.12); and the third-century writer Origen develops the same idea at greater length:

> The man who links together his prayer with deeds of duty and fits seemly actions with his prayer is the man who prays without ceasing, for his virtuous deeds or the commandments he has fulfilled are taken up as a part of his prayer. For only in this way can we take the saying 'pray without ceasing' as being possible, if we can say that the whole life of the saint is one mighty integrated prayer (*De Oratione* 12.2).

Such stress on the whole of life as prayer did not mean, however, that Christians of this period did not observe any specific, fixed times for praying. On the contrary, the passage just quoted from Origen's writings goes on to say that, 'of such prayer, part is what is usually called "prayer", and ought not to be performed less than three times a day'; and a similar pattern of threefold daily prayer is confirmed from other early Christian sources. In the West by the third century we find that praying at least five times a day is generally recommended—in the early morning; at the third hour (about 9 a.m.); at the sixth hour (noon); at the ninth hour (3 p.m.); and in the evening—and the faithful were further expected to break their sleep and rise for a time of prayer during the night as well. Indeed the African writer Tertullian uses this practice as an argument against mixed marriages: a Christian wife will be unable to escape her pagan husband's attention when she rises during the night to pray (*Ad Uxorem* 2.5). It was no doubt the New Testament warning that Christ would return 'as a thief in the night' which originally encouraged the custom of regular nocturnal prayer, just as the universal rule of facing East for all prayer, in private devotion as well as in public worship, seems to stem from the expectation that the Messiah would rise like the sun.

In general, the observance of the times of prayer must chiefly have been by individuals on their own, or with families, though perhaps occasionally groups were able to meet together for daily worship. Dugmore again argued that regular morning and evening services were held by the Christians of this period, continuing the pattern of synagogue worship. There were certainly some regular assemblies each week in a number of places, in addition to that for the Sunday Eucharist, but these seem to have been occasional services of the word rather than regular times of prayer. We know, for example, of the existence in several places of a service of the word at the ninth hour on Wednesdays and Fridays. This was apparently a parallel to the Jewish synagogue service held on Mondays and Thursdays, and was intended by the hour of its celebration to commemorate the crucifixion. There is also evidence of a daily early morning assembly for instruction both of the faithful and of candidates for baptism.

A further feature of early Christian church life was the *agape* or fellowship supper, apparently created when the Eucharist became separated from a genuine meal. At these gatherings there was a ceremonial lighting of the evening lamp, with thanksgiving for the gift of light, something also found in Jewish practice, from which it may very well be derived. The evening also included an informal style of ministry of the word, which we have already encountered above in the New Testament evidence. Here individuals sang to the assembled company a hymn of their own composition or alternatively one of the canonical psalms, which continued to be interpreted as prophecies of Christ. The rest of the people present made the response 'Alleluia' after each verse, again a custom derived from Judaism. This use of psalms and hymns gradually spread to the regular times of daily prayer, especially when the latter were observed by groups of people together.

4 The 'Cathedral' Office

With the cessation of persecution in the fourth century it became easier to hold public gatherings for prayer every day. Although evidence for this period is limited, it would seem that in most places they took place every morning and evening. These services have been given the name 'the cathedral office' by scholars, in order to distinguish them from monastic forms of daily worship, about which more will be said later. They were essentially corporate acts of the local church. Presided over by the bishop, or failing him a presbyter, they involved the participation of the whole community—deacons, lectors, cantors and laity—all fulfilling their proper liturgical functions. Each service comprised two main elements:

(a) A limited number of psalms and canticles, usually unchanging from day to day, and often chosen for their appropriateness to the time of day. The earliest evidence suggests that Psalms 148–50 were widely, if not universally, used as morning hymns of praise, and Psalm 63, which was at that time understood to refer to the morning in verse 1, is generally also found. Often additionally included were the canticles Gloria in excelsis and Benedicite, the latter frequently as a Sunday supplement to the pattern. The use of other biblical canticles seems on the whole to have been a later development. Psalm 51 tends to occur as an expression of penitence at the beginning of the service on weekdays, though this may be derived from monastic usage. A common feature of the evening service was a ceremonial lighting of the evening lamp and thanksgiving for the gift of light, taken over from the *agape*, often using the hymn 'Hail, gladdening light' (*English Hymnal* 269; *Ancient and Modern Revised* 18). Psalm 141, with its reference to prayer as the evening sacrifice in verse 2, was also widely used at this service, though Psalm 104 may have been an alternative in some places. The normal manner of singing the psalms was responsorial: a cantor would sing the verses, and the congregation responded with a refrain after each one, usually composed of a verse from the psalm itself. This was a development of the earlier practice at the *agape* in which individuals sang psalms to each other, and the response 'Alleluia' was made.

(b) A substantial element of intercession. Prayer was offered for various groups and individuals, and involved the whole community: our Eastern sources tell of the deacon pronouncing the biddings for each category in turn; the people then prayed for them, making the response, 'Lord, have mercy'; and the president summed up their petitions with a concluding prayer. This later become formalized as a litany. In parts of the West, on the other hand, verses from psalms came to be used as a response to the biddings. Eventually the biddings dropped out of the services there, presumably when the rites had become overlong and complex and the emphasis on intercession as an important part of the purpose of the office had declined, with the result that all that was left was a series of versicles and responses drawn from psalm verses, termed *preces* by scholars, together with a concluding collect.

Readings from Scripture were not generally included in these daily services, which were intended principally for praise and prayer and not instruction, and a public ministry of the word continued to be restricted mainly to the celebration of the Eucharist, to the Wednesday and Friday services mentioned earlier, and to the assemblies for instruction, which were now frequently held only for baptismal candidates during the Lent/Easter period.

5 The Monastic Office

The daily timetable of prayer recommended to Christians of the first few centuries, demanding though it may appear to be for ordinary people engaged in everyday life, was not considered enough by everyone. There were some who regarded it as no more than a second-best way of fulfilling the apostolic injunction to pray without ceasing. What was really requisite, they believed, was literally continuous praying. This attitude seems to have been particularly prevalent in Alexandria among those who had come under the influence of the philosophy of Plato, and although it is unlikely that their approach had much in common with the practice of the majority of ordinary Christians of the time, it came subsequently to exercise a profound influence on the development of the spirituality of early monasticism, which began in the deserts of Egypt in the fourth century, and through that upon the mainstream of later Christian thought and practice.

Here the ideal of ceaseless prayer was given a different interpretation. Instead of attempting to integrate prayer with the rest of life, the early hermits went into the desert in effect to depart out of life and give themselves literally to prayer without ceasing, or at least with the minimum interruption for sleep. For the nourishment of their prayer, they turned to the canonical psalms, believing them to have been inspired by the Holy Spirit and so free from the possibility of the taint of heresy which was beginning to attach to many non-canonical compositions. Abandoning the earlier selective use of the Psalter, they committed all the psalms to memory, together with other passages of Scripture, and recited them in order, so as to fill the whole of their day with meditation on the word of God and perpetual prayer.

In time, however, the common life of monasticism prevailed over the excessive individuality of the hermits, and daily communal worship became established, but was formed of those elements which were at the heart of the spirituality of the movement—the recitation of the psalms in their biblical order and the reading of portions of Scripture for the edification of the brethren, together with the silent prayer of the monks for their own individual spiritual growth—and not, as in the churches elsewhere, of intercession for the needs of the world. The Egyptian monks came together in this way only twice each day, when they rose early in the morning and again in the evening before they retired to bed. They sat and listened as a member of the community read aloud from the Psalter and/or other parts of the Scriptures, and then rose to their feet for a period of silent prayer. At the end of this, they sat again for a further reading, and thus alternated reading and prayer throughout the time of their assembly. During the rest of the day they continued the work of prayer alone.

Monastic communities which were growing up in other parts of the East, however, tended to be more in touch with the practice of the Church around them, and in their daily worship produced a fusion of the two traditions. On the one hand, they celebrated communally all the times of prayer during the day which the faithful of earlier centuries had observed (morning, third, sixth, and ninth hours and evening), and used at them selected psalms which had become associated with those particular hours. On the other hand, they kept a vigil during a part of the night, frequently leading directly into the morning office, and they included in that, and often also in the evening service, the recitation of psalms in consecutive order derived from the Egyptian custom. In order to maintain concentration, the method of psalm-singing was varied in the course of a service, both antiphonal and responsorial psalmody being used. Because of this, in the course of time the psalms came to be thought of not so much as God's word to human beings to which they responded, but as their praise and prayer to God.

As the monastic tradition developed, the number of prescribed hours of daily prayer tended to increase, as the monks strove to spend as much time as possible in formal prayer. Thus, gradually other offices were added to the daily cycle, in most places simply Prime (at the first hour of the day) and Compline (before retiring to bed), but in some places there were even attempts to maintain a more or less continuous round of worship, with offices following one another at every single hour of the day, or alternatively with groups of monks praying in turn on a rota basis, so that, in the words of a popular nineteenth-century hymn, 'the voice of prayer is never silent, nor dies the strain of praise away'.

Studies:

Robert Taft, 'Praise in the Desert: The Coptic Monastic Office Yesterday and Today' (*Worship* 56, 1982), pp. 513–36.

— 'Quaestiones Disputatae in the History of the Liturgy of the Hours: The Origins of Nocturns, Matins, Prime' (*Worship* 58, 1984), pp. 130–58.

Adalbert de Vogue, 'Monastic Life and Times of Prayer in Common' (*Concilium* 142, 1981), pp. 72–7.

6 Later Eastern Rites

Nearly all later Eastern forms of the daily office show the effects of a fusion of 'cathedral' and monastic traditions. In the Byzantine rite, for example, all the hours of daily prayer of the monastic tradition are now included, and both the morning and evening services have a monastic preamble composed of consecutive psalmody attached to them. In this way the whole Psalter is recited in the course of a week at these two services, in addition to the fixed psalms at these and the other daily offices, though in Lent the number of psalms at night/morning service is increased, and consecutive psalmody is also added to the lesser hours of the day, so that the Psalter is completed twice each week. The Lenten evening office includes Old Testament readings too, the remains of the earlier separate assemblies for instruction held daily at this season. Otherwise Bible readings are still only a feature of the festal form of the daily offices.

Because these rites have in the course of their history become so elaborate and complex, with many accretions and variations at different seasons of the year, it is impossible to present here a complete synopsis of their structure, but perhaps the Lenten forms of the Byzantine morning and evening services will offer an indication of the resultant shape of the fusion of cathedral and monastic elements. For the sake of simplicity, secondary elements such as prayers, litanies and hymns, which occur repeatedly throughout the services, have been omitted from this outline (see overleaf).

MORNING	EVENING
Pss. 3, 38, 63, 88, 103, 143	Ps. 104
Canticle of Isaiah (verses from ch. 26)	
3 divisions of the Psalter, each followed by a reading	1 division of the Psalter
Ps. 51	Pss. 141, 142, 130, 117 (and
Variable Old Testament canticle	lighting of lamps)
Benedicite	'Hail gladdening light'
Magnificat and Benedictus	
Pss. 148, 149, 150	2 Old Testament readings
Gloria in excelsis	
Litany	Litany

Texts:

I. F. Hapgood, *Service Book of the Holy Orthodox–Catholic Apostolic (Greco-Russian) Church.* Boston/New York 1906.

Mother Mary and Kallistos Ware, *The Festal Menaion.* 1969.

— *The Lenten Triodion.* 1977.

E. Mercenier, *La prière des églises de rite byzantin.* 3rd edn, Chevetogne 1975.

7 *Later Western Rites*

Western forms of the monastic office were varied, but displayed a growing tendency to include consecutive psalmody and Bible reading in all the daily services, following the Egyptian pattern, and not just at the morning and evening hours, and to reduce the selective psalmody and intercession of the cathedral tradition. This was particularly true of the version produced by St Benedict in his rule about 530, which was based partly on the Roman monastic tradition, and partly on another monastic rule known to us as 'The Rule of the Master'. On the other hand, he did include metrical hymns in his services, whereas earlier monasticism had often been rather doubtful about non-biblical compositions. His rule prescribed eight daily offices:

(a) *Vigils*, celebrated at about 1 a.m. in summer, and followed immediately by Lauds, but at about 2 a.m. in winter and followed by a period of private study. It consisted of an opening versicle (repeated three times); Ps. 3; Ps. 95; hymn; six psalms; three readings, each followed by a short responsory psalm; six more psalms; a reading; versicle; and Kyrie eleison. In summer there was only one reading between the two blocks of psalmody, and on Sundays and festivals there were additional readings and canticles.

(*b*) *Lauds*, the morning office, celebrated about 2.15 a.m. in summer and about 5 a.m. in winter. It consisted of Ps. 67; Ps. 51; two 'proper' psalms and an Old Testament canticle appointed for the particular day of the week; Pss. 148–50; a reading and responsory; a hymn; versicle; the canticle Benedictus; litany; and Lord's Prayer.

(*c*) *Prime, Terce, Sext, None*, the first, third, sixth, and ninth hours of the day. All had approximately the same main features, consisting of an opening versicle; hymn; three psalms; versicle; Kyrie eleison; and Lord's Prayer.

(*d*) *Vespers*, the evening office, consisting of four psalms; a reading and responsory; hymn; versicle; the canticle Magnificat; litany; and Lord's Prayer.

(*e*) *Compline*, consisting of Pss. 4, 91, 134; hymn; reading; versicle; Kyrie eleison; and blessing.

From the fourth century onwards the ordinary clergy and laity were constantly encouraged to participate, if only in part, in the full monastic cycle of daily prayer, especially by those bishops who were themselves products of the monastic tradition. With regard to the laity, success in this matter was rather limited and short-lived, and they tended on the whole to adhere conservatively to their older practice of attending only the morning and evening services of the cathedral tradition. Even here, however, they were eventually reduced to being little more than, as it were, spectators of the professionals, because of their ignorance of Latin and the growing complexity of the office, and especially of its music. In the course of time, therefore, their attendance at weekday services declined, though the evidence suggests that they continued to come to Sunday Lauds and Vespers throughout the Middle Ages.

The secular clergy, on the other hand, were increasingly not only encouraged but obliged to participate in the monastic pattern: firstly, the daily vigil or night office was added to the cycle of morning and evening services for which they were responsible in the churches; then the lesser hours of the monastic office tended to be distributed among different churches within a city so that between them the whole cycle might be maintained; and ultimately, later still, there arose the obligation on each church to celebrate the whole round of monastic daily offices. Thus, in the

West, it was not so much a matter of a fusion of cathedral and monastic traditions, but the former pattern of the daily office only survived for a few centuries before it was entirely supplanted by the latter, so strong was the monastic influence over the Church. Indeed at Rome the cathedral office has disappeared almost without a trace, since monastic communities there took responsibility for maintaining the daily round of services in the city churches at an early date. Gradually too the wide divergences of monastic practices in the West were assimilated in varying degrees to the pattern of Benedict's office or of the Roman monastic office, itself considerably influenced in its later form by the Benedictine version.

Because the monastic office was intended primarily as a means of furthering the monk's spiritual growth and not as the action of praise and prayer by the Church, as the cathedral office was, it was of great importance that every member of the religious community should be present at it. When, therefore, someone was unable to be there for some reason, monastic rules usually required the individual to say the psalms and prayers on his or her own. No such obligation was at first imposed on the clergy. In the cathedral tradition the obligation belonged to the Church, and the individual cleric was only required to take his turn on the rota to fulfil his particular liturgical function. The first evidence which exists for the extension to the clergy of the monastic ideal and pattern is the Rule of St Chrodegang, Bishop of Metz, who died in 766. Here is laid down the requirement that clerics should live together under a common rule and attend all the offices of the day. This model was adopted by others, and soon attendance at the full round of monastic services became a normal feature of clerical life. As in the monastic rules, anyone who was prevented from attending the corporate celebration of the office was required to make it up by private recitation. Inevitably there were many clergy, and even certain religious orders, as for example the itinerant Franciscans, whose way of life made corporate celebration rarely possible, and so individual recitation became the effective norm for them, even though corporate celebration continued to be the theoretical ideal throughout the Middle Ages.

In addition to the formal requirements of the daily cycle of services, members of religious orders and others continued to be encouraged to spend considerable time in private prayer, frequently of a strongly penitential kind, in order to express contrition for their sins. For this purpose the use of the psalms was still recommended, but generally in a selective manner, particular groups of psalms being thought appropriate for particular states of mind. Thus, for example, Pss. 6, 32, 38, 51, 102, 130 and 143 were known as the Seven Penitential Psalms; Pss. 22, 64 and 68 might be recommended for times of temptation, and so on. Groups of psalms were also employed as a form of intercessory prayer for a monastery's benefactors, living and departed. In the course of time some of these practices came to be formalized as supplementary offices, composed mainly of selected psalms or verses from psalms and attached to the main offices of the day. The most universally adopted of these were the Office of the Dead and that of the Blessed Virgin Mary. Moreover, at least from the fourth century, new converts to Christianity had been encouraged, as a private act of devotion, to recite the Lord's Prayer and the Apostles' Creed every day, those being the only fixed liturgical forms at this period. This practice continued through the centuries, and eventually led to the inclusion of these elements within the daily offices.

In the thirteenth century attempts were made to reduce the large number of different books required for the celebration of the office into a single volume, which later became known as the Breviary, and this process led, almost inevitably, to some abbreviation of the contents of the offices, chiefly the shortening of the readings and the elimination of alternatives to many collects, antiphons and responsories. On the other hand, a process of expansion also went on at the same time, and the offices became further elaborated in certain respects. In particular, more special forms of the office for saints' days, with their own 'proper' psalms and lessons, were added, thus steadily eroding the regular Sunday and weekday forms. Together with the supplementary observances of the Offices of the Dead and of the Blessed Virgin Mary, this meant that the old offices gradually became overlaid and obscured by a flowering of festal and subsidiary accretions, which made them extremely complicated to use and burdensome to recite, even for monastic communities with time to celebrate them, let alone for those with other duties to perform.

Thus, apart from some attendance on Sundays and greater feasts by the laity, the offices were an almost exclusively monastic and clerical preserve by the end of the Middle Ages. In any case, only those laity who had the ability to read and could afford to purchase a copy of a Primer, or layfolk's prayer book, had any real way of sharing in them, and the contents of these books tended to focus almost entirely upon the secondary additions to the offices and not on their older core—usually just the Office of the Blessed Virgin Mary, unvarying from day to day.

Texts and studies:

Luke Eberle (ed.), *The Rule of the Master*. Kalamazoo, Michigan, 1977.

Timothy Fry (ed.), *RB 1980: The Rule of St Benedict in Latin and English with Notes*. Collegeville, Minnesota, 1980, esp. Appendix 3: 'The Liturgical Code in the Rule of St Benedict', by Nathan Mitchell, pp. 379–414.

K. McDonnell, 'Prayer in the Ancient Western Tradition' (*Worship* 55, 1981), pp. 34–61.

P. Salmon, *The Breviary Through the Centuries*. Collegeville, Minnesota, 1962.

S. J. P. van Dijk and J. H. Walker, *The Origins of the Modern Roman Liturgy: The Liturgy of the Papal Court and the Franciscan Order in the thirteenth century*. 1960.

8 *The Reformation*

There was widespread dissatisfaction with the daily offices at the beginning of the sixteenth century, and reform was certainly needed. It began with a revised Breviary produced by the Spanish Cardinal Quiñones in 1535, originally commissioned by Pope Clement VII and authorized by Pope Paul III. This was a drastic recasting, and met with much opposition because it was so radical. All variation for liturgical seasons and saints' days was excluded, and, in recognition of the fact that in practice the office generally tended to be recited by individuals on their own, most of the specifically choral and communal elements were deleted, leaving a very simple structure indeed compared with what had gone before. The old Roman custom of reciting the whole Psalter in the course of a week was restored, but with virtually no attempt to allocate appropriate psalms to certain occasions. Each office had three psalms, and the night office also included three substantial readings, one from the Old Testament, one from the New Testament, and one non-scriptural, so that the majority of the books of the Bible were once again read through in the course of a year. The supplementary observances were suppressed, but hymns were retained. Although Quiñones produced a second edition of his work in 1536 which tried to counter the opposition by restoring certain traditional features, this Breviary was eventually suppressed in 1568.

Texts and studies:
J. A. Jungmann, *Pastoral Liturgy* (1962), pp. 200–14.
J. Wickham Legg, *Breviarium Romanum a Francisco Cardinali Quignonio Editum et Recognitum.* 1888; republished 1970.
— *The Second Recension of the Quignon Breviary*, vol. 1 (1908), vol. 2 (1911).

Quiñones' reform had continued to assume that the offices were for the clergy and religious alone, but Martin Luther and others began to produce forms of daily services which were intended for the laity. Although Luther strongly disliked the traditional forms of the daily office, having found them an intolerable burden when he was a monk himself, he believed that regular morning and evening services went back to the beginnings of Christianity and deserved to be restored to their proper form, which for him meant the inclusion of preaching as their central feature: 'when God's word is not preached, one had better neither sing nor read, nor even come together.' The orders of service which appeared, therefore, included the reading of a passage from the Old or the New Testament, on a continuous basis from day to day so as to work through the whole Bible, after which the preacher was to expound its meaning. The congregation was to give thanks to God, praise him, and pray for the fruits of the word, using selected psalms, responsories and antiphons in Latin from the old rites for this. Each service was to last about an hour. Though meant for congregational use, in practice such services tended to become largely restricted to schools and colleges, and the ordinary person was left only with private prayer. For this latter purpose Luther suggested in his *Small Catechism* forms of prayer for use each morning and evening which consisted principally of the Apostles' Creed, the Lord's Prayer, a prayer of thanksgiving and commendation, and a hymn.

Weekday services wholly in the vernacular appeared in the Reformed tradition. Once again these were basically much simplified vernacular versions of the medieval offices, but with Bible reading and preaching given a central place. Those used at Strasbourg, for example, typically included the singing of metrical translations of the psalms; the reading of a Bible passage and an explanation of its meaning; the singing of a canticle (often Benedictus in the morning and Magnificat in the evening); and prayers, concluding with the Lord's Prayer and blessing. Unfortunately, all such services eventually fell into disuse, and were replaced by private devotions.

Texts and studies:
J. Neil Alexander, 'Luther's Reform of the Daily Office' (*Worship* 57, 1983), pp. 348–60.
U. S. Leupold (ed.), *Luther's Works* 53 (Philadelphia 1965), pp. 9–14.
H. O. Old, 'Daily Prayer in the Reformed Church of Strasbourg, 1525–1530' (*Worship* 52, 1978), pp. 121–38.

9 The Church of England

The Church of England alone of the churches of the Reformation succeeded in retaining a form of daily office. Archbishop Cranmer drew up two potential schemes of revision of the offices, both strongly influenced by Quiñones' Breviary, before finally devising that which appeared in the first Book of Common Prayer in 1549 (see G. J. Cuming, *The Godly Order*, 1983, ch. 1). There had already been a tendency to recite all the offices of the day in two blocks, at the beginning and end of the day, and not to observe them at their traditional hours, and so it is hardly surprising that Cranmer provided only two services for each day, morning and evening, and incorporated into them material from five of the medieval offices, as the following table shows.

MORNING PRAYER		EVENING PRAYER	
Lord's Prayer		Lord's Prayer	
Versicles		Versicles	
Gloria Patri	from Mattins	Gloria Patri	from Vespers
Venite	(night office)		(evening office)
Psalms		Psalms	
O.T. reading		O.T. reading	
Te Deum		Magnificat	
N.T. reading	from Lauds	N.T. reading	
Benedictus	(morning office)	Nunc Dimittis	
Kyries		Kyries	from Compline
Creed	from Prime	Creed	
Lord's Prayer		Lord's Prayer	
Preces		Preces	
Collect of day	from Lauds	Collect of day	from Vespers
Collect for peace		Collect for peace	
Collect for grace	from Prime	Collect for aid	from Compline

The Preface to the Book of Common Prayer, which was modelled on that in Quiñones' Breviary, indicates that the primary purpose of these services was seen to be to provide a simple and uniform pattern of Bible reading in English for the whole country, by which

> the Clergy, and especially such as were Ministers in the congregation, should (by often reading, and meditation in God's word) be stirred up to godliness themselves, and be more able to exhort others by wholesome doctrine, and to confute them that were adversaries to the truth: and further, that the people (by daily hearing of holy Scripture read in the Church) might continually profit more and more in the knowledge of God, and be the more inflamed with the love of his true religion.

The services themselves confirm this to be the aim. Hardly anything is allowed to interfere with the consecutive reading of the Bible, so that the whole Old Testament is completed once each year and the New Testament three times, except for Revelation, of which only two chapters are prescribed; very few Holy Days are provided with proper lessons, and even where they are, the lectionary is so arranged that the continuous reading is resumed afterwards without any omission. The Psalter is also recited in its biblical order in the course of each month, with proper psalms being provided on only four occasions in the year. Many traditional features are omitted, including hymns—though Cranmer only abandoned the latter with reluctance, being unable to find adequate translations; and the result is an office of stark simplicity.

In 1552 the offices were provided with a lengthy penitential introduction, much of it from Reformed sources, and proper psalms were included as alternatives to the Gospel canticles, as the use of the latter was disliked by extreme Reformers. The Kyries were also placed after the Creed instead of before it. Moreover, whereas in 1549 both clergy and laity had been expected to attend the services, and no special obligation had been laid on the clergy, except for those who had the responsibility for leading congregational worship, now all priests and deacons were bound to say Morning and Evening Prayer daily 'either privately or openly', unless they were prevented by 'preaching, studying of divinity, or by some other urgent cause'. A cleric who ministered in a parish church was expected to say the offices there and to ring the bell beforehand so that 'such as be disposed may come to hear God's word and to pray with him'.

Although it was thus still obviously the intention that lay people should join with the clergy in saying Morning and Evening Prayer daily, this did not happen in practice. On the other hand, they did continue their ancient custom of attending those services on Sundays, and apparently in recognition of this fact proper first lessons for Sundays were introduced in the 1559 revision of the Prayer Book, so that they might encounter something more edifying than the next portion of the continuous reading from the weekdays. Injunctions issued at this time permitted the singing of a hymn at the beginning and end of the services, and in the 1662 revision of the Prayer Book a rubric was inserted to allow the singing of an anthem after the collects, and further prayers (the 'State Prayers') were also then appended to the conclusion of the services. The dispensation formerly granted to the clergy to omit the saying of the office if they were busy preaching or studying divinity now disappeared, and they were obliged to say Morning and Evening Prayer every day unless prevented by 'sickness or some other urgent cause'.

The orders of Morning and Evening Prayer thus came to exercise a dual function within the Church of England. On the one hand, they provided a twice-daily pattern of Bible reading and prayer for the clergy and such of the laity as were minded to join them, whilst, on the other hand, they constituted the regular forms of Sunday congregational worship, since throughout most of the history of the Church of England the laity have adhered to the pre-Reformation tradition of only receiving Holy Communion a limited number of times in the course of the year. Hence until the nineteenth century the normal Sunday morning service consisted of Morning Prayer, Litany, and Ante-communion, together with sermon and hymns, even though the Prayer Book itself made no specific mention of the latter, the metrical psalms from Elizabethan days eventually being replaced or supplemented by the new hymnody of Isaac Watts, John and Charles Wesley, William Cowper, and others. The Act of Uniformity Amendment Act of 1872, however, made it legal to use Morning Prayer, Litany, and Holy Communion as three separate services, and also permitted the abbreviation of Morning and Evening Prayer on weekdays.

These developments were subsequently reflected in the proposed Prayer Book of 1927/8. Here tables of special psalms and lessons (the latter taken from the Lectionary of 1922) for Sundays and Holy Days recognized the distinctiveness of the Sunday congregational services, and provision was also made for a greater variety of prayers to supplement or replace the State Prayers—45 Occasional Prayers arranged under 32 different headings, each with a bidding, versicle and response. Surprisingly enough there was still no official provision for the use of hymns, sermon or blessing at these services. A number of other changes were also made at this revision: permission was given to omit the penitential introduction on weekdays, whilst a shorter form of it was included as an alternative; introductory sentences for seasons and special occasions were provided; the first Lord's Prayer was removed from the services; Invitatories for the seasons of the year were included for optional use with the Venite, and its last four verses were deleted; Psalm 51 was added as an alternative to the Te Deum and Benedicite; and permission was given to omit both the penitential introduction and everything after the second canticle when another service, for example Holy Communion, was to follow immediately.

Whilst most of these variations came to be widely used, they received no formal authority until the Prayer Book (Alternative and Other Services) Measure was passed in 1965. Under this measure most of the 1928 variations were authorized in Series 1 Morning and Evening Prayer for experimental use for a period of seven years as from 10 June 1966, and this was later extended until 31 December 1979. The only differences from the 1928 proposals were that the Invitatories to the Venite and the Occasional Prayers were omitted; permission was given to use the 1961 Lectionary as well as those of 1871 and 1922; and a new set of proper psalms for Sundays and other Holy Days was provided by the Liturgical Commission. Hymns, sermon and blessing were therefore still without formal authority.

These Series 1 proposals were the responsibility of the House of Bishops in consultation with a few members of the Liturgical Commission; but the Commission's own proposals, Series 2, had already been completed in 1962 and were published in December 1965, before the Series 1 version was authorized. It was not until 1968, however, that the Series 2 offices completed their passage through the Convocations and the House of Laity and were finally authorized for experimental use. It was a very modest revision, with no new arrangements for psalms and lessons. The Preface claimed that 'no reviser would wish to depart from the principles

93

enumerated in the Preface to the first Book of Common Prayer, namely the systematic and straightforward reading of Bible and Psalter in a language understood by the worshippers', and it went on to emphasize the dual function of the services: 'the present revision is an attempt to make the Orders themselves more suitable for Sunday use, without impairing their value as the form of daily prayer which is a statutory obligation upon the clergy.' The most notable differences from Series 1 were:

(a) there was a new short form of penitential introduction, containing a form of confession identical to that in Series 2 Holy Communion; and permission was given to omit this introduction, except on Sundays;

(b) the Benedictus and Te Deum were transposed, and the Gloria in excelsis was permitted as an alternative to either, thereby not only restoring the Gloria to its original function as an office canticle, but also facilitating the use of Morning Prayer as part of the Ante-communion service;

(c) the concluding verses of the Te Deum were omitted, so that it ended at 'glory everlasting';

(d) permission was given to end the services after the first or second canticle, if Holy Communion were to follow;

(e) provision was made for a sermon;

(f) consideration was given for the first time to typography and layout as an aid to worshippers: the alternative canticles were put in an appendix, the Creed and the Lord's Prayer were lined out, and congregational responses were printed in italics.

This revision was destined to have a short life, however. It was allowed to lapse on 27 November 1971, being replaced by something rather more flexible. For some time there had been growing unease among clergy and in the theological colleges at the length and rigidity of the offices, features which all the proposals to date had failed to meet in the eyes of the critics. In August 1968 the Joint Liturgical Group published a set of proposals under the title *The Daily Office*. Although still based upon the same principles as the earlier Anglican forms, this office was extremely flexible, and could be used once or twice a day, and in full or abbreviated form. It was therefore suitable both as an office for clergy and also as a brief daily devotion for laity. Moreover, with a lectionary offering an Old Testament reading, an Epistle, and a Gospel for each weekday on a two-yearly cycle (the Old Testament being read over two years and the New

Testament over one) it could also provide a Ministry of the word for a daily Eucharist, Sunday readings having been included in the Group's proposals, *The Calendar and Lectionary*, published in the previous year. The daily prescription of psalmody was considerably reduced, being arranged on a thirteen-week cycle instead of on a monthly basis, and the number of canticles was increased so that each morning and evening was allocated its own proper canticle.

These proposals proved to be extremely popular: they were welcomed by the Liturgical Consultation of the 1968 Lambeth Conference, and by 1973 the book had already gone through ten impressions. The Church Assembly first discussed this work at a Liturgical Conference in 1969, and encouraged the Liturgical Commission to incorporate it in a new set of proposals for use in the Church of England. These were first published as *Common Prayer 1970*, and then in amplified form later in the year as *Alternative Services Second Series (Revised) Morning and Evening Prayer*. They were authorized for four years as from 28 November 1971, an authorization subsequently extended until 31 December 1979. In this version both Morning and Evening Prayer appeared in two forms, one following the traditional pattern as in the original Series 2, and one based on the Joint Liturgical Group's pattern, but each having a sufficiently rich provision of canticles for each weekday to have its own proper canticles if required. The Psalter could be used either on a monthly basis or on the thirteen-week cycle, and the Joint Liturgical Group's weekday lectionary was added to the existing authorized lectionaries.

By the time that these services were authorized for use, the demand for forms in more contemporary language had grown considerably. Already in February 1971 the General Synod had asked the Liturgical Commission to produce forms of the daily office in such language 'with all possible speed'. This was done, and Morning and Evening Prayer Series 3 were authorized in 1975 for use from 1 November 1975 to 31 December 1979. They were substantially the Series 2 Revised forms in modern language, supplemented by the Litany, Prayers for Various Occasions, and Endings. For the first time hymns were also given recognition and included in the rubrics. The typography and layout were improved by the use of two-colour printing and by clear distinction between rubrics, ministerial texts, and congregational texts. With some very minor changes, these were the forms which finally appeared in the Alternative Service Book.

B
MORNING PRAYER
COMMENTARY

The Sentences

The medieval Office began with the priest saying *In nomine Patris* ... followed by the silent recitation of the Lord's Prayer. Then came the opening versicles and responses. At the Vigils, the first of the eight daily services, a variable antiphon, which came to be known as an invitatory, also accompanied the Venite and psalms. The 1549 Prayer Book retained relics of this practice, but with variations. At Mattins and Evensong the priest was to 'begin with a loud voice the Lord's Prayer'; and after the versicles and responses, the Venite was said 'without any invitatory'. The one exception was Easter Day, when two sentences from the Sarum Breviary, Romans 6.9 and 1 Corinthians 15.20 were said or sung together with a versicle and response and a collect before Mattins began. 1552 changed the pattern, by prefacing the Lord's Prayer with an Exhortation, Confession and Absolution but all preceded by a selection of eleven sentences—eight from the Old Testament and three from the New Testament—expressing either penitence or the assurance of forgiveness. These sentences were in fact invitatories to the Venite for Lent in the Sarum Breviary; and they were retained in 1662.

A departure from the note of penitence was made in the American Prayer Book of 1789, when three sentences of a more general nature (Hab. 2.20; Mal. 1.11; Ps. 19.14) were added; another four were added, together with seasonal sentences in 1892. This practice of including general and seasonal sentences was followed in various revisions of the Prayer Book in the 1920s, including the Proposed Prayer Book of 1928 in England. Here not only twenty-seven sentences—penitential, general and seasonal— were provided, but invitatories to the Venite were restored for optional use on festivals and Holy Days. These invitatories were never popular; and when the 1928 services were authorized for experimental use in 1966, they were omitted. A much larger choice of seasonal material was included in Series 2 Revised; and this was further extended in the Alternative Service Book. It now provides that every week of the year, every season and Holy Day, and every special occasion has its own sentence. All the sentences are for optional use; and the offices can now begin on either a general, a penitential or a seasonal note.

The Exhortation, Confession and Absolution
(sections 1–6)

The inspiration for the penitential introduction in 1552 came from a variety of sources, including Quiñones' revision of the Breviary and a number of continental Reformed sources. So, for example, there is the phrase from Archbishop Hermann of Cologne: 'It is agreeable to true religion, that as often as we appear before God in his Church, we should first of all acknowledge and confess our sins, and pray for remission.' Some of the phrases are possibly of far earlier date—note the statement of the ninth-century Florus of Lyons: 'Although we ought at all times, to acknowledge from our hearts that we are sinners, yet ought we most chiefly so to do the more attentively and perform the same, when in that holy Mystery [the Eucharist] is celebrated the grace of remission and forgiveness of sins.' Or again, the purposes of the Office, as expressed in the Exhortation, showed affinities with the commentary on the fourth commandment in *The Bishops' Book* ('Institution of a Christian Man', 1537) and *The King's Book* ('Necessary Doctrine and Erudition for any Christian Man', 1543). Indeed, this whole section has been rightly described as a mosaic of phrases culled from a variety of sources, and was produced by someone unknown from among the 1552 revisers. It was retained in its entirety in 1662.

The Exhortation expressed the nature and purpose of the service—a corporate action to offer God praise and thanksgiving, to hear and receive his holy Word, to bring before him the needs of the world, to ask his forgiveness of our sins, and to seek his grace. The Confession, based on Romans 7.8–25, included sins of omission as well as of commission, a supplication for pardon, and prayer for help. The Absolution, evidently written with the Absolution of the Sarum Breviary before the authors, was a declaratory form which reconciled the Church daily to God, prepared those present to offer him worship and praise, and conveyed pardon of sin. This act was in marked contrast both in place and content to the penitential act in the Breviary offices of Prime and Compline. There it took the form of a mutual act between priest and congregation towards the end of the service, whereas in 1552/1662 it had become a Confession by the congregation, and an Absolution by the priest, prefixed by an Exhortation stating the function of the service—all at the beginning.

1928 provided alternative shorter forms of Exhortation, Confession and Absolution, fulfilling the same purpose as those of 1552–1662. The Confession and Absolution were modelled on the forms in Compline in the Sarum Breviary (J. Dowden, *Further Studies in the Prayer Book*, 1908, p. 99). As an alternative to the Exhortation, 1928 also permitted the Minister simply to say, 'Let us humbly confess our sins to Almighty God.' These alternatives, together with the 1662 form, were continued in Series 1; and one or other of the forms was mandatory. Series 2, however, made the Introduction optional, omitted the 1662 forms, revised the alternative Confession and Absolution, and omitted the alternative Exhortation. Series 2 Revised followed suit; but Series 3 reinstated and improved the 1928 alternative exhortation (General Synod, *Report 215. Proceedings*, February 1975, p. 133).

The Alternative Service Book provides various forms of introduction, all of which are optional. First there is the Series 3 Exhortation expressing the nature and purpose of the service, which now includes 'to hear and receive his holy word'—a feature missing in 1928. This can be followed by an appropriate sentence and/or a hymn; or these two items can be used without the Exhortation. Then follows the Confession and Absolution which may, if required, be introduced by the sentence 1 John 1.8–9 (taken from 1662), by any of the sentences from Ash Wednesday to Lent 5 (all penitential), or by the words, 'Let us confess our sins to almighty God'. Provision is also made in the Absolution, when pronounced by someone other than a priest, for 'us' and 'our' to replace 'you' and 'your'. Both Confession and Absolution are identical with the forms in Holy Communion Rite A. (For further information see pp. 190–1.) With the Exhortation and penitential material being entirely optional, it means that praise may be regarded as an equally fitting opening to the office; or if required, all the introductory material may be omitted, and the office may begin with the versicles and responses. But this does not necessarily preclude penitence in the office. A note (note 3, p. 46) does provide for the use of the penitential sections to be used after the collects if that is considered appropriate.

The Lord's Prayer

In the medieval Office the priest began by saying privately the Lord's Prayer without the doxology (later with the Ave Maria) as a personal devotion—a custom first mentioned by Benedict of Aniane (810). 1549 continued the custom, but required the priest to say it 'with a loud voice'. The introduction of the penitential material in 1552 meant that the Lord's Prayer was sandwiched between the Absolution and the versicles and responses. 1662 made two further changes: the doxology was added, and the people were required to join in aloud. 1928 and a number of other Anglican revisions of the period wisely removed the Lord's Prayer, and the omission has continued to the Alternative Service Book.

In its present position after the Creed, it is in a climactic position, introducing the prayers. To use it twice in one service was an unnecessary duplication. For a discussion of the prayer itself, see pp. 30–2.

The Versicles and Responses
(section 8)

The use of sentences at the beginning of Vigils was directed by St Benedict (*Monastic Rule* 9 and 18), and he probably adopted the custom from earlier practice. The order then was Ps. 70.1, Gloria Patri, and Ps. 51.15 repeated three times, probably by the entire congregation. In the Roman and Sarum Breviaries the two psalm sentences were transposed and used as versicles and responses, followed by Gloria Patri sung by all, and Alleluia, except in the period Septuagesima to Easter Day. Ps. 51.15 was peculiar to the first office of the day: all other offices except Compline began with Ps. 70.1, Gloria Patri and Alleluia. Apparently the whole of Psalm 70 was originally repeated entire on waking or on the way from the dormitory to the church. (For the Gloria Patri, see pp. 32–3.)

In 1549 Cranmer took the form from the Sarum Breviary for Mattins: Ps. 51.15, Ps. 70.1, Gloria Patri, and Alleluia to be said from Easter to Trinity Sunday; he also still omitted Ps. 51.15 from Evensong. But he made the unusual addition of 'Praise ye the Lord'—to be said by the priest—after the Gloria Patri and before Alleluia. It was unusual, for 'Praise ye the Lord' and Alleluia really have the same meaning; but possibly 'Praise ye the Lord' could be regarded as an unvarying form of the old variable invitatory which preceded the Venite. In 1549 the personal pronouns in the versicles and responses were still in the singular, as in the Psalter. 1552 changed the personal pronouns to the plural, included Ps. 51.15 in Evening Prayer, and dropped the Alleluia; while in 1662 the Gloria Patri became a dialogue between priest and people, and a response 'The Lord's name be praised' was added to the priest's 'Praise ye the Lord'. While it neatly rounded off the opening dialogue between priest and people, it added nothing to the meaning. It had first appeared in the Scottish Prayer Book of 1637 and owes much to Cosin and Wren for its appearance in 1662. This opening dialogue remained unchanged until Series 2, when the Gloria Patri was said by both priest and people.

In Series 3 and in ASB it was both abbreviated and simplified. The versicle and response from Ps. 70.1 were replaced by 'Let us worship the Lord—All praise to his name', partly because it was felt that no satisfactory modern form for the words could be found, and partly because the new form provided a satisfactory link between the opening versicle and response and the Gloria Patri, after which any further dialogue would be otiose. The new versicle and response find echoes in a number of psalms, e.g. Pss. 96.1–2; 99.3; and 100.3.

Venite, Jubilate, Easter Anthems
(section 9)

The contents of both Venite and Jubilate indicate that the Jews used them as liturgical psalms, and it is not surprising that they were accorded a similar use by the Christian Church. The earliest accounts of the Roman Daily Office indicated that the Venite, Psalm 95, introduced the psalmody in the first office of the day except on special occasions; while St Benedict appointed Psalms 3 and 95 with an antiphon to be used before the hymn and psalms for the day at the Vigils. It was singularly appropriate at the beginning of the day's services with its invitation to worship God and to listen to his voice. In the Roman and Sarum Breviaries it continued in a similar position, and it was the only psalm said with an antiphon in the ancient manner—at the beginning, at the end, and between verses.

1549 retained it as the introduction to psalmody, but with no alternative, and with no invitatory. 1552, however, provided the Easter Anthems as a compulsory alternative on Easter Day. In 1928 two changes were made. In the first place, in an attempt to recover the seasonal note, ten invitatories were provided: but these never became popular and were dropped in Series 1. Secondly, the last four verses were deleted, thereby making the Venite simply an invitation to worship. While this was done on account of possible difficulties of interpretation of these verses, nevertheless the command to hear God's voice was lost; and this was an undoubted impoverishment. Series 1 recognized this and restored the verses, although permission was given to omit them. Series 2, however, again deleted them. Practice was evidently divided in different parts of the Anglican Communion. One solution to the problem, however, had been employed in America as early as 1789. Here verses 9 and 13 of Psalm 96 had replaced verses 8–11. In 1968 the JLG proposals provided a variation on this suggestion, namely to include the first part of verse 8 with its demand to hear God's voice and to add to it Ps. 96.13 with its reference to God's judgement. In the Hebrew original the first part of verse was in fact part of the preceding verse, thereby providing good precedent for their inclusion. There is also good precedent in the Psalter itself for combining passages from different psalms to form a single unit. This composite psalm, which appeared in Series 2 Revised now came to be known as Venite, although both in Series 3 and in the Alternative Service Book Psalm 95 in its entirely could be used in its place.

In the medieval Office the Jubilate was the second of the fixed psalms at Lauds on Sundays and Holy Days, and it was also used in Prime. Cranmer made no use of it in 1549; but in 1552 it appeared as an alternative to the Benedictus, doubtless as a sop to those who objected to Gospel canticles. 1662 made further provision that it should replace the Benedictus on those occasions when the latter appeared in one of the readings appointed for the day. Its position as an alternative to the Benedictus was incongruous, however. It is essentially an invitation to worship, and the provision in Series 2 Revised that it should be an alternative to the Venite was eminently sensible.

The second alternative to the Venite in ASB is the canticle known as the Easter Anthems. 1549 prescribed a short devotion to be used before Mattins on Easter Day: Romans 6.9–11 with two Alleluias, 1 Corinthians 15.20–2 with one Alleluia, a versicle and response, and a collect. This order in the Sarum rite had accompanied a procession before Mass on Easter Day which went to the sepulchre, collected the host, and placed it on the high altar: the cross was then carried to a side altar and venerated. 1552 deleted the Alleluias, the versicle and response and collect, and ordered the two anthems to be used instead of the Venite on Easter Day. 1662 added 1 Corinthians 5.7–8 to precede the other two anthems and Gloria Patri at the end. No change in usage or content was made until Series 3 and the ASB. Here the Easter Anthems was made an alternative to the Venite or the Jubilate, to be used on any occasion, the only proviso being that its use on Easter Day was mandatory.

The Psalms
(section 10)

In 1549 Cranmer, with the daily Offices reduced to two, ordered a monthly recitation of the Psalter in strict rotation. The only exceptions with their own proper psalms were Christmas Day, Easter Day, Ascension Day and Whit Sunday. Adjustments were made for those months not having thirty days. Those with thirty-one days repeated the psalms for the thirtieth day on the last day of the month; while February began on the last day of January and ended on the first day of March. 1552 retained these arrangements: but 1662 made changes. Ash Wednesday and Good Friday were provided with their proper psalms, and a simpler plan was made for February—the psalms for the first twenty-eight or twenty-nine days were used, and January and March followed the same plan as other months with thirty-one days. 1928, recognizing that changes in the pastoral situation demanded a Sunday provision distinct from that on weekdays, provided every Sunday through-out the year with its own proper psalms. Red Letter days and special occasions were also given their proper psalms. Unfortun-ately permission was given to ministers to choose only one of the psalms appointed on these days: this resulted in the growth of a custom in some places of using only the shortest of the psalms; many congregations therefore found their experience of the psalter drastically reduced. 1928 also permitted on the thirty-first day of a month the use of any of the psalms which had been omitted in the regular course on Sundays. For the first time, too, psalms and portions of psalms were bracketed and could be omitted if considered to be unsuitable for public worship. Series 1 continued with the 1928 system, but with a new selection of proper psalms for Sundays and Holy Days: it also safeguarded against the use of only the shortest psalms by insisting that all the psalms appointed for a particular occasion should be used.

Meanwhile the Episcopal Church in America had made a notable departure from the monthly system. In 1943 it arranged for regular recitation on a seven-week cycle based on the ecclesiastical year. Every day in the Church's year was given its proper psalms, due consideration being given to the season, the time of the day and the day of the week. It indicated a growing concern—felt also in this country—that length and inflexibility were making the daily office unpopular in certain sections of the Church. This concern was indicated in the JLG proposals of 1968 (p. 32), where a new system was produced based not on four weeks but on thirteen weeks, whereby the number of verses used in each office was on average just over thirteen and never exceeded twenty-five. Nine psalms were also omitted, on grounds either of unsuitability or duplication. Series 2 Revised accepted these proposals as an alternative either to the 1662 system or the Series 1 system. There was a feeling, however, that the pendulum had perhaps swung too far, and less than justice was being done to the Psalter in daily devotion.

In June 1976, therefore, the Liturgical Commission proposed an entirely new system (GS 292), which was approved by the General Synod in July 1978 and eventually incorporated into the Alternative Service Book. As an alternative to the 1662 monthly plan, it provided a ten-week cycle (the Church in Wales produced a ten-week cycle in 1969) in which every day in the Church's year was provided with its own psalms—but in strict rotation, with an average of eighteen verses of psalmody per office. It was so arranged that the entire Psalter was recited at least twice a year both morning and evening, and for increased flexibility morning and evening psalms were interchangeable except on special occasions such as Christmas Day, Holy Week and Ascension Day. Furthermore, on those occasions when special psalms were appointed for use at Holy Communion, these could also be used instead of those appointed for Morning or Evening Prayer. No psalms were omitted from the cycle, but nos 58 and 109 were bracketed, as were certain portions of psalms, indicating that they could be omitted if thought unsuitable. The Sunday cycle of proper psalms were also chosen wherever possible to fit the theme of the day. One hundred and seventeen psalms were included in this cycle and efforts were made to keep repetitions as far apart as possible.

The Readings
(sections 11, 13)

Both 1549 and 1552 indicated by rubric how lessons should be read—'distinctly with a loud voice'—and how they should be introduced, e.g. 'The first, second, third or fourth chapter of Genesis' and concluded: 'Here endeth such a Chapter of such a book'. They also required that 'in such places where they do sing, there shall the lessons be sung in a plain tune after the manner of distinct reading'. 1662 modified these arrangements: directions on the manner of speaking and of singing were removed; the introduction became 'Here beginneth such a Chapter, or verse of such a chapter of such a Book'; and the conclusion became 'Here endeth the first/second lesson'. 1928 changed the order in the introduction, requiring the minister to name first the book, then the chapter, and finally, if necessary, the verse. In Series 2 Revised the reader was no longer required to say, 'Here beginneth', and no directions were given for the conclusion. Series 3 and ASB, however, changed the conclusion to a Versicle and Response: 'This is the word of the Lord/Thanks be to God' (see p. 33).

The rubric on the permissive keeping of silence first appeared in the JLG Daily Office in 1968 and then was introduced in Series 2 Revised. The Christian Church recognized silence as an integral part of liturgy at an early date, e.g. Canon 19 of the Council of Laodicea (c. 345). (cf. the *Apostolic Constitutions*, and the *Homilies of Narsai*.) Subsequently it was achieved, not only by the congregation remaining silent, but by the recitation of certain prayers, particularly in the Canon of the Mass, by the priest in silence. The Reformers saw little merit in the practice and it disappeared from Reformed worship. Even in 1662 there was only one specific provision for silence—in the Ordinal after the examination of candidates for the priesthood. But today most Churches recognize its value in public worship. It is an appropriate way of receiving the word of God—a restful waiting upon God, detached from outward distractions and receptive to the influence of divine grace. The silence can help meditation and move into thanksgiving, intercession, resolve, or other forms of prayer. While the silence is used individually and independently, the action is also corporate. Indeed, no other form of public prayer combines individual and corporate expression so admirably.

Benedictus, A Song of Creation, Great and Wonderful
(section 12)

One of three canticles follows the first reading: Benedictus, A Song of Creation, or Great and Wonderful.

1 Benedictus

Benedictus—the Song of Zechariah—is recorded in St Luke's Gospel (1.68–79) as having been said by the father of John the Baptist at his son's circumcision. The first six verses, which parallel the Magnificat, speak of the coming redemption of Israel as an accomplished fact; the second four verses, addressed to the infant John, depict him as the forerunner of the Messiah. Much of it is borrowed from phrases in the Septuagint. It was one of the biblical canticles appended to the Psalter, possibly as early as the fourth century; it certainly appears in that position in the Codex Alexandrinus in the fifth century.

In the Western medieval Breviary it was the canticle after the Gospel lessons at Lauds, and its position there has been ascribed to St Benedict: of this there is no complete certainty, although he does speak of a Canticum de Evangelio being used there. Some three centuries later Amalarius (820) definitely refers to its use in that position. In 1549 Cranmer placed it after the second lesson at Mattins, using the translation in *The King's Primer* of 1545. At the time there was apparently no theological rationale for its position. It had been the custom to use the Breviary offices in two batches, one in the morning and one in the evening, and Cranmer had simply used the canticles in the order in which they appeared there. Benedictus therefore followed Te Deum, which was the canticle at medieval Mattins. Cranmer and his successors were more concerned to meet Puritan objections to the use of any canticles in public worship. This was evident in the modification made in 1552. Whereas 1549 prescribed the use of Benedictus 'throughout the whole year' with no alternative, 1552 provided Psalm 100—Jubilate—as a general substitute. 1662, however, restricted the use of Jubilate to those occasions when Benedictus was read in the lessons. The transposition of Benedictus and Te Deum did not occur until Series 2 in 1967, when it was argued that this canticle, like the Magnificat, was a 'pre-Incarnation' song, whose logical position was between the Old and New Testament lessons. It has remained in this position ever since—a position generally accepted by other Anglican revisions.

The translation used in ASB is that of ICET, with minor variations. St Luke's Greek constructions are in places a little difficult to translate into straightforward English. This is particularly the case in verses 5–6: but by starting a new sentence in verse 5, and repeating the word 'free' at the beginning of verse 6, it becomes clear that these verses are an expansion of the covenant referred to in verse 4. 'The dawn from on high' in verse 9, recalling Malachi 4.2, presents a slight problem: it is difficult to interpret 'from on high' as dawn's appearing over the horizon. In the Septuagint the Greek word here used for 'dawn', *anatole*, is used to render the Hebrew word for 'branch', and so is almost a technical term for the Messiah: the dawning of the Messianic age is depicted, and the better attested reading of a future tense makes better sense than the past tense used in 1662.

2 A Song of Creation

This canticle, previously known as Benedicite omnia opera, is the second and longer part of the Song of the Three Children (vv. 35–65) which was added to the third chapter of the book of Daniel in the Septuagint. The first part (vv. 29–34) also came to be used as a canticle under the title Benedictus es—Bless the Lord. The whole section, now in the Apocrypha and not in the Old Testament, purports to be the hymn sung by the three young men in Nebuchadnezzar's fiery furnace. Its origin is uncertain; but it is thought to have been written by an Alexandrian Jew soon after the Maccabean struggle and was independent of the rest of the book of Daniel. Verse 66, referring to Ananias, Azarias and Misael, was probably added when the hymn was incorporated into the book in order to fit it into its context. It was a canticle to the Creator, summoning the hosts of heaven, the physical elements, the creatures of the earth including humanity, and the people of God—living and departed—to praise God.

It has had a long history in Christian worship, both East and West. It has been sung at the morning office in the East, probably since the fourth century. Both the Mozarabic and Gallican eucharistic rites used it before or after the Epistle. In the early Offices of the West, both Roman and monastic, it was also sung at Lauds on Sundays and festivals, and it retained this position in the medieval Breviaries. Here the canticle was normally shortened by extensive omission of the refrain; it also had its own Trinitarian doxology and concluded with the antiphon from the Benedictus es: 'Blessed art thou, O Lord, in the firmament of heaven: to be praised and magnified above all for ever.' It was in this form that it appeared in English in Primers of the late fourteenth and early fifteenth centuries, and also in the late Reformed Primers 1530–45.

In 1549 Cranmer used the translation from the Great Bible, restored the refrain to every verse and replaced the doxology and antiphon with the Gloria Patri. He prescribed it as a Lenten alternative to Te Deum—a position again very understandable. Medieval Mattins had ended with Te Deum and had been followed immediately by Lauds, in which Benedicite had occurred. 1552 removed the Lenten restriction, making it a general alternative to Te Deum; and 1662 continued this practice. 1928, however, made considerable changes. It omitted the refrain on Breviary lines, but retained the Gloria Patri (unlike America 1928 and Scotland 1929, who restored the original doxology as an alternative to Gloria Patri). It also divided the canticle into four sections, permitting the omission of the two middle sections, referring to the physical elements and earthly creatures, on weekdays. The unsuitability of Benedicite as an alternative to Te Deum in Lent was also indicated by the provision of Psalms 51 and 40 as additional alternatives.

An important but unofficial change took place in 1948 in the BBC Psalter—a revision which owed much to Professor E. C. Ratcliff. Here the reference to Ananias, Azarias and Misael was omitted, 'Israel' became 'People of God', and the original doxology and antiphon were restored. The whole canticle therefore became more explicitly Christian. The canticle was also divided into two, and each half could be used on its own, with the addition of the doxology and antiphon. This revision clearly had its influence on Series 2. The omission of Ananias, Azarias and Misael, the change from 'Israel' to 'the People of God', and the restoration of the doxology and antiphon were all adopted: but it followed 1928 in retaining the refrain in every verse and in dividing the canticle into four sections, with permission to omit the middle two. It was also permitted as a general alternative to either Benedictus or Te Deum. Series 2 Revised retained these arrangements, but with two further modifications—there were further excisions of the refrain in the longer form, reducing it from 33 verses to 21, and its use was restricted to that of an alternative to Benedictus. The long link with Te Deum was therefore finally broken. ASB continued with the longer and shorter forms, the latter simply achieved by the permissive omission of verses 4–17, and its use being permitted only on weekdays. The original doxology was retained, but the antiphon was omitted. Its use as a general alternative to Benedictus was also retained. The translation was that of NEB with minor modifications. The title Benedicite was dropped in favour of 'A Song of Creation'.

3 Great and Wonderful

This canticle, first known as Magna et Mirabilia, is based on two passages in the Revelation of St John. Verses 1–3 are from Revelation 15.3b–4 and the doxology is from Revelation 5.13. It is the Song of the Martyrs in the presence of God, and has links with the Song of Moses in Exodus 15. It has been suggested that this was an early Christian hymn which the author of Revelation incorporated into his book.

It first appeared in the draft proposals for the revised Roman Breviary; and from there JLG used it as the canticle for Saturday morning in its 1968 Daily Office. At that time it took the form of Revelation 15.3b–4 with the Gloria Patri. Series 2 Revised then incorporated it in its forms of Morning Prayer, either as an alternative to Te Deum or for use on Saturday mornings. The doxology from Revelation 5.13 was also substituted for Gloria Patri—a form which had already appeared in the 1933 Appendix to the Irish Prayer Book, and was also appended to the canticle 'Glory and Honour'. In ASB it is included as a regular alternative to Benedictus. The text is basically that of RSV. The canticle now appears in a number of new Anglican books—Australia, Ireland, New Zealand, South Africa—as well as in the new Roman Breviary.

The Sermon
(section 14)

There was no provision for a sermon at either Morning or Evening Prayer in 1549, 1552 or 1662; although all three books provided for the catechizing of the unconfirmed. In 1549 this was to take place half an hour before Evensong at least once every six weeks either on a Sunday or Holy Day. In 1552 it was ordered at the same time on all Sundays and Holy Days; while in 1662 it was ordered on all Sundays and Holy Days after the second lesson at

Evensong. Clearly this requirement was neglected in the eighteenth and nineteenth centuries: although by the late nineteenth century sermons on Sundays at both Morning and Evening Prayer had become increasingly common. 1928 took no cognizance of this fact, however, and the 1662 provisions remained unchanged. Series 2 provided for a Sermon before or after either Office or after the second Reading, while Series 2 Revised extended these options by also permitting a sermon after the first Reading. ASB provides for a Sermon either after the second Reading or at the end of the Office—the two most obvious places.

Te Deum, Gloria in excelsis, Saviour of the world
(section 15)

After the second Reading, three canticles are provided. Gloria in excelsis is a general alternative to Te Deum, while Saviour of the world meets a long-felt need for a penitential responsory to the New Testament in Lent.

1 Te Deum

This was one of a group of early hymns—Gloria in excelsis was another—known as *psalmi idiotici*—psalms by private individuals as opposed to those which appeared in Scripture. The Breviary called it 'Canticle of Ambrose and Augustine' and legend claimed that it was composed extempore by these two men at the latter's baptism: but there is no evidence to support the claim. Some scholars in the past have ascribed it to Niceta, Bishop of Remesiana in Dacia (*c.* 392–414), but this can neither be fully proved nor disproved. North Africa and Southern Gaul have been agreed as possible places of origin. All that can be said is that it is a Western Latin composition, probably of the fourth century. The earliest text appears in the late seventh-century *Bangor Antiphonary.*

Both Benedict and Caesarius of Arles prescribed its use at the end of the Night Office. The reference in the rule of the latter is of particular interest, for it spoke of specified psalms, Te Deum laudamus, Gloria in excelsis, and the 'capitellum'. A capitellum was a verse, usually from a psalm, recited as an antiphon or a prayer in the form of a versicle or response at the conclusion of a hymn. Both Te Deum and Gloria in excelsis had capitella: and it is evident that those of both hymns are now appended to Te Deum.

The actual hymn ended at 'glory everlasting' (verse 13). It seems likely that verse 14 was the original capitellum of Te Deum, verses 15–16 were the capitella of Gloria in excelsis, and verses 17–18 were a later addition. There is manuscript evidence for some early variation in these capitella, but the present set appear to have been in use since 800. The capitella to Gloria in excelsis still appear in the Eastern Office. Possibly when this hymn was transferred from the Office to the Mass in the West, Te Deum took its place with the capitella, for both hymns are similar in structure and content— a series of acclamations in praise of God.

In Te Deum, part I (vv. 1–7) is in praise of God the Trinity and falls into two sections: the first section (vv. 1–4) is praise by God's creation, earthly and heavenly, reaching its climax in the Sanctus: the second section (vv. 5–7) is praise by the Church living and departed, reaching its climax in a statement of Trinitarian faith. Part II (vv. 8–13) is in praise of God the Son and is concerned with salvation. These acclamations have some interesting affinities with the prefaces or *contestationes* of Gallican rites (CQR, April 1884, p. 227); and shortly afterwards parallels were detected in the Gothic Missal (pp. 270–1). Further study enabled Ernst Kähler in 1958 (*Studien zum Te Deum*, Göttingen) to argue that Te Deum was originally the Preface, Sanctus and Post Sanctus of a Mass for the Easter Vigil, and that certain elements of credal formulae (vv. 6, 7, 8b, 11b) were added later—a position which has won wide acceptance among scholars.

Despite these eucharistic affinities Te Deum has been an integral part of the Western Daily Office since the days of Caesarius and Benedict. In the Mozarabic Office it was used at Prime on Sundays and festivals, while in the Roman and Sarum Breviaries it was sung after the last lesson at Mattins on all Sundays except in Advent and from Septuagesima to Easter. In 1549 Cranmer appointed it to be used at Mattins after the Old Testament lesson except in Lent, when Benedicite was substituted. For translation he made use of the existing English forms, and he included the capitella as part of the hymn: it therefore appeared as a single entity without any divisions. 1552 retained this structure and removed the restrictions on its use in Lent. Indeed it was not until 1901 that any attempt was made to produce it in a more intelligent form. At the instigation of Dr John Wordsworth it was then arranged for the Accession Service in three sections: the two acclamations and the capitella. In 1928 the hymn appeared in two forms. In the Accession Service it was in its three sections; but in

Morning Prayer it was divided into four, the first acclamation being set out in its two halves, an unfortunate arrangement which gave the impression of two separate entities instead of a single coherent whole. The Episcopal Church in America was the first to suggest a more radical rearrangement: in its 1957 proposals for a revision of the office, it not only clearly distinguished between the two acclamations, but it removed the capitella from the hymn and used them as the Suffrages for Morning Prayer—a commendable suggestion which restored to this section its original purpose. It was a proposal which was unfortunately not taken up in this country.

Series 1 continued to print the whole hymn with capitella as a single unit of twenty-nine verses as in 1552 and 1662. Series 2 deleted the capitella altogether and printed the two acclamations as a single unit of sixteen verses: it did, however, transpose Te Deum and Benedictus. Series 2 Revised restored the capitella and printed the hymn in its three sections. Series 3 did likewise, but indicated that the capitella could be omitted. That is how it has remained in ASB; and a proposal by the Liturgical Commission that the capitella should be set out as versicles and responses was rejected by the General Synod. The new translation in ASB is that of ICET, which attempts to stay closer to the original Latin than the forms in the earlier Prayer Books.

The First Acclamation—to God the Trinity (vv. 1–7)

Verses 1–2: Three short shouts of praise, of the kind used for a ruler. All begin in Latin with *Te*, and the verbs—*laudare* (praise), *confiteri* (acclaim), *venerare* (worship)—are typical. *Deum*, like *Dominum* and *Patrem*, is an accusative, and not a vocative, as it was mistranslated in 1549 and successive Prayer Books. The literal meaning of the first shout is 'We praise you as God'. The new translation attempts to retain the original structure of the three 'shouts' and at the same time do justice to the three accusatives.

Verse 2: *Terra* means the whole of creation, not just 'the earth'.

Verse 5: A vision of the heavenly court, with each group being progressively greater in size, from a mere group of apostles to a whole army of white-uniformed martyrs.

Verses 6–7: The trinitarian conclusion. 'Unbounded' expresses the meaning of *immensae* better than 'infinite'. Likewise 'worthy of all worship' is closer to the original meaning of *venerandum* than

111

'honourable'; and 'advocate and guide' expresses *paraclitum* better than 'comforter'.

The Second Acclamation—to God the Son (vv. 8–13)

Verse 9: The translation of *horruisti* has presented problems. ICET used the verb 'spurn', feeling that 'abhor' had little usage or acceptance in some parts of the English-speaking world. The feeling of the Liturgical Commission, however, and endorsed by the General Synod, was that 'abhor' is still current usage and is the best translation available.

Verse 10: *Devicto mortis aculeo*. The verb 'overcome' covers both the interpretations 'draw or extract' and 'neutralize the effects of' when speaking of the sting of death.

Verse 12: *Subveni*. The meaning is better expressed by the literal 'come . . . and help' rather than by 'help'.

Verse 13: The Latin in the later Sarum Breviary had *numerari*, for which there is no manuscript authority: it appeared as a mistake for *munerari* in the late fifteenth century. Unfortunately the Reformers kept the error in the Prayer Book version. The translation 'bring us to' covers the ideas of both *numerari* ('numbered') and *munerari* ('rewarded').

The Capitella (vv. 14–18)

Despite the fact that these capitella are a mosaic of various psalm verses and added at different times, they have an intrinsic coherence. The dominant theme is expressed in verse 14: the rest is comment on it. Verse 14b specifies the salvation and blessing asked for in verse 14a; verse 15 describes the activity of those who are so blessed; verses 16–17 express the need of those who wish to continue the worship of God in their daily lives; then verses 17–18 bring the thought back from their needs to their trust in God.

Verse 14: Psalm 28.10.

Verse 15: Psalm 145.2.

Verse 16: Psalm 123.3.

Verse 17: Psalm 56.1,3 or 33.21.

Verse 18: Psalm 31.1. This verse—in the singular in the Psalter— is here put in the plural to conform with the rest.

2 Gloria in excelsis

Gloria in excelsis was another of the *psalmi idiotici*, of unknown authorship. It was a fourth-century composition, with variations in the early texts. There was, for example, an Arian version in the *Apostolic Constitutions*, 7.47 (*c.* 380): without the Arian additions it was almost identical with the text in the fifth-century Codex Alexandrinus, where it appeared with the Scripture canticles as a Morning Hymn. This Alexandrinus text was basically that found in the Byzantine Liturgy and agreed with the oldest Western Latin text in the seventh-century *Bangor Antiphonary*. In the *Apostolic Constitutions* it was the canticle in the Morning Office, a place it has retained in the Eastern Church ever since. In the West it was also in the Office. Caesarius (542) appointed it for use at Mattins; it was used at Prime on Sundays and feasts in the Mozarabic Office; and in the Celtic Church it was used at both Mattins and Vespers. Gradually, however, it was transferred to the Mass.

The Liber Pontificalis gives two traditions as to its transference:

(*a*) Pope Telesphorus (d. 139) appointed it for use in the Mass of Christmas night—a theory now discounted.

(*b*) Pope Symmachus (498–514) appointed it for use at episcopal Masses on Sundays and the feasts of Martyrs.

Certainly it appeared in the Gregorian Sacramentary (seventh century) to be used on Sundays and festivals; while *Ordo Romanus Primus* ordered its use on festivals, where the Pope began it *Si tempus fuerit*. For a long time priests were forbidden to use it except at Easter and this restriction was not removed until the twelfth century. Its use as a festival canticle in the Mass was a Roman peculiarity: it was not used in the Gallican rite, and its introduction into the Ambrosian and Mozarabic rites was a Roman importation. 1549 retained it as an element in the Eucharist and it remained exclusively so until relatively recent times. The first Anglican Prayer Book to restore it to the Office was the first American book (1789), where it was an alternative to Gloria Patri at the end of the psalms. In England it first appeared in 1967 in Series 2 Morning Prayer as an alternative to either Benedictus or Te Deum. In Series 2 Revised it became an alternative to Te Deum only, and it has remained so in ASB. When Morning Prayer is combined with Holy Communion its use is very appropriate.

In structure and content the canticle is a typical doxology, similar to the Te Deum. It consists of an antiphon from Luke 2.14 (v. 1), followed by three acclamations, the first to God the Father (vv. 2–3), and the second and third to God the Son (vv. 4–6 and

vv. 7–8). In ASB the translation is that of ICET; certain phrases and lines have been transposed in the interests of clarity, while some words have been omitted as redundant and unnecessary.

The Antiphon (v. 1)

In excelsis: 'in the highest'—literally 'in the highest heavens'—is closer to both the Greek and the Latin texts than the 1662 'on high'. The two lines have a series of parallels—Glory, God, heaven—Peace, men, earth. The meaning of Luke 2.14 is uncertain. The Eastern tradition refers the good will to God, i.e. it is God's peace and good will to men: but the Western tradition has generally referred the good will to men, i.e. it is God's peace among men of good will. Cranmer clearly followed the Eastern tradition on this point. There is also the question, does 'men' refer to mankind in general, or to the people of God who are the recipients of the divine favour? The ICET translation attempts to meet various interpretations.

The First Acclamation (vv. 2–3)

The 1662 order has been reversed, so that the person addressed— God the Father—comes first. The number of verbs in the Greek original—typical of an acclamation—has been reduced: 'bless' and 'glorify' have been omitted, being included in 'worship, thanks and praise'. The acclamation therefore now consists of two parallel lines, culminating in the word 'glory'. In Codex Alexandrinus this acclamation ended with a specific reference to the Trinity, which continued in some rites, especially in the Greek Office and in the Scottish Liturgy (both 1764 and 1929).

The Second Acclamation (vv. 4–6)

The transposition of 'Son of the Father' to follow 'Lord Jesus Christ' in line 7 not only provides parallel acclamations in both lines of verse 4, but also places 'Lamb of God' in immediate juxtaposition to what follows in verse 5. The double reference to 'the Son', which was in both the Greek original and in 1662, has been reduced to a single reference in verse 4, this being considered sufficient. The declaratory form in verses 5–6 is preferred to the relative form as being more suitable to an acclamation. The petitions in verses 5–6 have also been reduced to two: 'have mercy on us' and 'receive our prayer'. 1549 had three petitions: 'have mercy, receive our prayer, have mercy'; while 1552 and 1662 had four: 'have mercy, have mercy, receive our prayer, have mercy'. The increase in 1552 is of uncertain origin. Dr Brightman suggested that the duplication of 'have mercy' was in Codex Alexandrinus, and the Anglican revisers may have seen the Greek text and copied it. W. E. Scudamore (*Notitia Eucharistica*, 2nd edn, p. 795) suggested that the revisers deliberately reproduced the threefold plan of Agnus Dei; but Dr Dowden rejected the idea as far-fetched and fanciful, particularly when the 1552 revisers had already removed Agnus Dei from the rite. The duplication may also have been simply a clerical or a printer's error. Scotland 1764 and America 1928 had removed the duplication of 'have mercy', but it remained in English rites until Holy Communion Series 2, which followed the 1549 pattern. In ASB, in agreement with the ICET translation, it has been reduced to two. It is logical to put 'have mercy' in verse 5, linking it with 'Lamb of God', while 'receive our prayer in verse 6 is linked suitably with Christ's session at God's right hand. In verse 5 there is variation in the Greek texts between 'sin' and 'sins'. The Latin has 'sins', and this was retained from 1549 until Holy Communion Series 2, where 'sin' was used in accordance with John 1.29 and also *Apostolic Constitutions*. In verse 6 'are seated' is preferred to 'sit' in 1662: this conforms to what is in the Creeds in ASB and emphasizes the permanence of Christ's position.

The Third Acclamation (vv. 7–8)

The final acclamation, also addressed to Christ, concludes with a Trinitarian doxology. It resembles the people's response to the invitation to communion in the Eastern liturgies: 'One is holy, one is Lord, Jesus Christ, to the glory of God the Father'. The conjunction 'for' in verse 7 makes an effective link with what precedes. The use of 'alone' rather than the 1662 'only' is more emphatic and clarifies the meaning. All the titles of Jesus Christ are put together in these verses—Holy One, Lord, the Most High—before the reference to the Holy Spirit. 'Jesus' is in the Greek text and so it is included.

3 Saviour of the world

This penitential canticle, recommended for use in Lent, is of uncertain origin but is thought to have been written by Dr Henry Allon, a noted Congregational hymnologist of the last century.

Pastor of Union Chapel, Islington, from 1844 and subsequently editor of *The British Quarterly Review*, Dr Allon was, with John Hunter and Thomas Binney, a leader of the Liturgical Movement among Free Church Independents. The canticle appeared in the *Congregational Hymnal* of 1860, which he edited: most of the hymns in it are attributed to their authors; but since this hymn has no attribution, it is thought by experts to have been written by Allon himself. It also appeared in his later collection *Congregational Psalmist* and subsequently in most twentieth-century Free Church hymnbooks. It was included by the JLG in its Daily Office in 1968 as the canticle for Friday morning, and from there appeared in Morning Prayer Series 2 Revised as an alternative to Te Deum—a position it has retained not only in ASB but in a number of new Anglican Prayer Books.

The canticle is a series of biblical variations, taken from both Old and New Testaments, on the antiphon, 'O Saviour of the world, who by thy Cross and precious Blood hast redeemed us, save us, and help us, we humbly beseech thee, O Lord', which appeared in the Order for the Visitation of the Sick in the Sarum Manual, and then in the 1549, 1552 and 1662 Prayer Books. Texts which appear to have been used include Psalm 80.2; Isaiah 58.6; 63.9; Acts 21.13; 1 Peter 1.18–19; 1 John 3.2; and Revelation 21.5. The antiphon was also used in the 1928 Burial Service; and it is conceivable that the canticle may have been used in a Burial Service which Allon himself drew up and which was widely used in the nineteenth century.

The Apostles' Creed
(section 16)

The Apostles' Creed developed from short, simple, trinitarian confessions of faith made by catechumens when they were baptized. It could have taken shape as early as the middle of the second century; and baptismal confessions of faith which approximate to it were certainly in use at Rome and in other Western churches in the fourth century. One form was cited by Marcellus of Ancyra in 341. As a creed it was therefore not of apostolic origin, and the title was first found c. 390. Its use in the present form in the Office dates from the eighth century; and it was probably not in general use much before the ninth century. In England it was used in Anglo-Saxon times as a private devotion said at the end of Prime and Compline with the Lord's Prayer and the Suffrages. Like the Lord's Prayer, its two final clauses were recited aloud as versicle and response. It was known in the vernacular in these times, and a number of versions have been found in Anglo-Saxon and early English. Its use as a private devotion at the end of Prime and Compline remained until the Reformation. Until then the only profession of faith recited publicly in the Office was the Athanasian Creed, which was used daily at Prime after the psalms and before the prayers. In his reformed Breviary, Quiñones appointed the Athanasian Creed for use on Sundays, and the Apostles' Creed on weekdays.

In 1549 Cranmer retained the Creed, the Lord's Prayer and the Suffrages in their Breviary position but made them a public part of the Offices. The rubric directed that after the second canticle the people were to kneel and the Kyrie was to be said: 'Then the minister shall say the Creed and the Lord's Prayer in English, with a loud voice'. The congregation was expected to say only the end of the Lord's Prayer, for the suffrages began, '*Answer.* But deliver us from evil. Amen.' It is interesting to note that it was simply called 'the Crede' and no text was included. The Reformers were reticent about its title: Article 7 in 1552 described it as 'that which is commonly called the Apostles' Creed'. Cranmer also laid down in 1549 that on six festivals the Athanasian Creed should be used at Morning Prayer instead: Christmas, Epiphany, Easter, Ascension, Pentecost and Trinity. 1552 made a number of changes. In the first place it inserted the text of the Creed (though not the Lord's Prayer), using the current vernacular text found in the Breviary. Secondly, it required both Creed and Lord's Prayer to be said by both congregation and minister, and that the Creed was to be said standing. Thirdly, it added a further seven days on which the Athanasian Creed was to be said at Morning Prayer: the feasts of St Matthias, St John Baptist, St James, St Bartholomew, St Matthew, St Simon and St Jude, and St Andrew. This meant in practice that the Athanasian Creed was recited at approximately monthly intervals throughout the year. It was only in 1662 that the texts of both the Creed and the Lord's Prayer were set out in full, and that the former was given the title 'The Apostles' Creed': the requirements for the use of the Athanasian Creed remained as in 1552. Since 1662 provision for its use has been modified; and in the present century its public recitation has declined, particularly at the major festivals. In 1928 its use became permissive, although on three occasions it could be used at Evening as well as at Morning Prayer: Trinity Sunday, Christmas I and the Feast of the

Annunciation; on Trinity Sunday only Part I and on the other two occasions only Part II was required. Series 2 modified the provisions for its use even further: it became permissive at either Morning or Evening Prayer on Trinity Sunday 'and at other times'. Finally, in Series 2 Revised it was omitted altogether, and the same arrangement appears in ASB. The Apostles' Creed therefore remains an obligatory element of both Morning and Evening Prayer on all occasions.

The text of ASB is that of ICET.

Lines 1, 3, 13: 'I believe' is repeated at the beginning of each section, rather than linking them by 'and'. This is done in the interests of clarity. The use of the singular is appropriate for a personal declaration of faith made at baptism.

Line 2: 'Creator' is a correct translation of the Latin *creatorem*, in contrast to the Greek in the Nicene Creed—*poieten*, 'maker'.

Line 4: 'By the power of' safeguards the work of the Holy Spirit without any suggestion of a carnal operation.

Line 6: 'Suffered' has a wider meaning here than in line 11 of the Nicene Creed and includes more than the crucifixion.

Line 7: 'Died'—modern usage demands an active form, distinguishing it from 'was crucified ... was buried'.

Line 8: 'He descended to the dead'.

Descendit ad inferna has been subject to various interpretations: (*a*) It underscores the assertion of death in line 7. (*b*) It follows the idea expressed in 1 Peter 3.19 of our Lord proclaiming victory to the spirits in prison. (*c*) It describes our Lord doing battle with Satan, thus guaranteeing the deliverance of the saints. (*d*) It describes in general terms our Lord's presence with the departed, cf. Luke 23.43. But an adequate English expression for *ad inferna* has been difficult to find, particuarly in recent times. 'Into hell' appeared in virtually all Anglo-Saxon and early English versions and was used from 1549 to 1928. The first American Prayer Book did, however, add a rubric permitting the replacement of 'descended into hell' by 'went into the place of departed spirits', although this permission was withdrawn in 1892. Series 2 also added a footnote, pointing out that 'hell' meant 'the place of the departed': but this footnote was omitted in Series 2 Revised. The present text attempts to leave the interpretation open, but also do justice to the Latin.

Line 9: 'Rose again'. The active voice is retained as an accurate translation of *resurrexit*. 'Again' is an English colloquialism which is appropriate to the spatial metaphor and avoids the unnecessary repetition of 'from the dead'.

Line 10: 'Ascended'—this is unavoidable if the other metaphors of *descendit* and *resurrexit* are retained.

Line 11: To reiterate 'God, the Father almighty' from line 1 would make the line unnecessarily ponderous.

Line 15: 'Communion of saints'. Despite the interpretation favoured in some quarters of *sanctorum communionem* as a participation in holy things, e.g. the sacraments, the traditional rendering has been retained, both because of its general acceptance and because no satisfactory expression for 'holy things' has been found.

Line 17: 'Body' is really an undertranslation of *carnis*. In 1549, private and public Baptism translated *carnis resurrectionem* as 'resurrection of the flesh', although the Catechism used 'body'. 1552, 1559 and 1662 all used 'flesh' in Baptism, but 'body' in the Offices and the Catechism. The phrase may be said to guarantee the resurrection of the whole man.

The Lesser Litany and the Lord's Prayer
(sections 17–18)

In the Sarum Breviary the prayers at Prime were in the following order: Lesser Litany, Lord's Prayer, Creed, Suffrages with Confession and Absolution, Salutation, Invitation, Collect, Salutation, Benedicamus. In 1549 the order at Mattins became: Lesser Litany, Creed, Lord's Prayer, Suffrages, Salutation, Invitation, Collects: the congregation was required to kneel throughout, and only the priest was directed to stand for the Collects. 1552 changed to a more orderly arrangement: Creed, Salutation, Invitation, Lesser Litany, Lord's Prayer, Suffrages, Collects; the minister now stood for both Suffrages and Collects. This order was retained in 1662, 1928 and Series 1. Series 2 omitted the Salutation and Invitation as being unnecessary in the middle of prayers which were obviously corporate; and the omission was continued in ASB. Here no instruction is given for the minister to stand for the Suffrages and Collects, although he is free to do so under the provisions of General Note 3 (p. 32).

The Lesser Litany
(section 17)

The petition 'Lord, have mercy upon us' appeared in the Old

Testament (e.g. Isa. 33.2, Ps. 123.3); and it is probably from the Septuagint that it found its way into Christian worship in the fourth century among Greek-speaking Christians of the East. Here it not only appeared as the response to intercessions at the Eucharist in the *Apostolic Constitutions*, book 8 (*c.* 350), but also as a response to petitions at the Evening Office in Jerusalem, according to the account of Egeria (381–4). It gradually spread throughout the West via Rome. The Council of Vaison (529) prescribed its use at Mass, Mattins and Vespers, and by the time of St Benedict it was in general use in the Daily Office. The practice of interspersing Kyrie eleison with Christe eleison was clearly in use in the time of Gregory the Great; while the Roman *Ordines* provide evidence of the threefold use. However, it would be difficult to prove that this was deliberately introduced as a set of devotions to the Trinity: indeed in primitive Christian usage *kyrios* is normally applied to Christ. Furthermore, the Eastern Church only used Kyrie eleison.

The Lord's Prayer
(section 18)

From 1549 to 1662 the Lord's Prayer was said twice in the Office—at the beginning (cf. p. 96) and at this point. 1928 omitted the first Lord's Prayer, however; and since then the single use at the hinge of the Office—after the Word and Profession of Faith and before the Prayers—has persisted. Series 2 also introduced the practice of lining out the prayer—a procedure now followed for all corporate elements in ASB, and one which facilitates public recitation and helps to clarify the sense. It was not until 1662 that the doxology was added to the first Lord's Prayer, following the precedent set in the Scottish Prayer Book of 1637; but it was not added to the second Lord's Prayer. Indeed there is a general practice in 1662 that, if the Lord's Prayer followed the Lesser Litany, then the doxology was omitted. Nevertheless, there are exceptions to this practice in the Churching of Women and in Forms of Prayer to be used at Sea, and no strict principle can be applied. In Series 2 the doxology was omitted and so was the Amen, on the tenuous grounds that the following suffrages expressed the application of the Lord's Prayer to particular needs. Series 2 Revised, however, quickly restored both the doxology and the Amen; and in ASB the Lord's Prayer is always printed in this form. Not only does it make good theological sense, but its consistency is a guarantee against confusion. Further information on the Lord's Prayer may be found on pp. 30–2.

The Suffrages
(section 19)

The practice of concluding each office with a series of suffrages or capitella was evident from the Rule of St Benedict (*c.* 526) which ordered *missae fiant*—'*missae*' meaning verses of psalms comparable to our suffrages. The Rule of Caesarius of Arles also stated that the monastic office concluded with *capitella de psalmis*. In both cases the capitella were not necessarily followed by a collect, and they were devotional rather than intercessory. But the *Bangor Antiphonary* (*c.* 690) indicated that the Celtic monastic Office concluded with a series of capitella preceded by biddings and covering a wide variety of intercessions. Nor were these suffrages peculiar to the monastic Office: and in the later Middle Ages such forms of devotion were quite common—the *Preces Feriales* in the Sarum Breviary, in the Primer and in the Bidding of the Bedes. The suffrages in 1549 in fact closely resemble those in the Bidding of the Bedes in the Sarum Processional.

The first four came direct from the Bidding of the Bedes, although in a slightly different order, the second and third being transposed. Only the last two came from different sources. There was a suffrage for peace in the Bidding of the Bedes, but Cranmer preferred to use the antiphon which accompanied the Memorial for Peace from the Sarum Lauds of the BVM, and which he also included in Mattins as the Collect for Peace. Similarly, since he included the Collect for Grace from the Sarum Prime, he also took one of the accompanying sets of versicles and responses as the last of the suffrages. These suffrages have appeared in successive Prayer Books, and it was not until 1928 that any change was made. Unhappiness was felt in some quarters over the suffrage for peace: 'Give peace in our time, O Lord./Because there is none other that fighteth for us, but only thou, O God.' It suggested that a state of war did exist, and what was asked of God was simply peace for ourselves and in our own generation. 1928 therefore provided a new response to the same versicle: 'Because there is none other that ruleth the world, but only thou, O God.' This, too, had its critics, who argued that the whole world clearly did not accept God's rule. Series 2 therefore chose to follow the American and South African Prayer Books and use the response:

'For it is thou, Lord, only, that maketh us dwell in safety.' Series 2 Revised changed the response again, however, to: 'And let thy glory be over all the earth.' Finally, Series 3 and ASB undertook an extensive revision of the whole set of suffrages, producing a more satisfactory series of petitions, all based on passages from the Psalms.

1 Psalm 85.7: The ASB Psalter version of the 1662 versicle and response.

2 Psalms 20.9 and 105.22: A new response to the 1662 versicle— 'And teach her counsellors wisdom'—both from the ASB Psalter.

3 Psalm 132.8: The ASB Psalter version (adapted) of the 1662 versicle and response.

4 Psalm 67.2: A new versicle and response adapted from the ASB Psalter.

5 Psalms 122.7 and 72.21: A new versicle and response on peace adapted from the ASB Psalter, which avoids the limitations of the 1662 suffrage.

6 Psalm 51.10: The ASB Psalter version (adapted) of the 1662 versicle and response.

The Collects
(sections 20–2)

The Suffrages are followed by three collects, the Collect of the Day, the Collect for Peace, and the Collect for Grace. The first and third are mandatory, the second is optional.

1549 directed the priest to stand for the collects, while the congregation remained kneeling. This direction remained in successive Prayer Books and revisions until Series 2, when no directions as to the posture of the minister were given: and no further directions have been added subsequently. It might be assumed that the minister, in the absence of directions, would remain kneeling with the congregation; but under the provisions of General Note 3, the minister could stand for the collects, if it were desirable or customary. For further information on collects in general, see pp. 265–7.

1 The Collect of the Day (section 20)

The Collect was clearly not an original part of the Daily Office, and its place there is no earlier than the eighth century. In early days psalms were followed by private prayers and a collect which summed up the petitions. This devotion tended to disappear, being replaced by suffrages at offices other than Nocturns, with the Lord's Prayer forming the conclusion. The Collect then was borrowed from the Mass to form an alternative conclusion to the Lord's Prayer at Vespers. In the Sarum Breviary the Collect was confined to Lauds and Vespers on festivals, Sundays and station days. Quiñones also included the Collect in his reformed Lauds and Vespers. It is not surprising, therefore, that Cranmer included the Collect of the Day in both Morning and Evening Offices, and it has remained there as a mandatory element ever since.

2 The Collect for Peace (section 21)

The Collect of the Day at Lauds and Vespers was followed by Memorials, consisting of a collect—either of a saint or with some particular intention—preceded by an antiphon and a versicle and response. There was a memorial for peace said at Lauds, and Cranmer used its collect as an invariable second collect at Mattins in 1549. The collect was originally the post-communion in the Mass for Peace in the Gelasian Sacramentary, and it was still in that position in the Sarum Missal. It has remained the second collect at Morning Prayer since 1549; but in ASB it has become optional, for peace is already prayed for in the Suffrages. The ASB text makes little change from the earlier Prayer Books, except to replace 'knowledge' and 'service' by active verbs. Not only is this simpler and more direct, but it is closer to the original text: *quem nosse vivere, cui servire regnare est*—literally, 'whom to know is to live, whom to serve is to reign'. The phrase comes from St Augustine of Hippo.

3 The Collect for Grace (section 22)

Two prayers are provided, one of which is obligatory.

The first has been a constant element of the Morning Office ever since 1549. It was the ferial collect for Prime in the Sarum Breviary: and like the Collect for Peace, it had also appeared in the Gelasian and Gregorian Sacramentaries, where it was among the *Orationes ad Matutinas lucescente die*. The ASB text again shows a minimum of change from the traditional Prayer Book text:

'governance' is omitted as being no longer in common use and covered by the verb 'order'; while 'right in your eyes' replaces the archaic 'righteous in thy sight'.

The second is a modern prayer, first produced as the constant morning collect in the JLG Daily Office in 1968. It owed much to the inspiration of the Rev. James Todd, the Congregational liturgist and a member of the Group. In its original form, the words 'this day' were included in line 5, emphasizing the fact that it was a daily morning prayer: their removal, while making the collect more general in its application, is to be regretted. It indicates that divine creation and redemption are the basic facts to which we should respond in our daily lives, and to do this we need the help and guidance of the Holy Spirit.

The Final Rubric
(section 23)

The State Prayers have been omitted from Morning and Evening Prayer in ASB and instead have been included in the Prayers for Various Occasions. In their place a rubric has been inserted indicating a variety of ways in which the service may be concluded:

1   It may end at the third Collect.

2   Additional prayers may be added, which may or may not include the State Prayers.

3   For the service to assume the function of a principal Sunday service or a service for a special occasion, it may include a sermon, hymns and a blessing.

Furthermore, additional material is not confined to what exists in ASB, although a Subject Index of Prayers (pp. 110–12) indicates the richness of the material which is available there.

The provisions in Section 47 (p. 71) also indicate the way in which Morning and Evening Prayer can be combined with Holy Communion Rite A. The office may take the place of the Ministry of the Word: the Penitential Introduction, the first Canticle, the Apostles' Creed at Evensong, and the second Collect are optional; the Lesser Litany, the Lord's Prayer and the Suffrages are omitted; and the Eucharist begins with the Intercessions (see also pp. 133–5). Other services may also be combined with Morning or Evening Prayer: Thanksgiving for the Birth of a Child, Thanksgiving after

Adoption, Baptism and Confirmation. In the case of the two Thanksgiving services, these may be used either at the beginning of Morning or Evening Prayer, or after the second Reading, or after the Sermon. In the case of Baptism and Confirmation, they may be used after the second Reading.

C
EVENING PRAYER
COMMENTARY

The following sections are not covered by the Commentary on Morning Prayer.

Psalm 134 or O Gladsome Light or The Easter Anthems
(section 32)

An innovation at Evening Prayer, proposed by the Liturgical Commission in Series 2 Revised, was to make the structure of the service identical with that of Morning Prayer, by introducing items corresponding to the Venite and its alternatives. It might be argued that there is some kind of precedent, for in his revised Breviary Quiñones had proposed transferring the office hymn at Vespers from before the Magnificat to before the Psalms. But, in any case, if the Venite and its alternatives serve a useful purpose at the beginning of Morning Prayer, there is no reason why Psalm 134 and its alternatives should not perform a similar purpose at the beginning of Evening Prayer.

Psalm 134

Psalm 134, with its reference to evening worshippers in the Temple, is singularly appropriate for use at Evening Prayer. The Rule of St Benedict appointed it as one of the fixed psalms at Compline, and its use there has been constant.

O Gladsome Light

Phos hilaron is one of the earliest hymns in the Church, being an anonymous composition dating from the third century. St Basil (379) witnessed to its early established position in Eastern worship by claiming that the singing of this ancient hymn was one of the cherished traditions of the Church (*On the Holy Spirit*, xxix. 73). It was sung during the lighting of the lamps at Vespers and is still so used today.

The translation used in ASB is by Robert Bridges from the *Yattendon Hymnal*. It is considered by many expert hymnologists as the most felicitous. There are, however, a number of other translations available in various hymnbooks, including Keble's well-known 'Hail, gladdening Light', and any of these may be used.

The Easter Anthems

In view of the fact that some churches regard Evening Prayer as one of the principal Sunday services, attracting quite large congregations, it seems unwise to restrict the use of the Easter Anthems to Morning Prayer. For many worshippers Evening Prayer is still the main occasion on which they are reminded weekly of the significance of the resurrection. For further information on the Easter Anthems see pp. 101–2.

Magnificat or Bless the Lord
(section 35)

After the first reading at Evening Prayer two canticles are provided, Magnificat and Bless the Lord.

1 Magnificat

St Luke attributes this hymn to Mary, at the time of her visit to her cousin Elizabeth (Luke 1.46–55). Modelled on the Song of Hannah (1 Samuel 2.10), it is a mosaic of Old Testament phrases, e.g. 1 Samuel 2.7; 2 Samuel 22.51; Psalms 89.11; 98.3; Job 5.11; 12.19; Isaiah 41.8; Micah 7.20. Although used in the Morning Office in the East and in the Gallican churches, it was St Benedict who gave it its position as the Gospel Canticle at Vespers, and it has retained its position there ever since. Cranmer used it as the first canticle at Evensong in 1549 with no alternative, taking the translation from the Great Bible. Apart from the fact that it retained its position in the order of canticles in the Sarum Breviary, its position between the Old and New Testament lessons was appropriate, for it expressed the fulfilment of God's promises to his people through the coming of Jesus Christ.

The text used in ASB is that of ICET.

Verse 1: 'Magnify' is archaic in this particular sense—'proclaims the greatness' retains the essential idea of the verb.

Verse 7: 'Empty' is placed last as the emphatic word. It also makes clear the parallel with the preceding line: 'hungry—good things/rich—empty'.

Verse 9: It is not entirely clear in the Greek whether the phrase 'to Abraham and his children for ever' is in apposition to 'to our fathers', or whether it follows 'his promise of mercy' in the previous verse, with line 1 of verse 9 as a parenthesis. Both alternatives remain open in this translation, although the meaning is the same in either case.

(In the Sarum Breviary, Benedictus, Magnificat and Nunc Dimittis were all preceded by metrical office hymns proper to the service and the season. Cranmer retained them in his first scheme for a revised Latin Office, but omitted them in 1549; and they did not appear in subsequent Prayer Books. A general rubric at the beginning of 1928, however, permitting hymns and anthems at services without specifying their position, made the restoration of an office hymn before the Magnificat possible; and it is customary in some churches to have such a hymn. There is also precedent for an office hymn before the psalms. In the Sarum Breviary such a hymn preceded the psalms at Mattins, and Quiñones proposed in his revised Breviary to transfer the office hymn to this position at Vespers. There is something to be said for emphasizing the note of the season or the occasion as early as possible in the service.)

2 Bless the Lord—Benedictus es

This canticle comes from the Song of the Three Children in the Apocrypha (verses 28–34) and immediately precedes the Benedicite (see pp. 106–8). In fact, on occasions during its liturgical history, it has been used with the Benedicite. It has had a long history as a canticle in the Daily Office: at the Morning Office in the Eastern Church, and at Lauds in the Mozarabic Office. It entered Anglican liturgy in the 1920s when the new American and Scottish Prayer Books used it as an alternative to the Te Deum. In 1968 it appeared in the JLG Daily Office as the canticle for Tuesday evening; and from there Series 2 Revised adopted it as an alternative to Nunc Dimittis. In Series 3 and ASB it became an alternative to the Magnificat. The text follows the same pattern and structure as the Benedicite, and it concludes with the same doxology.

Nunc Dimittis, or the Song of Christ's Glory, or Glory and Honour
(section 38)

After the second Reading, a choice of three canticles is provided.

1 Nunc Dimittis

This canticle is recorded by St Luke (2.29–32) as being sung by Simeon after seeing the infant Jesus in the Temple at Mary's purification. It has had a long history in the evening worship of the Church, first appearing in the Evening Office in the fourth century in the *Apostolic Constitutions* (VII.48), and then continuing in the Eastern Church. In the West the Rule of St Benedict made no provision for it in the monastic office of Compline, nor was Compline originally part of the secular office: but by the eighth century Compline, with Nunc Dimittis as its canticle, was established. It has also served other liturgical uses: not surprisingly it came to be used in the procession before Mass on the feast of the Purification, and it was part of the celebrant's final devotions in the Eastern rite of St John Chrysostom.

As the last canticle in the Breviary Office, Cranmer made it the second canticle at Evensong in 1549, using the translation in the Great Bible of 1539. Its subject-matter, expounding the implications of the incarnation for the human race, made it a suitable response to the New Testament lesson. In 1552, again because of the prejudice against canticles, Psalm 67, Deus misereatur, was added as an alternative; and this remained until Series 2 Revised, when it was replaced by Glory and Honour, Dignus es.

The text of Nunc Dimittis in ASB is that of ICET.

Verse 1: 'Lord' is here used in the sense of 'master'—the Greek *despota*, not *Kurie*. It emphasizes the contrast between master and servant or slave.

'You let your servant go'. This is the indicative—a statement of fact, containing the technical idea of manumission of a slave. In this case the instrument of release is death: it is also used in the Septuagint with reference to the death of Abraham (Genesis 15.15), Aaron (Numbers 20.29) and others.

'Your word'. This refers to the divine promise in Luke 2.26.

Verse 3: 'Light' and 'glory' are in apposition to 'salvation'. The Messiah is the 'glory' in the midst of his people Israel, and he sheds universal 'light' on the nations of the world. This revelation of Christ needs a stronger verb than 'lighten'—hence the use of 'reveal'.

2 The Song of Christ's Glory

This canticle, from Philippians 2.6–11, is a new element in Anglican worship. It first appeared in Christopher Wansey's *A New Testament Psalter* in 1963; but it was not until 1975 that it received official recognition as a canticle in the new South African rite. It was first used in England in Series 3 as an alternative to Nunc Dimittis, and it retains that position in ASB. It also appears as an office canticle in the new Australian and Irish Prayer Books. The text used is that of RSV. New Testament scholars believe it to be an early Christian hymn, separate from the rest of the epistle. Its main theme that life is under the rule of Christ and derives its purpose from the meaning which his incarnation gives to it, makes it an appropriate canticle for Christian worship. 'It is best seen as a dramatic, imaginative composition, lofty in poetic tone, the bearer of the fervent devotion of early Christian congregations' (J. L. Houlden, *Paul's Letters from Prison*, 1970, p. 82).

3 Glory and Honour

This canticle first appeared in the Appendix to the Irish Prayer Book of 1926 as a canticle in the alternative form of Evening Prayer for use on weekdays. It received no further recognition, however, until recent times. The proposals for the new Roman Breviary included it as an evening canticle for use on Tuesday evenings, and from there the JLG Daily Office in 1968 appointed it as the evening canticle for Friday evenings. Series 2 Revised then used it as an alternative to the Nunc Dimittis under the title 'Worthy art thou'. It retained this position in Series 3 and in ASB, but under the new title 'Glory and honour'. In addition to the ASB and the new Roman Breviary, it is also included in the new American, Irish and South African Prayer Books.

The text, which is that of the Liturgical Commission, has been adapted from three passages in the Revelation of St John—4.11; 5.9; and 5.10—where they appear as hymns sung to the One seated on the Throne and to the Lamb in the vision of Heaven.

These hymns may again be early Christian hymns which the author of the Revelation incorporated into his book. They correspond to the acclamations at the enthronement of a king, and have affinities with the acclamations found in Gloria in excelsis and Te Deum. Some scholars have suggested that they may possibly be the thanksgivings of an early Eucharistic Prayer, reflecting what the author of the Revelation and his fellow Christians experienced in their Sunday worship.

The Collects
(sections 43–5)

As at Morning Prayer, the first and third collects are mandatory, and the second is optional.

1 The Collect of the Day

See pp. 122–3.

2 The Collect for Peace

Like the morning Collect for Peace, this collect has had a long history. It was originally the first collect in the Mass for Peace in the Gelasian Sacramentary, and it retained that position in the Sarum Missal. In the Sarum Breviary it was the Memorial for Peace after Vespers, and it was among the collects of the Sarum Litany. Cranmer's version in 1549 contained the rather clumsy rendering: 'that both our hearts may be set to obey thy commandments, and also that by thee we being defended from the fear of our enemies, may pass . . .'. Despite the fact that the Elizabethan Primer of 1559 contained a more literal and a more succinct rendering—'that our hearts being obedient to thy commandments, and the fear of our enemies taken away . . .'—the 1549 version persisted until Series 2, when a simpler and more felicitous version emerged: 'that our hearts may be set . . . and that we, being defended from the fear . . .'. The ASB version has improved this further by substituting 'freed from' for 'being defended from'.

3 The Collect for Aid against Perils

Another ancient collect from the Gelasian Sacramentary, where it was among the Vesper collects. It became the invariable Collect for Compline in the Sarum Breviary and was an almost inevitable choice by Cranmer in 1549. Its position has remained unchallenged.

D

ALTERNATIVE FORMS
COMMENTARY

Shorter Forms of Morning and Evening Prayer

A radical proposal of the JLG in 1968 was that the Office for each day should be regarded as a single entity, although said in two parts. Accordingly duplication was avoided. The Old Testament lesson and the Epistle were read in the morning and the Gospel in the evening. If the Creed and the Lord's Prayer were used in the morning, there was no need to repeat them in the evening: similarly, if the act of penitence were used in the evening, there was no need to use it in the morning. These arrangements, together with the provision of a single canticle in each part of the Office made Morning and Evening Prayer very much shorter. At the same time one was incomplete without the other. Provision was also made, for the benefit of the laity, of a single daily office with one psalm, one canticle and one lesson, which, while taking only a few minutes to recite, nevertheless enabled those who used it to feel they had taken some part in the Daily Office of the Church.

The Church of England accepted the principle of the two shorter morning and evening services, but not that of a single daily service. In Series 2 Revised, therefore, two shorter forms of Morning and Evening Prayer were provided on the JLG pattern; and these have now been included in the ASB. In Morning Prayer abbreviation is achieved by the omission of the penitential introduction, the first canticle and the suffrages; both readings therefore come together, while one particular canticle is assigned to each day of the week except Sunday, when any canticle may be used. At Evening Prayer the penitential introduction is included, but there is only one reading—from the New Testament—and there is a single proper canticle as at Morning Prayer; the Creed, the Lesser Litany and the Suffrages are omitted, and the Collect of the Day is optional; only the Lord's Prayer and the final Evening Collect are mandatory. The Lord's Prayer is, in fact, the only item which need be used both morning and evening.

It is hoped that the Daily Office will not be seen simply as a preserve of the clergy, but now with greater flexibility to meet a multiplicity of needs, it will be seen to provide a pattern of devotional material in which both clergy and laity can share in a way envisaged but never fulfilled by the first Prayer Book in 1549.

Canticles at Morning and Evening Prayer

A criticism levelled against 1662 Morning and Evening Prayer was their lack of variety and flexibility. Apart from the Benedicite, the only alternatives provided for Benedictus, Te Deum, Magnificat and Nunc Dimittis were psalms; and these had been provided in 1552 because of the objections to canticles raised by some Reformers. 1928 did little to extend the provision, except to add Psalms 51 and 40 to the alternatives to Te Deum. It was left to the JLG Daily Office in 1968 to make the first proposals for an extension to the number of canticles and to provide sufficient for each weekday morning and evening to have their own provision. This provision was modest, in that only one canticle was needed for each morning and evening and none was provided for Sundays. Nevertheless, it was a move in the right direction and was based on good precedent. The Roman Breviary, for example, had provided seven Old Testament canticles at Lauds, varying their use from day to day, while a number of Anglican Prayer Books had had a wider choice of canticles for many years.

This additional material was first introduced in the Church of England in Series 2 Revised, which also abandoned the principle of alternatives from the Psalter. Instead the four main canticles at Morning and Evening Prayer were each given two alternatives as follows:

Benedictus—alternatives Benedicite (long and short versions) or Saviour of the World (Lent).
Te Deum—Alternatives Gloria in excelsis or another varying canticle.
Magnificat—alternatives Great and Wonderful or the Easter Anthems (Easter Day).
Nunc Dimittis—alternatives Worthy art thou or another varying canticle.

The varying canticles, which were alternative to Te Deum and Nunc Dimittis, were so arranged—as in the JLG Daily Office— that each weekday had its own proper provision. Furthermore, if the shortened forms of Morning and Evening Prayer were used, requiring only one canticle each, each weekday again had its own proper provision.

In ASB the provision has been further extended, giving the following variety of choices:

1   Morning and Evening Prayer still have their two traditional canticles each, and each of these now has two alternatives except Magnificat, which has one.

Benedictus—alternatives A Song of Creation (long and short versions), and Great and Wonderful.

Te Deum—alternatives Gloria in excelsis or Saviour of the world (Lent).

Magnificat—alternative Bless the Lord.

Nunc Dimittis—alternatives The Song of Christ's Glory or Glory and honour.

2   At the same time, the table on p. 72 (section 48) provides each weekday morning and evening with its own two proper canticles, which may be used instead of those set out above in No. 1.

3   If Benedictus is used as the invariable first canticle at Morning Prayer, the second canticle may vary each weekday according to the table on p. 72 (section 49).

4   If Te Deum is used as the invariable first canticle at Evening Prayer, the second canticle may vary each weekday according to the table on p. 72 (section 50).

5   If the shortened forms of Morning and Evening Prayer are used requiring only one canticle each, each office is provided with its own proper canticle for each weekday.

The 1662 Form of the Canticles

The 1662 versions of the Canticles together with the Venite and the Jubilate are included in ASB, mainly for the benefit of those churches where these items are still sung to well-known musical settings.

Morning or Evening Prayer with Holy Communion Rite A

Provision is now made for combining Morning or Evening Prayer with Holy Communion, an arrangement whereby the Daily

133

Office fulfils the function of the Ministry of the Word. In the eighteenth and nineteenth centuries, when 'the morning service' on Sundays took the form of a combination of Morning Prayer, Litany and Holy Communion—more often than not ending at the Prayer for the Church Militant—it was a long and wearisome performance, with all the psalms for the day, four lessons, and a considerable amount of duplication. Official permission to split the three elements into separate services by the Act of Uniformity Amendment Act in 1872 provided welcome relief and at the same time encouraged the pattern of Holy Communion at 8 a.m. and choral Mattins at 11 a.m. This arrangement had disadvantages, however.

1   In many churches the Eucharist became simply a service for the pious few. Admittedly there were some attempts to combine choral Mattins with a said service of Holy Communion starting at 'Ye that do truly and earnestly repent'—an expedient which at least provided a combination of the right ingredients. Nevertheless, there was a sharp contrast between choral Mattins with a large congregation and a short said Communion Service with only a handful of worshippers, and it still gave the impression that the Eucharist was not central but simply an extra for the exclusive few. The same problem occurred if the Eucharist were to follow choral Evensong.

2   Those people who came only to Holy Communion at 8 a.m. or who attended a choral Eucharist with sermon at a later hour never heard the psalms and only very rarely a lesson from the Old Testament. Their biblical diet was unbalanced. It was not until 1966, in the Series 1 services, that a table of Old Testament lessons borrowed from the 1960 Indian Prayer Book was authorized for use, helping to redress the balance.

3   The saying or singing of Morning Prayer before Holy Communion involved a great deal of unnecessary duplication. For example, there could be two creeds, two confessions and absolutions, four recitations of the Lord's Prayer, and some duplication of intercessions.

As early as 1911 W. H. Frere in *Some Principles of Liturgical Reform* had pleaded for a combination of Daily Office and Eucharist (pp. 151–62), but nothing specific of an official nature was done until the Lambeth Conference of 1968, although the practice was evidently envisaged and even endorsed. 1928, for example, stated that, if Morning or Evening Prayer were 'immediately followed by another Service provided in this book', it was permissible to drop the penitential introduction and to end the Office either at the third collect or with the canticle following the second lesson. Presumably the Eucharist then continued from the Nicene Creed; but nothing was said on this point. Again, Morning and Evening Prayer Series 2 in 1967 included a general rubric permitting the office to end after the first or second canticle if the Eucharist were to follow immediately, presumably allowing for either two or three lessons; but here too no further directions were given. A significant step was taken, however, at the 1968 Lambeth Conference. Its Liturgical Consultation commissioned a second edition of the Pan-Anglican Liturgical Document, to be prepared by Bishop Leslie Brown and Dr Ronald Jasper; and when this was published in the following year, it argued for a closer relationship between Office and Eucharist, with specific proposals as to how this might be done. (The Church of South India had in fact indicated how this combination might be achieved some years earlier.) In 1970 specific provision for a combination of the services appeared in Morning and Evening Prayer Series 2 Revised. This provision was continued in Series 3 and then found a place in ASB.

If Morning or Evening Prayer are combined with Holy Communion Rite A, the following elements of the Office are omitted: the Lesser Litany, the Suffrages and the Lord's Prayer (sections 17–19, 40–2); and the following are optional: the penitential introduction (sections 1–7, 24–30) if penitence follows later in the Eucharist, the first canticle (sections 12, 35), and the Collect for Peace (sections 21, 44). After the Collects, the Eucharist begins at the Intercession. Two or three readings may be used, and the readings of both Morning and Evening Prayer and the Eucharist are interchangeable.

There are two combinations, however, for which no provision is made:

1 The combination of Morning or Evening Prayer with Holy Communion Rite B, mainly on account of the fact that the former is in a 'You' form and the latter in a 'Thou' form.

2 The combination of the shorter form of Evening Prayer with Holy Communion Rite A, mainly on account of the fact that the former has provision for only one reading—from the New Testament.

8
Prayers for Various Occasions

The Litany
(section 1)

For commentary on the Litany see pp. 35–43.

The State Prayers
(sections 2–4)

The only prayer of this group to appear in 1549 or 1552 was the Prayer of St Chrysostom, which was placed—without its title—at the end of the Litany. In 1559, however, it was joined by the Prayers for the Queen and for the Clergy and People, together with the Grace—still at the end of the Litany and immediately preceding six other Occasional Prayers. It was the Scottish Prayer Book of 1637 which made provision for their use at the end of Morning and Evening Prayer; and 1662, apparently at the instigation of Bishop Cosin, took similar action, setting out the prayers in full at the end of each Office. In 1928 they were again omitted from the Offices and were included in the Occasional Prayers and Thanksgivings, although a rubric permitted the minister to end either Office with one or more of the Occasional Prayers and Thanksgivings 'or such others as are authorized by the Bishop'. It meant, therefore, that the State Prayers could be totally ignored. Series 2, however, restored specific reference to the State Prayers in this rubric, although they remained optional; and this arrangement has continued to the ASB. The texts of the three prayers—for the Queen, for the Royal Family, and for the Clergy and People—are placed immediately after the Litany.

The Prayer for the Queen
(section 2)

The Prayer for the Queen which appeared in the Prayer Book from 1559 onwards has been replaced in ASB by the Prayer for the Queen and all in authority under her, which first appeared in 1928.

The address is the same as that of the Prayer for the Royal Family—the prayer as a whole first appeared in Report 517 of the Convocation of Canterbury in 1919. The revised form in ASB has two changes of significance:

1 The reference to 'the parliaments in all her dominions' is omitted as no longer expressing the truth of the contemporary situation.

2 'Equity' is added to 'wisdom', thereby providing a pair of doublets—'wisdom and equity, righteousness and peace'—and adding a quality not fully covered by the three original nouns.

The Prayer for the Royal Family
(section 3)

The authorship of this prayer is not certain, but it is usually attributed to Archbishop Whitgift. It first appeared under the title 'A Prayer for the Queen and Prince, and other the King and Queen's children' in the letters patent addressed to the Archbishop by King James I on 9 February 1604, confirming the decisions of the Hampton Court Conference. It was added to the prayers at the end of the Litany in the same year. One change, first made in 1625 and finally confirmed in 1633, was the substitution of the phrase 'the fountain of all goodness' for the relative clause 'who has promised to be a Father of thine elect, and of their seed'. No significant changes have been made in ASB.

The Prayer for the Clergy and People
(section 4)

This is an ancient prayer from the Gelasian Sacramentary, where it appeared in two forms—as a collect for a mass in a monastery, and as the collect for a blessing on any particular household. In the Gregorian Sacramentary it became the collect for a mass for an abbot or his congregation. It was widely known in pre-Reformation England, for it was in the Sarum Litany of the Saints and a version appeared in the Primer from the fourteenth century onwards. Cranmer included it in his 1544 Litany, adding 'curates' to 'bishops and all congregations'. 1928 and Ireland 1926 substituted 'clergy' for 'curates', failing to appreciate that bishops are clergy in any case. The American 'bishops and other clergy' was preferable. In ASB the phrase has been changed to 'bishops and other pastors', in view of the fact that pastoral ministries are now exercised by a wide variety of people, both clerical and lay. The phrase 'the healthful spirit of thy grace' has also been changed to the less archaic 'the spirit of your saving grace'.

A General Intercession
(section 5)

At the Savoy Conference the fourth of the Puritan Exceptions objected to the Litany:

> The Litany (though otherwise containing in it many holy petitions) is so framed, that the petitions for a great part are uttered only by the people, which we think not to be so consonant to Scripture, which makes the minister the mouth of the people to God in prayer, the particulars thereof may be composed into one solemn prayer to be offered by the minister unto God for the people.

It has been suggested that this general intercession was written to meet this objection, probably by Peter Gunning, Master of St John's College, Cambridge, subsequently Bishop of Chichester and then Ely. Other possible authors were Robert Sanderson, Bishop of Lincoln, and Edward Reynolds, Bishop of Norwich. It was inserted at the end of the Occasional Prayers under the title 'A Collect or Prayer for all conditions of men' together with a rubric enjoining it to be used 'at such times when the Litany is not appointed to be said', which meant at Morning Prayer on Mondays, Tuesdays, Thursdays and Saturdays.

It has been argued that in its original form the prayer must have been considerably longer: but in view of the fact that prayers for the king, the royal family, and the clergy and people had been said immediately before, the petitions for these groups were omitted. This would account for the strange appearance of the adverb 'Finally' at the beginning of the third sentence—quite unnecessary in so short a prayer. Unfortunately no earlier text of the prayer has yet been discovered. There is evidence for some dependence on scriptural phrases—Psalm 67.2, John 16.13 and Ephesians 4.3.

1928 retained the prayer with its rubric in the Occasional Prayers immediately before those for the faithful departed. The retention of the rubric made little sense in view of the fact that the recitation of the Litany had become optional, and that there was no obligation to use any material after the third Collect. In Series 2 Revised, however, three changes were made:

1 The prayer was printed without its rubric. It therefore became a general intercession for use on any occasion.

2 Despite its lack of reference to the faithful departed, it became an alternative form of intercession for use at Holy Communion.

3 It was converted into a short Litany of three petitions, each accompanied by the same versicle and response as appeared in the intercessions at Holy Communion, with permission to include individual subjects of prayer.

This arrangement continues in ASB, where it appears as 'A General Intercession' immediately after the State Prayers. The modern text is that prepared by the Liturgical Commission.

Petition 1

'All sorts and conditions of men' in modern usage could simply mean 'a wide variety of people'. But the phrase 'men of every race, and in every kind of need' clearly indicates that the petition is all-embracing and covers 'all mankind' of whom God is the creator and preserver.

Petition 2

While the petition for 'all who profess and call themselves Christians' was evidently originally framed with Puritans in mind, today it can happily bear a much wider meaning.

A General Thanksgiving
(section 6)

The General Thanksgiving, together with the Thanksgiving for restoring Public Peace at Home, were added to the Thanksgivings in the Prayer Book in 1662. The author was Bishop Edward Reynolds of Norwich. He possibly drew inspiration from three sources:

1 Various passages of Scripture, notably Psalm 51.15; Luke 1.75; and Colossians 1.27.

2 A thanksgiving composed by Queen Elizabeth after one of her

progresses in 1596: 'I render unto thee, O merciful and heavenly Father, most humble and hearty thanks for thy manifold mercies so abundantly bestowed upon me, as well for my creation, preservation, regeneration, and all other thy benefits and great mercies exhibited in Christ Jesus.'

3 The regulations for the construction of a eucharistic prayer in *The Directory for Public Worship* (1664): 'With humble and hearty acknowledgement . . . of our great unworthiness of the least of all God's mercies; To give thanks to God for all his benefits, and especially for that great benefit of our Redemption, the love of God the Father, the sufferings and merits of the Lord Jesus Christ the Son of God, by which we are delivered; and for all means of Grace . . . Earnestly pray to God, the Father of all mercies.'

1662 placed it first among the Thanksgivings with no directions as to how it should be said. 1928, however, indicated that it could be said by the minister alone, or by the minister and congregation. Series 2 Revised simply printed the prayer with no directions. ASB, by printing it in bold type and in lines, clearly assumes that it is a congregational prayer. Changes from the traditional text are minimal.

A Prayer of Dedication
(section 7)

At the request of the General Synod, a prayer was added to Morning and Evening Prayer Series 3 in 1975 to serve as a congregational devotion at the conclusion of services of the Word, parallel to the final prayer of Dedication and Thanksgiving in Holy Communion Rites A and B. Taking ideas from Psalms 118.14 and 119.105, it is similar in structure and length to the prayer in Holy Communion but sufficiently distinctive to avoid confusion. It was composed by Dr Ronald Jasper.

Concluding Prayers
(sections 8–14)

Prayers 8 and 9

These are both versions of the Prayer of St Chrysostom, a prayer which belongs to the Byzantine rite. Its earliest form dates from the ninth century, and it appears in medieval manuscripts of both the Liturgy of St John Chrysostom and the Liturgy of St Basil. Here, with the addition of a doxology, it concluded the Deacon's litany in the Mass of the Catechumens. Possibly it was this close connection with the Litany which inspired Cranmer to translate it and include it at the end of his 1544 Litany, although without the doxology. In 1549 and 1552 it bore no title; but in 1559 it appeared as 'A Prayer of Chrisostome'—a title which persisted through Scotland 1637 to 1662 and is misleading, for it suggested authorship; whereas the author is unknown. Cranmer probably knew the Liturgy of St John Chrysostom but not that of St Basil; for the former had been translated by Erasmus into Latin at the request of John Fisher, Bishop of Rochester, and this was printed in the Basle edition of Chrysostom's Works in 1539. Furthermore, St John Chrysostom's Liturgy—but not that of St Basil—also was published in Greek with a Latin translation in Venice in 1528. Possibly Cranmer was acquainted with both the Basle and the Venice editions. (But evidently he did not know the Rome edition of 1526 which contained both liturgies.)

The Latin of the Venice edition bears remarkable similarities to Cranmer's translation:

1 Two or three are gathered together in your name.' This was Cranmer's way of understanding the Venice text *duobus aut tribus convenientibus*. Erasmus, however, had given a more correct rendering in the Basle text with *quando duo aut tres concordant in nomine tuo*.

2 'Supplication' in Cranmer corresponds to the Venice *supplicationes*'. Erasmus had written *preces*.

3 Similarly Cranmer's 'petitions' corresponds to the Venice *petitiones*. Erasmus had written *postulationes*.

4 'Knowledge of your truth'. Cranmer again follows the Venice *cognitionem tuae veritatis*, which is a close rendering of the Greek. Erasmus omitted the *tuae*.

It is possible, however, that Cranmer knew both the Venice and the Basle texts: for his 'fulfil now, O Lord' follows Erasmus in the Basle text, whereas there is no 'O Lord' either in the Greek text or in the Venice Latin translation. Cranmer was also guilty of misquoting or misunderstanding the Greek of Matthew 18.19–20, on which the prayer is based. The verses actually say: 'If two of you agree on earth about any request you have to make, that request will be granted by my heavenly Father. For where two or three have met together in my name, I am there among them.' In other words, it is only when people *agree* in Christ's name, that God will grant their requests. Cranmer has conflated the two clauses, producing a different idea on prayer. Whether he did this deliberately or unwittingly is unknown.

Prayer 8 simply takes the Prayer Book version of the prayer, retaining Cranmer's conflation of Matthew 18.19–20, and making only the minimum of change. Prayer 9 is a much freer rendering, which attempts to express more precisely what Matthew says.

In 1662 this prayer with the Grace appeared at the end of Morning and Evening Prayer, and at the end of the Litany. 1928 placed them also at the end of the Occasional Prayers and Thanksgivings with three other conclusions, and inserted a rubric permitting the use of any of the four conclusions at Evening Prayer; Morning Prayer, however, still had to end with St Chrysostom and the Grace. It was not included either in Series 2 Revised or in Series 3: but in ASB it reappeared in these forms as the first of the Concluding Prayers.

Prayers 10–14

These prayers are modest modernizations of the group of prayers at the end of the Holy Communion service in 1662, omitting the third. Cranmer placed them at the end of the rite in 1549 together with the prayers for rain and fair weather, and a rubric indicated that one should be said after the offertory on those days when there was no communion. 1552 extended their use by permitting them 'after the collects, either of Morning and Evening Prayer, Communion or Litany'. This arrangement continued in 1559 and 1662. 1928 removed them, however, indicating at the end of the Communion service that collects in the book or sanctioned by the bishop could be said after the intercession or before the blessing. Series 3 restored five of the six prayers to 'Prayers for various Occasions' with no rubrical directions as to their use, and ASB has retained them with the same freedom.

Prayer 10

This ancient prayer comes from the Gelasian Sacramentary and was originally concerned with travellers. In the Sarum Missal it was still the collect for the *Missa pro iter agentibus*. It also appeared in the Sarum Breviary, in devotions said after Prime. Cranmer's adaptation of it to more general use is most felicitous.

Prayer 11

This also came from the Sarum Breviary and normally was said in the devotions after Prime. At the suggestion of Bishop Cosin it was also included as the final collect in the Order for Confirmation in 1662.

Prayer 12

Another ancient prayer from the Gregorian Sacramentary. In the Sarum Missal it was the fifth collect for the Saturday in Ember week in Lent; and in the rites of York and Hereford it was said before the Confiteor at Mass. The meaning of 'prevent' has clearly changed, and the sense of the Latin *prevenire* has been expressed by the verb 'guide'.

Prayer 13

A prayer composed for 1549 and inspired by various biblical phrases—Ecclesiasticus 1.5; Matthew 6.8; and Romans 8.26.

Prayer 14

Another new prayer in 1549, although it is remarkably similar to the collect for Trinity 23 in the same book, which came from the Gregorian Sacramentary. Again it is inspired by various biblical phrases—Psalm 17.6; John 14.13–14.

The Endings
(sections 15–17)

1 No. 15

Derived from 2 Corinthians 13.14, this ending has had a long and extensive use in Liturgy. From the fourth century onwards it introduced the Sursum corda in many Eastern rites–*Apostolic Constitutions* Book 8, St James, St John Chrysostom, St Basil. In the Sarum Breviary, it was also used as a chapter at Terce. In the Prayer Book, it was first used at the end of the Litany in 1559; and from there was transferred with the State Prayers to the end of Morning and Evening Prayer in 1662.

2 No. 16

Derived from Ephesians 3.20–1, this ending was used by Dean Milner-White in the 1930s in *After the Third Collect*. Its first official use was in Morning and Evening Prayer Series 3; and it has been retained in ASB.

3 No. 17

A traditional formula for concluding services. In Gallican rites *c.* 800 it was used at the end of Mass on High Festivals. It was introduced into the Roman rite *c.* 1000 as an alternative to Ite missa est. The latter was used when the Gloria was said or sung, while Benedicamus was used on other days. It was also the concluding formula at Lauds, Prime, Vespers and Compline in the Sarum Breviary. 1928 first used it in Anglican worship as an additional ending to Morning and Evening Prayer. Although not used in Series 2 and Series 2 Revised, it was restored in Series 3 and has been retained in ASB.

The Blessings
(sections 18–19)

No. 18

This ancient form, known as the Aaronic Blessing, is based on Numbers 6.24–6, and is found in Gallican and Anglo-Saxon Missals. Jeremy Taylor used in his *Collection of Offices*, 1658, and it was undoubtedly from there that Bishop John Cosin successfully proposed its introduction in the Visitation of the Sick and—in shorter form—in the Commination in 1662. Officially its use was confined to these services until 1977, when it was introduced into the Series 3 Initiation Services at the end of the Forms of Thanksgiving for the Birth of a Child and after Adoption. At the request of the General Synod, it was included in ASB for general use.

No. 19

A new form, prepared by the Liturgical Commission as an alternative to the above in the Series 3 Forms of Thanksgiving. It too was included in ASB for general use.

9
The Eucharist

A
HISTORY

General studies:
Donald Bridge and David Phypers, *The Meal that Unites?* 1981.
L. Bouyer, *Eucharist: Theology and Spirituality of the Eucharistic Prayer.* 1968.
Y. Brilioth, *Eucharistic Faith and Practice: Evangelical and Catholic.* 1930.
G. J. Cuming, *He Gave Thanks: An Introduction to the Eucharistic Prayer.* 1981.
Lucien Deiss, *It's the Lord's Supper: Eucharist of Christians.* 1980.
G. Dix, *The Shape of the Liturgy.* 1945: a classic work, but one which should be used with caution since some of its conclusions would not be entirely shared by many liturgical scholars of more recent years.
T. Klauser, *A Short History of the Western Liturgy.* 1969.
G. A. Michell, *Landmarks in Liturgy.* 1961.
Nathan Mitchell, *Cult and Controversy: The Worship of the Eucharist Outside Mass.* New York 1982.
Geoffrey Wainwright, *Eucharist and Eschatology.* 1971

Collections of texts:
F. E. Brightman (ed.), *Liturgies Eastern and Western*, vol. i: Eastern Liturgies. 1896, reprinted 1965.
R. C. D. Jasper and G. J. Cuming (eds), *Prayers of the Eucharist: Early and Reformed.* 1975.

1 *The Old Testament and Jewish Background*

Sacred meals have been a feature of many religions. They have generally been linked to an act of sacrifice, in which part of the animal or other food which is offered to the deity is consumed by the offerers. The purpose of such acts has often been to affirm and strengthen a communal bond among the participants, or between them and the god to whom it is offered. For Judaism, however, not only special sacrificial meals but all eating and drinking were religious acts, and were not to be performed without prayer.

The classic form of Jewish prayer is the *berakah* or blessing, and this has its roots in the Old Testament. A typical example is the prayer of Abraham's servant when he has been successful in finding a wife for Isaac (Gen. 24.27): 'Blessed be the Lord, the God of my master Abraham, who has not forsaken his steadfast love and his faithfulness towards my master.' As can be seen, it is composed of an opening formula of blessing, a further descriptive phrase, and a relative clause expressing the particular grounds for the blessing. By such a prayer the speaker thus *remembered* what God had done for him; *confessed* or acknowledged that it was the work of God and not the result of mere chance or human effort alone, by ascribing the praise and glory for it to him; and *proclaimed* the mighty works of God to any who were present to hear his prayer. The remembrance (in Greek *anamnesis*) might be expanded from a simple relative clause into an extended narrative description; and petition or intercession might follow on from it, and in subordination to it, the remembrance by the worshipper of God's past goodness constituting the ground upon which he might be asked to remember his people and continue his activity among them. The *berakah* would then return to the theme of praise in a concluding doxology.

A variant of this prayer-form was the *hodayah*, in which the passive opening formula was replaced by an active form of the verb *yadah*, usually rendered 'I give thanks' in English versions of the Old Testament but more accurately translated as 'I confess' or 'I acknowledge', the same verb being used for the confession of sins. In place of a relative clause, a subordinate clause introduced by 'that' was generally employed, as in Isaiah 12.1: 'I will give thanks to you, O Lord, that though you were angry with me, your anger turned away, and you comforted me.' When the *hodayah* was translated into Greek, some compound form of the verb *homologeo*, the equivalent word for 'confess', was used at first, as in the prayer attributed to Jesus in Matthew 11.25–6/Luke 10.21: 'I confess to you, Father, Lord of heaven and earth, that you have hidden. . . .' Later, however, the verb *eucharisteo*, 'I give thanks', tended to be used instead, and thus the note of gratitude was added to the themes of remembrance, acknowledgement, and proclamation already present in the prayer-formula. By the first century prayers might use a mixture of the *berakah* and *hodayah* forms, and the former was now generally found in the second person rather than the third person, 'Blessed are you, O Lord our God. . . .'

Such blessings or thanksgivings were used not only in formal liturgical services, but by pious Jews in their daily life, so that they might keep themselves constantly aware of their dependence on God for all the good things which they enjoyed. This applied especially to meals, where nothing was to be eaten or drunk without a blessing having been offered for it to God the giver. Although it was God who was blessed by this action and not the food, it could be said that, by acknowledging that the meal was given by God's bounty, it too was sanctified or consecrated. At a communal meal, such as the weekly Sabbath meal, when wine would be drunk to mark its significance, the blessings were not said by each person individually but performed corporately. First, all present would ritually wash their hands, and on certain occasions there might be an additional cup of wine before the meal or a preliminary dish, over which each would say grace individually. The first action of the meal proper, however, was performed by the head of the household, the host, or the senior person present. He would rise, take bread into his hands, and bless God for it in the name of all present, to which they would respond, 'Amen'. After this he would break it and distribute it to the others. The meal then began, with a blessing being said over each new course. At the end of the meal the host rose to say the blessing over a special cup of wine—sometimes called the cup of blessing (cf. 1 Cor. 10.16)—which he then passed round to all the participants. Although the wording of such prayers of blessing was not precisely prescribed until a later period, their general forms and themes were established, and they would have been along these lines:

(*over the bread*)
Blessed are you, O Lord our God, king of the universe, who bring forth bread from the earth.

(*over the wine after the meal*)
Blessed are you, O Lord our God, king of the universe, who feed the whole world with goodness, with grace, and with mercy.
We thank you, O Lord our God, because you have caused us to inherit a good and pleasant land.
Have mercy, O Lord our God, on Israel your people, and on

Jerusalem your city, and on Zion, the dwelling-place of your
glory, and on your altar and on your temple.
Blessed are you, O Lord, who build Jerusalem.

Certain meals, however, were particularly important, among
them the meals connected with the great annual pilgrimage
festivals, when people were expected to go up to Jerusalem to
participate in them, and especially the Passover, which commemorated the Exodus from Egypt. This meal had a number of
unusual features, in addition to the eating of a Passover lamb
sacrificed in the Temple, among them the use of unleavened bread
and bitter herbs. By tradition the youngest person present was
expected to ask about the meaning of these features, and in
response the head of the family, presiding over the meal, was to
tell the story of the Exodus. Thus both by word and also by
symbolic actions those participating remembered, acknowledged,
and proclaimed what God had done for them; time was tran-
scended, and present and past were united, since, in the words of
the Passover ritual, 'in every generation each Jew is duty bound to
think of himself as having personally taken part in the Exodus . . .
It was not only our forefathers that the Holy One, blessed be he,
redeemed; he redeemed us, the living, together with them.' The
Passover had a future dimension too: remembrance of what God
had done in freeing his people from slavery led inevitably to hope
and prayer for the coming of the Messiah and the consummation
of God's Kingdom.

2 The New Testament

According to the synoptic gospels (Matt. 26.17; Mark 14.12; Luke
22.7), the Last Supper was a Passover meal. John's Gospel, on the
other hand, states that Jesus died on the day of the Passover
sacrifice (John 19.14), and so the Last Supper would have been on
the previous day. There has been a considerable debate among
scholars as to which of these claims is historically correct, but the
answer is not particularly vital for an understanding of the origins
of the Christian Eucharist. On the one hand, even if the Last
Supper were not a Passover meal as such, it took place within the
context of the Passover season, and so the Eucharist quite
naturally attracted to itself Passover imagery and theology. On the
other hand, even if it were a Passover meal, none of the ritual
actions peculiar to that occasion seem to have become a part of the

Christian liturgical tradition, but only those which were to be found in all Jewish formal meals of the period, and since those meals followed a common pattern, we can use that to fill out the accounts of the Last Supper given in the New Testament.

We may presume that Jesus would have broadly adhered to the traditional ritual at the Last Supper, but it appears from the New Testament accounts (Matt. 26.26–9; Mark 14.22–5; Luke 22.14–20; 1 Cor. 11.23–6) that, as he distributed the bread and the cup after the prayers, he interpreted them in a new sense, as representing his body and his blood, and, according to the account in 1 Corinthians 11, commanded his followers to remember him when they performed these customary actions at future meals. Luke's account of the Supper differs from the others in including an additional cup of wine before the taking of the bread, and in some manuscripts of the Gospel the cup of wine after the meal is omitted, leaving simply the inverted order, wine–bread. Biblical scholars are divided over the question as to which version of the text is the original, and what conclusions should be drawn from it.

The Christian Eucharist, however, was not merely a re-enactment of the Last Supper. Had it been so, one might have expected it to have taken place only once a year on the anniversary of that event. The New Testament describes many of the resurrection appearances of Jesus as taking place within the context of a meal, often on 'the evening of the first day of the week' (see, for example, Luke 24.30f.), and this suggests that in the continuation of their regular common meals together after the death of Jesus, his followers experienced the presence of their risen Lord as a living reality, uniting into one body the individuals gathered there, and they looked forward in hope to the final consummation of God's Kingdom and the fulfilment of the messianic banquet, of which their meal was a foretaste.

References to Christian eucharistic practice in the New Testament are only fragmentary or indirect, so that it is impossible to say very much with any certainty about the earliest period of liturgical history, but it is generally agreed by New Testament scholars that the earliest Eucharists were in fact complete meals shared by the local Christian community, apparently taking place regularly in the evening of the first day of the week, which came to be called 'the Lord's day' (see, for example, Rev. 1.10). Here they performed the familiar Jewish meal-ritual, but now in remembrance of Jesus. No doubt because of the fluidity of their wording, it was not long before the prayers of blessing, or

149

thanksgiving as the Christians increasingly tended to call them, began to include some explicit reference to Jesus and to what God had done through him (cf. 1 Cor. 11.26). Something of this sort seems to be preserved in the document known as the *Didache*.

St Paul implies that the participants were expected to contribute food and drink to the meals themselves (1 Cor. 11.21), as was the case in Jewish practice: although when guests were invited to someone's home to share a meal, the host would naturally have provided everything himself; when a group of friends or associates, sometimes called a *haburah*, met together for a common meal, it was customary for all to bring some contribution to the food and wine. He also suggests that the meals were followed by an informal style of ministry of the word (1 Cor. 14.26), which also seems to have sometimes been the case in Jewish practice.

Studies:
Gillian Feeley-Harnick, *The Lord's Table: Eucharist and Passover in Early Christianity*. Philadelphia 1981.
David Gregg, *Anamnesis in the Eucharist*. 1976.
J. Jeremias, *The Eucharistic Words of Jesus*. 1966.

3 The Second and Third Centuries

Before the end of the first century this pattern was already running into difficulties: in a Gentile environment the sacred nature of the meal could easily be lost in the festal atmosphere surrounding it, and antisocial behaviour could emerge, as appears to have been the case at Corinth (see 1 Cor. 11.17f.); periods of persecution and Roman legislation against meetings of clubs could also make it difficult to maintain a full evening assembly; and there were also no doubt practical catering difficulties. It is not so surprising, therefore, that in our earliest full account of eucharistic practice outside the New Testament, given by Justin Martyr at Rome in the middle of the second century, a dramatic transformation has taken place. The Eucharist has now become separated from a meal, and is an early morning Sunday service instead of an evening assembly. The meal, or *agape* as it was often called, however, continued to survive on its own for several centuries as an occasional congregational supper before it finally died out.

Two other significant changes have also occurred, apparently as a consequence of this upheaval. Firstly, the eucharistic action has been prefixed with a synagogue-style Service of the word and prayers, which had almost certainly existed as a separate entity prior to this. Justin provides only a few details of this part of the rite. A reader read from the Old Testament and the Gospels for as long as time allowed; the president (as Justin calls him) then delivered a homily, and intercessions followed. These were concluded with the kiss of peace, and then bread and wine mixed with water (the normal Eastern way of drinking wine) were brought to the president to begin the second part of the service. On occasions the ministry of the word might be replaced by a baptism of new converts.

Secondly, the shape of the eucharistic action itself has altered. The brief ritual which had originally preceded the meal (taking bread, blessing God over it, breaking it, and sharing it) has now become fused with the more substantial ritual after the meal (taking the cup of wine, giving thanks to God over it at some considerable length, and sharing it), and forms what has been called a fourfold shape: (i) taking bread and wine together; (ii) saying the thanksgiving over both; (iii) breaking the bread; and (iv) distributing both bread and wine to all present. Justin tells us that there was still considerable freedom with regard to the wording of this eucharistic prayer: 'the president offers prayers and thanksgivings to the best of his ability', and the people associate themselves with this by saying 'Amen' at the end. Deacons then distribute the bread and wine to those present and take it to those unable to be there for some reason; apparently it was considered very important that all the faithful were able to share in the communion in some way.

Later sources both fill out this description and also indicate how the structure of the Eucharist subsequently developed. Tertullian and Cyprian, writing in North Africa in the third century, tell us that there could be as many as four scriptural readings in the ministry of the word: the Law and the Prophets, as in synagogue usage, followed by a reading from the earliest Christian writings, the Epistles, and finally one from the Gospels. After the ministry of the word all those who had not yet been baptized and those undergoing ecclesiastical discipline were dismissed before the Christian community began its prayers. These authors also confirm that the communicants each brought a contribution of bread and wine for the service, and afterwards they were able to take home a little of the consecrated bread and make their communion from it on weekdays.

The *Apostolic Tradition* of Hippolytus, which is believed to originate in Rome early in the third century, provides a specimen form of Eucharistic Prayer which the president may use, though he is still free to pray as he wishes, provided that what he says remains 'orthodox'. This model prayer begins with the dialogue which was to become standard in the West: 'The Lord be with you'; 'And with your spirit'; 'Lift up your hearts'; 'We lift them to the Lord'; 'Let us give thanks to the Lord'; 'It is fitting and right'. It then proceeds to give thanks to God for his work in Christ and to recount his mighty acts; with only a brief reference to creation, it passes quickly on to the incarnation, the redemption on the cross, and the sanctification of the people of God. It also includes an account of the institution of the Eucharist at the Last Supper, an offering to God of the bread and the cup, and a petition for the descent of the Spirit (or epiclesis as it has been called by scholars) on the oblation of the Church and for the fruits of communion. Some scholars suspect that parts of the prayer, and especially the epiclesis, may have been altered or added by later hands. E. C. Ratcliff, in particular, believed that the prayer had been substantially rewritten in the fourth century, and that originally it had culminated in the Sanctus, now missing from the text, but his theory has not been widely accepted.

Studies:

R. P. C. Hanson, 'The Liberty of the Bishop to improvise prayer in the Eucharist' (*Vigiliae Christianae* 15, 1961), pp. 173–6.

— *Eucharistic Offering in the Early Church.* 1979.

L. Ligier, 'The Origins of the Eucharistic Prayer: from the Last Supper to the Eucharist' (*SL* 9, 1973), pp. 161–85.

E. C. Ratcliff, 'The Sanctus and the Pattern of the early Anaphora' (*JEH* 1, 1950), pp. 29–36, 125–34; reprinted in A. H. Couratin and D. H. Tripp (eds), *E. C. Ratcliff: Liturgical Studies* (1976), pp. 18–40.

T. J. Talley, 'The Eucharistic Prayer of the Ancient Church according to Recent Research: Results and Reflections' (*SL* 11, 1976), pp. 138–58; also appeared in an expanded version as: 'From Berakah to Eucharistia: a Reopening Question' (*Worship* 50, 1976), pp. 115–37.

— 'The Eucharistic Prayer: Tradition and Development', in K. W. Stevenson (ed.), *Liturgy Reshaped* (1982), pp. 48–64.

4 Later Developments

From the fourth century onwards evidence of liturgical practice becomes more plentiful, and we can discern the existence of different 'families' of rites, with distinctive variations in the form and manner in which the service was celebrated in different geographical areas. The Eucharistic Prayer of the Syrian tradition, for example, had a much more extensive thanksgiving for creation than that in the *Apostolic Tradition*, and included a reference to angels, culminating in the Sanctus, the angelic song, 'Holy, Holy, Holy . . .' The use of this hymn of praise was derived from Jewish worship, and it slowly spread from its Syrian home to become a universal feature of all Eucharistic Prayers, Eastern and Western.

In the changed situation of the Church after the conversion of Constantine in the fourth century the style of celebration became much more formalized and elaborate, as congregations grew in size and the Christian liturgy absorbed many of the elements of court ceremonial. The Eucharist was now 'public' and open to all, and so the dismissal of the unbaptized and those undergoing ecclesiastical discipline, which had formerly taken place after the ministry of the word and before the prayers, now either disappeared altogether or remained as an anachronistic feature of the rite. The prayers of the faithful and the Eucharistic Prayer ceased to be the only prayers in the rite, and additional ones began to appear at various points throughout the service. Moreover, the Eucharistic Prayer itself began to include a substantial element of intercession, both for the living and for the departed, as prayer for the fruits of communion was extended from those participating in the sacramental act to others for whom they desired its benefits.

Alongside the emphasis on the community-event as the means by which Christ's presence was experienced, at least since early in the second century when the ritual of the Eucharist was separated from a full meal, there had also been an increasing stress on the food, the bread and wine themselves, as the *locus* of his presence. This grew even more strongly in the fourth century, when because of the great expansion in numbers consciousness of the local church as a tight-knit community began to decline, and it led to a number of new developments in eucharistic rites. These included the emergence in the Eucharistic Prayer of a specific petition for the consecration of the bread and wine that they might become the body and blood of Christ. In the Syrian family of rites this was usually formed by expanding the petition for the descent of the Spirit, the 'epiclesis', in the latter part of the prayer; in the Egyptian (or Alexandrian) rites, where the original epiclesis came between the Sanctus and the narrative of the institution of the Eucharist, a second, consecratory, *epiclesis* was inserted in the latter part of the prayer; and in the Roman rite a similar petition, though not strictly speaking an epiclesis in its form, appeared before the narrative of institution. Two main theories emerged among ancient scholars as to which part of the prayer it was which effected the consecration: some held that it was the epiclesis, others that it was the recital of the narrative of institution. Eventually, the East adopted the view that both were necessary, while the West regarded the latter as constituting the moment of consecration.

Perhaps one of the most significant developments in the history of the Eucharist was the stress on awe and fear as the proper attitudes towards the presence of Christ in the bread and wine which began to emerge in Syria from the fourth century onwards. This reverential disposition, which for example can be very clearly seen expressed in the well-known Eastern hymn, 'Let all mortal flesh keep silence', once again gradually spread throughout the Christian Church, and brought about profound changes in eucharistic practice. Not only did it lead to an increase in gestures and expressions of adoration towards the consecrated elements, but it also led, albeit indirectly, to the decline in the regular reception of communion by lay people. Because of the fact that many of the new converts flooding into the Church in the wake of the conversion of Constantine had only a very limited grasp of the Christian faith and were inclined towards irreverent behaviour at the Eucharist, the bishops and clergy began in their teaching to stress the need for a proper interior holiness in approaching the sacred mysteries. Unfortunately, far from encouraging a more reverent attitude when receiving communion, it had the opposite effect and discouraged most people from the frequent reception of communion altogether, as they judged themselves to be unworthy of it.

One other consequence of this development may also be noted. In earlier times the table, or altar as it now began to be called, had been placed towards the centre of the room and the bishop or priest presiding at the Eucharist had stood behind it facing the congregation and surrounded by his assistant ministers. Later, however, it began to be moved away from the people and placed within a more enclosed area at the end of the building, so as to create a distinct sanctuary or holy space, and eventually this tended to be cut off from the rest of the church by a substantial screen.

Studies:
For the later development of the Byzantine rite, John Fenwick, *The Eastern Orthodox Liturgy* (1978), provides a brief introduction, and Casimir Kucharek, *The Byzantine–Slav Liturgy of St John Chrysostom* (Allendale, Canada, 1971), a more substantial commentary, though as it is based on the Ukrainian rite it needs to be used with caution. Robert Taft, *The Great Entrance* (Rome 1975), is a masterly study of one particular part of the rite.

For the theology of eucharistic consecration see Richard Buxton, *Eucharist and Institution Narrative* (1976); J. H. McKenna, *Eucharist and Holy Spirit* (1975); J. H. Srawley, *The Early History of the Liturgy* (2nd edn, 1947), ch. 9.

5 The Roman Rite

It is not possible within the limited space available here to trace all the various ways in which the Eucharist was celebrated in ancient tradition, and we must content ourselves with looking at the development of eucharistic practice at Rome, the principal ancestor of the Western medieval Mass. Had we been present at a Eucharist celebrated by the Pope around 700, we would have found that in the course of the preceding centuries the rite had grown and changed, and was now composed of the following main elements:

(a) *Introit Psalm*

This was sung during the entry of the ministers through the great basilica churches of the city, and may have been included in the service in imitation of the practice of the imperial court, where the entry of rulers was greeted with music. Some consider that it may have found its way into the rite during the papacy of Celestine I (422–32).

(b) *Kyries*

These were the remains of a litany which had been added to the beginning of the service some time earlier, possibly during the papacy of Gelasius I (492–6), in imitation of Eastern practice. Subsequently the petitions of the litany were omitted, in order to save time, leaving only the response, *Kyrie eleison*, 'Lord, have mercy', repeated over and over again until the Pope signalled the choir to stop. Eventually the number of repetitions came to be fixed at nine: 'Lord, have mercy' three times, 'Christ, have mercy' three times, and 'Lord, have mercy' again three times.

(c) Gloria in excelsis

This ancient canticle, which had been a regular part of the daily morning service in the East since at least the fourth century, was introduced from there into the morning service in Gaul. Its presence here may be the result of celebrating the morning Office immediately before the Eucharist, though that is merely conjecture. For several centuries it was only used in the Roman tradition at Eucharists on Sundays and feasts presided over by a bishop. Later, priests were allowed to include it at Easter, and gradually its use spread until in the eleventh century it formed a regular part of all Sunday and festal services, except in Advent and between Septuagesima and Easter.

(d) Salutation and Collect

The salutation ('The Lord be with you'; 'and with your spirit') as the opening greeting of the service is first mentioned by Augustine of Hippo (354–430), though its use may well go back to New Testament times. The collect is a distinctive prayer-form of the Roman tradition, and receives its name from its function of 'collecting' or summing-up the prayers of the people. The date of its introduction into this service cannot be fixed precisely, but was probably around the middle of the fifth century, though scholars dispute the purpose of its inclusion at this particular point in the rite. At first collects were improvised by the minister presiding, but eventually specific collects were assigned to particular occasions. Until the tenth century at Rome only one collect was said at any one service, but thereafter the number tended to increase (to as many as seven!), following the tendency to elaboration already prevalent elsewhere in the Western Church.

(e) The Readings

We now reach part of the service which derives from early times. We have already seen that it was possible for there to be as many as four readings in the ministry of the word, two from the Old Testament and two from the New Testament. The Roman rite seems originally to have had three, one from the Old Testament, one from the Epistles, and one from the Gospels, but the number was apparently reduced to two during the fourth century. It then became customary to have Epistle and Gospel on Sundays, and the Old Testament reading and Gospel on weekdays.

(f) Chants between the Readings

This is the most ancient point in the service at which a psalm was sung, the first firm evidence for the practice dating from the fourth century, though it is not entirely clear whether it was viewed as a further independent reading from the Old Testament, or as a response to the preceding lection. The method was responsorial: a cantor chanted the psalm, and the people responded with a refrain after each verse. At Rome the psalm always followed the first reading, and an 'alleluia' chant preceded the Gospel. The result of this was that, when the number of readings was reduced to two, these elements then followed one after the other.

(g) The Sermon

In the West it came to be the general rule that only bishops were allowed to preach, and by the fifth century the sermon was in any case beginning to be considered to be an optional element in the service. Thus, as time went on, preaching became very infrequent in many places. As yet the Creed had not found a regular place in the Roman eucharistic rite (though it was already used in other traditions), and it was not adopted until 1014, after the coronation of the Emperor Henry II, when it became obligatory on all Sundays and feast days. A notable omission of primitive practice from the Roman rite at this period is the intercessory prayers of the faithful. Their disappearance may possibly have been the result of a desire to abbreviate a service which was growing rather long, or they may have been dropped when the litany was introduced at the beginning of the rite (see Kyries above). They survived only on one occasion in the year—Good Friday.

(h) The Offertory

The bishop and the clergy collected the gifts of bread and wine which the people had brought. During this lengthy process a psalm was sung, and at the end a variable prayer, called the 'secret', was said, to some extent anticipating the Eucharistic Prayer itself.

(i) *The Eucharistic Prayer, or 'Canon of the Mass'*

The wording of this central prayer had now become fixed, and athough the principal features of the prayer found in the *Apostolic Tradition* of Hippolytus can still be discerned in this text, its character was markedly different. Unlike Eastern rites, which tended to have evolved a number of complete Eucharistic Prayers as alternatives to one another, the Roman rite had only the one prayer, but with certain parts of it varying according to the particular occasion or season of the year. Thus it still began with the customary dialogue and proceeded with thanksgiving, but this element was now very brief and general in tone: specific thanksgiving for what God had done in Christ belonged only to 'proper prefaces' which were used at appropriate points in the liturgical year when that particular aspect of salvation was being celebrated. Instead the prayer moves on to the Sanctus, and the rest is composed chiefly of petition for the acceptance of the offering of the gifts of the people, intercession for those who had offered the gifts and for those on whose behalf offering was being made, and petition for the consecration of the bread and wine, which led into the narrative of the institution of the Eucharist and prayer offering the bread and wine to God.

(j) *The Lord's Prayer*

We do not know when Christians first started to include this prayer in the eucharistic rite as distinct from their regular daily prayers, but Augustine of Hippo tells us at the end of the fourth century that 'nearly every church' said it after the breaking of the bread and before communion, though conservative Rome may still have been one of the exceptions. Gregory the Great (*c.* 540–604) is credited with having altered its position within the Roman rite so that it formed the conclusion of the Eucharistic Prayer.

(k) *The Kiss of Peace*

We have encountered this in primitive practice as the conclusion of the prayers of intercession, but by the fifth century in both Africa and Rome it came after the Lord's Prayer, perhaps as a symbolic expression of the clause, 'as we forgive those who sin against us'.

(*l*) The Breaking of the Bread, or 'Fraction'

This was another primitive utilitarian feature which had begun to have symbolic elaboration. The custom of singing the Agnus Dei, 'O Lamb of God ...', during it was introduced from Syria by Sergius I (Pope from 687 to 701), himself of Syrian descent.

(*m*) The Distribution of Holy Communion

The people came up to the altar to receive the bread and wine, and a psalm was now sung during this process. The words of administration seem to have been simply 'The body of Christ', 'The blood of Christ', to which the recipient replied, 'Amen'.

(*n*) Post-communion Prayer

Like the collect and the offertory prayer, this varied according to the day.

(*o*) Dismissal

This feature is mentioned as early as the third century, and probably goes back to the very beginnings of the Church. In some places a blessing had been introduced somewhere in the service, before or after communion, but it does not seem to have had a formal place in the rite at Rome.

Studies:
J. A. Jungmann, *The Mass of the Roman Rite.* 1959.
G. G. Willis, *Essays in Early Roman Liturgy.* 1964.
— *Further Essays in Early Roman Liturgy.* 1968.

6 The Medieval West

Although the texts of the later medieval missals are substantially derived from the rite just described, in the course of the Middle Ages the character of the eucharistic celebration in the West underwent a number of significant changes.

Firstly, there was the growth of presbyteral masses. Although priests had on occasions presided at eucharistic services in place of the bishop at least since the third century, nevertheless the corporate celebration presided over by the bishop and involving priests, deacons, lectors, acolytes, and laity, all fulfilling their proper roles, remained the norm for some considerable time.

Eventually, however, the spread of Christianity into distant parts of the world and the large size of dioceses meant that it became usual for people to experience a service which was presided over by one priest alone with no more than a single assistant minister, and to regard this as the norm with episcopal High Mass as peculiar and exceptional. This obviously brought about an enormous change in the way in which the Eucharist was generally celebrated.

Secondly, there was what might be called the dissolution of the liturgical community—the growing clericalization of the liturgy until it became something done *by* the priest *for* the people, who need not even be present, so it was thought, in order to receive the spiritual benefits of the celebration. This movement was linked to the stress on the need for awe and fear towards the sacred mysteries which we have referred to earlier and which had led to a growth of the sense of unworthiness among lay people and a decline in the frequency of the reception of Holy Communion. Thus by the end of the Middle Ages the majority of people made their communion no more than about once or twice a year, and attended the service as passive observers without receiving the sacrament on all other occasions.

The emphasis on reverence and awe led to other changes, such as the silent recitation by the priest of certain 'sacred' parts of the service, especially of the heart of the Eucharistic Prayer itself; the custom of kneeling rather than standing for prayer and for the reception of Holy Communion; the practice of receiving the bread directly into the mouth instead of in the hand and the wine through a tube instead of directly from the chalice; and the eventual withdrawal of the chalice from the laity altogether, lest they should spill any of the consecrated wine. Participation in the offertory also disappeared. With the decline in regular communion, bread and wine were no longer required in large quantities, and so the people stopped bringing their contributions. In any case, under the influence of the Old Testament account of the Passover, the Western Church began to use unleavened bread in place of the ordinary bread baked by the faithful.

The laity, therefore, no longer participated in the service on most occasions when they were present. They simply *saw* and *heard* it celebrated by the priest, but because he now stood between them and the altar, facing East, and because of the ignorance of Latin among ordinary people, even these two activities were rather limited, and by the end of the medieval period the most that they could do was to get on with their own private devotions and look up when a bell was rung at what was considered the moment when the bread and wine were changed into the body and blood of Christ, when the priest repeated the words spoken by him in the narrative of the institution of the Eucharist during the Eucharistic Prayer. At this point the priest would hold the bread and cup high up in the air for the people to catch a glimpse of them and so be able to adore their Redeemer. Thus the Eucharist was no longer viewed as a meal, nor even as heavenly food or the medicine of immortality, as formerly, but principally as an object of devotion: the rite had in effect been transformed into a visually dramatic ceremony by which, it was thought, the bread and wine became Christ's body and blood through the action of the priest on behalf of the people, to be worshipped from afar but not approached; and Christ's sacrifice of himself was offered to the Father so that the benefits of his passion might be appropriated by those for whom it was offered, whether present or absent.

On the other hand, a measure of pastoral concern for the needs of the people can be discerned in the emergence of an unofficial vernacular element in the Sunday Mass known as 'Prone'. This was included in the rite between the ministry of the word and the eucharistic action, and consisted of a sermon preceded or followed by 'the bidding of the bedes' and instruction in such things as the Ten Commandments and the Lord's Prayer. The bidding of the bedes was a form of intercession, which was flexible and so allowed the priest to include specific objects of prayer within it, although with the passage of time it did tend to assume a fixed form.

Finally, mention should be made of one other medieval development, the growth from the eighth century onwards of the private Mass. This originated in the idea that each priest ought to fulfil what was thought of as his priestly function every day and say Mass, regardless as to whether any pastoral need for it existed or not, and also in the idea that the more Masses were celebrated, the more one's own salvation and that of those for whom the offering was being made could be advanced—a quantitive attitude towards the sacrament which was applied particularly to the departed. Hence there was a multiplication of Masses without any congregational presence and of altars at which they might be said, and also a considerable change and adaptation of ceremonial to this new situation, which in turn tended to influence the way in which other celebrations of the Eucharist were carried out. These included the emergence of the Missal, a single book containing the whole text of the service for the sole minister to use; the inclusion in this text, as essential parts of the service, of what had originated as the private devotional prayers of the priest, and which tended to bring a strongly penitential tone to the rite; and the abbreviation of the various psalms of the service to a single verse and antiphon, since there were no longer any lengthy ceremonies involving the whole congregation at these points.

7 The Reformation

With regard to the Eucharist, the prime concerns of the Reformation debate centred around the doctrines of the nature of the presence of Christ in the sacrament and of the nature of the rite as a sacrifice. The Reformers were united in condemning the idea that in any sense Christ could be offered in the Eucharist. The Eucharist could only be considered a sacrifice in the sense that in it Christians could offer themselves, along with their thanks and praise, through Christ to the Father. They were also united in demanding that there should be no celebration of the Eucharist which did not include the communion of the people and not just of the priest alone, and that this reception should be of both bread and cup and not just of bread alone.

They were more divided, however, over the way in which Christ could be understood to be present in the Eucharist. While Martin Luther rejected the medieval doctrine of transubstantiation as popularly understood, he retained a literal understanding of Jesus' words, 'This is my body ... This is my blood', which caused him to hold on to the notion of the real, objective presence of Christ in the bread and wine. This he explained in a modified version of the medieval theory. The scholastic theologians of the Middle Ages had taught that in the eucharistic consecration, whilst the external characteristics, or 'accidents', of bread and wine remained, the inner 'substance' was changed from that of bread and wine into the body and blood of Christ. Luther argued that what happened was not 'transubstantiation' but 'consubstantiation': the substance of bread and wine remained, but *along with* that of the body and blood of Christ.

Luther's liturgical reform was quite conservative. It was in effect just a simplification and translation into the vernacular of the traditional rite, with more prominent preaching, and the deletion of the element which Luther regarded as most offensive, the

Eucharistic Prayer which enshrined the doctrine of the sacrifice of the Mass, and its replacement by a simple reading of the narrative of the institution. Otherwise in its externals it had a very traditional appearance.

Towards the other extreme of the Reformation spectrum stood Ulrich Zwingli of Zürich in Switzerland. He could not accept Luther's belief that Christ could be both in heaven and in the eucharistic bread and wine. Since he was convinced of Christ's presence in heaven, it followed that he could not be present in the bread and wine—a view which has sometimes, and somewhat unfairly, been described as 'the doctrine of the real absence'. Zwingli believed that Christ intended the bread and wine to *signify* his body and blood, and the celebration of the Eucharist was thus a memorial of Christ's death, performed in obedience to his command to 'do this in remembrance of me', an aid to the worshipper but not in itself the means of grace: the real communion took place between the believer and God independently of the reception of the elements of bread and wine.

Perhaps not surprisingly, Zwingli was not particularly anxious for there to be frequent celebrations of the Eucharist: four times a year was judged sufficient by him, and the normal Sunday service became a ministry of the word alone. When the Eucharist was celebrated, the service was very simple. It began with a sermon and prayers, including intercession and the confession of sins. Then followed two fixed readings, 1 Corinthians 11.20–9 and John 6.47–53, separated by the Gloria in excelsis. The Apostles' Creed was recited, and a deacon exhorted the people to receive communion with trust, faith, and confidence in Christ. The Lord's Prayer and another prayer followed, the narrative of institution was read, and the people then received communion. Psalm 113 was said after this, and the minister prayed a final brief prayer of thanksgiving and dismissed the congregation.

Between these two positions stood John Calvin in Geneva. He rejected Luther's doctrine, but took a more positive view of the Eucharist than Zwingli. He believed that, through the communion, 'Christ offers himself to us with all his blessings, and we receive him in faith', though he was careful to avoid too precise a definition of the mode of Christ's presence in the Eucharist. Though, therefore, he was not unhappy with the kind of service drawn up by Zwingli, and the forms he produced were broadly similar, he would have wished to have had at least a weekly celebration of the sacrament. However, he was not able to persuade others of the desirability of this, and quarterly communions eventually became the norm in the Reformed Church throughout the world.

8 The Church of England

Texts and studies:
Colin Buchanan (ed.), *Background Documents to Liturgical Revision 1547–1549.* 1983.
— (ed.), *Eucharistic Liturgies of Edward VI: A Text for Students.* 1983.
— *What did Cranmer think he was doing?* 1976.

It is difficult to determine which of these Reformation views formed the foundation of the eucharistic theology of Thomas Cranmer in England. Indeed the probable answer is that he had his own unique blend of them. Like the continental Reformers, he rejected transubstantiation and the doctrine of the sacrifice of the Mass. Since he believed that Christ was in heaven, he concluded that the bread and wine remained as bread and wine before, during and after the celebration of the Eucharist. Yet, when they were received *by faith*, then in the act of communion Christ was truly present to the believer, and the believer could feed on him. Cranmer did not, however, give his theology full expression in his first revision of the eucharistic rite, but proceeded to it by stages.

The first step was taken in 1547, when an element of vernacular teaching was introduced into the medieval mass. A set of injunctions was issued which included the directions that the Epistle and Gospel were to be read in English; and that when there was no sermon, the Creed, the Lord's Prayer, and the Ten Commandments were to be read in English after the Gospel every Holy Day; and one of the official homilies published that year was to be read every Sunday.

In December 1547 the administration of communion in both kinds, bread and wine, was ordered by Parliament, and *An Order of the Communion* for this purpose was produced in March 1548. This contained an exhortation to receive communion, which was to be read to the people on the preceding Sunday, and, not a complete English eucharistic rite, but simply a further vernacular element to be inserted into the Latin Mass immediately after the priest's communion. This consisted of another exhortation, an invitation to confession, a form of general confession, an absolution, the 'Comfortable Words', the 'Prayer of Humble Access', words of administration ('The body of our Lord Jesus Christ which was given for thee preserve thy body unto everlasting life'; 'The blood of our Lord Jesus Christ which was shed for thee preserve thy soul unto everlasting life'), and a concluding blessing. Much of this material was drawn from continental reformed sources, and especially from the work of Hermann von Wied, and the whole was to be said by the priest, even the confession, which he was to say on behalf of the people. The congregation, most of whom would not have been able to read and none of whom would have known the prayer or had their own copies of the service, were simply expected to say 'Amen' to the blessing.

1549

The table on page 166 indicates the general structure of the first complete English eucharistic rite, and the way in which the material from the 1548 order was incorporated within it. It was designated as 'The Supper of the Lord, and the Holy Communion, commonly called the Mass', and had the general appearance of a much simplified vernacular version of the medieval service which it was to replace. Moreover, it was still to be celebrated at the altar and the priest would wear vestments. It could appear to ordinary congregations, therefore, that little besides the language had been changed, and indeed it may have been intended to convey that impression. There were, however, a number of relatively small but doctrinally significant alterations. The 'offertory' now had an entirely new meaning. The scriptural sentences to be used at it in place of the old offertory psalm had nothing to do with offering bread and wine or with the liturgical season as before, but were all concerned with the offering of alms, and at that point in the service the congregation were required to come up to place their money in the 'poor men's box', which by Royal Injunction in 1547 had been set up near the altar. Having done this, those who desired to receive communion were to remain in the chancel near the altar, and the rest were to return to the nave of the church.

The Eucharistic Prayer, the whole of which was now to be recited aloud, was also carefully worded so as to exclude any suggestion of the sacrificial doctrine of the medieval Mass. The offering spoken of in it was of oneself and of praise and thanksgiving. Similarly, there was to be no elevation or showing of the bread and wine to the people at the supposed moment of

A COMPARISON OF THE STRUCTURE OF
THE EUCHARISTIC RITES OF THE FIRST TWO
ENGLISH PRAYER BOOKS

(Elements in italics in the first column indicate material drawn from the 1548 'Order of the Communion')

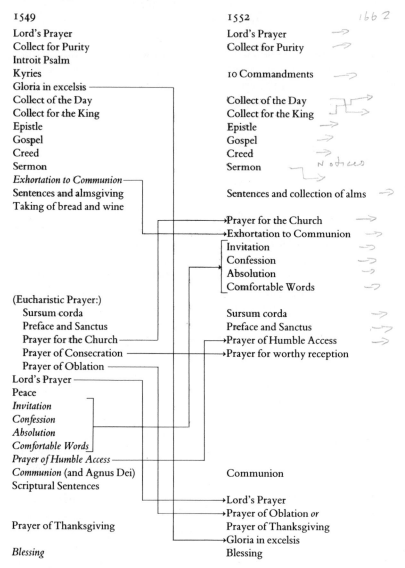

1549	1552	1662
Lord's Prayer	Lord's Prayer	
Collect for Purity	Collect for Purity	
Introit Psalm		
Kyries	10 Commandments	
Gloria in excelsis		
Collect of the Day	Collect of the Day	
Collect for the King	Collect for the King	
Epistle	Epistle	
Gospel	Gospel	
Creed	Creed	
Sermon	Sermon	Notices
Exhortation to Communion		
Sentences and almsgiving	Sentences and collection of alms	
Taking of bread and wine		
	Prayer for the Church	
	Exhortation to Communion	
	Invitation	
	Confession	
	Absolution	
	Comfortable Words	
(Eucharistic Prayer:)		
Sursum corda	Sursum corda	
Preface and Sanctus	Preface and Sanctus	
Prayer for the Church	Prayer of Humble Access	
Prayer of Consecration	Prayer for worthy reception	
Prayer of Oblation		
Lord's Prayer		
Peace		
Invitation		
Confession		
Absolution		
Comfortable Words		
Prayer of Humble Access		
Communion (and Agnus Dei)	Communion	
Scriptural Sentences		
	Lord's Prayer	
	Prayer of Oblation *or*	
Prayer of Thanksgiving	Prayer of Thanksgiving	
	Gloria in excelsis	
Blessing	Blessing	

consecration in the narrative of institution, and in the petition which preceded this, Cranmer substituted the phrase 'may *be* unto us the body and blood ...' for 'may *become* unto us ...' of the medieval rite. There was to be no celebration of the Eucharist unless some were willing to receive communion along with the priest. Since the laity were generally reluctant to receive communion much more often than the few times a year to which they had previously been accustomed, this meant that eucharistic celebrations tended to become somewhat infrequent in the Church of England, and the usual Sunday morning service consisted of Morning Prayer, Litany and Ante-Communion (i.e. the first part of the eucharistic rite only).

1552

It is quite probable that the 1549 service was always intended as an interim stage, but the fact that a number of bishops and eminent divines claimed that it was still possible to interpret the rite in accordance with the traditional eucharistic theology no doubt encouraged its demise and rapid replacement by the eucharistic rite of the 1552 Prayer Book. Here there was no ambiguity, but instead a clear, logical, liturgical expression of the theological conviction that the essential action of the Eucharist was simply the eating of bread and the drinking of wine in thankful remembrance of Christ's death. Not surprisingly, therefore, the title 'the mass' now disappears, and the priest is to wear only a surplice and not full eucharistic vestments. The altar becomes a table, of wood instead of stone, and stands in the chancel or in the body of the church, running east–west (so that it could not be visually mistaken for an altar) with the priest on the north side of it. It was to be covered with a fair linen cloth and nothing else.

Virtually everything which was not considered absolutely necessary to the service was removed from it, including all singing, except for the Gloria in excelsis, and the whole rite has a more penitential tone, especially with the Ten Commandments placed near the beginning, so that the people might prepare themselves to receive Holy Communion by careful self-examination. As can be seen from the comparative table, there was a considerable rearrangement of the structure of the rite. The intercessions from the Eucharistic Prayer have been moved to an earlier point in the service, and purged of all reference to the saints and petition for the departed, so as to avoid the suggestion that the

Eucharist was in any sense a propitiatory sacrifice offered for those for whom intercession was being made. Even the word 'offertory' is no longer used, and the churchwardens are now to collect the alms from the people and place them in the 'poor men's box'.

The communion devotions from the 1548 Order have also been moved, so as to enable the communion to follow directly after the reading of its scriptural warrant, the narrative of the Last Supper, and the petition which precedes this no longer asks God to 'bless and sanctify these thy gifts and creatures of bread and wine', but instead to 'grant that we, receiving these thy creatures of bread and wine . . . may be partakers of his most blessed body and blood': the prayer of consecration has thus been turned into a prayer for fruitful reception of the bread and wine. Ordinary, leavened, bread is now to be used, and since neither bread nor wine are any longer thought of as being consecrated, the priest may have any remains for his own use. The people receive the bread in their hands, instead of its being placed directly in their mouths, but they continue to receive communion kneeling, contrary to the desires of extreme Reformers who wished it to be done while sitting, so as more precisely to imitate what was thought to have been the posture at the Last Supper. A note at the end of the service explains, however, that kneeling is not intended to signify any adoration of the bread and wine or of 'any real and essential presence there being of Christ's natural flesh and blood'. Moreover, the words of administration have been changed, so as to remove any implication that the bread and wine are the body and blood of Christ. The priest now says simply, 'Take and eat this, in remembrance that Christ died for thee, and feed on him in thy heart by faith, with thanksgiving'; 'Drink this in remembrance that Christ's blood was shed for thee, and be thankful.'

The Lord's Prayer follows the Communion, and then comes what had in 1549 been the final part of the Eucharistic Prayer, in which we offer ourselves to God. This may now be used as an alternative to the Prayer of Thanksgiving. For, since the worshippers are unworthy to make any offering to God themselves, only after they are united with Christ through communion may they make their self-oblation and ask God to accept their sacrifice of praise and thanksgiving. The moving of the Gloria in excelsis to a position after this is probably intended to provide an expression of such praise and thanksgiving.

THE EUCHARIST

1559

In the Elizabeth Prayer Book an attempt was made to broaden slightly the doctrinal position expressed in the earlier book. The words of administration combined the formula used in 1549 with that used in 1552, so that one might be interpreted in the light of the other, though individuals were left free to decide which that should be, and the declaration on kneeling with its strong doctrinal affirmation was entirely removed from the service. Moreover, the book now permitted the priest to wear whatever vesture had been legal in the second year of the reign of Edward VI. Quite what vestments were intended by this is unclear, and perhaps this lack of clarity was deliberate. Injunctions issued subsequently allowed the table to be placed in the position originally occupied by the altar when it was not being used, and directed that unleavened bread was once again to be used for communion.

1662

In the seventeenth century many bishops and clergy attempted to give expression to a more catholic doctrine of the Eucharist by wearing a cope during the service and by leaving the table in its 'altar' position. They tried to obey the rubrics of the Prayer Book, however, by continuing to stand on the north side of the table, which had now, of course, effectively become the north end. They would have wished for a restoration of something akin to the 1549 eucharistic rite which would have more fully expressed their doctrinal position, and indeed there was an attempt to include just such a rite in the ill-fated Scottish Prayer Book of 1637.

When, therefore, after the restoration of the monarchy in 1660 the question of a further revision of the Prayer Book was raised, the 'High Church' party would have wished to amend the Eucharist in the direction of the Scottish rite. On the other hand, prudence dictated that this was not an appropriate time to press for a full-scale remodelling of the English liturgy, since there was little sympathy for change in Parliament, and much opposition from the Puritans. They contented themselves, therefore, with effecting the minimum number of alterations in the rite which they considered necessary to make it acceptable to their theological interpretation of the Eucharist. These were mostly in rubrics rather than in the text of the prayers themselves. The word 'offertory' reappeared in the rubric preceding the scriptural sentences, and directions followed them which instructed that the alms were not to be placed in the poor men's box but on a dish and given to the priest. He was then to 'present' them and place them on the table, together with bread and wine for the communion. The intercessions which followed once again included a commemoration of the departed, but no direct prayer for them and no commemoration of the saints. The prayer before communion was now called 'the Prayer of Consecration', and during the narrative of institution the priest was directed at appropriate points to take the bread and cup into his hands and to break the bread, but the actual text remained unchanged. Because the bread and wine were now thought of as being consecrated, provision was made for the further consecration of either, if there should prove to be insufficient for all the communicants, by the recitation of the appropriate part of the narrative of institution, and directions were also included for the reverent consumption of any consecrated remains. Finally, the declaration on kneeling was substantially restored, as a concession to the Puritans, but with a significant alteration: the words 'corporal presence' replaced the earlier 'real and essential presence', thus turning it into a denial of one particular mode of Christ's presence in the bread and wine and not of that presence altogether.

1927/8

The 1662 eucharistic rite was thus a compromise which did not really reflect fully any one theological position, and though it became well-loved by many, there were in the course of the following centuries many others who wanted changes made in it so that it might express more fully their particular eucharistic theology. It is hardly surprising, therefore, that in the process of liturgical revision at the beginning of the twentieth century, this rite was the most controverted feature. The controversy centred mainly around the form which should be taken by the Prayer of Consecration. What emerged in the proposals for the 1927/8 Prayer Book was something which broadly followed the lines of the 1549 Eucharistic Prayer, though without the insertion of the Prayer for the Church, but with the addition of an invocation of the Holy Spirit on the bread and wine (epiclesis) in the latter part of the prayer. This had the support of many liturgical scholars, since it was in line with the general structure of early Eucharistic Prayers. But whatever the liturgical merits of the prayer, it was unacceptable to many on doctrinal grounds: Evangelicals objected to the inclusion of self-oblation before communion, and Anglo-Catholics to the addition of the epiclesis, believing that its position after the narrative of institution implied the denial of the traditional Western doctrine of the consecratory effect of that narrative.

Other features of the eucharistic rite in this book included the deletion of any reference to the priest having to stand 'at the north side' of the table; the possibility of using Christ's summary of the Law instead of the Ten Commandments on Sundays, providing that the latter were used on one Sunday each month, and of using the Kyries instead of either on weekdays; and permission to omit the Creed and Gloria in excelsis except on Sundays and Holy Days. The Prayer for the Church was extended in scope, and included another controversial feature—prayer for the departed; the exhortation was made optional; and alternative, shorter forms of the invitation, confession and absolution were provided for use on weekdays. The Lord's Prayer was once again placed before the administration of communion, and it could be followed by the versicle and response: 'The peace of God be alway with you; And with thy spirit.'

Since 1928

After the defeat of the proposed book in 1927 and 1928, although the bishops were generally prepared to sanction the use of parts of it in their dioceses, they excluded the Communion Service from this, because of its controversial form. What began to be used instead by those who desired a more traditional shape of Eucharistic Prayer was the so-called Interim Rite—a minimal shuffle of the 1662 order so as to place the Prayer of Humble Access before the Sursum corda, and the Prayer of Oblation immediately after the Prayer of Consecration, followed by the Lord's Prayer. Meanwhile, the spread of the Liturgical Movement and the growing popularity of a Parish Communion service as the main Sunday morning worship in many parishes, instead of Morning Prayer, led to the desire for further changes in the eucharistic rite, including more opportunity for corporate participation, and provision for an Old Testament reading in the ministry of the word.

When, therefore, a 'Series 1' version of the Eucharist was produced under the 1965 Alternative Services Measure, for both these reasons it was not identical with the 1928 service. It included additional features, such as provision of Old Testament readings, taken from the 1961 Indian Prayer Book, and it did not reproduce the controversial Eucharistic Prayer in its original form. Instead it allowed three options: to end the prayer after the narrative of institution, as 1662 did; to continue with the Prayer of Oblation, as in the 'Interim Rite'; or to do the same, but excise the actual element of self-oblation from the prayer, and place that after communion. In spite of this attempt at compromise, it was opposed by Evangelicals, both because of the possibility of self-oblation before communion and also because of the presence of prayer for the departed in the intercessions of the service; and it only just managed to secure a sufficient majority for authorization for experimental use in November 1966.

Meanwhile, the Liturgical Commission had indicated the lines on which it was thinking of more radical revision in a discussion booklet, *Reshaping the Liturgy*, published in July 1964 and written by two of its members, Henry de Candole, Bishop of Knaresborough, and Arthur Couratin, Canon of Durham. It envisaged starting afresh, settling structure and basic principles before proceeding to a text, rather than simply tinkering with material from 1662 and 1928. An incomplete draft order was then included as an appendix in the book of proposed Series 2 services published in 1965. An ante-communion service of Bible readings, sermon, creed and prayer (both intercessory and penitential) was followed by the eucharistic rite itself with four clearly defined actions—the preparation of bread and wine, the thanksgiving over bread and wine, the breaking of the bread, and the sharing of bread and wine—a structure which owed much to the researches of Gregory Dix into the primitive pattern of the Eucharist in his book, *The Shape of the Liturgy*, published in 1945. Considerable flexibility was built into the rite, and (to quote the introduction) 'we have also, where matters of eucharistic doctrine are involved, tried to produce forms of words which are capable of various interpretations' (p. 146).

Bearing in mind the difficulties in securing the authorization of the Series 1 rite, the Commission presented this draft to a Liturgical Conference of the Convocations and the House of Laity in February 1966 with some misgivings, not least because the proposals included both prayer for the departed and an explicit oblation of bread and wine in the Eucharistic Prayer. To their great surprise, however, the reception was enthusiastic, and they were asked to complete the task as quickly as possible. This was then done, and the completed rite was published in April 1966. Nevertheless, considerable debate ensured, centred mainly on the two controversial elements. Solutions to the problems were not made any easier to find by a decision not to resort to alternative texts which simply catered for the interests of particular parties.

Perseverance eventually brought its rewards. The problem of prayer for the departed was met by the formula, 'Hear us as we remember those who have died in faith, and grant us with them a share in thy eternal kingdom'; while a solution to the difficulty of oblation in the Eucharistic Prayer was found with the words, 'wherefore, O Lord, with this bread and this cup we make the memorial of his saving passion. . . . We pray thee to accept this our duty and service'—a formula not very different from that used in 1549. At the time the latter was held out as a 'stop-gap' arrangement, in order to provide time and opportunity during the experimental period for a search for something more satisfactory. In practice it proved itself to be increasingly durable and acceptable, and it still remains in the second Eucharistic Prayers of both Rite A and Rite B in the Alternative Service Book. The Series 2 rite was finally authorized for use from July 1967 by large majorities, and it soon became extremely popular.

The next stage was to produce a rite in contemporary language. Here the Liturgical Commission undertook some important pieces of preparatory work. First, it published in 1968 a further discussion booklet, *Modern Liturgical Texts*, in which, with help from the Poet Laureate, C. Day Lewis, it introduced the Church to the problems and possibilities of services in 'you' form. Secondly, it sought information at grass-roots level on reactions to the use of the Series 2 rite by means of a widely distributed questionnaire. Thirdly, three members of the Commission— Canon Ronald Jasper, the Chairman, Canon Kenneth Ross, an Anglo-Catholic, and the Rev. Colin Buchanan, an Evangelical— made an attempt to find a more satisfactory solution to the thorny problem of oblation in the Eucharistic Prayer. The Commission was also helped by the International Consultation on English Texts, which in 1970 published its first set of texts in contemporary language in *Prayers we have in common*.

The proposals for Holy Communion Series 3 were eventually published in September 1971. They were radical, not only in language but also in format. With help from a leading expert, Keith Murgatroyd, a new typographical style for liturgical texts had been devised, distinguishing clearly between text and rubric, between optional and mandatory material, and between the text of the minister and that of the congregation. Indeed, so effective was the format that it became the standard for all services in the Alternative Service Book, and was highly influential in the production of new service books in other churches both at home and overseas. The Commission, conscious that many members of the Church might regard such a radical piece of work with suspicion, also published a number of documents to help commend it—a short general commentary in 1971, a guide on *The Presentation of the Eucharist* in conjunction with the Council for the Care of Churches in the same year, and a filmstrip with the help of the same body. A little later it also supported the publication of two musical settings, one by John Rutter, and another by Alan Wicks and Christopher Dearnley. Inevitably its consideration by the General Synod was fairly lengthy, and there was considerable amendment in matters of detail. The structure and the basic principles survived intact, however, and it was finally authorized for use by overwhelming majorities in November 1972.

Compared with Series 2, Series 3 provided a much richer supply of seasonal material: the number of proper prefaces was increased from four to eleven, while seasonal introductory sentences, post-communion sentences, and blessings were all entirely new. The congregational texts were drawn from the proposals of ICET, with one or two small exceptions, and the intercessions were extended to include the local community, families and friends. Some of the most interesting developments, however, were in the Eucharistic Prayer. Here the Sursum corda began with an unusual version of *Dominus vobiscum/et cum spiritu tuo*: 'The Lord is here/ His spirit is with us'; there was a greater element of congregational participation through the inclusion of acclamations after the narrative of institution and also at the end of the prayer; and there was a new formula to replace the 'stop-gap' anamnesis-oblation of Series 2: 'Therefore, heavenly Father, with this bread and this cup we do this in remembrance of him: we celebrate and proclaim his perfect sacrifice ... Accept through him, our great high priest, this our sacrifice of thanks and praise.' Despite its radical approach in so many different ways, Series 3 proved to be remarkably popular, and with the passage of time substantially replaced Series 2.

Soon after its advent in 1973 the General Synod began to make preparations for the production of the Alternative Service Book. A decision therefore had to be made about the future of the three eucharistic rites alternative to that of 1662 now in use. These were eventually reduced to two by combining Series 1 and Series 2 into a single rite, Series 1 and 2 Revised. This was essentially the Series 2 rite with a great deal of additional material: from Series 1 it included an alternative intercession, Eucharistic Prayer, and prayer of thanksgiving; and from Series 3 it adopted the seasonal material and the typography. By a judicious use of rubric it also provided a greater degree of flexibility. For example, it still permitted the Series 1 Eucharistic Prayer to end after the narrative of institution and the Lord's Prayer to be said after communion, thereby producing a pattern similar to that of 1662. After the usual revision process in the General Synod this rite was authorized for use in July 1976, and it eventually appeared in the Alternative Service Book as Rite B, the only service in that book in traditional language.

It was then decided to subject Series 3 to a thorough revision before the publication of the Alternative Service Book. Another questionnaire sent to all the dioceses in the autumn of 1976 revealed that over 85 per cent of both clergy and laity who had used the rite were generally satisfied with it. Consequently, when the Liturgical Commission published its proposals for Series 3 Revised (GS 364) in May 1978, while there were no really radical changes, there were some improvements and enrichments, no-tably an increase in the seasonal material, provision for the act of penitence to take place either at the beginning of the rite or after the intercession, and the addition of the Series 1 and 2 Revised Eucharistic Prayers in 'you' form. In July 1978 this report was remitted to a Revision Committee of the General Synod, which faced a marathon exercise of dealing with over a thousand proposals for amendment. This by no means reflected a deep dislike of either Series 3 or of the Commission's proposals for its revision. The results of the questionnaire had been substantially correct: most of the users of the rite were 'generally satisfied'. But as the various services were revised by the General Synod before inclusion in the Alternative Service Book, so the revision process tended to become more extensive; and Holy Communion Series 3 Revised marked the culmination of the process. In fact, most of the proposed amendments were concerned with matters of detail rather than with matters of fundamental principle, and inevitably many proposals cancelled each other out.

In the event the Revision Committee's own proposals (GS 364A) faced a further two hundred amendments on the floor of the

General Synod when it was debated in February and July 1979. These were dealt with, however, in time for authorization to be given in November 1979. The revised rite became Rite A in the Alternative Service Book. Despite the massive revision exercise, Series 3 Revised as it had originally appeared in GS 364 was still recognizable, but it had now undergone considerable modification and enrichment. The most significant changes were additional forms of intercession and penitential material; alternative forms of the Peace and of the Dismissal; the addition of an entirely new Eucharistic Prayer based on that in the *Apostolic Tradition* of Hippolytus; provision for a form of service following the pattern of the Book of Common Prayer; and the inclusion of a shorter Eucharistic Prayer for use with the sick.

B

RITE A
COMMENTARY

THE TITLE

The early Church used a variety of titles for the service, each one expressing some particular aspect of it. In the New Testament there is 'The Breaking of the Bread' (Acts 2.42), 'The Communion' (1 Cor. 10.16), and 'The Lord's Supper' (1 Cor. 11.20). By the second century 'The Eucharist' is found (e.g. in Justin); while a little later 'The Sacrifice' (e.g. Cyprian and Augustine) and 'The Offering' (Egeria) emerge. By the fifth century the West was using 'The Mass'; although it would appear that, when first used, this term described any service from which the congregation was sent away with a blessing. There is a relic of this in the Swedish Lutheran Church of today, where the principal Sunday service is a 'High Mass' whether it involves the sacrament or not. It was still used in the sixteenth century without particular doctrinal significance in the German Church Orders: Luther used it in his *Formula Missae et Communionis* (1523), while Cranmer used it in 1549. In the Eastern Churches the usual title from the ninth century was 'The Liturgy', indicating the corporate aspect of the rite; for the word means 'the work of the people', derived from the two Greek words *laos* (people) and *ergon* (work). Although the title 'The Lord's Supper' came to be associated with Protestantism, it was nevertheless used in Roman medieval books for the rite of Maundy Thursday: it was the *Caena Domini*—Supper of the Lord.

In 1549 Cranmer used a composite title, 'The Supper of the Lord and the Holy Communion, commonly called the Mass'. 1552 modified this and dropped the third title—'The Order for the Administration of the Lord's Supper, or Holy Communion'—a formula which was retained in both 1662 and 1928. While the single title 'Holy Communion' appeared in Series 1, 2 and 3, ASB uses a triple title, 'The Order for Holy Communion also called The Eucharist and The Lord's Supper'. The first and the third reflect Anglican usage since the Reformation, while the second— probably the oldest outside the New Testament—is widely used in ecumenical circles.

THE PREPARATION AND THE MINISTRY OF THE WORD

The structure of the rite is based on two main elements of Word and Sacrament, together with an Introduction and an Epilogue. The Introduction and the Ministry of the Word form a 'Bible Service' which can be used for a variety of situations and is interchangeable with Morning and Evening Prayer. Indeed, if the Prayers of Penitence (sections 4–8) are used in the Preparation, the structure of the first two main elements of the rite is remarkably similar to that of the Daily Office. Much of the material (e.g. canticles and readings) is interchangeable; and considerable progress has been made towards breaking down the barriers between the Ante-Communion and the Daily Office—a proposal made in the Pan-Anglican Document published after the Lambeth Conference of 1968.

THE PREPARATION
(sections 1–29)

The Entry
(section 1)

It was probably not until the fourth to fifth century, from the time of the Emperor Constantine, with the development of church buildings and increased congregations, that a formal entry with a procession of ministers and assistants developed. While Pope Celestine is reputed to have introduced the singing of psalms with antiphons as introits in the early fifth century, the practice was certainly established by the middle of the sixth century. In the later Middle Ages the amount of text required for an introit was much reduced, for various reasons. In some places the size of buildings precluded a lengthy procession, or the facilities for music were virtually non-existent; in others, where choirs were available, the music had become so complicated that only short texts were required. In Sarum the entrance rite was reduced to an antiphon, one verse of psalmody, Gloria Patri, and a repeat of the antiphon.

1549 provided psalms or portions of psalms to be said or sung as introits, and in addition the Litany was to be said or sung on Wednesdays and Fridays. From Advent to Trinity Sunday complete psalms were chosen, all short and many appropriate to the season, while for most of the Trinity season portions of Psalm 119 were used. In 1552 all these introit psalms disappeared, although the use of the Litany was extended to Sundays; and under Elizabeth a metrical psalm or a hymn was permitted before or after any rite. This situation remained unchanged until Series 2, when provision was made for a psalm or a hymn as an introit. This provision was then extended in Series 1 and 2 Revised and Series 3, by the introduction of seasonal sentences, and the addition of a canticle as an alternative to a psalm or a hymn. These elements, all optional, now exist in ASB.

The service may begin with a sentence of Scripture, establishing the theme of the collect and readings; and it may be said or sung. Alternatively, or in addition, a hymn, a psalm, or a canticle may be sung. Two passages of psalmody are appointed for every occasion, and either of these may be used. While no restriction is placed on the choice of canticle, Note 8 (p. 116) suggests the use of the Gloria in excelsis. As a series of acclamations with an antiphon, it is eminently suitable as an introit, particularly on festal occasions. Equally Salvator mundi or even the Kyries might be used on penitential occasions. It is also important to bear in mind that the ministers may enter in complete silence and begin the rite with the Salutation (section 2) and the Collect (section 11).

Whatever form the entry might take, it is desirable that the president, with any assistants, should pass through the congregation rather than come in through a side door as if they were actors coming on stage. The Eucharist is a corporate act and anything which helps to establish the unity of ministers and congregation is to be welcomed. Furthermore, since the first part of the rite is concerned with reading and expounding the word, proper emphasis should be given to the book containing the readings by bringing it in procession, wherever that is possible.

The Greeting by the President
(section 2)

The first mandatory action is the President's greeting of the congregation. No indication is given as to where this or the Ministry of the Word is to take place. 1549 enjoined the priest to stand 'humbly afore the middle of the altar' to begin the rite, and he or the reader should then move to 'a place assigned for the purpose' to read the Epistle. In 1552 he was to stand 'at the north side of the Table'—although it must be remembered that 1552 also required the Table to be moved into the body of the church or into the chancel and set at right angles to the building. The 1559 Elizabethan Injunctions stated that this was to permit the congregation to hear the service better or communicate more conveniently, and that out of service time the Table should be restored to its normal place against the east wall. 1662 retained the 1552 directions, although by then the Table was permanently against the east wall within communion rails. To stand at the north side of the Table in these circumstances was therefore not a particularly convenient place for the Ministry of the Word. But clearly some, if not all, of that Ministry was expected to be conducted elsewhere; for after the Sermon the priest was directed to 'return to the Lord's Table', although he had never been told when to leave it. 1928 was equally imprecise: at the beginning the priest was to stand 'at God's board', while the minister reading the Epistle and Gospel was to 'so stand and turn himself as he may best be heard of the people'; the priest was then back 'standing at the Lord's Table' for the Offertory. Series 1 gave no directions as to where the Ministry of the Word should be conducted except that the reader was to 'so stand and turn himself' for the readings as in 1928. But Series 2 and subsequent rites, including ASB, have given no directions, thereby permitting maximum freedom. Position should, however, be guided by two important principles:

1   At the beginning the president should clearly establish his presidency over the whole rite. He should therefore be so placed as to be seen visibly presiding.

2   The Ministry of the Word should be so conducted that the Word is *audible*, and the minister *visible*.

The rubric should be read in conjunction with Note 2 (p. 115), which not only stipulates that the president must be an episcopally ordained priest (Canon B12), but that he presides over the whole service. There are certain elements which are specifically his—the Greeting, the Collect, the Absolution, the Peace, the Taking, the Eucharistic Prayer, the Fraction, and the Blessing: they are his contribution to a corporate action. He should also communicate on every occasion. Note 2 also indicates that the president gives the Greeting and presides at both the Preparation and the Ministry of the Word except 'when necessity dictates'. This refers to a situation where a priest has to take services at different places in quick succession. This may involve a deacon or a layman starting the service while the priest is travelling from elsewhere.

The description of the chief minister as 'president' is not an attempt to dilute the Anglican concept of priesthood—Note 2 makes the position very clear. The term emphasizes, not what the minister *is*, but what he *does*. The entire congregation 'celebrates' the liturgy, and within that corporate action the president has a distinctive role.

> In their mutual relations, the eucharistic gathering and its president live their dependence on the one Lord and great High Priest. In its relation to the minister, the congregation is exercising its royal priest-hood conferred on it by Christ, the priest. In his relation to the congregation, the minister is living his presidency as the servant of Christ, the pastor. (ARCIC, *Modern Eucharistic Agreement*, 1972, p. 63.)

It is interesting to note that in the earliest description of the Eucharist outside the New Testament, in Justin Martyr's *First Apology* (*c.* 150), the minister is described as the *proestōs*, 'he who presides over the brethren'.

The Greeting at the beginning of the Eucharist has assumed different forms. An early form in *The Apostolic Constitutions*, Book 8, was the Grace from 2 Corinthians 13.14 with the response, 'And with your spirit'. This has been a customary form in the East, and it was also found in Gallican rites. An early Western form, in *Ordo Romanus Primus* was 'Peace be with you/And with your spirit': by the Middle Ages 'The Lord be with you' was the norm. 1549 used the Greeting three times in the Eucharist—before the Collect, at the Sursum corda, and before the Post-communion prayer. These were omitted in 1552 and 1662; but 1928 restored its use before the Collect and at the Sursum corda. This has remained in all subsequent rites, the only exception being Series 2, where it was also included before the Dismissal. ASB has retained it before the Collect and at the Sursum corda, but also permits its use (Note 5, p. 115) before the Gospel and before the Dismissal.

Four forms of greeting are available in Section 2:

1 Appropriate words of the president's own choosing.

2 and 3 Two versions of 'The Lord be with you'.

4 A seasonal greeting in Easter-tide.

For a discussion of the meaning of 'The Lord be with you', see pp. 34–5.

The Collect for Purity
(section 3)

This is an ancient prayer, reputedly of English origin and attributed to St Gregory, Abbot of Canterbury c. 780. It is reminiscent of Psalm 51. In the Sarum Missal it followed the Veni Creator in the priest's devotions said before Mass while vesting. It was also the collect in the Mass for the grace of the Holy Spirit. With the Lord's Prayer it was the only relic of the priest's preparation retained in 1549. Every rite down to Series 1 retained it as a prayer to be said by the priest. In recent times, however, it has become a prayer of preparation for the entire congregation. Series 2 began the transition, prefacing it with the rubric, 'Then may be said', thereby leaving it open as to who should say it; but Series 1 and 2 Revised clearly made it congregational by printing it in bold type, and this has continued in Rite A. Since Series 2 it has also ceased to be mandatory. If he so wishes, the president may omit virtually all the preparatory material and simply begin the rite with the Salutation and the Collect of the Day.

The Prayers of Penitence
(sections 4–8, 24–8)

Penitential prayers at the beginning of the Eucharist derive from the private act of penitence which the Pope made at the altar when attending stational services in Rome. By the eleventh century this had developed into the mutual confession and absolution by the priest and his attendants. By the same date there were also penitential prayers before the act of communion; but these could be rare for the congregation, since communion itself was rare, and in any case this would normally be preceded by private confession to a priest. A third place for penitential prayers with confession and absolution developed in the Middle Ages in the little vernacular service of Prone after the Gospel and Sermon—although this penitential element of Prone was evidently better known on the Continent than it was in England. This came to be adapted by the continental Reformers, including Hermann, for their own purposes. Hermann had an office of preparation on the day before communion, while in the communion rite itself he had a confession, comfortable word and absolution said by the priest before the introit at the altar in the name of the whole congregation. Cranmer borrowed Hermann's scheme and some of his language for his *Order of the Communion* in 1548, intending it as a preparation for communion to be inserted in the Latin Mass before the priest made his communion.

Cranmer's Order contained eight elements:

1 An Exhortation to be read on the previous Sunday urging self-examination before communion, and, where necessary, auricular confession. From Hermann.

2 An Exhortation drawing on 1 Corinthians 11, to be read at the Mass. From Hermann.

3 A warning to open and impenitent sinners not to communicate.

4 The Invitation—'Ye that do truly'. Cranmer's own composition.

5 Confession—borrowed from Hermann, who in turn took it from Bucer's Strasbourg rite.

6 Absolution—borrowed partly from Hermann and partly from one of the Roman forms.

7 Four Comfortable Words. Cranmer took Matthew 11.28 from Zwingli; and John 3.16, 1 Timothy 1.15 and 1 John 2.1 from Hermann.

8 The Prayer of Humble Access. Cranmer's own composition.

In 1549 Cranmer slightly rearranged and modified this material (see p. 166): the Exhortations came after the sermon, as in Prone; the preamble to the Absolution was changed, and the rest came before communion. In 1552 the Kyries at the beginning were replaced by the Decalogue with a more penitential form of Kyrie eleison as a congregational response. As for the later penitential material, the Exhortations—now three in number—came after the Intercessions and were followed by all the other items except for the Prayer of Humble Access, which followed the Preface and Sanctus: it therefore occupied a position very similar to the act of penitence in Prone. It could therefore be argued that 1552 had two acts of penitence, one at the beginning and one in the middle of the rite. In 1662 the Exhortations were revised, but the material remained in the same positions. 1928 made modifications to both sets of material:

1 At the beginning the Summary of the Law and the Kyries were included as alternatives to the Decalogue, provided the latter was said once a month on Sundays.

2 In the middle, two of the three Exhortations were placed in an appendix, and the Prayer of Humble Access was moved to follow the Comfortable Words.

Series 1 retained the Decalogue and its alternatives as a mandatory element at the beginning, while in the middle the Exhortations were omitted; the Prayer of Humble Access was also made a congregational prayer and was permitted in either its 1662 or its 1928 position. The changes in Series 2 were more radical: the Decalogue and its alternatives were made optional, while the Invitation, Confession and Absolution in the middle were replaced by new and shorter forms; the Prayer of Humble Access and Comfortable Words were also made optional. The penitential element in the rite could therefore be so brief as to be microscopic. Little was done to redress the balance in Series 1 and 2 Revised, the only change being the provision of the 1662 Invitation as an alternative to that of Series 2. But Series 3 provided new elements which gave the penitential material in the rite a new aspect:

1 All vestiges of an act of penitence at the beginning really disappeared by the removal of the Decalogue and the Summary of the Law. All that remained in this position were the Kyries, which become alternative to the Gloria in excelsis, and both were optional.

2 The penitential rite in the middle began with either an expanded form of the Decalogue (see pp. 185–7) or the Summary of the Law. While this remained optional, it added substantial weight to this element, particularly in seasons such as Lent and Advent.

3   New forms were provided for the Invitation, the Confession, and the Absolution.

4   An abbreviated form of the Prayer of Humble Access remained optional.

Series 3 Revised and ASB further developed the penitential material. It is made available either at the beginning or after the Intercessions; and while the provision in both places is similar, more scope is given to the minister at the beginning (section 6) to adapt the Invitation to the needs of the situation, rather than use the Comfortable Words (section 25). Improvements have also been made to the Confession, and alternative forms of Confession (section 80) and the Prayer of Humble Access (section 82) have been provided. Both places for the penitential material—the beginning and after the Intercessions—have had a long history, and modern revisions of the Eucharist have established no single pattern: some use one place, some the other, some both. There are also sound theological arguments for both places:

1   In favour of the beginning it can be said that any act of worship should begin with an acknowledgement of our unworthiness to approach God. This creates a right attitude for what follows. The Collect for Purity expresses the idea admirably: 'Cleanse the thoughts of our hearts . . . that we may perfectly love you and worthily magnify your holy name.'

2   In favour of a position after the Intercessions, three things can be said:
    (a) The hearing of God's word can be a valuable preparation for self-examination and confession.
    (b) The later position not only brings all 'the Prayers' together: it also indicates the natural link between the Penitence and the Intercessions. The Church first prays for the world and its needs; it then identifies itself with the world and its shortcomings. It is a confession of corporate sin as well as individual sin. Justin clearly thought of this corporate aspect when he spoke of the faithful identifying themselves with the catechumens in penitence (*Apology* 1.61).
    (c) Penitence immediately preceding the Peace is a liturgical expression of Matthew 5.23–4: 'If you are offering your gift at the altar, and there remember that your brother has something against you, leave your gift there before the

altar and go; first be reconciled to your brother, and then come and offer your gift.' It also makes the point dear to the Reformers: 'Let a man examine himself, and so eat of the bread and drink of the cup' (1 Cor. 11.28).

The Decalogue or the Summary of the Law
(sections 5, 78)

The Decalogue had a long history in the catechetical instruction of the Church, dating at least from the time of St Augustine in the fifth century. In the Middle Ages it was a regular feature in the office of Prone, and so it was a familiar adjunct to eucharistic worship at the time of the Reformation. The Injunctions of Henry VIII in 1538 ordered that no one should be admitted to Holy Communion unless he could recite the Creed, the Lord's Prayer, and the Decalogue, while the Injunctions of Edward VI in 1547 ordered the Decalogue to be recited in English after the Gospel at Mass. It was therefore not exactly an innovation when the Decalogue appeared in the 1552 rite of Holy Communion with an expanded form of Kyrie eleison, drawn from continental Reformed rites, as a penitential congregational response. Its role was evidently partly catechetical and partly penitential, for the second Exhortation in 1552 suggested to communicants to 'examine your lives and conversation by the rule of God's commandments'. The penitential aspect was also indicated by the accompanying rubric, 'Then shall the Priest rehearse distinctly all the Ten Commandments: and the people kneeling shall after every Commandment ask God's mercy for their transgression of the same'. The catechetical aspect, however, was indicated by the different response to the tenth Commandment, with its prayer to 'write all these thy laws in our hearts'—based on Jeremiah 31.33 (cf. Deut. 5.29). The use of Kyrie eleison as a refrain was found in Luther's metrical paraphrase of the Decalogue, an English translation of which Coverdale included in his *Ghostly Psalms*. 1662 retained the Decalogue in the 1552 form, but supplemented the rubric 'for their transgression thereof for the time past, and grace to keep the same for the time to come'.

With 1928 came two important changes: the Decalogue appeared in an abbreviated form, and the Summary of the Law and the Kyries were added as alternatives, provided the Decalogue was recited once on a Sunday in each month. The abbreviated Decalogue was by no means new, for it had appeared with minor

variations in the 1549 Catechism and before that in *The Bishops'
Book* (1537) and *The King's Book* (1543). The Summary of the Law
had first appeared in its Matthean form in the Nonjurors' Liturgy
of 1718, and then in the Scottish Liturgy of 1764. It has been
suggested that its introduction was due to a desire to express a
Christian rule of life in a more positive way, coupled with a dislike
of the too frequent recitation of the Decalogue. The 1928 form
was a combination of the two versions in Matthew 22.37–40 and
Mark 12.29–31. The Kyries, which were printed in both English
and Greek, were only permitted as a week-day alternative. Series 1
continued the 1928 arrangement with two small modifications: the
Decalogue was printed in its 1662 form but with the abbreviations
indicated by brackets, and no restriction was placed on the use of
the Kyries. While the use of one of the three alternatives was still
mandatory, the emphasis on penitence was markedly less. The
change in emphasis was even more noticeable in Series 2. The
Decalogue, shorn of its rubric indicating penitence on the part of
the worshipper, together with its alternatives—all in their 1928
form—were relegated to an appendix, while their place in the text
of the rite was taken by a brief rubric indicating that one of the
three 'may be used'. It was therefore possible to eliminate even a
vestigial element of penitence at the beginning of the rite. The
same arrangement was followed in Series 1 and 2 Revised.

In Series 3 several important experiments were made. At the
beginning of the rite the Kyries were set out as an alternative to the
Gloria in excelsis with a note suggesting that they were to be
preferred in penitential seasons; but both were still optional. The
texts of the Decalogue and the Summary of the Law continued to
be printed in an appendix; but a rubric was inserted after the
Intercessions indicating that either of them might be used before
the Confession. The use of the Decalogue as a help to self-
examination was also enhanced by an addition inspired by Michael
Peck, a former Dean of Lincoln. The whole Decalogue was
encapsulated within the Summary of the Law, the first half of the
Summary following the first commandment and the second half
following the tenth. All the other commandments were then
followed by short passages from the New Testament, each one
providing either by interpretation or by amplification some facet
of the Christian understanding of each commandment. In this
way, the worshipper was taken beyond the limitations of the Old
Testament, even though he was not presented with a complete
code of Christian ethics. Finally a new, and rather less abject,

response was provided for the congregation: 'Amen. Lord have mercy.' The 'Amen' signified the worshipper's acceptance that this is indeed the commandment of God; the 'Lord have mercy' expressed the sorrowful awareness of not having kept the commandment.

Series 3 Revised and ASB have now revised these forms in the light of experience:

1   Section 5 indicates that the Decalogue or the Summary of the Law is still the first, but optional, element in the Prayers of Penitence, preceding the Invitation and Confession. Only the text of the Summary of the Law is included in the rite, however, and this now appears in its Marcan form (Mark 12.29–31).
2   The Decalogue is included in an Appendix (section 78) in two forms: the Series 3 form with the New Testament additions, and the 1662 form with the abbreviations indicated by brackets. In both cases the response is in its Series 3 form.

It is hoped that these arrangements will meet the needs of worshippers who favour the continued use of the Decalogue, on the grounds that it has had significant value in the life of the nation in setting a hallowed statement of fundamental morals. On the other hand, the inclusion of the New Testament passages may help to allay the misgivings of others who fear that constant use can lead to a mistaken assumption that the Decalogue is a satisfactory summary of Christian ethics, when in fact it is only an incomplete code of an ancient Jewish nomadic community.

The Invitation to Confession
(sections 6, 25–6)

The desire to revive the practice of communion at the Reformation was tempered by the desire to guard against unworthy reception, and forms of preparation were a feature of many German Church Orders. Cranmer borrowed much of his *Order of the Communion* from Hermann, but the Invitation to confession was his own composition. In its original 1548 form, which was also included in 1549, communicants were invited to confess their sins not only to almighty God but also 'to his holy Church gathered together in his Name'. Three conditions were required of them: repentance of sins, love for their neighbour, and the intention to lead a good life. It also asked them simply to 'draw near and take this holy Sacrament to your comfort', indicating in this case a physical movement to the place of communion. In 1552 communicants were no longer asked to confess their sins to the Church but 'before this congregation', and the whole phrase disappeared in 1662. 1662 also added the phrase 'with faith' to 'draw near', indicating that the approach was now an approach of the heart. In any case the rubric preceding the third Exhortation in 1662 indicated that the communicants were to be 'conveniently placed for the receiving of the Holy Sacrament' at that stage. 1928 and Series 1 retained the same Invitation but also provided a shorter alternative form, which was in fact the second half of the 1662 form, beginning at 'Draw near with faith'. Series 2 produced a new, brief Invitation with a preamble based on Hebrews 4.14 and requiring of the communicant 'a true heart in full assurance of faith'. Series 1 and 2 Revised provided both the Series 1 and the Series 2 forms as alternatives; but the Series 2 form met with a number of critics who deplored the loss of the earlier references to 'the commandments of God' and to being 'in love and charity with your neighbours'. Series 3 therefore produced a new Invitation which not only restored both these elements but in fact returned to the three requirements of Cranmer's original. It also had a new preamble based on three of the four Comfortable Words:

1   God so loved the world that he gave his only Son—John 3.16.

2   Jesus Christ came . . . to save sinners—1 Timothy 1.15.

3   We have an advocate with the Father—1 John 2.1.

4   Whoever believes in him should . . . have eternal life—John 3.16.

This is the form which appeared in Series 3 Revised and in ASB. As an alternative the rubric of section 6 permits the minister to use an invitation of his own choice, which may meet the needs of a particular situation; or he may use the Comfortable Words in full, which are set out in section 25. The three Words used in the Series 3 Invitation were passages which Cranmer had borrowed from Hermann; the fourth—Matthew 11.28—Cranmer had borrowed from Zwingli's Latin Mass. The introduction 'Hear what comfortable words our Saviour Christ says' were probably borrowed by Cranmer from *The King's Book* (f.1.1): 'The penitent may desire to hear of the minister the comfortable words of remission of sins'. Cranmer had used the Comfortable Words after the Absolution, providing scriptural assurance for the forgiveness of sins, and this had continued in all rites up to and including Series 2. In Series 3, however, they preceded Confession and Absolution, providing courage and confidence to make the confession. Series 1 and 2 Revised permitted them in either place; but ASB has now clearly opted for the Series 3 position before Confession, although their use is entirely optional. ASB also describes them as 'Words of Comfort' rather than 'Comfortable Words', for in current usage 'comfortable' lacks some of the idea of solace and strength which the word possessed in earlier centuries.

The Confession
(sections 7, 27)

Cranmer borrowed almost the whole of the Confession in 1548 and 1549 from Hermann: he omitted the latter's reference to original sin, but added the phrase 'by thought, word and deed' from the old Roman confession. This form remained in use in successive rites until Series 2, when a new short form of two sentences appeared. The first sentence was borrowed from the old Roman confession, the second was a slightly abbreviated version of the conclusion of 1662. It was criticized both for its brevity and for its lack of any expression of sorrow for sin. Both these criticisms were met in the Series 3 form, which not only expressed sorrow for sin but indicated more fully the means by which human beings come to sin: in this respect the phrases 'through ignorance, through weakness, through our own deliberate fault' were borrowed from the new New Zealand rite. It also contained an acknowledgement that sin affects our relationships with other people as well as relationships with God. In Series 3 Revised and ASB this confession has been modified by the omission of the phrases 'in the evil we have done and in the good we have not done' and the substitution of 'negligence' for 'ignorance'— changes which undoubtedly improved both the style and the content.

The Absolution
(sections 8, 28)

The basis of the Absolution in ASB is still the old Roman form. In 1548 Cranmer had used the Roman absolution but had added the preamble from Hermann: 'Our blessed Lord, who hath left power to his Church (Hermann: 'congregation') to absolve penitent sinners from their sins, and to restore to the grace of the heavenly Father such as truly believe in Christ, have mercy . . .'. In 1549 he changed the preamble to: 'Almighty God, our heavenly Father, who of his great mercy hath promised forgiveness of sins to all them, which with hearty repentance and true faith, turn unto him: have mercy . . .'. This remained unchanged until 1928, which permitted an abbreviation by the omission of the preamble, viz. 'Almighty God have mercy . . .'.

Series 1 provided both the 1928 options, but Series 2 only provided the shorter form, but with one important amendment: the final phrase was changed from 'bring you to everlasting life' to 'keep you in life eternal', resting on the Johannine concept of eternal life as a present reality and the possession of Christians as well as their promised destiny. This change was retained in Series 3, and a short relative clause was added after 'Almighty God', viz. 'who forgives all who truly repent', thereby producing a simplified form of Cranmer's preamble. This is the form which has been retained in both Rite A and Rite B in ASB. The pronouns 'you/your' are printed in italics to allow for the fact that the Ministry of the Word may be used separately or may in certain cases be taken by a Reader, in which case the pronouns are changed to 'us/our'. This conforms with the practice in Morning and Evening Prayer, where the same Confession and Absolution are used.

The Kyries
(sections 9, 79)

There is evidence for the use of Kyrie eleison as a congregational response in the East in the fourth century. Egeria (c. 390) spoke of its use in Jerusalem as the response to the deacon's list of petitions at the evening office, while at approximately the same date it was the response in the deacon's litany at the Eucharist in Antioch (*Apostolic Constitutions*, Bk 8). The Litany spread to the West in the fifth century and evidence for its use in Rome was found in the *Deprecatio Gelasii* (c. 494) (cf. pp. 35f.). By the time of Pope Gregory the Great, Christe eleison had been added, and on ferial days the petitions of the litany were omitted, leaving only the Kyries. In *Ordo Romanus Primus* (c. 700) not only had they become an independent element at the beginning of Mass, they had also become a choral performance, the duration of which was controlled by signals from the Pope. From the ninth century onwards, where they were sung, the music became quite complicated: an extensive literature of tropes developed, which lasted until the sixteenth century. Originally the priest took no part in their recitation, and it was not until the thirteenth century that the principle was accepted that they were a joint activity of priest and congregation.

In 1549 Cranmer took the Kyries over from the Sarum rite, using them in a ninefold form after the Introit Psalm. In 1552, however, they assumed a penitential character as a response to the Decalogue: 'Lord, have mercy upon us, and incline our hearts to keep this law.' It was 1928 which reintroduced them as an independent element, permitting them as a weekday alternative to the Decalogue or the Summary of the Law. Series 1 extended their use to any occasion, but in Series 2 the use of all three items became optional. From this time the practice gradually developed of regarding the Kyries and Gloria in excelsis as alternatives, the latter being used on Sundays and Holy Days, the former being used on penitential and ferial occasions. The practice was officially recognized in Series 3; but ASB has reverted to the more flexible approach of Series 2, where either or both (or neither) could be used.

In section 8 the Kyries are set out in a sixfold form as three sets of versicles and responses; but other permitted variations— long and short, English and Greek—are set out in section 79. Note 7 (p. 116) indicates the permitted freedom of use. One possibility is the use of a musical setting as an introit (section 2) in penitential seasons.

The Gloria in excelsis
(section 10)

This fourth-century hymn of unknown authorship was first used as an office canticle both in the East and the West. It was introduced into the Roman Mass by Pope Symmachus (498–514), who ordered its use on certain festive occasions when he himself was the celebrant. By the time of Gregory the Great it had an established place for use on Sundays and festivals, except in Advent, Pre-Lent and Lent. Many continental Reformers, including Luther and Hermann continued to use it at the beginning of the rite, while Zwingli placed it between the Epistle and Gospel. Cranmer also placed it in the Roman position after the Kyries in 1549, but with no regulation as to its use except permission to omit it on weekdays. In 1552, however, it was transferred to the end of the rite, where it became a hymn of praise shared by those who had just shared in the heavenly feast. Since the rite now began on a much more subdued note with a penitential response to the Decalogue, there was much to be said for its new position after the Prayer of Thanksgiving. It occupied a position which was occupied in many Reformed rites by a psalm. 1662 and 1928 continued to use it in its 1552 position: 1662 made it mandatory on all occasions, 1928 permitted its omission on any day except Sundays and Holy Days. Series 1 and Series 2 made its use optional, and allowed it either at the beginning or at the end; but whereas Series 1 emphasized the 1662 position by printing the text at the end and legislating for its use at the beginning by a rubric, Series 2 did the exact opposite, thereby emphasizing the 1549 position. The same situation has continued in Series 1 and 2 Revised, and Series 3. ASB provides for its use and prints the text in both positions. It can also be used as a hymn at Section 50, while Note 8 (p. 116) permits its use as an Introit (section 1) or a Gradual (section 16). It may also be omitted in Advent and Lent, and on weekdays which are not Principal or Greater Holy Days. For further information, particularly on the text, see pp. 112–15.

The Collect
(section 11)

For the history and composition of collects, see pp. 265–7. In 1549 and 1552 the Collect was introduced by the rubric, 'Then shall follow the Collect of the day, with one of these two Collects following, for the King', the latter being a 'memorial', subsidiary to the Collect of the Day. Unfortunately 1662 followed the 1637 Scottish rite and transposed them, presumably to keep the Collect and the Readings of the day together and to avoid unnecessary page-turning. In 1549 the Collect was also preceded by the Salutation and 'Let us pray', but this was omitted in 1552. 1928 gave the Collect its former prominence by restoring the Salutation and 'Let us pray' and omitting the prayers for the sovereign, who in any case was mentioned by name in the Intercessions. This arrangement continued in Series 1 and Series 2. In Series 3, 1 and 2 Revised, and ASB, however, the Salutation and 'Let us pray' have been placed at the beginning of the Preparation, which is a more logical position. The Rules to Order the Service encourage the use of only one collect as the norm, in view of the fact that it is intended to 'gather up' the theme of the readings, or the season, or the occasion. This can be helped by the provision in Note 9 (p. 116), whereby the president may preface the Collect by 'Let us pray', a brief bidding, and silence. The Collect is part of the president's liturgy, and it should only be said by some other minister if the president is unable to be present for the first part of the rite.

THE MINISTRY OF THE WORD
The Readings
(sections 12–18)

For the origin and development of the eucharistic lectionary, see pp. 298–310.

From 1549 to 1928 it was the custom to have two readings at the Eucharist—the Epistle and the Gospel: the occasions on which an Old Testament passage was chosen to represent the Epistle were extremely rare, and from 1552 with the abolition of the Introit Psalms, the use of Old Testament material in the Eucharist was virtually nil, except for the recitation of the Decalogue. It could be argued that this represented a permanent, invariable Old Testament reading. Series 1 increased the provision from two readings to three, however, by the inclusion of the Old Testament readings from the 1960 Indian Prayer Book, which fitted in with the 1662 Epistles and Gospels. There were two reasons for this development. In the first place there was the growing preference for the 'parish communion' over Morning Prayer on Sundays, bringing with it a recognition of the lack of Old Testament provision in 1662 and 1928. Secondly, biblical theology encouraged people to see the whole of Scripture, both Old Testament and New, as the Word of God. St Augustine had truly commented, 'The Old Testament opens out into the New, the New lies hidden in the Old'. Since Series 1 all revisions have made provision for three readings, but have only insisted on two, regarding the Gospel as mandatory, and leaving the choice between the other two. A further development came in Series 3, and continued in ASB, with the idea of a 'controlling lesson', whereby the Old Testament reading is to be given preference in the pre-Christmas period, and the New Testament reading preference in the post-Pentecost period.

It is important that the whole of the Word of God, including the sermon, should be proclaimed in a place where it is audible and the

193

ministers making the proclamation are visible. This is by no means a trite observation. Care is often taken that the printed word is visible to the reader, but the reader is either hidden behind a huge lectern which obscures both sight and sound, or his face is shrouded in darkness. Or again, an attempt to proclaim the Gospel in the midst of the congregation can result in a reader being 'lost' in a crowd of people, audible and visible only to the immediate bystanders. To achieve maximum impact, a reader must be both heard and seen. Furthermore, there is much to be said for conducting the whole of the Ministry of the Word from a single place, thereby emphasizing the fact that it should be a coherent whole and not a set of single items, proclaimed from two or three different places. The Injunctions of 1547 were wise in directing all readings to be done from the pulpit. Admittedly the custom of Gospel processions has a long tradition—it can be found in *Ordo Romanus Primus* (*c*. 700); and there is a long tradition for proclaiming the Gospel towards the north—inevitable when a southern-based Western church faced the pagan Northern Europe—but the situation today is different. Attitudes towards the Bible have changed, and the Church is faced with a missionary challenge in all directions. The Gospel can always be given added dignity by means of lights, and by requiring the congregation to stand; but the fact must also be faced that all the readings from Scripture are the Word of God, and on some occasions the Gospel is not the key passage to be proclaimed.

The Use of Psalmody with the Readings

The use of psalmody with the readings has had a long history. In the Middle Ages this had become the Gradual or antiphon with the Alleluia. The name 'Gradual' probably derived from the *gradus* or step either of the altar or the ambo from which it was sung. The original form of the Gradual may have been a psalm in which the note of praise was expressed by 'Alleluia'. With the passage of time the psalm was replaced by a set piece comprising a twofold Alleluia, an antiphon, and a third Alleluia, the Alleluias being sung to music which could be extremely complicated. In penitential seasons it was replaced by the Tract—a psalm sung straight through to a simple chant without any response or Alleluia. It derived its name from a Greek technical musical term denoting a particular kind of tune. Luther was prepared to keep the Gradual on a limited basis in his Latin Mass, but in his German Mass replaced it by a metrical hymn. A similar pattern was followed in the German Church Orders. Cranmer, however, deleted the Gradual and the Tract in 1549, but included an Introit Psalm: 1552 deleted the latter as well, and psalmody was not restored until Series 2 permitted it between the readings but provided no texts. With the advent of Series 3 two passages of psalmody were appointed for every occasion on which a collect and readings were appointed, and this has continued in ASB. ASB indicates three places where psalms are likely to be used: as an introit (section 1) or between the readings (sections 14 and 16); and either piece of selected psalmody can be used at any of the places. The two passages should suffice, for it is unlikely that a church will want to use psalms at all three places in one service. As far as possible they relate to the readings or the occasion, and at all times their use is optional.

The Announcement of the Readings and the Responses

In 1549 the Priest was directed to read both Epistle and Gospel from 'a place assigned for the purpose'. No directions were given as to whether the congregation should stand or sit. The announcements for both readings were simple: 'The Epistle of Saint Paul/ The Holy Gospel, written in the . . . Chapter of. . .'. They have remained substantially the same ever since. In the case of the Epistle no other directions were given, but for the Gospel the congregation replied, 'Glory be to thee, O Lord'. There was no congregational response at the end of either Epistle or Gospel. 1552 made far less provision: no directions were given as to place or posture, and apart from the priest's announcements of Epistle and Gospel, there were no responses of any kind. To the bareness of 1552, 1662 added a little: the priest was to conclude the Epistle with 'Here endeth the Epistle', and the people were directed to stand for the Gospel. 1928 added still more: the reader of both Epistle and Gospel was directed to 'so stand and turn himself as he may best be heard of the people'; the 1549 response to the Gospel announcement was restored; and a further congregational response at the end of the Gospel was added: 'Praise be to thee, O Christ'. This arrangement was continued in Series 1, with an alternative response at the end of the Gospel, 'Thanks be to thee, O Christ, for this thy holy Gospel'. *Deo gratias* was an ancient Roman acclamation of approval, certainly in use by the eighth century, and was used not only after the end of the Gospel, but at the end of the entire rite. But here, addressed not to God, but to Christ, it had greater significance than a mere expression of thanks or approval. It was a recognition that God had spoken to his people through his Son, and still continued to do so through his Gospel—Jesus Christ is supremely the Word. This was made much clearer in Series 3, where all three readings concluded with a versicle and response. In the case of the Old and New Testament readings they took the form: 'This is the word of the Lord/Thanks be to God'. In the case of the Gospel, it was 'This is the Gospel of Christ/Praise to Christ our Lord', while the response to the announcement before the Gospel was 'Glory to Christ our Saviour'. This arrangement has continued in ASB. Note 11 (p. 116) provides alternatives for Holy Week: the announcement may take the form 'The Passion of our Lord Jesus Christ according to N', and the conclusion 'This is the Passion of the Lord'. In neither case is there a response by the congregation.

The Sermon
(section 18)

From the days of the early Church the sermon had followed the Scripture readings: but with the advent of the Creed into the rite the custom developed in some places of the sermon following the Creed. It was a practice adopted by many of the continental Reformers—Zwingli, Luther, Calvin, Hermann—and Cranmer followed suit in 1549. In the Middle Ages preaching had tended to become rare, due largely to the ignorance of the clergy. The deficiency was to some extent met by the activities of the Friars, but in the process the sermon tended to become an activity in its own right, divorced from the liturgy. The Reformers denounced this decay of the sermon as an abuse, and attempted to restore it to its rightful place. Luther, for example, required a sermon to be preached at every Mass. It is not surprising, therefore, that Cranmer also made the preaching of a sermon or the reading of a homily obligatory, although the obligation was lifted when the Eucharist was celebrated on a 'workday' or in private houses with the sick. Books of homilies or 'postils'—mainly expositions of the Epistles and Gospels—to help the clergy had not been unknown in the Middle Ages. In 1542 Convocation had approved a plan to prescribe homilies for the use of illiterate clergy, and a collection of a dozen was produced in the following year, although it was not officially authorized until 1547. A second book of a further twenty-one was authorized in 1571.

1552 and 1662 continued to prescribe the sermon or homily as mandatory and even withdrew the permitted omission on week-days and for the sick. 1928, however, made them optional, a concession continued by Series 1. Series 1 also permitted a choice: the sermon could be preached either in its accustomed place after the Creed or immediately after the Gospel—a practice adopted by the Liturgy for Africa, the Church of South India and a number of Anglican provinces, e.g. South Africa, New Zealand, Japan and Korea. Since Series 2 the sermon has consistently followed the Gospel and has been regarded as an essential element of the Ministry of the Word, although ASB makes it clear in Note 12 (p. 116) that the requirement should be approached with a degree of common sense: 'The sermon is an integral part of the Ministry of the Word. A sermon should normally be preached at all celebrations on Sundays and other Holy Days.'

The Nicene Creed
(section 19)

The Nicene Creed was in origin the baptismal creed of the Church of Jerusalem, being used by Cyril (c. 350) as a basis for teaching candidates for baptism. Known as the Niceno–Constantinopolitan Creed, it is probably a revised form of the Jerusalem Creed, summing up the beliefs proclaimed at the Councils of Nicaea (325) and Constantinople (381). It is described in the acts of the Council of Chalcedon (451) as the profession of 'the 150 holy Fathers who were assembled at Constantinople'. Apparently its use in the Eucharist began in Antioch in the fifth century, and from there it spread gradually through both the East and the West. In the West the third Council of Toledo (589) ordered its use to confirm Spain's conversion from Arianism to orthodoxy. From here it spread to Gaul and Britain, and ultimately Charlemagne accepted its use in Aachen. Development was slow, however, and it was not until the eleventh century that Rome accepted it, using it like the Gloria in excelsis as a festive addition on Sundays and festival occasions.

In its early days it was not recited until the catechumens had been dismissed and the Mass of the Faithful had begun. But when the dismissal of catechumens became obsolete, the Creed was placed after the Gospel and the sermon followed. This was its position in the thirteenth century and it was followed by continental Reformers and by Cranmer in 1549, although some Reformers rejected it in favour of the Apostles' Creed. Cranmer made it obligatory on all occasions: the priest began 'I believe in one God' and then 'the clerks shall sing the rest'. Both 1552 and 1662 continued its obligatory use, but 1928 permitted its omission 'on a day not being a Sunday or a Holy Day' at the discretion of the minister. All subsequent rites, including ASB, have continued to use it in the same way.

The text used in ASB is that of ICET. The following significant features should be noticed:

Line 1: 'We believe'. The plural follows the Greek, as in the original conciliar confession. The statement at Chalcedon made it clear that it was regarded as a corporate profession of orthodoxy, and not as an individual profession by a candidate for baptism, as in the Apostles' Creed. Nevertheless, the use of the plural does not preclude an individual affirmation of faith when it is used today.

Line 2: 'the almighty'. The article is included, for the Greek *Pantocrator* is a noun, not an adjective. It is the Septuagint rendering of the Hebrew divine name (cf. Revelation 1.8; 4.8).

Line 5: 'seen and unseen'. This refers to 'all that is' in the previous line, and applies to 'heaven and earth' in line 3. The comma at the end of line 4 makes this clear.

Line 6: 'We believe'. The repetition of the phrase is found in several early creeds. It assists in dividing the Creed into three paragraphs.

Line 8: 'eternally begotten'. The original translation 'before all worlds' is not only archaic; it also does not mean the same as 'eternally'. The Council of Nicaea safeguarded two facts against Arianism: (a) the Son exists eternally with the Father; and (b) his relationship with the Father *is* that of Son to Father. St Athanasius argued that 'the Son must exist eternally alongside the Father'. The explanation of this is that his generation is an eternal process (cf. J. N. D. Kelly, *Early Christian Doctrines* (2nd edn, 1960), p. 243; *Early Christian Creeds* (3rd edn, 1972), p. 238).

Line 9: 'God from God'. 'From' is a clearer and more literal translation of the Greek preposition *ek*.

Line 12: 'of one Being'. 'Being' comes nearest to the Greek philosophical term *homoousios* and is preferable to 'substance'. The word is used to safeguard the unity of the Godhead.

Line 13: 'Through'. cf. Hebrews 1.2. The reference is still to the Son, who is the Father's agent in creation. It relates to line 3.

Line 16: 'by the power of'. The phrase safeguards the work of the Holy Spirit in the incarnation, making it clear that no carnal activity is implied.

Line 17: 'became incarnate of'. The one point where the ICET text was not followed, 'of' being preferred to 'from'. The latter suggests birth rather than conception. The point to safeguard is that Christ was both *conceived* and *born* of the Virgin Mary.

Line 19: 'suffered death'. The greek *pathonta* is made to bear the notions of both suffering and death. 'Death' provides the link between 'suffered' and 'buried'.

Line 21: 'In accordance with'. A better translation than Cranmer's 'according to', which suggests that Scripture says one thing, while other authorities say something else.

Lines 22–3: 'ascended—is seated'. See pp. 115, 118.

Line 28: 'the Lord, the giver of life'. These are two distinct phrases, both applying to the Holy Spirit. They avoid the misunderstanding of the older version 'the Lord and giver of life', which might suggest 'the Lord of life' and 'the giver of life'.

Line 29: 'and the Son'. The famous *filioque* clause, which was not part of the original ecumenical formulation of the Creed, but was introduced unilaterally by the West at the Council of Toledo in 589. It has not appeared in Eastern texts of the Creed, and Anglican–Orthodox Conversations in 1977 led to a recommendation that it should be omitted. Until there is general agreement on the matter, there should be no unilateral action. The problem of the phrase is not its truth, but its authority—or lack of it.

Line 32: 'We believe in one holy'. While the Latin translation omits the preposition 'in', the Greek original *eis mian* clearly requires 'belief in' the Church, as well as 'in God' and 'in Christ', although 'belief in' the Church is of a different order from 'belief in' God. The adjective 'holy', which was omitted by Cranmer, is now restored: it is in the Greek original.

The Intercession
(sections 20–2)

Section 20

Despite the title of this section of the service, the rubric allows for the inclusion of thanksgiving as well as intercession. If thanks are offered to God for his mighty acts in the Eucharistic Prayer, it is reasonable to provide some opportunity to offer him thanks for the bestowal of specific mercies, particularly on individuals. This part of the rite seems to be the most suitable place. Considerable freedom is permitted. The prayers may be conducted by the president or by others, and choice can be made between a variety of methods:

1 The form set out in section 21.

2 One of the two forms set out in section 81.

3 'Other suitable words', which may include *either* other set forms of prayer, *or* free or extempore prayer with or without the versicle and response provided.

Section 21

Intercession was included in the Eucharist from the earliest times. Justin, for example, spoke of offering up 'sincere prayers in common for ourselves, for the baptized person, and for all other persons wherever they may be' (*Apology*, 1.65). These were offered after baptism and were clearly part of the prayers of the faithful. Hippolytus too made the same point: people must be baptized and confirmed before they can join in with these prayers of the faithful (*Apostolic Tradition*, xxii. 5). In the East, by the time of Cyril of Jerusalem in the fourth century, these intercessions came at the end of the Eucharistic Prayer in the form of a litany. This litany form was then introduced to Rome in the fifth century by Pope Gelasius, who placed it at the beginning of the rite, supplanting the old prayers of the faithful, which only survived on the Wednesday and Friday of Holy Week in the form of biddings followed by silence and a collect (see p. 36). By the time of Pope Gregory the Great (590–604), the introductory litany had disappeared and prayers for the living and departed were found in the Eucharistic Prayer. Obviously these prayers meant little to the congregation when the canon came to be recited silently, but with the advent and growth of the office of Prone in the Middle Ages, intercessions in the vernacular came to be included. The position of these prayers served as a guide to many of the continental Reformers, who included substantial prayers of intercession between the sermon and the Eucharistic Prayer. Calvin, Bucer and Hermann all followed this pattern.

In 1549 Cranmer made provision for the 1544 Litany to be said before Mass on Wednesdays and Fridays, but he also followed the pattern of the Roman canon by prefixing intercessions to his Eucharistic Prayer. These were introduced by the bidding, 'Let us pray for the whole state of Christ's Church', which was similar to the rubric preceding the intercessions in Hermann. Cranmer's prayer was a pastiche, with phrases culled from Scripture, from the Roman canon, from the rite of St Basil, and from Hermann. The order of the intercessions was in fact the same as Hermann's: Church, King and Council, Clergy, God's people, the assembled congregation, the afflicted, and the departed. Three changes were made in 1552: the intercessions were detached from the Eucharistic Prayer and placed after the creed and sermon; the phrase 'militant here in earth' was added to the bidding, thereby producing a form almost identical with one appearing with the bedes in the *Liber Festivalis* (a Primer frequently reprinted down to 1532); and in answer to Bucer's criticism, the prayer for the departed was omitted. 1662 then omitted 'pastors' from the phrase 'bishops, pastors, and curates' because of the Puritan connotation of the word, and restored a commemoration of the departed developed from the bidding prayer in the Elizabethan Injunctions of 1559. Despite this addition, the 1662 form was unsatisfactory, for it limited intercession strictly to the Christian Church; and 1928 attempted to remedy this by including 'all nations', 'all kings and rulers', 'those who are labouring for the spread of thy Gospel among the nations', 'all places of education and learning', together with a thanksgiving for 'all thy Saints'. Series 1 included both 1662 and 1928 prayers and permitted their division into paragraphs, with a congregational response after each: either 'Hear us, we beseech thee', or 'Lord, hear our prayer/And let our cry come unto thee'.

The approach of Series 2 was much more radical, being a return to the principle of the old Roman *Orationes Solemnes*. Intercession was still for the 'whole Church of God', but it was now divided into four sections: the Church, the nations of the world, the sick and afflicted, and the departed. Biddings could be made on these subjects, extending as far as the minister might choose; then in each case there was silence, a versicle and response, and a short prayer. If desired, these short prayers could also be joined together and said as a continuous whole. The versicle and response, adapted from Kyrie eleison, were also new: 'Lord in thy mercy/ Hear our prayer'. The Kyrie was therefore restored to its primitive use as a response to intercession. Successive revisions—Series I and 2 Revised, Series 3, and Series 3 Revised—have adhered to this pattern but have considerably developed and improved it. Intercession is now clearly 'for the Church and for the world' and is divided into six categories:

1   For the Church universal, including the local bishop.
2   For the state and the nations of the world.
3   For the local community and families (missing in Series 2).
4   For the suffering.
5   For the departed.
6   A commendation of the worshippers and all Christians to God.

Considerable flexibility is permitted. The sections of the prayer may be used separately, with their individual concluding prayers, as in Series 2, or they may be used as a continuous whole. Biddings may be used with the whole prayer or with each section, and there is no obligation to use all the sections on every occasion. Individual names may also be inserted in each section of set prayer; while the versicle and response may be used before or after each set prayer, according to preference. The final versicle and response are different, ending with a prayer that God will accept the prayers offered through Jesus Christ. The form the intercessions take depends on the occasion and the time available: but the increased flexibility obviously demands strict discipline and careful preparation on the part of the minister responsible.

Section 22

It is at this point in the service that the Order following the pattern of the Book of Common Prayer continues at section 57 on p. 146.

Prayers of Penitence
(sections 23–9)

Sections 24–8 have already been dealt with in sections 4–8, pp. 181–90.

The Prayer of Humble Access
(section 29)

This prayer, which first appeared in the 1548 *Order of the Communion*, was Cranmer's own composition, intended to provide the communicants with a prayer for worthy reception, analogous to the priest's prayers before communion in the Roman rite. In fact it begins with a phrase from a priest's private prayer found in some missals before 1548. The whole prayer is a pastiche of phrases which may be found in a variety of sources, few of which could be reliably identified as *the* original source: the Liturgies of St Basil and St James, Daniel 9.18, Mark 7.28, John 6.56, Leviticus 17.11, the Hereford and Westminster Missals, the German Church Orders, Thomas Aquinas, Florus of Lyons, and Paschasius Radbert.

The original form in 1548–9 contained an additional phrase 'in these holy mysteries' in the second half, and the clauses came in a different order. It ran:

> Grant us therefore, gracious Lord, so to eat the flesh of thy dear Son Jesus Christ, and to drink his blood *in these holy mysteries*, that we may continually dwell in him, and he in us, that our sinful bodies may be made clean by his body, and our souls washed through his most precious blood.

1552 deleted the additional phrase, and inverted the final clauses, producing the prayer in its familiar form. Whatever the theological result, the 1552 form undoubtedly runs more smoothly. Its position in the rite also changed in 1552. In 1549, when the entire penitential section appeared between the consecration and communion, the Prayer of Humble Access immediately preceded communion: but in 1552 it immediately preceded the Eucharistic Prayer. Its move to this position is said to have been due to Gardiner's criticism that the prayer, said kneeling after consecration, taught the adoration of Christ's flesh in the sacrament. While it could also be argued that in its new position it destroyed the natural sequence of Preface, Sanctus and Eucharistic Prayer, the alternation of praise and penitence is sound, with the thought of the approaching communion in mind.

Gilbert Burnet, the Latitudinarian Bishop of Salisbury, argued in his *History of the Reformation* (3 vols, 1679–1714) that the final clauses caused grave disquiet to many people, because they seemed to suggest that the body of Christ was given to preserve the body of the communicant, and the blood of Christ was given to preserve his soul. This was undoubtedly what was said in the words of administration in the 1548 *Order of the Communion* (drawn from the Sarum rite for the Communion of the Sick), as well as in the Prayer of Humble Access, and the two formulae said together in close juxtaposition would seem decisive. But a modification was made in 1549, for the words of administration were changed to 'body and soul' in both cases. The doctrine of concomitance, together with the question of reception in one kind, had been a leading topic of medieval theologians, such as Anselm and Thomas Aquinas. The distinction was of long standing, and with the safeguard inserted in 1549, it should not be pressed too far. These two lines were in fact omitted in Series 2 and Series 3, and were bracketed as optional omissions in Series 1 and 2 Revised, arrangements which have continued in Rite A and Rite B respectively in ASB.

A further problem was raised by critics who argued that the clause 'Grant us *so* to eat the flesh . . . *that* we may evermore dwell in him' implies the possibility of partaking of Christ's body and blood otherwise than to the soul's health. Such an interpretation is admittedly possible, especially in the light of clause in the 1549 Prayer of Oblation—omitted in 1552—'that whosoever shall be partakers of this holy communion may *worthily* receive the most precious body and blood'. Bishop Dowden has pointed out, however, that such an interpretation is not necessary: it simply means, 'Grant us to eat . . . so that our sinful bodies'; and instances of 'so' separated from 'that' are frequent in 1662, e.g. second post-communion prayer in Holy Communion; collects for SS Simon and Jude, Advent 3, All Saints, Trinity 13 (Dowden, *Further Studies in the Prayer Book*, pp. 339–43).

1928 changed the position of the prayer by attaching it to the end of the penitential section—a position it had occupied in 1549, although the entire penitential section now preceded consecration instead of following it. It has retained this position in successive revisions and remains there in ASB. Some critics would argue that no such prayer is really necessary at this point, when communicants have already confessed their sins and received absolution. Questionnaires have revealed, however, that this is one of the best-loved prayers in the rite, and its disappearance would cause considerable distress. Despite the preceding absolution, it finds wide acceptance as an expression of unworthiness before reception of the sacrament. The only significant change in wording in ASB has been the substitution of 'nature' for 'property', a word which expresses the meaning more clearly in current usage. An alternative form of the prayer is provided in section 82 (p. 253).

THE MINISTRY OF THE SACRAMENT

The Peace

(sections 30–1)

There are a number of references in the New Testament to the use of the Peace as a sign of brotherly love in the faith: Romans 16.16, 1 Corinthians 16.20, 2 Corinthians 13.12, 1 Thessalonians 5.26, 1 Peter 5.14. References to its appearance in the Eucharist are also both early and frequent. Justin, for example, commented, 'At the conclusion of the prayers we greet one another with a kiss. Then, bread and a chalice containing wine mixed with water are presented to the president.' (*First Apology*, 65.3) Clearly the peace came between the prayers of the faithful and the offertory—a position also mentioned by Origen—'after the prayers'—and Tertullian, who called it 'the seal of prayer'. Matthew 5.23f., stating the need for reconciliation with one's brother before offering one's gift at the altar, may have led to the placing of it at this point. In early Eastern rites the Peace seems to have extended throughout the period during which the offerings were brought from the sacristy to the altar. It was therefore introductory to the eucharistic action itself. The Gallican and Mozarabic rites also placed the Peace before the Canon.

By the fifth century, however, the Peace occupied a different position in the Roman rite. Pope Leo I, in his letter to Decentius, Bishop of Gubbio (416) insisted that it should come after the Canon, as indicating the assent of the people to all that was done in the mysteries. It was a position with which St Augustine and the African Church agreed; and it is a position which the Roman rite has maintained consistently to the present day. In this position, as an immediate preparation for communion, it has associations with the Lord's Prayer—'Forgive us our sins, as we forgive those who sin against us'—and with the Agnus Dei—'grant us peace'. 1549 retained it in the Roman position after the Canon and Lord's Prayer, but 1552 removed it altogether. It did not appear again until 1928, when it reappeared in its 1549 position as an optional element, an arrangement which continued in Series 1. In Series 2, however, it became a mandatory element, was restored to its

primitive position between the prayers of intercession and penitence and the offertory, and was prefaced by the quotation based
on 1 Corinthians 12.13, 27 and Ephesians 4—with its exhortation,
'Endeavour to keep the unity of the Spirit in the bond of peace'. In
all subsequent revisions the Peace has remained mandatory, but
changes have occurred in the introductory exhortation. Some
criticism was expressed at the Series 2 use of Ephesians 4.3, in that
it could imply that the Christian community was simply strug-
gling to maintain an existing situation, whereas it should be seen
as a pilgrim community reaching out and striving towards an
ideal. In Series 3, therefore, this passage was replaced by Romans
14.19, 'Let us then pursue all that makes for peace and builds up
our common life'. This in its turn had its critics, who considered it
to be too hortatory in character and who wished for something
more clearly Christocentric. In Series 3 Revised, therefore, the
Series 3 form was supplemented by a form borrowed from the
experimental Scottish Episcopalian rite of 1977. It is a pastiche of
Ephesians 2.14, 16, Matthew 18.20–1, and 1 Thessalonians 5.13.
In addition five seasonal alternatives are appended in section 82,
p. 170: these are, however, only a guide, and choice is not limited
to this particular selection.

The Sign of Peace
(section 31)

No form of action is prescribed: each congregation must work this
out for themselves. But a cue is given for the appropriate moment
of exchange in the form of a statement from the president. Its use,
however, is optional. Whether demonstrated by word or gesture
or both, the purpose of the Peace is to strengthen the congregation's sense of unity and brotherly love, and to overcome
factional interests. Normally, a handclasp accompanied by the
words, 'Peace be with you' is sufficient. The rubric—'All may
exchange a sign of peace'—is so worded to avoid the mistaken
idea that the Peace must be handed down in an unbroken line from
the president. This was encouraged by the medieval custom of the
Peace being handed down from the president, either after he had
kissed the altar or the host or chalice, or after he had kissed the
'pax brede' or board, which was then passed round and kissed.
There is, however, no kind of spiritual procession from the
president: the whole action should be spontaneous, but restrained.

The Preparation of the Gifts
(sections 32–5)

References to the collection of alms for the relief of the needy, to the reception of the gifts of the bread and wine to be used at the Eucharist, and to the necessary preparations for the eucharistic action are frequent in the liturgies of both East and West. Justin, Hippolytus, *Apostolic Constitutions* Book 8, and St Mark, for example, all refer to them. As has already been noted (p. 205) in the Eastern liturgies the deacons and others brought the necessary gifts from the sacristy while the Peace was being exchanged. In the West, by the time of the *Ordo Romanus Primus* the offertory was surrounded by an elaborate ceremonial, including processions, censing, hand-washing and music.

At first there was only one prayer—the *oratio super oblata*; but gradually the various ceremonies each attracted their own prayers, some of doubtful theology, for the tendency arose of confusing the offering of oblations at this point with the later act of oblation in the eucharistic canon. The Reformers reacted against this, some quite violently. Luther, for example, in his *Formula Missae* of 1523 wrote:

> There follows that complete abomination, into the service of which all that precedes in the Mass has been forced, whence it is called *Offertorium*, and on account of which nearly everything sounds and reeks of oblation. In the midst of these things those words of life and salvation have been placed, just like in times past the ark of the Lord was placed in the temple of idols next to Dagon ... Therefore repudiating all those things which smack of sacrifice and of the offertory, together with the entire canon, let us retain those things which are pure and holy. (Jasper and Cuming, *Prayers of the Eucharist*, pp. 136–7)

The bread and the wine were therefore prepared without prayer and ceremony, while those who were to communicate 'gathered together by themselves in one place' near the altar. Hermann followed the same practice, instructing that communicants, 'as soon as they have made their oblation, must go together to that place that shall be appointed unto them, nigh to the altar' (ibid., pp. 158–9).

In 1549 Cranmer followed suit. All private prayers and ceremonies disappeared, and the Prayer for the Church made no reference to alms and oblations. The Offertory Chant became the Offertory Sentences, taken from Scripture and emphasizing the duty of almsgiving, the maintenance of the clergy, and the relief of the poor. While these were said or sung, the people came into the chancel to make their offerings in 'the poor men's box'. The communicants then remained, the men on one side, the women on the other, while the non-communicants departed. The priest without further ado set the bread and the wine upon the altar and began the Sursum corda. 1552 was even more drastic. The altar was already in the body of the church or chancel, so there were no instructions for the people to draw near; the churchwardens gathered their alms and placed them in the poor men's box, while the priest said one or more of the Sentences; a petition that God would accept the alms was only included in the Prayer for the Church if there were 'alms given unto the poor'; nothing at all was said about placing bread and wine upon the table—apparently it was often done prior to the service; and the term 'Offertory' was studiously avoided. With 1662 the balance was slightly redressed. The term 'Offertory' reappeared; the deacons, churchwardens or other fit persons were instructed to receive the alms in a decent basin and bring them to the priest, who then presented them and placed them on the table; the priest was then required to place sufficient bread and wine on the table; and the petition in the Prayer to the Church was expanded to 'alms and oblations'. The precise meaning of this phrase has been a matter for considerable debate, particularly in view of the Scottish 1637 rite's inclusion of a requirement for the presbyter to 'offer up and place the bread and wine prepared for the Sacrament upon the Lord's Table'—a requirement which Bishop Cosin would have liked to introduce into 1662. In the seventeenth century Patrick argued that 'oblations' referred to the bread and wine, a view widely accepted, not least by the Nonjurors and Wheatly. But a lengthy examination of the historical evidence by Bishop John Dowden has since encouraged the view that 'oblations' referred to 'other money offerings for pious uses' (Dowden, *Further Studies in the Prayer Book*, 1908, pp. 176–222). Nevertheless, whatever meaning is given to the phrase, Dowden admits that 'a ceremonial offering of the bread and wine seems to me a primitive and edifying rite' (ibid., p. 222). 1928 made no changes to 1662, except to add the comment that it was 'an ancient tradition of the Church to mingle a little water with the wine'.

With Series 1 came the first small, but significant, move

towards an Offertory of Bread and Wine. The alms and other devotions of the people were still collected and presented before the Prayer for the Church: but the Priest was then given a choice. He could place the bread and the wine upon the table either at this point, before the Prayer for the Church, or later, immediately before the Prayer of Consecration: and in both places it was given its own sentence from 1 Chronicles 29.11, 14. The sentence is itself important, for it summarizes the true spirit of the Offertory—a recognition that God is the giver of all gifts, and what we offer is no more than a return of what he has already given us. In Series 2 the Offertory occurred at only one point, immediately before the Eucharistic Prayer, under the heading 'The Preparation of the Bread and Wine'. It was confined to a single rubric, with no accompanying sentences of any kind. The bread and the wine were simply placed upon the holy table, and it was permitted to collect and present the gifts of the people at the same time: the whole action could be accompanied by a hymn. Clearly a great deal was left to the priest and his congregation as to the way in which all this should be done; but the emphasis has now shifted from the offering of money to the presentation of the bread and wine. As may be expected, Series 1 and 2 Revised marked a further development on similar lines. The title remained 'The Preparation of the Bread and Wine'; the offerings of the people could be collected and presented either before the Intercessions or before the Eucharistic Prayer, to the accompaniment, if required, of a hymn or sentence of Scripture, although none of the latter were provided; the bread and the wine were brought to the holy table; and the sentence from 1 Chronicles 29 reappeared. Similar provision was made in Series 3, but with one very important change: after the sentence from 1 Chronicles 29, a further rubric appeared—'The President takes the bread and wine'. The title of this section of the service had also been changed from 'The Preparation of the Bread and Wine' to 'The Taking of the Bread and Wine'. For the first time, therefore, 'Taking' appeared as an action in its own right, to be distinguished from the setting of the bread and wine upon the Holy Table. The significance of the 'Taking' became even clearer in Series 3 Revised and ASB, where it was associated with the Eucharistic Prayer rather than with the Preparation of the Gifts (see pp. 211–13).

Section 32

The rubric is so worded that there is scope for a variety of methods for the placing of the bread and wine on the holy table, from a simple transference by the president from a near-by credence to an elaborate ceremonial involving a solemn laying of the table, an offertory procession with cross, lights and members of the congregation, and the use of incense. Note 20 (p. 117) also permits this preparation to take place earlier in the rite, for example in the 1662 position before the intercessions.

Section 33

This section, which is optional, permits the president to 'praise God for his gifts in appropriate words'. The congregational response from the new Roman rite suggests that for some people the Roman prayers might be acceptable at this point. The new South African rite has included them: but since other people might not find them theologically desirable they are not included in ASB. The texts are as follows:

The Bread:

Blessed are you, Lord, God of all creation. Through your goodness we have this bread to offer, which earth has given and human hands have made. It will become for us the bread of life.

The Wine:

Blessed are you, Lord, God of all creation. Through your goodness we have this wine to offer, fruit of the vine and work of human hands. It will become our spiritual drink.

Section 34

This may be followed by the collection and presentation of the offerings of the people, accompanied by the words from 1 Chronicles 29, if this collection has not taken place earlier. No other Scripture sentences are provided, but a suitable hymn may be sung (section 35).

Through the entire Preparation of the Gifts, or the Offertory, as it was called in 1662, two actions take place, one functional and the other symbolical. The functional action is that of preparing the table for the eucharistic action. The symbolical action is the offering of our lives and the fruits of our labours to God. To a considerable degree the two actions take place together; and it is quite possible to undertake the functional without overlaying it with the symbolic. In any case the dangers of a Pelagian attitude to the Offertory have been well aired (e.g. Archbishop Michael Ramsey, *Durham Essays and Addresses*). Nevertheless, the Roman prayers and the text from 1 Chronicles 29 made it clear that throughout the initiative lies with God. It should also be remembered that in the contemporary situation the 'collection' is a very realistic symbol of human labours.

A procession of the bread and wine, together with the sacred vessels, to the holy table, is also a reminder that the focal point has now moved from the Bible to the Sacrament.

THE EUCHARISTIC PRAYER
THE TAKING OF THE BREAD AND CUP
and THE GIVING OF THANKS

The Taking
(*section 36*)

The sections on the Eucharistic Prayer have a sub-heading—'The Taking of the Bread and Cup and The Giving of Thanks'—which refers to the first two of the four dominical acts stated in the institution narrative: taking, blessing, breaking, and giving. The custom of the priest performing certain ceremonies as he said this narrative during the Eucharistic Prayer, expressive of a desire to fulfil our Lord's command to do as he had done was widespread and of long standing, although they have not always been identical in every instance. The manual acts, as performed in the medieval Roman rite, were abolished by Cranmer in 1549 but were restored in 1662, following the example of the Scottish rite of 1637. They were continued in Series 1; but at the same time the first step towards a new approach to the manual acts was seen by the introduction of a rubric permitting the fraction to take place after the consecration and before the distribution of the consecrated elements. This was taken a step further in Series 2. The provision for breaking the bread during the institution narrative was omitted altogether, and it became an action in its own right with its own text between consecration and distribution. Three of the four dominical acts now clearly followed one another—blessing, breaking, and giving. The first dominical act, the taking, still remained obscure, however. It could be identified with one of two acts. It could be identified with the Offertory, or it could be identified with the 'taking' which accompanied the institution narrative: the priest was still required to 'take' the bread and the cup into his hands at this point. Series 3 went still further towards an identification of the 'taking'. The rubrics requiring 'taking' during the institution narrative were removed altogether, and a new section of the rite under the heading 'The Taking of the Bread and Wine' appeared before the Eucharistic Prayer. This at least had the merit of indicating the four actions following one another in their correct sequence, although there was still some room for confusion because the section began with the Offertory. The section did conclude, however, with the clear rubric—after the completion of the Offertory—'The president takes the bread and wine'. This new arrangement was not included in Series 1 and 2 Revised; but the matter was placed beyond all doubt in Series 3 Revised and in ASB.

Here it becomes clear that the 'taking' is not to be confused with the Offertory and other preparatory acts. The rubric on 'taking' now becomes the necessary preliminary to the Eucharistic Prayer under the new subheading 'The Taking of the Bread and Wine and the Giving of Thanks'. The action therefore occurs after the bread and the wine are on the holy table and is performed in silence. The president takes both elements in his hands, raises them for everyone to see, and then replaces them on the holy table before the Eucharistic Prayer begins, indicating that these are the elements over which thanks are to be given. This would appear to be the survival of a Jewish table custom with which our Lord was familiar. In the Passover ceremonies, the head of the family took the bread and the wine, and held them above the table before giving thanks over them. This action certainly appeared in the Mishnah, in which the Passover ceremonies were written down in considerable detail about AD 200. While it might be argued that this was a long time after the Last Supper, it might also be argued that it was not a particularly long time after the Gospel accounts; furthermore, in such matters the Jews were conservative, and the ceremonies written down in the Mishnah were more likely to be of long standing than recent innovations.

The fact that all four dominical actions are now clearly defined does not imply that all four are of equal significance. 'Taking' and 'breaking' are preliminaries to the 'blessing' and 'giving'; but they are necessary preliminaries which the New Testament accounts of the Last Supper considered sufficiently important to include. Admittedly Note 16 (p. 117) permits 'traditional manual acts' during the Eucharistic Prayers; but this permission is given in deference to people who have always been accustomed to such acts, regarding them as a re-enactment of our Lord's actions. The fact remains that the 'taking' in section 36 is mandatory, clearly indicating the first of the four actions required in the Eucharist. Its position also reinforces the view that there is no specific moment or formula of consecration. The whole prayer is consecratory.

THE EUCHARISTIC PRAYERS
(sections 38–41)

General Introduction

Unlike 1662, where the single prayer was called 'The Prayer of Consecration', the prayers in Rite A are called 'Eucharistic Prayers', indicating a return to the Jewish concept of blessing or consecration by thanksgiving. They denote the second of our Lord's four actions: after taking bread and wine, he gave thanks over them. It was a pattern clearly followed in the early Church. Justin, for example, says that the president, having taken the bread and the cup 'offers praise and glory to the Father of all in the name of the Son and of the Holy Spirit, and gives thanks at some length that we have been deemed worthy of these things from him'. (Jasper and Cuming, *PEER*, p. 18)

The multiplicity of Eucharistic Prayers within a single rite is a new feature in the liturgy of the Church of England, and indeed in the Church of Rome. But it is again clear that in the early Church, a variety of prayers within an agreed pattern was found acceptable. Hippolytus, having provided the text of a prayer, commented: 'It is not at all necessary for [the bishop] to say the same words as we said above ... when giving thanks to God, but let each pray according to his ability ... Only, let his prayer be correct and orthodox.' (ibid., p. 24) Indeed, the lack of variety is quite unique. Cipriano Vagaggini, a noted Roman Catholic liturgist, commented some years ago: 'In the anaphora tradition of large liturgical groups, the Roman liturgy is almost alone in never having known the possibility of using simultaneously more than one anaphora.' (C. Vagaggini, *The Canon of the Mass and Liturgical Reform*, 1967, p. 122) There should be room, within a given pattern, for providing for various theological, spiritual and pastoral needs and insights. The fact that Rite A provides four Eucharistic Prayers (five if the Prayer Book order is included) and Rite B provides two is therefore neither unusual nor new-fangled.

At the same time, while recognizing the legitimacy and desir-

213

ability of variety, the fact remains that certain words, phrases and prayers, through constant use over the centuries, have strong roots in the devotional life of both Churches and individuals. They cannot be cast aside lightly: indeed, in many cases there is no reason why they should. There is much to be said for combining the old with the new. A good example of this may be seen at the very beginning of the Eucharistic Prayer, as the general structure is first examined.

The Structure of the Eucharistic Prayer

1 The Opening Dialogue and Sursum corda

The three versicles and responses at the beginning of the Eucharistic Prayer are found in the *Apostolic Tradition* of Hippolytus (215), the earliest (more or less) complete text of a Eucharistic Prayer so far discovered. They were also found in their entirety in the Roman Canon and in 1549. 1552 omitted the first versicle and response—'The Lord be with you/And with thy Spirit'—and 1662 followed suit. 1928 restored them, however, and they remained in Series 1, 2 and 3. They are a peculiarly Western form, Eastern rites preferring either 'Peace be with you' or the Grace from 2 Corinthians 13.14. But Professor van Unnik has argued cogently that, although many Churches use this salutation in a number of places in various rites, the beginning of the Eucharistic Prayer is its true home, and without it the whole prayer loses an important dimension: it contains a vital reference to the Holy Spirit, and 'a true Eucharist can only be celebrated where the Spirit of God is present'. (For a more detailed discussion, see pp. 34–5.)

ASB therefore provides two forms, and there is no case of preference: either can be used on any occasion. One is a paraphrase, indicating the presence of the Holy Spirit. The other is a more traditional and literal form, which, while not committing itself to the 'Holy Spirit' interpretation, is at least important in renewing the association of president and congregation at this vital point in the rite and in recognizing their unity in the action about to be undertaken.

The second versicle and response takes the congregation in heart and mind into the heavenly places—the true locus of Christian worship, as the New Testament frequently points out, e.g. Ephesians 2.6, Hebrews 4.14–16, 10.19–22. The Eucharist is both a meeting with the Lord who comes to us here on earth, and also

214

an ascending on our part to the heavenlies to meet him there. A further reminder of this heavenly context comes at the end of the Preface and the singing of the Sanctus with the company of heaven. The third versicle and response reaffirms that the essential element of the Eucharistic Prayer is praise and thanksgiving.

2 The Preface

The Preface recited the 'mighty acts' of God: that in the *Apostolic Tradition* of Hippolytus, for example, referred to creation, incarnation, passion, death and resurrection. But the way in which this has been expressed in different parts of the Church and at different times has varied. The Gallican rites produced a different preface for every mass. The Eastern rites, on the other hand, had no variable element; but each rite had its own invariable preface, some of them extremely long and detailed. In the Roman rite, the Leonine Sacramentary had a proper preface for each of its 267 masses, but with the passage of time these were considerably reduced to a mere eleven, a common preface being supplemented by a proper preface on specific occasions. Many of the prefaces of the Reformed rites were clearly influenced by the Eastern prefaces, which had become available in print during the sixteenth century.

In 1549 Cranmer used the first part of the Roman preface, but omitted the ferial preface and reduced the Proper Prefaces to five—Christmas, Easter, Ascension, Pentecost, and Trinity—a provision which 1552 and 1662 retained (see pp. 249–50). The result was a short and impoverished Common Preface, containing no reference to any of the 'mighty acts' for which thanks and praise were offered. 1928 attempted to remedy this by increasing the number of Proper Prefaces to eleven, including a Preface for use on Sundays which had no special provision. Series 1 further increased the Proper Prefaces to fourteen: and while Series 2 reduced them to four, the Common Preface itself was considerably enriched to include references to the mighty acts of creation, redemption and sanctification. Series 3 retained this extended Common Preface, but supplemented it with eleven Proper Prefaces; and Series 1 and 2 Revised similarly increased its preface material.

ASB has continued with the process of variety and enrichment. Eucharistic Prayers 1 and 2 have an identical Common Preface covering the mighty acts of creation, redemption and sanctification; Eucharistic Prayer 3 has a different Common Preface, similar to that of Hippolytus, and concentrating more fully on the work of Christ; while Eucharistic Prayer 4 has a much shorter Common Preface, similar to that of Series 1. In the case of Prayers 2 and 4 there is further special provision. In the former the Proper Preface may replace instead of supplement the Common Preface, if so desired; in the latter the Proper Preface must always replace the Common Preface—they may not be used together. In all four Prayers the Preface culminates in the Sanctus with the optional addition of the Benedictus.

3 The Sanctus and Benedictus

The early history of the Sanctus is obscure. Some scholars have argued for its existence as early as the late first century, while Professor Ratcliff claimed it to have been part of the rite in the *Apostolic Tradition* of Hippolytus: but the evidence is not conclusive. What is clear is its existence in the rites of Antioch, Jerusalem and Egypt by the fourth century and of Rome by the sixth century. In nearly all rites the Sanctus was accompanied by Hosanna in excelsis and Benedictus qui venit. In the rite of *Apostolic Constitutions*, Book 8, Benedictus was sung before communion as part of the people's response to *Sancta sanctis*, 'Holy things to holy people', and it was also repeated in this position in the Byzantine rite.

In the Roman rite the pattern was Sanctus–Hosanna–Benedictus–Hosanna—a pattern followed by Cranmer in 1549, although he substituted 'Glory to thee, O Lord, in the highest' for the second Hosanna. 1552 omitted the Benedictus and second Hosanna, while the first Hosanna became 'Glory be to thee, O Lord most high'—a form which was retained both in 1662 and 1928. Series 1 restored Benedictus and Hosanna to their traditional place after the Sanctus on an optional basis; but Series 2, possibly as a first stage towards subscribing to the Ratcliff theory that in Hippolytus the Sanctus etc. had come at the end of the Eucharistic Prayer, placed Benedictus and Hosanna at that point for optional use. Series 3, aware that opinion was divided on the use of Benedictus, placed it with Agnus Dei, leaving complete freedom as to where it should be used, if at all. ASB, however, has restored it to its traditional position after the Sanctus, although its use is still optional; and the rubric of section 47, permitting hymns or anthems during the distribution of the sacrament, clearly envisages its use by some people at that point also.

216

It should be emphasized that the Sanctus is a constituent element of the Eucharistic Prayer, just as the Sursum corda and the Preface are constituent elements. The practice of some congregations standing until the Sanctus is over and then kneeling for the rest of the prayer is to be discouraged. There is no precedent—certainly in Anglican liturgy—for suddenly changing posture in the middle of a prayer. It is not only illogical, but it destroys the unity of the second of the dominical acts. Whether the congregation stands or kneels, the same posture should be retained throughout the whole prayer.

The texts of Sanctus (from Isaiah 6.3) and Benedictus (from Mark 11.9–10) are those of ICET.

Line 1: The punctuation is a problem. In 1549 a comma was placed after the third 'holy', a practice continued in successive Prayer Books. Printed editions of the old *Missale Romanum* omitted the comma between Sanctus and Dominus; and this has now been followed. It is treated as an address to God, which is supported by the rendering of line 3.

Line 2: The translation of *Deus sabaoth* has also caused problems. Cranmer's rendering was 'God of hosts' in 1549, and this was retained until Series 3. 'Sabaoth' literally means 'heavenly hosts of Angels'; but the word 'hosts' is open to misunderstanding— particularly at this point in the rite. ICET has therefore used the phrase 'power and might', which fits with the Sanctus of Revelation 4.8: here 'Sabaoth' has become 'Pantocrator' ('the Almighty'); and it avoids any misconceptions.

Line 3: Hosanna in excelsis—this has followed the pattern in the Gloria in excelsis (see pp. 112–15). As in the traditional Roman text, the same refrain is used in both lines 3 and 5.

4 The Link between Sanctus and Invocation

In the past Sanctus and Benedictus have been linked to the rest of the Eucharistic Prayer in a variety of ways. Often 'tie-words' have been used. The rite in *Apostolic Constitutions*, Book 8, and that of St John Chrysostom, for example, used the word 'holy', taken up from the Sanctus: 'holy also is your only-begotten Son...' Sarapion, on the other hand, used 'fill' taken up from 'full of your glory': 'Full is heaven ... fill also this sacrifice'. The Roman rite had no such tie-word, but simply used 'therefore': 'We therefore pray and beseech you, most merciful Father ... to accept and bless these gifts'.

In 1549, however, any attempt to link Sanctus and Benedictus with the rest of the prayer was blocked by the intrusion of the Prayer for the Church; while in 1552/1662 it was blocked by the intrusion of the penitential material. 1928 returned to the principle of a tie-word by the use of 'glory', taken up from the 1662 response to the Sanctus: 'All glory be to thee, Almighty God...' It disappeared in Series 1; but Series 2 produced its own link, not by a tie-word, but by means of a petition in response to the Sanctus: 'Hear us, O Father, through Christ thy Son our Lord; through him accept our sacrifice of praise, and grant...' Series 3 followed the Series 2 pattern with a petition: 'Accept our praises, heavenly Father, and grant...'; while in Series 1 and 2 Revised, Prayer A followed 1928, and Prayer B followed Series 2. In ASB all four prayers employ links, but of different kinds. Prayer 1 uses the Series 3 'Accept our praises'; Prayer 2 the Series 2 'Hear us'; Prayer 3 the tie-word 'holy'; and Prayer 4 the 1928 'All glory to you'.

5 The Invocation or Epiclesis

In its broadest sense an epiclesis was an invocation of God, and was not necessarily confined to the Holy Spirit. But the Holy Spirit connection was evident at an early date. In the rite of Hippolytus, for example, there was an invocation of the Holy Spirit which followed the institution narrative: 'We ask that you would send your Holy Spirit upon the offering of your holy Church; that gathering them into one, you would grant to all who partake of the holy things [to partake] for the fullness of the Holy Spirit for the confirmation of faith in truth.' (PEER, p. 23) The text is a little doubtful; but it would appear to be essentially a prayer for a good communion, that the communicants might be filled with the Holy Spirit. There was no indication here of a 'consecratory epiclesis', with the Holy Spirit effecting a change upon the elements. With the passage of time, however, the Eastern liturgies came increasingly to regard this invocation of the Holy Spirit as the effective element of consecration. Cyril of Jerusalem in the late fourth century certainly regarded the epiclesis in this consecratory sense: 'We beseech God, the lover of man, to send forth the Holy Spirit upon [the gifts] set before him, that he may make the bread the body of Christ, and the wine the blood of Christ; for everything that the Holy Spirit has touched, has been sanctified and changed.' (PEER, p. 53) The epiclesis, following the institution narrative, and bearing this consecratory significance, became a feature of Eastern liturgies: while Egyptian rites, as in the Liturgy of St Mark, had two invocations, one before and one after the institution narrative.

In the West, however, with the possible exception of the Mozarabic rites, the story is rather different, mainly because consecration came to be linked with the institution narrative. The old Roman rite had no explicit epiclesis, although it could be that the vestiges of one remained in the petition before the institution narrative asking that God might bless the oblation 'that it may be unto us the body and blood of your dearly beloved Son Jesus Christ'. Some scholars have also argued that the relics of an epiclesis also existed in the *Supra quae* and *supplices te* clauses after the institution narrative, though there is no general agreement on this point. In 1549 Cranmer took over the petition before the institution narrative from the Roman rite, but prefaced it with an invocation from the Eastern rite of St Basil: 'Hear us, O merciful Father: and with thy Holy Spirit and word...' If 'word' is correctly equated with the institution narrative, Cranmer could be said to have combined both Eastern and Western emphases in a novel and effective manner. In 1552, in the face of Bucer's criticisms, these phrases largely disappeared, being replaced by a simple prayer for a good communion: 'Hear us, O merciful Father, and grant that we, receiving these thy creatures of bread and wine..., may be partakers of his most blessed body and blood.' Despite a return to the 1549 form in the Scottish 1637 rite, 1662 remained loyal at this point to 1552. 1928, in a well-meaning but misguided attempt to produce a Eucharistic Prayer on primitive and Trinitarian lines, introduced an epiclesis after the institution narrative, by transferring the 1552–1662 'Hear us' petition and adding to it 'and with thy Holy and Life-giving Spirit vouchsafe to bless and sanctify both us and these thy gifts of Bread and Wine that they may be unto us the Body and Blood of thy Son...' As is well known, it raised a storm of protest from both Anglo-Catholics and Evangelicals and was one of the factors contributing to the defeat of the 1928 Book as a whole. The fact that other Reformers had supported the idea of an epiclesis—notably the Westminster Directory and Richard Baxter—counted for little or nothing; and when liturgical revision began again in this country in the 1960s, despite the evident willingness of other churches both inside and outside the Anglican Communion to use epicleses of varying kinds, revisers moved with extreme caution. In Series 1, therefore, the 1928 Eucharistic Prayer was replaced by that of the interim rite, which contained nothing more than the 1552/1662 prayer for a good communion; while Series 2's advance on this was minimal: 'Hear us, O Father, through Christ thy Son our Lord . . . and grant that these gifts of bread and wine may be unto us his Body and Blood.' What undoubtedly helped to produce a new attitude towards the epiclesis was the publication of the Anglican–Roman Catholic Agreed Statement on Eucharistic Doctrine on 31 December 1971. Paragraph 10 stated: 'Through this prayer of thanksgiving, a word of faith addressed to the Father, the bread and wine become the body and blood of Christ by the action of the Holy Spirit, so that in communion we eat the flesh of Christ and drink his blood.' (*Modern Eucharistic Agreement*, 1973, p. 29) In Series 3, therefore, the appearance of an epiclesis upon the elements before the institution narrative and an epiclesis upon the communicants after it was accepted without demur. The former prayed God 'that by the power of your Holy Spirit these gifts of bread and wine may be to us his body and his blood'; while the latter prayed that 'as we eat and drink these holy gifts in the presence of your divine majesty, renew us by your Spirit'.

In the four prayers of Rite A this pattern is largely followed. In Prayers 1, 2 and 3 there is still the double epiclesis, one before and one after the institution narrative, and in Prayer 1 the language is identical with that of Series 3. Prayer 4 is more conservative, with only one epiclesis which comes before the institution narrative: 'Grant that by the power of your Holy Spirit, we who receive these gifts of your creation, this bread and this wine . . . may be partakers of his most blessed body and blood.'

6 The Institution Narrative

The institution narrative fulfils two functions:

1 It indicates our Lord's warrant for what is done.
2 It is part of our memorial of and thanksgiving for his redeeming work.

It has been used in eucharistic rites since the earliest days of the Church; and although one rite—the third-century Syrian rite of Addai and Mari—lacked the narrative, its absence is a matter of dispute among scholars and should not be regarded as establishing a precedent (cf. R. C. D. Jasper, *The Eucharist Today*, 1974, pp. 108, 126). The wording of the narrative varies considerably from liturgy to liturgy, and even in early rites never conformed exactly to the words of Scripture. Professor Jungmann has suggested that its origin lay in pre-biblical tradition, and that it had three phases of development. First, the two sections on bread and wine were fashioned to gain symmetry and could be quite simple. Some idea of this can be seen in the text of Hippolytus: 'He took bread and gave thanks to you, saying, "Take, eat; this is my body, which shall be broken for you". Likewise also the cup, saying, "This is my blood, which is shed for you; when you do this, you make my remembrance."' (*PEER*, p. 22) Secondly, more serious note was taken of the biblical accounts, and words and phrases from Scripture began to be incorporated into the texts. Finally words and phrases from outside Scripture were added, either to fit local customs of etiquette or worship, or to introduce or emphasize certain theological ideas (cf. J. A. Jungmann, *The Mass of the Roman Rite* (1 vol. edn), 1959, pp. 418–19). The text of the traditional Roman rite is worth quoting as an illustration:

> Who, on the day before he suffered, took bread in his holy and reverend hands, lifted up his eyes to you, his almighty God and Father, gave thanks to you, blessed, broke, and gave it to his disciples, saying 'Take and eat from this, all of you; for this is my body.' Likewise after supper, taking also this glorious cup in his holy and reverend hands, again he gave thanks to you, blessed, and gave it to his disciples, saying 'Take and drink from it, all of you; for this is the cup of my blood, of the new and eternal covenant, the mystery of faith, which will be shed for you and for many for forgiveness of sins. As often as you do this, you will do it for my remembrance.' (*PEER*, p. 107)

In 1549 Cranmer produced a much briefer and simpler narrative which rejected all non-scriptural material and was in fact a conflation of the New Testament accounts. But it was still part of a prayer addressed to the Father and not merely a narrative. This text, with the exception of one or two small changes noted here, has remained the form of the narrative in successive Prayer Books and subsequent revisions including Series 2.

1　In 1549 Cranmer introduced the bread by 'when he had blessed and given thanks'. In 1552, 'blessed' was omitted: the advanced Reformers disliked it, preferring to regard it as a synonym for 'given thanks'.

2　In 1662, 'the' was added before 'remission of sins'.

3　In 1928 'Covenant' replaced 'Testament'.

4 In Series 2 'to thee' was added after 'when he had given thanks', thus emphasizing that the narrative was still part of the prayer.

The form in Series 3 was not radically different from that in Series 2, although it used more contemporary language. The most important changes were:

1 'For' replaced 'who' at the beginning as a more logical link with what had gone before;
2 'Drink this, all of you' replaced 'Drink ye all of this', indicating that 'all' referred to the people and not to the contents of the cup; and
3 'forgiveness' replaced 'remission'.

In 1549 Cranmer also considerably simplified the manual acts accompanying the narrative: the priest was merely directed to take the bread and the cup into his hands at the appropriate points. This was omitted in 1552; but they returned in greater detail in 1662 in a form suggested by the Scottish Prayer Book of 1637 and in response to the demands of both Puritans and High Churchmen for a more 'explicit' consecration. There were now five manual acts: taking the bread and the cup into the hands, laying the hand on both bread and cup, and breaking the bread (cf. p. 170). These manual acts not only reproduced the actions as well as the words of our Lord; they also indicated the elements which were being mentioned—something effected in medieval rites by the sign of the cross. A fraction at this point was unusual. It was found in only two Eastern rites, the Coptic and the Abyssinian (Brightman, *LEW*, pp. 177, 233). Some medieval missals did instruct the priest to make 'a show of breaking' the bread at this point, but the Sarum Missal merely instructed him to touch the host. The elevation of the elements, although retained by Luther, was specifically forbidden by rubric in 1549 and has never returned. The five manual acts remained in 1928 and Series 1; but Series 2 reduced them to the two acts of 1549, while Series 3 removed them altogether and they have not been reintroduced in ASB. Note 16 (p. 117) does permit the use of manual acts (unspecified) with the institution narrative; but this is not to be regarded as a return to the concept of using the narrative as a consecration formula, but simply as a permission for those who wish to follow both the words and the actions of our Lord to do so.

The narrative in all four Eucharistic Prayers of Rite A is identical and is substantially that of Series 3, but with three modifications:

1 'Who' reappears instead of 'for' as the link with the preceding material, simply because it makes more sense. The preceding material is not the same in all four prayers.
2 The 'four action' shape is emphasized by a careful rephrasing:
   '(He) *took* (1) bread and *gave you thanks* (2);
   he *broke* (3) it and *gave* (4) it to his disciples,'
3 A parallel rephrasing is provided for the cup, introduced by 'In the same way' instead of 'again':
   'He *took* (1) the cup and *gave you thanks* (2);
   he *gave* (3) it to them, saying,'.

7 The Acclamations

The institution narrative is followed by three congregational acclamations, focusing attention on our Lord's death, resurrection and second coming. Eastern rites have been familiar with such acclamations for many centuries, using them both after the narrative and after the anamnesis. The most traditional form, found in the Palestinian and Egyptian liturgies, is:

> Dying you destroyed our death,
> Rising you restored our life,
> Lord Jesus, come in glory.

The CSI rite understandably pioneered the use of such acclamations in modern liturgies, dividing a long Syrian acclamation into two, and placing the first half after the institution narrative and the second half after the anamnesis. This enabled the congregation to be further associated with the Eucharistic Prayer, over and above their participation in the Sursum corda and the Preface, and it enabled them to recall our Lord's redemptive activity as it is experienced in the Eucharist. Other Churches followed the CSI example. Rome provided a choice of four acclamations, introduced by the bidding, 'Let us proclaim the mystery of faith'. This bidding had been part of the institution narrative in the traditional Roman rite, referring to the chalice—an ancient, but nevertheless inexplicable insertion. Professor Jungmann had said of it, 'How, or when, or why this insertion was made, or what external event occasioned it, cannot readily be ascertained.' (Jungmann, op. cit., p. 422) A desire was expressed in Rome in 1967 for its removal from the narrative, but Pope Paul VI urged its retention. In the event, it was retained in the revised Roman rite, but as an introduction to the acclamations. The meaning of the phrase therefore changes: the 'mystery of faith' was no longer simply the chalice, but the whole of our Lord's redemptive activity in the Eucharist. Logic demands that such acclamations would come better after the anamnesis; and there is Eastern precedent for such a position. But the tendency in all modern liturgies is to place them after the institution narrative, and Rite A has followed suit. It is to be regretted, however, that Rite A provides no choice, as in the Roman rite, particularly as the chosen form is the baldest of those available, without any specific mention of the congregation itself. Note 15 (p. 117) makes it clear that the acclamations are optional and may be introduced by a bidding, such as the Roman form.

8 The Anamnesis

The anamnesis indicates the way in which the command 'Do this in remembrance of me' is fulfilled. Different liturgies have expressed this in different ways over the centuries, but the general pattern is similar. It has usually followed the line, 'We remember Christ's saving work, and so we undertake some particular action'. Hippolytus expressed it simply and briefly, 'Remembering therefore his death and resurrection, we offer to you the bread and the cup'. What that action should be has often been a matter of controversy, involving as it does the doctrine of the eucharistic sacrifice, and by no means everyone would accept the Hippolytan formula 'We offer the bread and the cup' (see p. 172). First of all, however, the meaning of 'remember' should be examined.

It is important to consider this in the light of Jewish ideas of 'remembrance'—particularly with reference to the Passover; although such ideas are not limited to the Passover (L. Bouyer, *Eucharist*, Engl. tr., Notre Dame USA, 1968, pp. 103–5). Scholars are not fully agreed that the Last Supper was a Passover meal; but at least the Supper was held in a Passover context. In the Passover, remembering involved the commemoration of God's deliverance of the children of Israel from bondage in Egypt; but it also recognized that that deliverance applied to those who celebrated the Passover year by year. The implications of this were well expressed by the Anglican–Roman Catholic Agreed Statement on Eucharistic Doctrine:

The notion of *memorial* as understood in the passover celebration at the time of Christ—i.e. the making effective in the present of an event in the past—has opened the way to a clearer understanding of the relationship between Christ's sacrifice and the eucharist. The eucharistic memorial is no mere calling to mind of a past event or of its significance, but the Church's effectual proclamation of God's mighty acts ... In the eucharistic prayer the Church continues to make a perpetual memorial of Christ's death, and his members, united with God and one another, give thanks for all his mercies, entreat the benefits of his passion on behalf of the whole Church, participate in these benefits and enter into the movement of his self-offering (*Modern Eucharistic Agreement*, pp. 27–8).

There is, however, another dimension to 'remembrance' in the Passover which must not be forgotten. The Passover included four cups of wine, each one attached to a particular Old Testament text—Jeremiah 25.15; 51.7; Psalm 75.8; 11.6—and all of these spoke of God's judgement over evil and the final deliverance of his children. 'Remembrance' in the Passover therefore not only involved past and present, it also looked forward into the future. This also applies to 'in remembrance of me' in the Eucharist: it anticipates the final parousia and is a foretaste of the heavenly banquet. Anamnesis in these dynamic senses involves much more than the English word 'remember'. Indeed it has no single English equivalent, and can be expressed in a variety of ways. Note, for example, the Liturgy of St Mark, which said, 'We *proclaim* the death, we *confess* the resurrection, ascension, and heavenly session, we *look for* the second coming'. Another example appears in the first Eucharistic Prayer of Rite A, where the verb 'celebrate' is used. An extensive study of the verb has produced the following conclusion: 'It can mean no more than "to do" or "to perform" in a liturgical context; on the other hand, it can carry all the meaning which is conveyed by the expression "to make the anamnesis of", depending upon the contexts in which it is used' (P. Bradshaw, in *The Eucharist Today*, p. 139). Professor Jeremias has also pointed out that 'in remembrance of me' is not related simply to human activity. It can also mean 'that God may remember me'. God, remembering his mercies in Jesus Christ, may bestow the fruits of Christ's redeeming work on his people and bring about the consummation of the Kingdom (J. Jeremias, *The Eucharistic Words of Jesus*, 1966, pp. 237–55; cf. M. Thurian, *The Eucharistic Memorial*, pt II, 1961, pp. 40–2).

The way in which the 'doing' has, however, presented problems. The solution of Hippolytus has already been indicated— 'Remembering his death and resurrection, we offer the bread and the cup'. This combination of 'remember—offer' has been followed by many liturgies, both Eastern and Western. This is precisely what the unrevised Roman rite did: 'having in remembrance the blessed passion ... his resurrection ... and also his glorious ascension ... we offer to your excellent majesty from your gifts a pure victim ... the holy bread of eternal life and the cup of everlasting salvation'. In 1549 Cranmer produced a more ambiguous form: 'We do celebrate and make here before thy Divine Majesty with these thy holy gifts, the memorial ...; having in remembrance his ... passion ... resurrection and ... ascension ... accept this our sacrifice of praise and thanksgiving'. But in 1552 the approach was much more drastic: nothing was said after the institution narrative; communicants proceeded immediately to 'eat and drink', and the expanded words of administration made it clear that this was what was being done 'in remembrance'. 1662 produced no further solution, while 1928 simply reverted to 1549. For many people, however, any 'Godward' action of offering is thought to be unacceptable. When Series 2 in its original form therefore sought to follow Hippolytus by 'offering the bread and the cup', it was rejected, and a compromise was found with 'we make with this bread and this cup the memorial of Christ your Son our Lord. Accept through him this offering of our duty and service'. It was intended as a temporary solution on 1549 lines; instead it has proved to be surprisingly durable and is embodied in the second Eucharistic Prayer of Rite A. The first Eucharistic Prayer, as has already been indicated, based its solution on the use of the verb 'celebrate': 'We remember (his death) ... proclaim his resurrection and ascension ... look for his coming in glory [and] we celebrate with this bread and this cup his one perfect sacrifice. Accept through him ... this our sacrifice of thanks and praise'. The third prayer, although owing much to Hippolytus, nevertheless avoided the contentious phrase: 'Calling to mind his death ... rejoicing at his resurrection and ascension, and looking for his coming in glory, we celebrate this memorial of our redemption ... Accept this our duty and service'. The fourth prayer used traditional Prayer Book phrases: 'In remembrance of the death ... resurrection ... and ascension, we offer you through him this sacrifice of praise and thanksgiving ... Although we are unworthy to offer you any sacrifice, yet we pray that you will accept . . . the duty and service that we owe'.

9 Fruitful Reception

After the anamnesis came the prayer for the benefits of communion, introduced by some form of epiclesis, either upon the
elements, or upon the communicants, or both. Hippolytus, for
example, prayed that the Holy Spirit might be sent upon the
communicants that they might be gathered into one and their faith
confirmed. The rite in *Apostolic Constitutions*, Book 8, had an
epiclesis upon both elements and communicants, followed by a
prayer that the latter might be strengthened, and then by wide-
ranging intercessions. Cyril of Jerusalem commented that this was
the appropriate place to make intercession for all kinds of people
and for the departed, and to pray for the peace of the churches and
the stability of the world. Much later the Roman rite prayed for
the communicants, that they might be filled with all heavenly
blessing and grace and admitted to the company of the saints, and
then went on to pray for the departed.

In 1549 Cranmer, who had already placed the prayer for the
Church at the beginning of the Eucharistic Prayer, followed his
anamnesis by petitions for the communicants and for the whole
Church; and for all he asked for forgiveness of sins and all other
benefits of Christ's passion, for worthy reception, grace, and
being made one body with Christ. 1552 had no intercessions, but
if the eucharistic action is considered to continue after communion, the prayer of oblation and the prayer of thanksgiving can
be said to continue a list of petitions identical with those of 1549.
In this respect the same may be said of 1662; while 1928 and Series 1
followed 1549, including them all after the anamnesis. By contrast
Series 2 was very brief, merely praying that the communicants
might be 'filled with thy grace and heavenly blessing'. Series 3 was
also brief but far richer in content, reiterating the petitions of
Hippolytus and including the concept of unity: 'renew us by your
Spirit, inspire us with your love, and unite us in the body of your
Son'. This form was repeated verbatim in the first Eucharistic
Prayer of Rite A. Prayers 2 and 3 continue to pray for the
communicants and for their unity, but express it in different ways:
the former prays that they may grow into the likeness of Christ
and become a living temple to God's glory; the latter prays that
they may be joined with the company of the saints and engaged in
everlasting praise. Prayer 4 maintains the 1928/Series 1 pattern.

10 The Doxology and Amen

A Trinitarian doxology was the normal conclusion to most eucharistic prayers, summarizing the movement of the eucharistic action. The people stand with Christ and 'in Christ', and through him are brought by the power of the Holy Spirit to the Father. The local church is at one with the whole Church, both in earth and heaven. The doxology therefore reiterates the theme of both Sursum corda and Sanctus. The doxology of the Roman rite was taken over by Cranmer in 1549, only 'in whom' being omitted. This has been used consistently ever since down to Series 3. Even in 1552 and 1662, when the prayer ended at the institution narrative, the doxology was still used at the end of the Prayer of Oblation. Series 3, however, broke new ground. Its doxology began in the usual way: the congregation are with and in Christ; and through him are brought by the Spirit to the Father. But it then went on to associate the congregation 'with all who stand before you in earth and heaven'. The phrase 'to stand before you and minister or worship' occurred at the end of the Eucharistic Prayer in Hippolytus and is clearly rooted in Scripture (Deuteronomy 10.8; 18.5; 18.7; Daniel 7.10), where it indicated not only the worship of earth but also the worship of heaven. It contributed to Professor Ratcliff's theory that the Hippolytan prayer ended with the Sanctus, combining the worship of earth and heaven ('The Sanctus and the Early Pattern of the Anaphora', *JEH*, vol. i, nos 1 and 2, 1950). Series 3 therefore concluded its doxology with a further congregational acclamation based on Revelation 5.13, thereby bringing the congregation once again into active association with the president, and guaranteeing a convincing 'Amen'. This doxology and acclamation were used at the end of Prayer 1 in Rite A. Prayers 2 and 3 also made use of the phrase 'stand and minister' although they included no acclamation: Prayer 2 used the phrase in the penultimate line of the doxology, while Prayer 3 made use of it immediately after the anamnesis. The doxology of Prayer 4 is the traditional form, substantially that of 1549/1928 with the addition of 'in whom'. The Amen is the final assurance that the congregation is identified with the president in the prayer just offered. It should be said with conviction and not resemble a subdued moan. In the Middle Ages, when most of the prayer was recited silently, the priest raised his voice just before the end, so that the people might know when to say Amen.

Note 16 (p. 117) permits the use of traditional manual acts

during the Eucharistic Prayer: and this presumably allows for an elevation of the bread and the cup at the end of the prayer. It is a practice of long standing, occurs in most Eastern rites, and is found in *Ordo Romanus Primus* in the West.

The Eucharistic Prayers: Origins and Sources
First Eucharistic Prayer

The first prayer is a direct development of the Series 3 prayer, first published in draft form in June 1971, and this in its turn was developed from Series 2. The 1971 Report stated:

> It is clear from the use which has been made of *Holy Communion: Series 2* both at home and abroad during the past four years that the rite has served a useful purpose. It has been a valuable means of experiment at home, while its influence on the new rites of other Churches has been far from negligible. Nevertheless, it was never intended to be a finished product; and experience has revealed its limitations. We believed that it was simply a step in the right direction. That belief has been justified: for we have been able to build Series 3 on the foundations of Series 2; and although there are all kinds of changes in language and detail, we have found no solid reason to make any serious departure from the structure of our original rite. (Foreword, *Report of the Liturgical Commission on Series 3*, June 1971)

Since its authorization in 1973, it was first revised by the Liturgical Commission in 1977–8 and then by the Revision Committee of the General Synod in 1978–9. Prayer 1 is still substantially the original prayer of Series 3. Its distinguishing features are:

1 Its reference to the atonement: 'the offering of himself made once for all upon the cross'.

2 Its variety of verbs in the anamnesis: 'we remember—we proclaim—we look for', culminating in 'we celebrate with this bread and this cup his one perfect sacrifice'.

3 The use of active verbs in the petition for a fruitful communion: 'renew—inspire—unite'.

4 The inclusion of a congregational acclamation at the end of the doxology.

Second Eucharistic Prayer

The second prayer is the direct descendant of the Series 2 prayer, which was the Liturgical Commission's first essay in eucharistic liturgical construction. It owes much to the CSI rite and to the popularity of Hippolytus among liturgists, and marked the first break in the Church of England with the idea of a Eucharistic Prayer centred exclusively on the Cross. As has already been noted, its original attempt to use the Hippolytan phrase 'we offer this bread and this cup' was rejected in favour of a phrase more in keeping with 1549. Since its original Series 2 form, an epiclesis on the elements before the institution narrative has been added, while a more detailed petition for a fruitful communion has been included. Slightly shorter than the first prayer, it can be further abbreviated on special occasions by the use only of the Proper Preface and the omission of the General Preface. This also has the effect of a greater concentration on the special occasion itself. Its distinguishing features are:

1 Its reference to the atonement: 'his death once for all upon the cross'.

2 The anamnesis controlled by 'in remembrance—and looking for', culminating in 'we make with this bread and this cup the memorial of Christ your Son our Lord'.

3 The use of the concept 'become a living temple to your glory' in the petition for a fruitful communion.

4 The inclusion of the Hippolytan phrase 'all who stand before you' in the doxology.

Third Eucharistic Prayer

The third prayer owes much to the initiative of the Rev. R. T. Beckwith and the Rev. B. D. F. T. Brindley, although the draft was subsequently worked over by the Revision Committee of the General Synod and by the General Synod itself. Its primary source is Hippolytus together with the second canon in the revised Roman rite, which is also based on Hippolytus. It is distinctive and has less of the recognizable Anglican pattern of the other three Eucharistic Prayers. Its most notable features are:

1 The use of the tie-word 'Holy' to link the Sanctus/Benedictus with the rest of the prayer.

2 Its reference to the atonement: 'This perfect sacrifice made once for the sins of all men'.

3 The choice of verbs in the anamnesis: 'calling to mind—rejoicing—looking for', culminating in 'we celebrate the memorial of our redemption'.

4   The use of the Hippolytan phrase 'to stand in your presence and serve you', although its link with the worship of heaven is less well defined.

Fourth Eucharistic Prayer

The fourth prayer is based on the Series 1 prayers and should be compared with the second Thanksgiving of Rite B. Since Series 1 a reference to God's work in creation has been added to the Preface, and an epiclesis has been included before the institution narrative. Because of its origin this prayer is more 'cross-orientated' than its three companions. As far as possible the traditional forms from 1662 have been retained. Its distinguishing features are:

1   The epiclesis before the institution narrative.

2   The use of the single verb in the anamnesis: 'in remembrance', culminating in 'we offer you through him this sacrifice of praise and thanksgiving'.

3   The absence of any reference in the anamnesis to the second coming, although it is referred to early in the prayer before the epiclesis: 'until he comes again'.

THE COMMUNION
THE BREAKING OF THE BREAD AND THE GIVING OF THE BREAD AND CUP

This is the second part of the sacramental action, involving the third and the fourth of our Lord's acts.

The Lord's Prayer
(section 42)

The early history of the Lord's Prayer as a devotion before communion is obscure. There is no reference to it in Hippolytus and in the rite of *Apostolic Constitutions*, Book 8, and it is not until the late fourth century that there is clear evidence for its existence—from St Chrysostom, St Cyril of Jerusalem, and St Ambrose. Nor was there in early centuries any uniformity of position. Early Western custom—the Ambrosian, Mozarabic, African and Roman rites—clearly favoured a position between the fraction and communion. Eastern custom, however, favoured a position between the Eucharistic Prayer and the fraction. Gregory the Great (590–604) is now regarded as being responsible for changing its position in the Roman rite to conform to Eastern practice—since when this has been the normal position in the West. Despite its close proximity to the Eucharistic Prayer, it should not be regarded as part of that prayer. It is still clearly a communion devotion. By the Middle Ages the Roman rite had also acquired an introduction and a conclusion to the Lord's Prayer. The former, said by the priest, ran, 'Instructed by thy saving precepts, and following thy divine institution, we are bold to say'. The latter, in common with non-Byzantine Eastern rites, was an additional prayer for forgiveness, based on the final petition, 'Deliver us from evil', and known as the Embolism. The pattern was for the priest to say 'Our Father . . . into temptation'; the people or choir responded, 'but deliver us from evil'; and the priest then resumed, 'Deliver us, we beseech thee, O Lord, from all evils . . .'

In 1549 Cranmer retained the Lord's Prayer immediately after the Eucharistic Prayer, together with a simplified form of the Roman introduction, 'As our saviour Christ hath commanded and taught us, we are bold to say'. He also retained the requirement that it should be said by the priest, with the congregation responding, 'But deliver us from evil'; but there was no Embolism. 1552 and 1662 saw a complete change. The introduction was omitted; and it became a congregational prayer, complete with doxology, immediately after the act of communion, becoming in effect a prayer of thanksgiving. Its manner of recitation was also rather odd: the priest was to say the prayer, 'the people repeating after him every petition'. 1928, however, restored the prayer to its 1549 position, complete with 1549 introduction, and retaining it as a congregational prayer; while Series 1 permitted its use either in the 1549 position with introduction, or 1662 position without introduction. Series 2 made a significant change, returning to the primitive Western position after the fraction, and retaining the 1549 introduction, but omitting the doxology. Series 3 kept the same position, but restored the doxology and provided a simpler, briefer introduction. Criticism had been expressed of the continued use of the phrase, 'We are bold to say'; and it must be admitted that it is not the ideal translation of *audemus dicere*; nor is it true to say that our Lord had 'commanded' us to say the prayer at this point. These criticisms were met by the new form, 'As our Saviour has taught us, so we pray'.

It is now evident that, although modern liturgies are divided over the position of the Lord's Prayer, the great majority favour a pre-fraction position. Rite A has therefore reverted to this position, at the same time retaining the Series 3 introduction and the doxology. By placing it beneath the heading 'The Communion', the Rite also makes it perfectly clear that it is a communion devotion, and not a part of the Eucharistic Prayer. The rubric permits the prayer to be said in either its traditional or modern form.

Finally, a comment is needed on the difficult line 9. Series 3 had used a slightly modified form of the ICET text—'Do not bring us to the time of trial'. Despite the fact that this was a perfectly sound translation of the Greek in St Matthew's Gospel, it had by no means met with general acceptance. In the interests of ecumenicity and almost universal usage, therefore, the General Synod agreed to revert to the traditional form 'Lead us not into temptation'. For further information, see pp. 30–2.

The Fraction
(section 43)

The fraction can be viewed in four different ways:

1 It is simply a utilitarian action—bread must be broken in pieces in order that it may be given to the communicants.

2 It is an imitation of what Jesus did at the Last Supper; and this is how 1662 seems to view it.

3 It is a symbolic representation of our Lord's body being broken on the cross. But was our Lord's body broken? Cf. John 19.36.

4 It is a symbolic sharing of the one Bread among the many of the one Body—1 Corinthians 10.17. St Augustine (354–430) was an early exponent of this. In Sermon 272, commenting on 1 Corinthians 10.17 he said: ' "We being many are one bread, one body". Understand and rejoice; unity, truth, piety, charity . . . (Christ) willed that we should belong to Him, and consecrated the mystery of our peace and of our unity on His table.'

Early liturgies say little about the fraction, apparently regarding it as a utilitarian action. The main task was to divide the loaves into pieces for distribution. Even when wafers began to be used the fraction remained. In the Rome, however, certain ceremonies had developed around the fraction which had theological significance. First, there was the commixture, in which a piece of the consecrated host was placed in the consecrated wine. Theodore of Mopsuestia had already pointed out some centuries before that just as our Lord's death was represented in the Eucharist, so his resurrection was represented by reuniting the sacramental Body and Blood. Secondly, there was the fermentum: a portion of the bread consecrated at the bishop's mass was sent to outlying parishes, where it could be added to their chalice as a symbol of their unity under the bishop. Thirdly, there was the sancta: a portion of the consecrated bread was reserved and placed in the chalice at the ensuing mass as a symbol of unity in time.

Cranmer retained none of these ceremonies in 1549, nor did he refer to the fraction in the rite itself: but in the final rubrics he specified wafers: 'unleavened, and round, as it was afore, but without all manner of print, and something more larger and thicker than it was...; and every one shall be divided in two pieces, at the least, or more'. 1552 likewise had no reference to the fraction, and specified that 'the bread be such as is usual to be eaten at the Table with other meats, but the best and purest wheat bread, that conveniently may be gotten'. 1662 retained this, but added a fraction at the recital of the institution narrative—an arrangement which continued in 1928. Series 1, however, permitted a further fraction—and this was clearly a utilitarian fraction—between the Lord's Prayer and the communion.

New ground was again broken in Series 2. The fraction was removed from the institution narrative and placed immediately after the Eucharistic Prayer under a new heading 'The Breaking of the Bread'. It was also accompanied by the whole of 1 Corinthians 10.16–17, referring both to the bread and the cup of blessing, and by the Agnus Dei, described by the rubric as an anthem to accompany the fraction. For the first time in an Anglican rite, therefore, the fraction was clearly set out in its own right as the third of the eucharistic actions. The position of the text and the accompanying words indicated that the fraction now fulfilled two purposes—a necessary breaking of the bread for distribution, and a symbol of the unity of the Church in Christ. Series 3 retained this new arrangement with one small change: the reference to the cup, which is irrelevant at this point, was omitted. Rite A has made only one further change and that has already been indicated: the fraction no longer precedes the Lord's Prayer, but follows it.

The Agnus Dei
(section 44)

The Agnus Dei, familiar from Isaiah 53.7, John 1.29 and Revelation 5.6f., and derived from the Gloria in excelsis, was of Eastern origin, probably in Syria, where the Lamb of God was the focus of special devotion, being used to designate both Christ and the bread of the Eucharist. In the Liturgy of St James (fifth century) it was a formula to be said by the priest after the fraction. According to the *Liber Pontificalis*, it was introduced into the Roman rite by Pope Sergius I (687–701), himself a Syrian, to be sung by the choir and the people after the Peace, while the bread was broken. For several centuries the single line was repeated as often as was necessary; but with the diminution of communion and the introduction of unleavened bread, the repetitions were reduced to three—probably by the tenth century. With the close proximity of the Peace, the third response also changed to 'Grant us your Peace'. It therefore became an anthem, often sung to elaborate music, extending not only through the Communion of the priest, but also through the Communion of the people as well.

The Agnus Dei was found in Luther, Hermann and various German Church Orders, and it is not surprising that Cranmer retained it in 1549 as a communion anthem. 1552 omitted it, however, and it did not appear again until Series 1, where it was used as an optional communion anthem. Both Series 2 and Series 1 and 2 Revised used it as an optional anthem during the fraction, but Series 3 reverted to its use during Communion. Rite A permits its use either during the fraction or during Communion.

ASB provides two versions of the anthem, both of which are ICET texts. The first is a traditional form; but the second, the work of Dr J. G. Cuming, is a freer version. There is some precedent for introducing each line by 'Jesus', for some of the German Reformed versions of the anthem prefixed each line with 'Christ'. In fact the name rather than the title is used as the focal point. Lines 2 and 3 provide free renderings of the Latin *qui tollis peccata mundi*. The verb *tollis* can be interpreted 'bear' or 'take away', so the use of 'bearer' and 'redeemer' give the dual meaning.

In line 3 'your peace' provides a link with John 14.27: 'My peace I give to you'.

The Distribution
(sections 45–7)

This is the fourth of the dominical acts.

The posture for Communion in the early Church was standing—a posture the Eastern Churches have always maintained. Various reasons were given for this: it was a sign that the communicants were God's children, not his slaves; it was also a sign of being raised by Jesus Christ; and it conformed to the Passover requirement to eat with haste and be ready to do the Lord's business. Even where rails existed, they were apparently of a height to require standing reception. But later practices varied. In the Roman *ordines* communicants remained in their places and ministers brought them the sacrament. Elsewhere—in Gaul and in Africa—communicants approached the altar. Kneeling to receive Communion only gradually became the norm in the West between the eleventh and the sixteenth centuries. It was also the practice in the early Church for communicants to receive in both kinds, and to receive the bread in their hands. The instruction of Cyril of Jerusalem is well-known: 'When you approach . . . make your left hand a throne for the right, since it is to receive a king' (*PEER*, p. 54). But changes in eucharistic piety and the risk of purloining the consecrated bread for profane or superstitious use gradually resulted in changes of methods of distribution. In the East and in some parts of the West intinction came to be used with the aid of a spoon. In Rome, from the ninth century onwards, wafers gradually replaced bread and were placed directly into people's mouths, while the chalice was no longer given to the laity. Throughout it was the general practice for the presiding minister, be he Pope, bishop, or priest, to communicate first, being followed by the other ministers and then the laity.

Early forms of words to accompany distribution were simple. Hippolytus provided the form for the bread only—'The bread of heaven in Christ Jesus'—to which the communicant responded 'Amen'. The form was even briefer in *Apostolic Constitutions*, Book 8—'The body of Christ. Amen' and 'The blood of Christ, the cup of life. Amen'. Liturgies in the East tended to expand these forms by adding reverential epithets. The Liturgy of St Mark, for example, used, 'The holy body/The precious blood of our Lord and God and Saviour Jesus Christ'; while the Byzantine rite added to the end of the St Mark formula 'unto remission of sins and unto everlasting life'. In Rome the various sacramentaries and *Ordo Romanus Primus* are silent on the early medieval forms, and the only evidence in the York and Sarum Missals is the formula used when communicating the sick. This took the form of a prayer or blessing: 'The body of our Lord Jesus Christ keep your body and soul in eternal life'.

It is therefore interesting to note Cranmer's arrangements in *The Order of the Communion* in 1548. Communion was given in both kinds and communicants were bidden to kneel, but nothing was said about the manner of receiving the bread. The words of distribution were particularly interesting, being substantially the Sarum form just given but with two modifications: (1) the phrase 'which was given/shed for thee' was added—words which clearly came from Hermann, Luther, and various German Church Orders; and (2) the body of Christ preserved the communicant's body, while the blood of Christ preserved the communicant's soul. (On this point see the discussion on the Prayer of Humble Access, pp. 203–5.) Changes were now made in almost every successive rite, and these are noted briefly seriatim:

1549

The direction to kneel was omitted; the 1548 words were retained, but 'body and soul' were included for both bread and cup; and the bread was to be delivered into people's mouths, because 'they many times conveyed the same secretly away, and diversely abused it to superstition'.

1552

Some of the continental Reformers who came to England as refugees began the practice of sitting for Communion. In reaction 1552 required communicants to kneel, both to show humble and grateful acknowledgement of the benefits of Christ and to avoid profanation and disorder. At Bucer's suggestion it also required people to receive into their hands. There were also new words of distribution, strongly reminiscent of forms put out by the Reformer, John a Lasco: 'Take and eat this, in remembrance that Christ died for thee, and feed on him in thy heart by faith, with thanksgiving./Drink this in remembrance that Christ's blood was shed for thee, and be thankful.' Although these forms expressed the desire of extreme Reformers to avoid any identification of the elements with the Body and Blood of Christ; and although the declaration on kneeling was added, denying that 'adoration is intended unto any real and essential presence there being of Christ's natural flesh and blood', they were tempered by the Prayer of Humble Access and the Prayer of Thanksgiving after Communion.

1559

The 1549 and 1552 words of distribution were combined, and the declaration on kneeling was omitted.
(The Scottish rite of 1637 reverted to the 1549 words of distribution, each followed by Amen.)

1662

The 1559 words were retained, and the declaration on kneeling returned but with one important modification: 'corporal' replaced 'real and essential'.

Series 1

This rite broke new ground; and the growing popularity of the Parish Communion had presented the problem of regularly dealing with larger numbers of communicants. Communicants were still required to kneel and to receive the bread 'into their hands'; but alternative words of distribution were provided—either:

(a) the 1662 form; or
(b) a general invitation to the congregation to draw near and receive—substantially the 1559 words—followed by either the 1549 or the 1552 words said over each communicant or row of communicants.

Series 2

Nothing was said about kneeling or receiving into the hands, nor did such directions appear again in subsequent rites. A general invitation to communicate was followed by the primitive forms 'The Body/Blood of Christ' with the response 'Amen'.

Series 1 and 2 Revised

A great variety of words of distribution:

(a) the 1662 form;
(b) the general invitation, plus (i) the 1549 words; (ii) the Series 2 words; (iii) the old Roman form.

Series 3

A return to a single form: the general invitation plus 'The Body/Blood of Christ keep you in eternal life', with the response 'Amen'.

ASB retained the Series 2 and the Series 3 forms, and the rubrics of sections 46 and 66 also permitted the 1662 forms. But some variation is also permitted in the general invitation of section 45. Note 17 (p. 117) provides for its omission, except on Sundays and Holy Days; while section 85 provides forms associated with other traditions of worship which may be added to the general invitation on Sundays and Holy Days, or substituted on weekdays. The general invitation precedes all Communions, including those of the president and any other ministers: and the rubric of section 46 has been so worded that they may communicate after the congregation. There is much to commend this practice, especially at large services: in the first place it allows ministers to communicate only once—from what remains of the consecrated elements; and secondly, it sets an example of good 'table manners', of serving others before serving oneself.

Supplementary Consecration
(section 48)

In the early Church, if further supplies of bread and wine were required during a Eucharist, they were consecrated by contact— unconsecrated wine being added to consecrated wine, and unconsecrated bread being intincted with consecrated wine. This expedient was apparently permitted in the Roman rite before the chalice was withdrawn from the laity; but in the later medieval period 'reconsecration' of the chalice was only permitted in the event of an accident. This Sarum contingency was included in the 1548 *Order of the Communion*, where the consecration of further wine was permitted by means of the recital of the relevant words from the institution narrative: *Simili modo postquam coenatum est . . . in remissionem peccatorum.* 1549, 1552 and 1559 were silent on 'reconsecration'; although in 1573 the Puritan, Robert Johnson, was brought to trial and condemned for attempting to supplement the consecrated elements without reciting any words at all, despite his argument that there was no rubric to prove him wrong. The Canon of 1603 (No. 21) remedied this deficiency by requiring the institution narrative to be said over bread and wine 'newly brought', and this was followed by the Scottish rite of 1637 and by 1662. But there were evidently reservations as to the adequacy of this arrangement, for Wheatly was found arguing in 1710 that it was insufficient, and that either the whole prayer should be said again, or at least from the words, 'Hear us, O merciful Father'

C. Wheatly, *A Rational Illustration of the Book of Common Prayer*, 1858 edn, pp. 345–8). The Scottish rite of 1764 did in fact require the whole of the prayer to be said, from the beginning to the end of the invocation; but the recommendations of 1928 were more modest: only the institution narrative and the invocation. Series 1 and Series 2 made no provision; but by the late 1960s the subject had become a matter for discussion.

On the one hand, it was recognized that simply to use the institution narrative was inadequate, for it was contrary to the general understanding of the Eucharistic Prayer, and perpetuated the idea of a moment of consecration with a formula. On the other hand, to repeat the whole of the prayer was cumbersome and constituted a separate sacramental action. What was needed was an extension of the original consecration. The Liturgical Consultation of the 1968 Lambeth Conference and the Doctrine Commission were both asked to consider the matter, and finally there was general agreement with the Liturgical Commission on the principle of bringing further bread and/or wine into the sacramental action before the exhaustion of the original supplies of consecrated elements. The new provision appeared in Series 3 and was repeated in Series 1 and 2 Revised. Before the consecrated elements were exhausted, the president was required to return to the holy table and add more. He then used the words, 'Having given thanks to you, Father, over the bread and the cup according to the institution of your Son, Jesus Christ, who said, "Take, eat; this is my body" (and/or "Drink this; this is my blood"), we pray that this bread/wine also may be to us his body/blood, and be received in remembrance of him'. In this way identity was established with what had already taken place. ASB has repeated this arrangement with one modification: the present tense 'giving thanks over the bread and wine' is preferred to the past 'having given thanks' as indicating more clearly that the same Eucharistic Prayer is being extended. Some pleas have been made that such an action could be done in silence, causing the least possible disruption in the service; but words do define and clarify what is being done and therefore serve a didactic purpose.

The Ablutions
(section 49)

The primitive custom, which seems to have lasted for some centuries, was for any remaining consecrated elements to be kept until the end of the service, or until the next day, either on the altar or in the sacristy. They were then either consumed, or used for Communion on the following day. Cleansing also took place. Chrysostom referred to the cleansing of the mouth by means of bread and water, and in the medieval West the cleansing draught of wine for communicants was general. *Ordo Romanus Primus* also spoke of the Pope washing his hands after Communion, and later the cleansing of the chalice was combined with the cleansing of the hands. Sarum provided for the ablutions at the end of Communion before the post-communion was said, and the priest was required to consume what was left in the chalice. 1549 made no reference to these matters; while 1552 was vague, stating that 'if any of the bread or wine remain, the Curate shall have it to his own use'. Presumably this applied to both consecrated and unconsecrated remains. Thanks to Bishop John Cosin, the two were clearly distinguished in 1662, for there had been cases where the curate had taken consecrated bread and wine out of church and used them as common food and drink (Cosin, *Works*, vol. V, p. 519). 1662 therefore directed: unconsecrated bread and wine remaining the curate could have to his own use; but consecrated bread and wine remaining was not to be carried out of church but consumed immediately after the blessing by the priest, assisted if necessary by some of the communicants. In this respect 1662 agreed with primitive custom, both East and West. 1928 followed the 1662 provisions, but also permitted the reservation of some of the consecrated elements for the communion of the sick. At the time it created no little controversy, but it was retained in subsequent revisions from Series I onwards and still remains in ASB. Section 49 requires that 'any consecrated bread and wine which is not required for purposes of Communion is consumed at the end of the distribution or after the service'. The option to do the 'washing up' after Communion, which has also been provided in all rites since Series I, accords with ancient practice.

AFTER COMMUNION
A Sentence or Hymn

(section 50)

The chanting of psalms during Communion was an ancient and universal practice. But in the West, with the decline of Communion during the Middle Ages, the need for such singing dwindled.

All that remained by the thirteenth century was an antiphon, bearing the name *communio* and used after the Communion of the priest. This then came to be used as a thanksgiving after Communion with the title *antiphona post communionem* or simply *post communio*. Cranmer provided twenty-two such post-communion sentences in 1549, 'to be said or sung every day one', but these were omitted in 1552 and did not reappear until Series 3. Here and in Series 1 and 2 Revised, eleven sentences—mostly seasonal— were provided for optional use. Rite A now has a complete set of such sentences, one provided for every occasion on which there are propers, and each related to the theme or occasion. Note 20 (p. 117) suggests that such sentences could introduce a short period of silent prayer. Provision is also made for a hymn at this point. There is much to be said for this arrangement. The final part of the service is brief: the prayer in section 53 points to the Dismissal; and the Dismissal should be the final act.

Post-communion Prayers
(sections 51–3)

Rite A provides two prayers after Communion, the first to be said by the president alone, the second by the president and congregation. The president may also add other suitable prayers at his discretion. The use of a formal conclusion after Communion was a development following the post-Constantinian peace in the fourth century, with the growth in numbers and the development of church buildings. The form of the conclusion varied; and the East, in contrast to the West, came to include hymns. In some rites the final prayers were fixed, in others they were variable. The Roman rite developed a form which was both brief and simple— usually a variable collect for grace and perseverance and a dismissal. Cranmer's pattern in 1549 was similar—the salutation, a fixed prayer of thanksgiving, and the blessing. The prayer of thanksgiving was one of his own compositions, borrowing phrases from Sarum and Hermann: it has been described by Professor Massey Shepherd as 'one of the most remarkable summaries of doctrine to be found in all the formularies of the Prayer Book' (M. H. Shepherd, *The Oxford American Prayer Book Commentary*, New York, 1950, pp. 83–4). 1552, however, produced a much more elaborate pattern of praise and thanksgiving, associated with the worship of heaven—the Lord's Prayer, the prayer of thanksgiving or the prayer of oblation, the Gloria in excelsis, and the blessing.

Parallels to such a pattern can be found in a number of Reformed rites, including Zwingli's rite at Zürich. The position of the Lord's Prayer is, of course, consistent with Cranmer's use of it in other rites (see p. 31), while the prayer of oblation was another of his compositions, culled from phrases in the old Roman canon. 1662 retained the 1552 form; but 1928 reduced it to the prayer of thanksgiving, the Gloria in excelsis, and the blessing, while the Gloria could also be omitted on weekdays. Series 1 and Series 2 both provided a range of options, which could assume either a brief 1549 type of conclusion or an extended 1552 type, the only innovation being the inclusion of a short congregational prayer (see below). Series 3, however, produced the pattern presented in ASB of a new prayer to be said by the president, or the short Series 2 prayer to be said by the president and congregation.

Section 52

The first post-communion prayer, the work of Professor David Frost, has been described as an extended thanksgiving for redemption in Christ, with a prayer for the final victory of his Kingdom. It is rich in imagery. Sentence 1 recalls Christ's description of the divine love given in the parable of the Prodigal Son: we, like the Prodigal Son, were 'still far off'; but God came to meet us in the person of Christ and through him reconciled us to himself—he 'brought us home'. Sentence 2 summarizes the process and the results of Christ's redemptive activity. Sentence 3 prays that, having shared in the sacrament of his body and blood, we may live his risen life and be his active agents in the world. Sentence 4, in an image by which the writer of Hebrews captured the paradox of free will, prays that we may be kept in the living hope of Christ, so that we may be—as his slaves—truly free; then in consequence of our freedom, it prays that the whole world may genuinely live, by praising God through Christ. It is to be regretted that the General Synod rejected the original imagery of Hebrews 6.19 in the last sentence—'Anchor us in this hope'—replacing it with the weaker 'Keep us'. In the early Church the anchor was a familiar symbol of hope: Clement of Alexandria spoke of it as a device engraved on Christian rings, and it occurred frequently on inscriptions in company with the symbol of the fish.

Section 53

The second post-communion prayer, produced by the Liturgical

Commission, first appeared in Series 2 as a prayer of dedication and was expanded in Series 3 to include an element of thanksgiving. Sentence 1 echoes the opening clause of the 1662 prayer of thanksgiving. Sentence 2 is drawn from the 1662 prayer of oblation. Sentence 3 refers—as the whole service does at the outset—to the work of the Holy Spirit: 'The Lord is here, his Spirit is with us'; his presence is necessary if the communicants are to live and work in the world to the praise and glory of God.

THE DISMISSAL
(sections 54–6)

The Blessing
(section 54)

There is no evidence of a blessing at the Eucharist before the fourth century; but Sarapion (*c.* 350) had a prayer to be said by the president with his hands 'laid on' or 'stretched out' over the congregation, and this was followed by many Eastern liturgies. A similar feature appeared in the West; and in the Leonine Sacramentary a prayer *super populum*—a prayer by the president for a blessing upon the people—was the feature of every Mass. In the Gelasian Sacramentary it was used throughout the year; but in the Gregorian Sacramentary it was limited to Lent—and with good reason. Taking into account the requirements of penitential discipline, Gregory retained this blessing, because penitents were obliged to receive a regular blessing from the Pope or bishop. But with the passage of time the formulas ceased to refer to penance and began to refer to the communicants; they remained in use, however, for many centuries during Lent as a piece of ancient tradition. But *Ordo Romanus Primus* referred to another type of blessing given by the Pope as he left church. This episcopal blessing was a private form for which no texts were provided in the liturgical books. In the Middle Ages the bishop gave this blessing from the altar, and the practice spread throughout the Western Church. As a result of Gallican influence, these blessings also came to assume standard texts. The Gallican rites included a blessing, reserved to the bishop, which was proper to the season and was given prior to Communion. Some scholars have claimed this to be a blessing on communicants given before Communion; others have argued that it was a blessing on non-communicants given just before they left church. Whatever its purpose, this blessing was retained as the Roman rite replaced the Gallican, and by the eleventh century texts had appeared in pontificals and benedictionals.

In the light of this development, the content of Cranmer's blessing in 1549 is of particular interest. The first clause, from Philippians 4.7, comes from the 1548 *Order of the Communion*, where it was used to dismiss the communicants from the altar after communion. The second clause is akin to some of the medieval episcopal blessings found before Communion; it is in fact almost identical with a form in Lacey's *Exeter Pontifical*, and is closely parallel to the final blessing used by Hermann.

The 1549 blessing has been and remains the standard form; but Series 3 introduced for optional use ten seasonal blessings, constructed in the style of the medieval episcopal blessings, and largely the work of Canon E. C. Whitaker. In ASB these alternative blessings have now increased in number to twenty-one. Since Series 2 the blessing has become optional, while the dismissal which follows has become mandatory. Many would argue that after receiving Communion no further blessing is necessary. Others would argue that the blessing said by the president is of a different kind, and would justify it, not only on the grounds of long Anglican tradition, but also on account of the large numbers of non-communicants who attend the Eucharist.

The Dismissal
(sections 55–6)

The first unambiguous evidence of a formal dismissal occurred in the *Apostolic Constitutions*, Book 8. Here, and in other Eastern rites, the deacon issued the command, 'Depart in peace', and the congregation responded, 'In the name of Christ'. The traditional Roman form was *Ite, missa est*; and although there is no evidence for it before the *Ordines*, the formula is probably earlier. Similar formulas were evidently a part of Roman social life. Gallican rites used the form 'Let us bless the Lord'; and as the Roman rite supplanted the Gallican, the former's dismissal came to be used as the festal form, while the latter's came to be used as the ferial or penitential form. Both used the response 'Thanks be to God', which was regarded as an acknowledgement on the part of the congregation that they had heard what was said. 'Alleluias' were added during Easter, while by the twelfth century, *Ite* was replaced at requiems by 'May they rest in peace', because the former was regarded as an expression of joy.

Neither 1549 nor successive Prayer Books included a dismissal, although it was used by some continental Reformers, e.g. Zwingli and Bucer. It first appeared in Series 2 as a mandatory element, and has remained so in Series 3 and in ASB. ASB provides two forms, the first Eastern, the second Western. In Eastertide 'Alleluia, Alleluia' may be added to both versicle and response.

Of the dismissal Canon Douglas Webster has commented: 'In that early Church, mission cohabited with worship as a dual concern, the glorious realities of worship driving those first Christians out into mission, the harsh realities of mission sending them back into worship, to enable them to go out once more' ('The Mission of the People of God', in *The Parish Communion Today*, ed. D. M. Paton, 1962, p. 109).

THE ORDER FOLLOWING THE PATTERN OF THE BOOK OF COMMON PRAYER

To meet the needs of those worshippers who prefer the 1662 structure but wish to use contemporary language, a fifth eucharistic pattern is provided. It owes much to the Revs R. T. Beckwith and B. D. F. T. Brindley, although both the Revision Committee of the General Synod and the General Synod itself have revised their proposals. The Ministry of the Word is that of Rite A, and wherever possible texts have been drawn from those of Rite A. It was thought to be too confusing, however, to include this Order within Rite A itself. It has therefore been added as a separate unit; and a rubric in Rite A after the Intercession indicates where this Order is to commence (section 22, p. 125). In this Order the term 'priest' is used instead of 'president', since that is the term in 1662.

The Preparation of the Gifts
(section 57)

The Preparation of the Gifts takes place immediately after the Intercessions. For comment see pp. 207–11.

The Prayers of Penitence
(sections 58–62)

The only difference here from Rite A is that the Comfortable Words follow the Confession and Absolution, providing scriptural assurance of the forgiveness of sins. The use of these words derives from Hermann. For comment see pp. 181–90.

The Sursum corda, Preface and Sanctus
(section 63)

As with 1662, the Sursum corda lacks the introductory *Dominus vobiscum* and response. The Preface also makes no reference to the 'mighty acts' of God in creation, redemption and sanctification. For comment see pp. 214–17.

The Prayer of Humble Access
(section 64)

In 1549 this prayer was placed immediately before the act of Communion. Bishop Gardiner contended, however, that in this position it taught the adoration of Christ's flesh in the sacrament. In 1552, therefore, it was transferred to its place between the Sanctus and the Prayer of Consecration. While some would regard this as breaking the unity of the Eucharistic Prayer, others would commend it as a laudable alternation of penitence and praise, keeping the thought of the approaching sacrament constantly in mind. It was well expressed at the beginning of the eighteenth century by Wheatly:

> The nearer we approach to these holy mysteries, the greater reverence we ought to express; for since it is out of God's mere grace and goodness, that we have the honour to approach his table; it is at least our duty to acknowledge it to be a free and undeserved favour. . . . And therefore, lest our exultations should savour of too much confidence, we now allay them with this act of humility. (C. Wheatly, *A Rational Illustration of the Book of Common Prayer*, Cambridge 1858, pp. 342–3)

For comment see pp. 203–5.

The Prayer of Consecration
(section 65)

The prayer was drafted in the light of similar prayers in the Australian 1978 Prayer Book (First Order) and in the Liturgical Commission's draft for Series 3 Revised (Thanksgiving A) in GS 364. Much of the text has been incorporated into the fourth

Eucharistic Prayer of Rite A. The institution narrative conforms to that in the other Eucharistic Prayers of Rite A. All the manual acts of 1662 are included, together with the 1662 provision for further consecration (section 67). The breaking of the bread should not be seen as a symbolic breaking of our Lord's body (cf. John 19.33), but as a faithful representation of our Lord's actions as well as his words. The 1662 provision for further consecration, requiring the institution narrative to be said over the additional bread and wine, together with Canon 21 of the Canons of 1603, do seem to suggest that 1662 does tie consecration to the institution narrative. The rubric states: 'The priest is to *consecrate* more according to the form before prescribed'; while Canon 21 states: 'No Bread or Wine newly brought shall be used; but first the words of Institution shall be rehearsed, when the said Bread and Wine be present upon the Communion Table.' For further discussion on this point see R. F. Buxton, *Eucharist and Institution Narrative* (Alcuin Club Collections, No. 58, 1976), who questions whether seventeenth-century Anglican divines really did tie consecration to the institution narrative.

For comment on the Eucharistic Prayer, see pp. 214–31.

The Distribution
(section 66)

The Words of Distribution are those of 1662: but those of Rite A may be used instead if required. For comment see pp. 236–9.

The Ablutions
(section 68)

The rubric for the Ablutions is identical with that of Rite A, section 51. See pp. 240–1.

The Lord's Prayer
(section 69)

The Lord's Prayer may be said in either its contemporary or traditional form. In 1552 the Lord's Prayer was placed after Communion, thereby becoming the first element of thanksgiving. It is also consistent with its position in other 1552/1662 rites, e.g. Baptism and Marriage, where it becomes the first prayer after the reception of God's gift. For comment see pp. 231–3.

Post-Communion Prayers
(sections 70–2)

Either the 1662 Prayer of Oblation or Prayer of Thanksgiving, or one of the post-communion prayers of Rite A (sections 52–3) may be used, provided one of the four is said. The two forms provided here in sections 71–2 are taken from the First Order of the 1978 Australian Prayer Book. The change from 1662 is minimal. For comment see pp. 242–4.

Gloria in excelsis
(section 73)

As in 1552/1662 this now becomes part of the extended act of thanksgiving following Communion, and links the communicants with the worshipping company of heaven. The worship of earth and heaven is therefore linked both before Communion in the Sanctus and after Communion in the Gloria in excelsis. The printing of the text again at this point avoids unnecessary confusion and page-turning.

For comment see pp. 112–15, 191–2.

The Blessing
(section 74)

For comment see pp. 244–5.

APPENDICES

Proper Prefaces
(section 76)

One important difference between Eastern and Western liturgies was their approach to seasonal material. Eastern liturgies indicated a change of season or occasion, not by the inclusion of a proper preface in the Eucharistic Prayer, but by a change of the entire prayer. Western liturgies, on the other hand, had Eucharistic Prayers with basic structures of certain fixed elements into which varying seasonal material was inserted; and some liturgies had more variable elements than others. The Gallican rites, for example, had almost a plethora of variables, with only the Sursum corda, the Sanctus and the institution narrative being fixed. In the Roman rite only the preface varied, and even here the number of variations decreased with the passage of time. The Leonine

Sacramentary had Proper Prefaces for each of its 267 masses: but the Gelasian Sacramentary had only just over fifty, while the Gregorian Sacramentary had a mere eleven—a figure which remained constant throughout the centuries.

Under the influence of the German Church Orders, Cranmer reduced the Proper Prefaces to five: Christmas, Easter, Ascension, Pentecost and Trinity. The Sarum prefaces for Epiphany, Ash Wednesday, Apostles and Evangelists, Holy Cross, and the Blessed Virgin Mary were eliminated. Furthermore, whereas the Sarum prefaces could be used on a number of days, the 1549 prefaces were only to be used on the five feast days. 1552 made some concession by allowing the Proper Prefaces of Christmas, Easter and Ascension to be used throughout the octaves, and of Pentecost to be used until Trinity Sunday—an arrangement which continued in 1662. 1928 was much more liberal in its provision: seven new prefaces were added—Epiphany, Maundy Thursday, the Blessed Virgin Mary, the Transfiguration, Saints' Days, and Dedication and Sundays; and some were given extended use—the Christmas preface could be used until Epiphany, the Easter preface until Ascension, the Ascension preface until Whitsun, and Epiphany was given an octave. This provision continued in Series 1; but in Series 2 there was a radical change. Because the normal fixed preface now contained an extended recital of God's mighty acts, it was felt that an extensive supply of Proper Prefaces was not really necessary; only four were therefore provided: Christmastide, Passiontide, Eastertide, and Ascension–Pentecost. Experience proved this to be insufficient, and Series 3 considerably extended the provision to all those occasions provided for in 1928 and Series 1, and adding Advent and Lent.

Series 3 Revised and ASB have now extended the provision even further. It now comprises Advent, Incarnation, Lent, the Cross, Maundy Thursday, the Blessing of Oils, Resurrection, Ascension, Pentecost with Baptism and Confirmation, Trinity, Transfiguration, Michaelmas, All Saints, Apostles and Evangelists, Martyrs, Saints' Days, Dedication, Marriage, Ordination, Unity, Baptism and Sundays. These Proper Prefaces may be used with all four Eucharistic Prayers of Rite A and with the Order following the 1662 pattern. Only the last three (nos 31–3) are restricted to use with the fourth Eucharistic Prayer (section 41) and the Order following the 1662 pattern (section 63). Guidance as to the use of these Proper Prefaces is given with the collects and readings. For further information on prefaces see pp. 215–16.

Alternative Blessings
(section 77)

Seasonal blessings were provided in Series 3 and have continued in Series 1 and 2 Revised, Series 3 Revised and ASB. Rite A has twenty-one such blessings which are optional alternatives to the first part of the blessing provided in section 45. These forms, modelled on medieval episcopal blessings, were the work of Canon E. C. Whitaker. For further information on blessings see pp. 244–5.

The Commandments
(section 78)

The text of the Commandments is printed here to avoid undue disruption of the text in sections 24–5. Two forms of the Commandments are provided:

(A) (pp. 161–3). The abbreviated form of the Commandments to which is appended in each case a New Testament passage. The whole Decalogue is introduced by a brief exhortation based on two sayings of our Lord from John 14.15 and Luke 11.28.

(B) (pp. 163–4). The Decalogue in its full 1662 form, with permitted abbreviations indicated by brackets.

For further information on the Commandments see pp. 185–7.

Kyrie eleison
(section 79)

The complete texts in English and Greek are provided. For further information see pp. 190–1.

Alternative Confessions
(section 80)

Three forms of confession, alternative to that provided in sections 7 and 27, are provided:

(A) (p. 165). The original Confession in contemporary language as it appeared in Series 3. It sought to meet the criticism of undue brevity levelled against the Confession in Series 2. An attempt was therefore made to set out more clearly certain categories of sin—sins of omission and commission, sins done in ignorance and weakness, and deliberate sins. For this purpose lines 6–7 were borrowed from the 1970 New Zealand rite. After use some disquiet was expressed about lines 4–5, and in particular about 'in the good we have not done'. In Series 3 Revised these two lines were omitted. In view of the wide use of this particular form of confession, however, it has been retained for optional use.

(B) (p. 165). The short Series 2 form has been retained, with 'You/your' replacing 'thee/thy'. It has also been used extensively, despite the criticism levelled against it; and it might still be found to be an appropriate alternative on informal occasions.

(C) (p. 166). An entirely new Confession, the work of Professor David Frost, and originally proposed by the Liturgical Commission for use in Series 3. Although rejected by the General Synod in November 1971, it has now been included in Rite A as a third alternative. The attempt to include some new elements of imagery deserves comment. It owes something to Dame Julian of Norwich: 'The Holy Spirit leads [a man] on to confession, so that he deliberately reveals his sins in all their nakedness and reality and admits with great *sorrow and shame* that he has *befouled the fair image* of God' (*Confessions of Divine Love*, 39). The reference to God as giver of light and grace in line 1 links with the final petition in lines 13–14, where we ask to be led out of darkness, to walk as children of light—a reference to 1 Peter 2.9, which speaks of God calling us out of darkness into his marvellous light. Lines 7–8, indicating the effects of sin, refer back to Julian of Norwich—'we have . . . marred your image in us'.

Alternative Forms of Intercession
(section 81)

Two alternative forms of Intercession are provided:

(A) (pp. 166–7). The modernized form of the Prayer for all Sorts and Conditions of Men, introduced by the Series 2 Bidding to Intercession. For further information see pp. 138–9.

(B) (pp. 167–9). A portion of the Litany, with an Eastern form of introduction. Sections 1 and 2 of the Litany have been omitted, but the whole of sections 3, 4 and 5 are included. The concluding prayer is borrowed from the concluding prayer to the Litany in the Ordinal. For further information see pp. 35–43.

Alternative Prayer of Humble Access
(section 82)

Another new prayer, again the work of Professor David Frost, and originally proposed by the Liturgical Commission in Series 3. This too was rejected by the General Synod in November 1971, but has now been included in Rite A as an alternative form. It was not only another attempt to introduce some new forms of imagery, but also tried to meet the difficulties of those worshippers who have misgivings about the phrases 'eating flesh' and 'drinking blood'. It is related to George Herbert's poem 'Love', with its opening

> Love bade me welcome; yet my soul drew back
> Guilty of dust and sin

and its conclusion

> 'You must sit down,' says Love, 'and taste my meat'.
> So I did sit and eat.

We are led to see ourselves as those unworthy persons in the poem whom the Lord of the Feast in his love sent for and 'compelled to come in'. Lines 3–4 come from Psalm 24.4: those who would ascend the hill of the Lord and stand in his holy place must have 'clean hands and a pure heart', cf. James 4.8: 'Cleanse your hands, you sinners, and purify your hearts'. Lines 5–6 refer to the Canaanite woman's reply to Jesus in Matthew 15.27, while lines 7–8 refer to the feeding of God's rebellious children with manna in the wilderness. Lines 9–10 overcome the problem of 'eating flesh and drinking blood' by 'Cleanse and feed us with the precious body and blood'. The concluding lines speak of incorporation into Christ and the anticipation of the Messianic Banquet.

A Selection of Other Introductory Words to the Peace
(section 83)

Five optional seasonal introductions to the Peace, all based on Scripture:

1 Advent, Christmas and Epiphany: Isaiah 9.6–7.
2 Lent: Romans 5.1.

3   Easter, Ascension: John 20.21.
4   Pentecost: Galatians 5.22, 25.
5   Saints' Days: Ephesians 2.19, 17.

For further information on the Peace see pp. 205–6.

A Eucharistic Prayer for Use with the Sick
(section 84)

This prayer is an abbreviation of the first Eucharistic Prayer in Rite A, retaining all the essential elements and, where possible, the same wording. Apart from the Sursum corda, there are no congregational elements, which in any case may not be convenient. This involves a slight rewording in the section preceding the doxology. The prayer is approximately two-thirds its original length. It has now been incorporated in the rite of Communion with the Sick in the series of services *Ministry to the Sick* authorized for use by the General Synod in 1983.

Additional Words of Invitation to Communion
(section 85)

The words of invitation to Communion set out in section 45 are mandatory; but they may be followed, if the president so desires, by any of the three forms provided here. They provide a link with other traditions of eucharistic worship.

(A) (p. 172). This form has been associated with the Roman rite from the time of the Synod of Aix (1585). The versicle clearly has links with the Agnus Dei; and the response, from Matthew 8.8, was used in the priest's preparatory prayers for communion from the tenth century onwards.

(B) (p. 172). An Eastern form, which appeared in the rite of *Apostolic Constitutions*, Book 8, as early as 380 and is still in the rites of St John Chrysostom and St Basil.

(C) (p. 173). The traditional Easter Greeting based on 1 Corinthians 5.7–8. For further information see the Easter Anthems, pp. 101–2.

Alternative Final Prayer
(section 86)

This is the original Series 2 post-communion prayer set out in 'You' form. It omits the two lines of thanksgiving (lines 2–3, section 53); and it retains the phrase 'into the world'—a cause of concern for many people who argued that it encouraged the wrong idea of Church and world as two separate compartments, whereas in fact the Church is already in the world.

C
RITE B
COMMENTARY

Rite B is Holy Communion Series 1 and 2 Revised—a combination of the Series 1 and Series 2 services effected after Series 3 had appeared and to some extent influenced by it. It is the only service in ASB in traditional language. While its provision of seasonal material is rather more limited than that of Series 3, it is nevertheless a very flexible rite. By a careful use of its options and alternatives it is possible to produce on the one hand an order very similar to that of Series 3, and on the other an order very similar to that of 1662. Most of the commentary on Rite A applies to Rite B, and only differences are dealt with here in detail. Sentences, collects and readings of Rite A or of 1662 may be used, together with any others which may be authorized by the General Synod.

THE WORD AND THE PRAYERS
The Preparation
(sections 1–6)

The Entry (section 1)

See pp. 177–9.

The Greeting (section 2)

Only the traditional form is provided here, with no special provision for Eastertide. See pp. 179–81.

The Collect for Purity (section 3)

See p. 181.

The Decalogue, The Summary of the Law, Kyrie eleison (section 4)

While the prayers of penitence may not be used at the beginning of the rite, one of the options in this section may be used instead of or together with the Gloria in excelsis in section 5; or both sections may be omitted. See pp. 185–7, 190–1.

Gloria in excelsis (section 5)

See pp. 112–15, 191–2.

The Collect (section 6)

See pp. 192–3, 265–7.

The Ministry of the Word
(sections 7–14)

The Ministry of the Word is identical with the Ministry of the Word in Rite A (see pp. 193–9) with two exceptions:

1   *Section 12:* The congregational responses before and after the Gospel are the traditional forms. In 1549 only the first response was provided, and this was omitted in 1552 and 1662. Bishop Cosin claimed that the responses were still used in his time, and the Scottish Book of 1637 introduced the response after the Gospel; but attempts at their introduction in 1662 failed. Both responses appeared in 1928, however, and remained in Series 1, 2, and 1 and 2 Revised. Both the Gospel and the book itself symbolize the presence of Christ in the proclamation of the Word. In some places, both East and West, the announcement of the Gospel was greeted with the Benedictus; but the most common form, which was in the Roman rite by the Middle Ages was 'Glory to thee, O Lord'. The concluding 'Praise to thee, O Christ' came from the Gallican rites.

2   *Section 14:* The Creed begins in the singular. After the people ceased to participate vocally in the Mass, the custom of the priest beginning to say the Creed in the singular began to spread.

Prayers of Intercession
(sections 15–18)

Section 15

If desired, banns and notices may be read and the offerings of the people may be collected and presented at this point. This follows the 1662 pattern. But the bread and the wine are not to be prepared and placed upon the holy table.

Section 16

Two forms of intercession are provided, the first based on 1928 and Series 1, the second on Series 2. Unlike Rite A, no provision is made for the minister to use his own form. Both are introduced by the Series 2 form.

First Intercession (section 17)

As in Series 1 the prayer is divided into paragraphs, identifying the various subjects. Specific items of prayer may be mentioned before each paragraph, while the versicle and response may be used after each paragraph; or biddings may be used before the prayer begins, and the prayer can then be read as a continuous whole. This prayer first appeared in 1549 as the first part of the Eucharistic Prayer. Cranmer had put the material together from the intercessions in the Roman canon, and he followed the same order. The address comes from 1 Timothy 2.1. 1552 removed the prayer to its position after the Creed and Offertory and omitted the prayer for the departed—an omission which 1662 restored. 1928 then made further additions: the missionary work of the Church, places of education and learning, and a thanksgiving for the saints. Note 2 (p. 177) permits the use of the 1662 prayer as an alternative. For further information see pp. 200–1.

Second Intercession (section 18)

Both in content and structure the second intercession closely follows the intercession in section 21 of Rite A. See pp. 201–2.

Prayers of Penitence
(sections 19–23)

The Comfortable Words (section 19)

The Comfortable Words, which are optional, precede the Confession, as in Rite A. But unlike Rite A, there is no introductory Word comprising elements of all the Words. See pp. 188–9.

The Invitation (section 20)

The invitation to confession may take one of two forms. The first is the 1662 form, which may be used in its entirety or in part, as indicated by brackets. The words 'with faith' were added after 'Draw near' in 1662, for it now refers to a disposition of the heart and not to the physical approach of the communicants into the area around the holy table. The content of the invitation is essentially that of the invitation in section 26 of Rite A. See pp. 187–9.

The second form is that which originally appeared in Series 2. While it included the need for 'a true heart, in full assurance of faith'—a quotation from Hebrews 10.21–2—it was criticized by many people for its lack of reference to 'the commandments of God' and to 'love and charity with your neighbours'. See pp. 188–9.

The Confession (section 21)

The Confession is the second of the alternative forms in the Appendix to Rite A (section 80, p. 165). The only change is the substitution of 'thee/thy' for 'you/your'. See pp. 189, 252–3.

The Absolution (section 22)

The Absolution is the same as in section 28 of Rite A. See pp. 189–90.

The Prayer of Humble Access (section 23)

This prayer is included in its 1662 form, with the option of omitting lines 12–13, which are in brackets. See pp. 203–5.

THE MINISTRY OF THE SACRAMENT
The Peace
(sections 24–5)

This form, which appeared originally in Series 2, is based on Ephesians 4.3. At first it was extremely popular; but later it was criticized as not being sufficiently outward-looking. See pp. 205–6.

The Preparation of the Bread and Wine
(sections 26–8)

Section 26 clearly designates this action by the 1928 term 'The Offertory'. It is much less flexible than that of Rite A, and there is no scope for the use of the Roman offertory prayers. But the text from 1 Chronicles 29 can apply much more directly to the bread and the wine if the offerings of the people have been collected and presented before the Intercession. No reference is made here to 'The Taking', nor does it appear before sections 29–30. The first of the four dominical acts therefore remains undefined. See pp. 207–11.

The Thanksgiving
(sections 29–33)

Section 29

Although the heading of this part of the rite is 'The Thanksgiving', section 29 also retains the 1662 title 'The Prayer of Consecration'.

The First Thanksgiving (section 30)

This prayer is a direct descendant of the Eucharistic Prayer in Series 1, and is substantially the same as the fourth Eucharistic Prayer in Rite A, but in traditional language. The only noteworthy differences between this prayer and the fourth Prayer in Rite A are as follows:

1 Here there is only one form of salutation in the Sursum corda—the traditional form.

2 The 1662 manual acts accompany the institution narrative, as in Series 1.

3 The prayer may end after the institution narrative, as in 1662. See Note 9, p. 178.

4 The Prayer of Humble Access may be said after the Sanctus and Benedictus, as in 1662. See Note 9, p. 178.

For the whole prayer see pp. 213–29, 231.

The Second Thanksgiving (section 31)

This prayer is a direct descendant of the Eucharistic Prayer in Series 2, and is substantially the same as the second Eucharistic Prayer in Rite A, but in traditional language. The only noteworthy differences between this prayer and the second Prayer in Rite A are as follows:

1 There is only one form of salutation in the Sursum corda, as in the first Thanksgiving.

2 There is no reference to 'the living Word' as God's agent of creation in the Preface.

3 The common Preface is said on all occasions, and there is no permission to omit it as in Rite A.

4 There is no invocation of the Holy Spirit before the institution narrative.

5 The manual acts are inserted in the simple Series 2 form at the institution narrative, viz. The priest is 'to take the bread/ cup into his hands'; but there is no mention of breaking the bread.

6 The extended reference to becoming 'a living temple' is missing from the benefits of communion.

The prayer marks an interesting stage in the development from Series 2 to Series 1 and 2 Revised and to ASB Rite A, second Eucharistic Prayer. See pp. 213–30.

The Benedictus (section 32)

If the Benedictus has not already been said or sung with the Sanctus, provision is made for its use here after the Thanksgiving. There is some historical precedent for this position. It appeared here in the *Apostolic Constitutions*, Book 8 (*c.* 380).

The Lord's Prayer (section 33)

The Lord's Prayer is permitted either here, or after the Fraction (section 36), or in its 1662 position after Communion (section 44). Before the Fraction is the Series 1 and Rite A position; after the Fraction is the Series 2 position. See pp. 30–2, 231–3.

THE COMMUNION

The Breaking of the Bread and the Giving of the Bread and Cup
(sections 34–42)

The Fraction (section 34)

Typographically the Fraction is seen as one of the fundamental elements of the rite, following the 'Blessing' and preceding the 'Giving'. It is also mandatory to break the bread here at section 34 if the second Thanksgiving has been used, because there is no previous instruction for a Fraction. But if the Fraction has already occurred with the institution narrative in the first Thanksgiving, that is regarded as sufficient. See pp. 233–5.

The Agnus Dei (section 35)

In this rite the Agnus Dei only appears in its traditional form. See pp. 235–6.

The Lord's Prayer (section 36)

The text of the Lord's Prayer is given here in its Series 2 position, but it may also be used at section 33 or section 44. Note 2 (p. 177) also permits the 1662 text of the prayer. See pp. 30–2, 231–3.

The Giving of the Bread and Cup (sections 37–40)

A variety of methods of distribution are provided:

1   The 1662 words may be used with each communicant (section 38).
2   The same form of invitation as in Rite A may be said to all communicants, followed by one of three forms of words said to each communicant, who then replies 'Amen'.

   (*a*)   The short statement—'The Body/Blood of Christ'—as in Rite A.
   (*b*)   A slightly longer statement—'The Body/Blood of Christ preserve your body and soul unto everlasting life'. This abbreviation of the 1549 words can be regarded as a traditional equivalent of the Rite A form. The end follows the Roman form, using the accusative, *in vitam aeternam*, and suggesting that eternal life is still something in the future. Rite A, however, with 'Keep you in eternal life'

261

indicates with St John that in a real sense 'eternal life' is a present reality rather than a future hope.

(c) The 1549 words, i.e. the first half of the 1662 words (section 39). See pp. 236–9.

Supplementary Consecration (section 41)

The provision here is the same as in Rite A with one small exception. In Rite A, the verb is the present tense 'Giving thanks', suggesting a continuing action. Here in Rite B, the verb is in the past tense, 'Having given thanks', implying that the action has already been completed. See pp. 239–40.

The Ablutions (section 42)

See pp. 240–1.

AFTER COMMUNION
(sections 43–8)

Post-communion Sentence (section 43)

In addition to the sentences provided with the collects and readings, attention is drawn to the seasonal sentences on pp. 42–3. Series 1 and 2 Revised had its own provision of eleven post-communion sentences inserted in the rite at this point. These have now been extended and placed at the beginning of ASB with a provision of introductory seasonal sentences.

The Lord's Prayer (section 44)

Permission is given to use the Lord's Prayer and the Gloria in excelsis in their 1662 positions, provided they have not already been used. They should not be duplicated. See pp. 30–2, 231–3.

Prayers after Communion (sections 45–7)

Two post-communion prayers are provided. Either or both may be used, and two further alternatives appear in the Appendix (section 58). The first is the 1662 Prayer of Thanksgiving. See pp. 242–3. The second is the short post-communion prayer from Rite A, with 'thee/thy' substituted for 'you/your'. See pp. 243–4.

The Dismissal
(sections 49–51)

The Blessing (section 49) with its provision of seasonal options (section 54) is the same as in Rite A. The Dismissal (section 50) is the same as in Rite A with one exception: the first form is printed as it was in Series 2—'Go in peace and serve the Lord', omitting the Rite A command to 'love'. See pp. 244–6.

APPENDICES

Proper Prefaces for the First Thanksgiving (section 52)

Each Thanksgiving in Rite B has its own Proper Prefaces. Those for the first Thanksgiving are those of 1928 and Series 1 and are less extensive than those for Rite A. They provide for Christmas with Presentation and Annunciation, Epiphany, Maundy Thursday, Easter, Ascension, Pentecost, Trinity Sunday, Transfiguration, Saints' Days, Consecration or Dedication of a Church, and Funerals (two). Note 8 (p. 178) makes these mandatory. See pp. 249–50.

Proper Prefaces for the Second Thanksgiving (section 53)

Fifteen prefaces are provided, all from Series 1 and 2 Revised. They provide for Advent, Christmas with Presentation and Annunciation, Epiphany, Lent, Passiontide, Maundy Thursday, Easter, Ascension, Pentecost, Trinity Sunday, Transfiguration, Saints' Days, Consecration or Dedication of a Church, and Funerals (two). Of these Christmas, Passiontide, Easter and Ascension are mandatory—Note 8 (p. 178). See pp. 249–50.

Alternative Blessings (section 54)

All these are drawn from the provision in Rite A, but they are slightly fewer in number. There is only a single blessing for Christmas, Easter and Saints' Days, and there are no additional general blessings. But Note 10 (p. 178) permits the priest to supplement these with others at his discretion: the Rite A provision could therefore be used. See p. 251.

The Commandments (section 55)

A single form is provided—the abbreviated version of 1928. See pp. 185–7.

The Summary of the Law (section 56)

The form from section 5 of Rite A is included with two variations:

1 This is a slightly longer text as in 1928, including elements from both Mark 12.29–31 and Matthew 22.37–40.
2 The response is a fuller form, which appeared in 1552–1662 as the response to the Tenth Commandment of the Decalogue. It is based on Jeremiah 31.31 (cf. Hebrews 8.8–12, 10.15–17). See pp. 185–6.

Kyrie eleison (section 57)

This is identical with the form in section 79 of Rite A. See pp. 190–1.

Alternative Post-communion Prayers (section 58)

These prayers are alternative to those in sections 46 and 47. The first is the 1552–1662 Prayer of Oblation. Since much of this appears in the second part of the first Thanksgiving (section 30, p. 192), it would not be desirable to use it with this Eucharistic Prayer unless it ended after the institution narrative. As in 1552/ 1662 this prayer is to be said by the priest alone.

The second is the second half of the 1552/1662 Prayer of Oblation, beginning at 'we offer and present unto thee', and used as a congregational prayer. This would clearly be suitable as an alternative to the prayer in section 47, particularly if the prayer of thanksgiving in section 46 had already been said. See pp. 242–3.

10

The Collects

A

HISTORY

The collect is a distinctively Western type of prayer with which an act of worship or part of an act of worship was concluded: and the name has primarily come to be associated with the prayer which concludes the entrance rite at the Eucharist. Its origin and its original purpose are by no means clear. Prayers constructed on the same lines can be found not only in Hebrew religion but also in classical literature, both Latin and Greek. It is therefore probably another case of the Church using a form of prayer which had already been found acceptable in other religions. The earliest source for collects in the Christian Church is to be found in the Leonine and Gelasian Sacramentaries. Precise dating is difficult; but some of the collects could be as early as the late fourth or fifth centuries. In these sacramentaries four such prayers were provided for each day or occasion: at the end of the entrance rite, at the offertory, after communion, and at the conclusion—the blessing; and they came under the general title of *oratio*. In the Gregorian Sacramentary, however, the title became *ad collectam*; and it may have been a title taken from Gallican sources, where the term *collectio* was used to describe a short, public prayer which a priest used to sum up the prayers of all those present. *Collecta* is a later Latin form of *collectio* and means assembly. Whether *ad collectam* therefore meant originally the prayer of the 'collected' or gathered people, or whether it meant a 'collecting together' of their prayers is not clear. But it came to be used for the short public variable prayer said by the priest at the end of the entry rite, related to the day or the occasion, and so often related to the appropriate readings which followed. This was certainly its meaning and purpose in 1549/1662, for there the other three variable prayers— offertory, post-communion and conclusion—had disappeared; the collect was, of course, also used in the Office, closely related to the concluding prayers (see p. 123).

265

The collect has a distinctive pattern; and whereas Gallican forms could be rather diffuse, Roman collects were marked by brevity and conciseness, containing normally a single petition. They were also prayers noted for their rhythm. Many were written in the fifth and sixth centuries, when classical oratory flowered; and care was taken that they conformed to the rules of the *cursus*. Many people who subsequently attempted to translate collects from the Latin, or to write new collects in the vernacular attempted to follow the same pattern and style; and here Cranmer was undoubtedly outstanding. Those which were written for 1662 tended to be a little less concise; but on the whole those responsible for writing collects for the various prayer books have done their best to be faithful to the traditional form. The collect normally has five elements:

1   An address to God the Father (cf. John 16.23). Some later collects were addressed to the Son—Lent 1 in 1662: 'O Lord, who for our sake didst fast forty days and forty nights'. Where such examples have been used in ASB, they have been adapted in order to conform to the traditional pattern. In this case, therefore, Lent 1 becomes, 'Almighty God, whose Son Jesus Christ fasted forty days . . .'.

2   A relative clause, sometimes missing, stating some divine attribute or some proposition which is the introduction to or ground for the petition—ASB Lent 1: 'whose Son Jesus Christ fasted forty days in the wilderness, and was tempted as we are, yet without sin'. While this worked well rhythmically in 1549/1662 with the second person singular, it often presented problems in ASB with the second person plural. This was overcome principally by two devices: (a) by the use of 'you' with the indicative, e.g. Easter 5: 'Almighty and everlasting God, you are always more ready to hear . . .'; (b) by the use of a noun in apposition, e.g. Pentecost 17 where 'Lord of all power and might, who art the author and giver' becomes simply, 'Lord of all power and might, the author and giver . . .'

3   The petition itself, normally a single request which is for the Church or for those present when the prayer is used. It is therefore customary for the first person plural to be involved, e.g. Pentecost: 'Give us the same mind that was in Christ Jesus'.

4   The purpose of the petition, although this is also sometimes missing. So, in Pentecost 10, we ask for the mind that was in Christ Jesus 'that, sharing his humility, we may come to be with him in his glory'.

5   The mediation. Prayer is offered to God the Father, but through his Son, Jesus Christ. This, too, is based on Scripture, e.g. 1 Timothy 2.5; Hebrews 4.14; 1 John 2.2. Traditionally the mediation concluded with a Trinitarian doxology; and General Note 8 on p. 32 indicates the form which this can take. Any collect ending with 'Christ our Lord', may, if the Minister so wishes, be supplemented with, 'who is alive and reigns with you and the Holy Spirit, one God, now and for ever'. It should be noted that this ASB translation of the traditional doxology differs from the current translation in the Roman Catholic Missal and Breviary. The Latin is *qui vivit et regnat*; and the Liturgical Commission believed the translation 'who lives and reigns with the Father . . .' to be inadequate and ambiguous. While it is not incorrect, it suggests that the Son lives with the Father and reigns with the Father; furthermore, the true significance of *vivit* is lost—indeed it suggests *habitat* rather than *vivit*. *Vivit* indicates that the Son is alive, and it is as the living Lord that he reigns with the Father. The translation 'is alive' is therefore felt to be more vivid and more accurate.

The Western collect is such a unique and treasured piece of devotion, that ASB has endeavoured to preserve as many of the 1662 collects as possible together with their traditional wording. Nearly seventy of them appear in whole or in part; while a number of ancient collects which did not appear in 1662, e.g. Christmas 1, Epiphany 2 and Pentecost 16, have now been introduced. This body of collects is the result of wide consultation with other Churches, Anglican and non-Anglican, both at home and overseas; and most of them are now common property. It is therefore difficult to indicate all the original sources in every case. No contemporary writers can claim the genius of a Cranmer; but the ASB collects do represent a brave attempt to produce a distinctively Western form of prayer which is contemporary in outlook yet faithful to the traditional style. For the sake of clarity and to assist in public recitation, the collects are set out with their various elements on separate lines.

B
COMMENTARY

(a) Sundays and Seasons

Ninth Sunday before Christmas

Theme: The Creation.

A new collect by the Liturgical Commission. The preamble is borrowed from the CSI collect for the ninth Sunday before Easter and is based on Genesis 1.1 and 1.27.

Eighth Sunday before Christmas

Theme: The Fall.

The original form of this collect was probably written by Bishop John Cosin for Epiphany 6 in 1662, a Sunday for which there was no provision in 1549 or 1552. It is based on 1 John 3.1–9, which is the epistle for Epiphany 6 in 1662.

Seventh Sunday before Christmas

Theme: The Election of God's People; Abraham.

An adaptation by the Liturgical Commission of the CSI collect for Pentecost 4. Its main sources are Genesis 12.1–3 and Romans 4.16–18, passages which occur in the Old Testament and New Testament readings for Year 1.

Sixth Sunday before Christmas

Theme: The Promise of Redemption; Moses.

A new collect by the Liturgical Commission and inspired by the CSI collect for Pentecost 22. It is based primarily on Exodus 6.2–8, the Old Testament reading for Year 2.

Fifth Sunday before Christmas

Theme: The Remnant of Israel.

1   The first collect is an adaptation by the Liturgical Commission of the CSI collect for Advent 2. It is based primarily on Isaiah 10.20–3 and Romans 9.19–28, the Old Testament and New Testament readings for Year 2.

2   The second collect was one of the Advent collects in the Gregorian Sacramentary, which Cranmer used in 1549 for Trinity 25. The opening word *Excita*, 'Stir up' was commonly used in the early sacramentaries for the Advent collects, being applied either to God's power or to men's hearts and wills.

Advent Sunday

Theme: The Advent Hope.

Cranmer composed this collect for 1549, basing it on two ancient prayers:

1   Another *Excita* Advent collect from the Gregorian Sacramentary, based on Romans 13.12, a verse from the traditional Advent reading appointed for Year 2.

2   A post-communion Advent collect from the Gelasian Sacramentary, which also appeared in the Gregorian Sacramentary among 'Other Prayers for Advent'.

Advent 2

Theme: The Word of God in the Old Testament.

Another collect composed by Cranmer in 1549 for Advent 2. It is inspired by another *Excita* Advent collect in the Gelasian Sacramentary, and is based on Romans 15.4, a verse from the traditional Advent reading appointed for Year 2.

Advent 3

Theme: The Forerunner.

The Liturgical Commission has slightly adapted the collect which Bishop John Cosin composed for this Sunday in 1662. The most significant change is the replacement of 'the wisdom of the just' by 'the law of love'.

Advent 4

Theme: The Annunciation.

This collect, which appeared as No. 556 in *Parish Prayers* by Canon F. Colquhoun, has been adapted by the Joint Liturgical Group. No authorship is attributed to it; but it clearly owes its origin to the Angelus.

Christmas Eve

Theme: The Incarnation.

In the Gelasian Sacramentary this was one of the collects for the Advent Masses. In the Gregorian Sacramentary and in the Sarum Missal it was the collect for the Vigil Mass of Christmas. Cranmer changed its preamble and included it in 1549 as the collect for the first Mass of Christmas. 1552 dropped it; but 1928 restored it for use on Christmas Eve. Its original Advent associations are evident in line 6—'when he shall come to be our judge'.

Christmas Day

Theme: The Incarnation.

1   Although this is regarded as one of Cranmer's compositions for 1549, it was undoubtedly inspired by an ancient Christmas collect which appeared in both the Gelasian and the Gregorian Sacramentaries. In 1549 it was appointed for use at the second Mass of Christmas; but in 1552 and in subsequent Prayer Books it became the only collect.

2   In the Gelasian Sacramentary this was the collect for the Vigil Mass of Christmas. In the Gregorian Sacramentary it was the collect for the stational Mass of Midnight at St Mary Major. In the Sarum Missal it became the collect for the first Mass of Christmas at cockcrow. Its early origin and its theme of light are reminders of the origin of Christmas as a rival festival to the pagan celebration of the winter solstice.

Sunday after Christmas Day

Theme: The Incarnation.

Year 1: In the Leonine Sacramentary it was the collect for the first Mass of Christmas. In the Sarum Missal, it was the collect for the octave of Christmas, which was also the feast of the Circumcision. Cranmer did not use it in 1549; and it only reappeared in 1928 as the collect for Christmas 1. The phrases in lines 5–6 'share—humanity, share—divinity', attempt to copy the parallelism of the Latin *particeps humanitatis—consortes divinitatis*.

Year 2: This first appeared as the collect for the feast of the Purification of the Blessed Virgin Mary in the Gregorian Sacramentary. It retained this position in the Sarum Missal and in successive Prayer Books. The Liturgical Commission has now made important changes:

1 Line 3 has been added—'and acclaimed the glory of Israel and the light of the nations'—a direct reference to the Nunc Dimittis.

2 Lines 4–5 are new, referring to 1 Peter 2.9, which is part of the New Testament reading for the feast of the Presentation, an occasion on which this collect is also used.

Christmas 2

Theme: The Holy Family/The Wise Men.

Year 1: A new collect by the Revision Committee of the General Synod. The preamble is borrowed from a collect in the 1928 Order for the Baptism of Infants.

Year 2: An adaptation of the CSI collect for Christmas 2 by the Joint Liturgical Group. In CSI it was 'the wise and the great in every land' who were to be led; this has now been extended to 'the nations of the earth'.

Epiphany of our Lord

Theme: Revelation: the Wise Men.

The same collect as Christmas 2, Year 2. See above.

Epiphany 1

Theme: Revelation: the Baptism of Jesus.

In its original form, this collect, appointed by CSI for Christmas 4, was addressed to Jesus Christ and had no reference to the Holy Spirit. It was then revised by the Liturgical Commission, addressing it to the Father, and including a prayer for the gift of the Holy Spirit. Finally, the Revision Committee of the General Synod amended the petition in lines 4–6, producing the present form.

Epiphany 2

Theme: Revelation: the first Disciples.

In the Leonine Sacramentary this was a collect for one of the masses for September. It was translated by Dr Armitage Robinson and included in the 1928 Occasional Prayers and Thanksgivings in the familiar form, 'Remember, O Lord, what thou hast wrought in us'. The Liturgical Commission has adapted it to its present form in the Alternative Service Book.

Epiphany 3

Theme: Revelation: Signs of Glory.

This collect first appeared in the South African *Modern Collects*, 1972, as the collect for the seventh Sunday before Easter. The Liturgical Commission has amended the petition from 'Look with mercy on our weakness, and in all trouble and danger, help and defend us...', to 'Renew your people with your heavenly grace, and in all our weakness sustain us....'.

Epiphany 4

Theme: Revelation: the new Temple.

This collect, originally the CSI collect for Christmas 6, was amended to substantially its present form in the South African *Modern Collects*. The Liturgical Commission subsequently made one or two minor verbal amendments. It is based on 2 Corinthians 5.17 and 2 Corinthians 6.

Epiphany 5

Theme: Revelation: the Wisdom of God.

This collect came from one of the masses for September in the Leonine Sacramentary. Both in the Sarum Missal and in successive Prayer Books it was the collect for Trinity 9. In 1549/1552 it ran, 'that we, which cannot be [i.e. exist] without thee...'—a correct translation of the Latin *qui sine te esse*... But 1662 changed this to 'that we, who cannot do anything that is good without thee...'. This has been retained in the present ASB form.

Epiphany 6

Theme: Revelation: Parables.

This collect first appeared in 1662 as the collect for Epiphany 6. It was probably written by Bishop John Cosin and is based on 1 John 3.1–9, the Epistle for Epiphany 6 in 1662.

Ninth Sunday before Easter

Theme: Christ the Teacher.

This is a new collect, prepared by the Liturgical Commission and based on John 14.6—'I am the way, and the truth, and the life: no one cometh unto the Father, but by me.' There are also echoes of 1 Corinthians 13.6, Colossians 2.6 and Colossians 2.12.

Eighth Sunday before Easter

Theme: Christ the Healer.

This new collect first appeared in the South African *Modern Collects*, 1972, for this particular Sunday. The Liturgical Commission has made one small amendment, substituting 'Jesus Christ healed the sick and restored them...' for 'Jesus Christ came healing the sick and restoring your people'.

Seventh Sunday before Easter

Theme: Christ the Friend of Sinners.

This collect came from the masses for September in the Gelasian Sacramentary. In the Sarum Missal and in successive Prayer Books it was the collect for Trinity 21. The Liturgical Commission has made one small change in accordance with the principle that collects should include the people who use them: the first person has therefore replaced the third person—'that *we* may be cleansed from all *our* sins'.

Ash Wednesday

This collect, composed by Cranmer for 1549, was clearly based on Psalm 51 and the Sarum form for the imposition of ashes. The Liturgical Commission has made only one change—'perfect remission and forgiveness' becoming 'perfect forgiveness and peace'.

Lent 1

Theme: The King and the Kingdom: Temptation.

This collect, composed by Cranmer for 1549, was related to Matthew 4.1–11—the traditional Gospel reading for the day. The Liturgical Commission has made some significant changes:

1 Line 3: The addition of 'and was tempted as we are, yet without sin' (Hebrews 4.15).
2 Line 4: The substitution of 'discipline' for 'abstinence', and 'in obedience to your Spirit' for 'our flesh being subdued to the Spirit'.

3 Lines 5–6: The substitution of 'as you know our weakness, so may we know your power to save' (1 Corinthians 6.14) for 'we may ever obey thy godly motions in righteousness, and true holiness, to thy honour and glory'.

Lent 2

Theme: The King and the Kingdom: Conflict.

An ancient collect from the Gelasian Sacramentary, which in the Sarum Missal and in successive Prayer Books became the collect for Trinity 18. Cranmer's translation in 1549 was faithful to the original Latin: 'to avoid the infections of the devil'—*diabolica vitare contagia*. 1662 expanded this to 'withstand the temptations of the world, the flesh, and the devil'. Cranmer also translated *mente* as 'hearts and minds'—a translation he repeated on Ascension Day— indicating that something more than mental effort is required in discipleship.

Lent 3

Theme: The King and the Kingdom: Suffering.

This collect was composed in 1882 by Dr William Reed Huntington, an eminent American liturgist and divine. It first appeared in the 1928 American Prayer Book as the collect for the Monday in Holy Week, a position it still retains in the 1979 American Prayer Book. Dr Huntington borrowed the preamble from *The Pious and Religious Consultation* of Hermann.

Lent 4

Theme: The King and the Kingdom: Transfiguration.

This is a slightly adapted form of the collect for the feast of the Transfiguration which first appeared in the 1928 and Scottish 1929 Prayer Books. It is based on the concluding verses of 2 Corinthians 4, which is the New Testament reading for Year 1.

Lent 5

Theme: The King and the Kingdom: the Victory of the Cross.

This Passiontide collect from the Scottish 1929 Prayer Book appeared in a more contemporary version in the South African

Modern Collects, 1972. The Liturgical Commission has slightly modified this South African form: the address has been changed from 'Holy God and Lord of Life' to 'Most merciful God'; the word 'suffering' has been omitted in the relative clause; and 'his sacrifice' has been replaced by 'him who suffered'.

Palm Sunday

Theme: The Way of the Cross.

In its original form this collect was in the Gelasian and Gregorian Sacramentaries. Cranmer made one addition in 1549, adding to the preamble 'which of thy tender love toward man'; 1662 then modified this to 'who of thy tender love towards mankind'. The Revision Committee of the General Synod has changed the petition. Originally the collect referred to Christ's death 'that all mankind should follow the example of his great humility', and then went on to pray that we might 'both follow the example of his patience'. These two 'examples' have now been combined in a single petition that 'we may follow the example of his patience and humility'. The word 'patience' clearly indicates 'suffering' as well as 'endurance'.

Maundy Thursday

1 This collect is attributed to Thomas Aquinas, who is said to have composed it for the new feast of Corpus Christi. Originally addressed to Jesus Christ, it is now addressed to God the Father. The Revision Committee of the General Synod expanded the purpose of the collect. In its earlier form it ran 'that we may ever perceive within ourselves the fruit of his redemption'. It now runs: 'that we may know within ourselves and show forth in our lives the fruits of his redemption'.

2 This is a modern collect, originally composed by the Joint Liturgical Group for use on Maundy Thursday, and making use of some phrases from a prayer attributed to St Augustine. The Liturgical Commission has now expanded and adapted the collect, addressing it to the Father instead of to the Son.

The Blessing of the Oils

A new collect by the Liturgical Commission, based on Peter's speech in Acts 10, and particularly on verses 38–9: 'God anointed Jesus of Nazareth with the Holy Spirit and with power . . . he went about doing good and healing all that were oppressed by the devil . . . we are witnesses to all that he did'.

Good Friday

1   This collect from the Gregorian Sacramentary was later used in the Sarum Missal both as the post-communion for Good Friday and also as the collect *super populum* on the Wednesday in Holy Week, when its reference to our Lord's betrayal was particularly appropriate.

2   This was the third of the Solemn Prayers for Good Friday from the Gelasian Sacramentary. It has now been slightly adapted from Cranmer's translation in 1549. Cranmer translated *pro universis ordinibus* as 'for all estates of men in thy holy congregation'; this has become 'for all your faithful people'. 'Truly and godly serve thee' has also become 'serve you in holiness and truth'.

3   A slightly amended version of the collect which Cranmer produced in 1549 by combining a series of phrases from the Solemn Prayers for Good Friday—principally from the seventh, eighth and ninth. It is, however, clearly set in the context of the final Solemn Prayer: 'Almighty, everlasting God, who wouldest not the death of sinners but ever seekest their life; mercifully receive our prayer, and deliver them from the worship of idols, and gather them into thy holy Church.'

Easter Eve

No collect for Easter Eve appeared in 1549 and 1552. This collect first appeared in the Scottish Prayer Book of 1637. It then appeared in a slightly shorter form in 1662, having been revised by Bishop John Cosin. The Liturgical Commission has now made one change: the phrase 'so by continual mortifying our corrupt affections, we may be buried with him', is replaced by 'we . . . may continually put to death our evil desires and be buried with him'.

Easter Day

Theme: The Resurrection.

1   In its original form this collect appeared in the Gregorian Sacramentary as the second collect for the Wednesday in Holy

Week. Cranmer used it in 1549 as the collect for his vestigial Easter Procession (see pp. 101–2). It did not appear in 1552 and 1662, but 1928 provided it as an additional collect for use during the octave of Easter. The Liturgical Commission has now provided a new preamble, concentrating entirely on the Resurrection and based on 2 Corinthians 5.17.

2   This collect was in both the Gelasian and the Gregorian Sacramentaries. The translation which Cranmer provided in 1549 has been retained with only one significant change: 'preventing' has been replaced by 'going before', thereby providing the literal meaning of *preveniendo*.

Easter 1

Theme: The Upper Room/The Bread of Life.

A new collect composed by the Liturgical Commission. It is based primarily on the Gospel reading for Year 1, especially John 20.20—'The disciples were glad when they saw the Lord'—and on the New Testament reading for Year 1, especially 1 Peter 1.4–5—'You, because you put your faith in God, are under the protection of his power until salvation comes'.

Easter 2

Theme: The Emmaus Road/The Good Shepherd.

A new collect, based on Hebrews 13.20–1, first appeared in the South African *Modern Collects* in 1972. This has now been revised by the Liturgical Commission, resulting in a collect which is almost identical with the RSV, which now reads 'make us perfect in every good work to do your will' instead of 'equip you with everything good that you may do his will', and is a perfectly sound rendering of the Greek text.

Easter 3

Theme: The Lakeside/The Resurrection and the Life.

This collect has been adapted from the final prayer in the 1662 Burial Service, which in 1549 was the collect for the funeral Eucharist. Cranmer probably borrowed this from a collect in the *Dirige* in Bishop Hilsey's Primer of 1539. The first half is based on John 11.25–6, and the second half on Colossians 3.1.

Easter 4

Theme: The charge to Peter/The Way, the Truth, and the Life.

In both the Gelasian and Gregorian Sacramentaries, in the Sarum Missal, and in successive Prayer Books this collect has been appointed for use on Easter 4. Until 1662 the theme of the collect was unity, the preamble being, 'Almighty God, which dost make the minds of all faithful men to be of one will'. 1662 changed the preamble to its present form, however, thereby changing the thrust of the prayer. *Mundanas varietates* is now translated as 'the changes and chances of this world' in place of 'the sundry and manifold changes of the world'.

Easter 5

Theme: Going to the Father.

In the Leonine Sacramentary this was a collect for the autumn Ember Days; but in the Gregorian Sacramentary, the Sarum Missal, and in successive Prayer Books it became the collect for Trinity 12. The only significant change was made in 1662: the final clause 'giving unto us, that that our prayer dare not presume to ask', became 'giving unto us those good things which we are not worthy to ask'.

Ascension Day

Theme: The Ascension of Christ.

This collect from the Gregorian Sacramentary is based on Colossians 3.1–2. In 1549 Cranmer slightly modified it: *redemptorem nostrum* was translated 'our Lord'; *mente* was translated 'in heart and mind' (see p. 274); and the phrase 'and with him continually dwell' was added. The only change in the present form has been the addition of 'Jesus Christ' in line 2, which improves the balance of the line: 'your only-begotten Son our Lord Jesus Christ'.

Sunday after Ascension (Easter 6)

Theme: The Ascension of Christ.

This collect was composed in 1549 by Cranmer and was based on the antiphon to the Magnificat at Vespers on Ascension Day. The antiphon, addressed to Christ, spoke of men as *orphanos*. Cranmer addressed the collect to the Father, and translated *orphanos* as 'comfortless' evidently with Pentecost in mind.

Pentecost

1 In the Gregorian Sacramentary this collect was appointed for the morning Mass of Pentecost at St Peter's Basilica. It has continued as the collect for Pentecost in the Sarum Missal and in successive Prayer Books.

2 This is a new collect by the Liturgical Commission, drawing on three sources: Acts 2.2–3, the hymn *Veni Creator*, and a similar collect from the South African *Modern Collects*, 1972.

Trinity Sunday (Pentecost 1)

1 Trinity Sunday was only incorporated into the Calendar in 1334; but this collect, which is much older, was used in the Gregorian Sacramentary for the octave of Pentecost. In 1549 Cranmer kept closely to the original: 'that through the steadfastness of this faith, we may evermore be defended from all adversity'. 1662 modified this: 'that thou wouldest keep us steadfast in this faith, and evermore defend us from all adversities'.

2 This is an adaptation by the Liturgical Commission of the CSI collect for Trinity Sunday.

Pentecost 2 (Trinity 1)

Theme: The People of God/The Church's Unity and Fellowship.
The collect is the same as the second collect for Good Friday. See p. 276.

Pentecost 3 (Trinity 2)

Theme: The Life of the Baptized/The Church's Confidence in Christ.

A new collect by the Liturgical Commission, based on three sources: the collect for Easter Eve, the collect for the rite of Baptism and Confirmation, and the collect for Pentecost 3 from the South African *Modern Collects*, 1972.

Pentecost 4 (Trinity 3)

Theme: The Freedom of the Sons of God/The Church's Mission to the Individual.

A new collect by the Liturgical Commission, based on Galatians 3.23—4.7, which is the New Testament reading for Year 1.

Pentecost 5 (Trinity 4)

Theme: The New Law/The Church's Mission to all Men.

In the Leonine Sacramentary this collect was appointed for one of the masses for April and clearly referred to those who had recently been baptized on Easter Eve. It retained this paschal link in the Gelasian and Gregorian Sacramentaries; and both in the Sarum Missal and in successive Prayer Books it has been the collect for Easter 3. The present form of the collect differs from earlier Prayer Book forms on two points:

1 Line 4: The petition includes 'we' as well as 'all who have been admitted to the fellowship of Christ's religion'. This maintains the principle of including in the collect the congregation which prays it.

2 Line 5: The archaic verb 'eschew' has been replaced by the modern 'reject'.

Pentecost 6 (Trinity 5)

Theme: The New Man.

This collect first appeared with one of the sixteen Sunday masses in the Gelasian Sacramentary. In the Gregorian Sacramentary, in the Sarum Missal, and in successive Prayer Books it has been the collect for Trinity 19. In the original, and in 1549/1552, it prayed that 'the working of thy mercy may in all things direct and rule our hearts'. 1662 replaced 'the working of thy mercy' by 'thy Holy Spirit', and this form has been retained.

Pentecost 7 (Trinity 6)

Theme: The more excellent Way.

This collect was produced in 1549 by Cranmer for Quinquagesima Sunday, and was based on 1 Corinthians 13, the epistle for the day. Since 1549 two small amendments have been made:

1 Cranmer wrote, 'O Lord, which dost teach us'. 1662 changed this to 'O Lord, who has taught us'.

2 The noun 'charity' has been replaced by the modern 'love'.

Pentecost 8 (Trinity 7)

Theme: The Fruit of the Spirit.

A new composition by the Liturgical Commission, based on two sources: (i) Galatians 5.16.22—'Walk by the Spirit . . . the fruit of the Spirit is love, joy, peace'. (ii) The post-communion collect for Pentecost in the 1929 Scottish Prayer Book.

Pentecost 9 (Trinity 8)

Theme: The whole Armour of God.

In the Gregorian Sacramentary this was the collect for Lent 2. It remained the collect for that Sunday in the Sarum Missal and in successive Prayer Books. This collect is a fine example of the succinctness of the Roman collect, and also of the ability of Cranmer as a translator:

Deus qui conspicis omni nos virtute destitui: Almighty God, which dost see that we have no power of ourselves to help ourselves;

interius exteriusque custodi: keep thou us both outwardly in our bodies, and inwardly in our souls;

ut ab omnibus adversitatibus muniamur in corpore: that we may be defended from all adversities which may happen to the body;

et a pravis cogitationibus mundemur in mente: and from all evil thoughts which may assault and hurt the soul.

Pentecost 10 (Trinity 9)

Theme: The Mind of Christ.

An adaptation by the Liturgical Commission of the 1549/1662 collect for Palm Sunday, based on Philippians 2.1–11, the New Testament Reading for Pentecost 10, Year 1: 'Let your bearing towards one another arise out of your life in Christ Jesus . . . he made himself nothing, assuming the nature of a slave . . . he humbled himself, and in obedience accepted . . . death on a cross. Therefore God raised him to the heights'.

Pentecost 11 (Trinity 10)

Theme: The Serving Community.

The same as the second collect for Maundy Thursday. See p. 275.

Pentecost 12 (Trinity 11)

Theme: The Witnessing Community.

A new collect by the Liturgical Commission, based on 2 Corinthians 5.14—6.2 and particularly on verses 19–20, from the New

Testament reading for Year 1: 'God was in Christ reconciling the world to himself ... he had enlisted us in this service of reconciliation ... we come therefore as Christ's ambassadors ... we implore you, be reconciled to God.'

Pentecost 13 (Trinity 12)

Theme: The Suffering Community.

An adaptation by the Liturgical Commission of the collect for the Wednesday in Holy Week in the 1979 American Prayer Book. The author is unknown; but it first appeared in 1892 and was included in the 1928 American book. It is based on the Old Testament reading for Year 1—Isaiah 59.4–9a—and especially verse 6, 'I gave my back to the smiters ... I hid not my face from shame and spitting.' Cf. also Isaiah 53.10–12; Romans 8.18.

Pentecost 14 (Trinity 13)

Theme: The Family.

In the Gregorian Sacramentary, in the Sarum Missal and in successive Prayer Books this was the collect for Trinity 4. It is based on 2 Corinthians 4.13–18, and especially verses 14 and 18: 'He who raised the Lord Jesus will raise us also with Jesus and bring us with you into his presence ... we look not to the things which are seen but to the things that are not seen; for the things that are seen are transient, but the things that are unseen are eternal.'

Pentecost 15 (Trinity 14)

Theme: Those in Authority.

In its original form this was the collect in the unrevised Roman Missal for the feast of Christ the King. It has now been adapted by the Liturgical Commission to fit its new theme. The line 'govern the hearts and minds of those in authority' is not in the original: *peccati vulnere disgregatae* is translated 'divided and torn apart by the ravages of sin': *suavissimo* is translated 'just and gentle'.

Pentecost 16 (Trinity 15)

Theme: The Neighbour.

This collect appeared in the Leonine Sacramentary as the collect for one of the September masses. It has now been adapted by the Liturgical Commission. Based on our Lord's Summary of the Law (Matthew 22.37–40, Mark 12.29–31), it has appeared in various anthologies of prayer, but has not been used in earlier English Prayer Books.

Pentecost 17 (Trinity 16)

Theme: The Proof of Faith.

In the Gelasian Sacramentary this was the collect for the second of the sixteen masses for Sunday. In the Gregorian Sacramentary, the Sarum Missal, and successive Prayer Books it was the collect for Trinity 7. Cranmer's translation in 1549 did not exactly agree with the Latin original. The Latin said: *Quae sunt bona, nutrias, ac quae sunt nutrita, custodias*—literally, 'nourish that which is good and . . . preserve what you have nourished'. Cranmer wrote, 'nourish us with all goodness and . . . keep us in the same'. While Cranmer's rendering was preserved in successive Prayer Books, the Liturgical Commission has now restored the original meaning with the minimum of change. The preamble is based on James 1.17, from the New Testament reading for Year 1.

Pentecost 18 (Trinity 17)

Theme: The Offering of Life.

A new collect by the Liturgical Commission, based on three sources:

1   The well-known prayer of St Augustine: 'Thou hast made us for thyself, and our hearts find no rest, until we rest in thee.'
2   St Matthew 5.8: 'Blessed are the pure in heart, for they shall see God.'
3   1 Corinthians 13.12: 'Now we see in a mirror darkly, but then face to face.'

Pentecost 19 (Trinity 18)

Theme: The Life of Faith.

A new collect by the Liturgical Commission, based on two sources:

1   Philippians 3.13: 'Forgetting what lies behind and straining forward to what lies ahead, I press on towards the goal for the

prize of the upward call of God in Christ Jesus.'

2   A collect from the Gelasian Sacramentary for one of the sixteen masses for Sunday, which in the Gregorian Sacramentary, the Sarum Missal, and successive Prayer Books was the collect for Trinity 11. Cranmer's was a correct translation of the Latin original in 1549—*ut ad tua promissa currentes, celestium bonorum facias esse consortes*—'that we, running to thy promises, may be made partakers of thy heavenly treasure'. 1662 expanded this to 'that we running the way of thy commandments, may obtain thy gracious promises, and be made . . .'.

Pentecost 20 (Trinity 19)

Theme: Endurance.

A new collect by the Liturgical Commission, based on Hebrews 10.19–23 and John 4.24. Jesus has given the Christian direct access to God, 'by the new and living way which he opened for us through the curtain, that is, through his flesh'. Therefore, 'let us draw near with a true heart in full assurance of faith . . . let us hold fast the confession of our hope without wavering'. The final line is from John 4.24: those who worship God 'must worship in spirit and in truth'.

Pentecost 21 (Trinity 20)

Theme: The Christian Hope.

A new collect by the Liturgical Commission, produced by combining two Ascensiontide collects which first appeared in the South African *Modern Collects*, 1972. The preamble is based on the South African collect for Ascension Day, in its turn derived from a collect in the Leonine Sacramentary; this appeared in the 1912 Scottish Prayer Book as the post-communion collect for the Ascension. The petition is based on the South African collect for the Sunday after Ascension Day, which has affinities with the Prayer for all Sorts and Conditions of Men: 'We pray for your Church: guide and govern us by your Holy Spirit, that all may . . . hold the faith in unity of spirit, in the bond of peace'. Cf. also Ephesians 4.10 and Colossians 1.15–20.

Pentecost 22 (Trinity 21)

Theme: The Two Ways.

The same as the second collect for the fifth Sunday before

Christmas. See p. 269. It will only be used rarely.

Last Sunday after Pentecost

Theme: Citizens of Heaven.

In the Gelasian Sacramentary this was the collect for the first of the Sunday masses. In the Gregorian Sacramentary, the Sarum Missal, and successive Prayer Books it was the collect for Trinity 6. In 1549 Cranmer again showed his ability as a translator: he rendered *bona invisibilia*—literally 'invisible good things'—as 'such good things as pass man's understanding'. He also omitted one phrase: the Latin ran *te in omnibus et super omnia diligentes*—'loving you in all things and above all things'; but Cranmer omitted 'above all things'. 1662 preferred 'above all things' and omitted 'in all things'. The English does not distinguish between the two words used for 'love': in lines 2 and 5 it is *diligere*, literally 'to choose'—an act of the will; in line 4 it is *tui amoris affectum*, literally 'the affect of thy love'—indicating rather the emotion.

(b) Festivals and Holy Days

The Naming of Jesus, or The Circumcision of Christ (1 January)

This is a composite collect. Lines 1–3 come from the 1549/1662 collect for the Circumcision, composed by Cranmer, and based on a Benediction in the Gregorian Sacramentary. Lines 4–7, referring to the Name of Jesus, are by the Liturgical Commission, and are based on Peter's speech in Acts 4, and particularly verses 10 and 12: 'There is salvation in no one else, for there is no other name under heaven given among men by which we must be saved.'

The Conversion of St Paul (25 January)

In 1549 Cranmer adapted the collect for this day as found in the Gregorian Sacramentary and the Sarum Missal, and in so doing changed its thrust: the Latin collect emphasized the example of St Paul, but Cranmer emphasized his teaching. In 1662 the collect was given a longer preamble: instead of 'God, which has taught all the world', it became, 'O God, who . . . has caused the light of the Gospel to shine throughout the world'. The Liturgical Commission has retained the 1662 preamble, but returns to the thrust of the Latin collect by introducing a new last line: 'Grant that we . . . may follow him in bearing witness to your truth'.

The Presentation of Christ in the Temple (2 February)

The same as the collect for Christmas 1, Year 2. See pp. 270–1.

St Joseph of Nazareth, Husband of the Blessed Virgin Mary (19 March)

A new collect by the Liturgical Commission, based on one of the Gospel passages appointed for the day—Matthew 1.18–end, and especially verses 20–1, 24–6—'an angel of the Lord appeared to him in a dream, saying, "Joseph, son of David, do not fear to take Mary your wife, for that which is conceived in her is of the Holy Spirit" . . . When Joseph woke from sleep, he did as the angel of the Lord commanded him'.

The Annunciation of our Lord to the Blessed Virgin Mary (25 March)

This collect was the post-communion collect for the feast of the Annunciation both in the Gregorian Sacramentary and in the Sarum Missal. Cranmer used it as the collect in 1549, and it has been retained in successive Prayer Books virtually unchanged.

St Mark the Evangelist (25 April)

Cranmer composed this collect in 1549. 1662 made one change, transposing the two final clauses, so that the substantive petition became 'we may be established in the truth of thy holy Gospel'. A revised form of the collect appeared in the South African *Modern Collects*, 1972, which avoided the phrase 'being not like children carried away with every blast of vain doctrine' but at the same time retained the positive elements of the 1662 collect. It is the South African collect which appears here in ASB.

St Philip and St James, Apostles (1 May)

In 1549 Cranmer produced a new collect, based on John 14.6—'Jesus said, I am the way, and the truth, and the life'—and John 17.3—'This is eternal life, that they know thee the only true God, and Jesus Christ whom thou hast sent.' His ending, however, was rather abrupt: 'Grant us to know the Son . . . as thou hast taught St Philip, and other the Apostles'. 1662 expanded this to, 'that, following the steps of thy holy Apostles, St Philip and St James, we may steadfastly walk in the way that leadeth to eternal life'. ASB retains the 1662 form with two small modifications:

1 'Eternal life' is preferred to 'everlasting life' in the preamble.

2 'Glory' is preferred to a repetition of 'eternal life' in the conclusion.

St Matthias the Apostle (14 May)

Cranmer produced a new collect for St Matthias in 1549, basing it on the account of the choosing of the Apostle in Acts 1. This collect has been retained in successive Prayer Books. The Liturgical Commission has made only one modification, expanding the petition to include the congregation which uses the collect: 'Preserve your Church from false apostles, and *by the ministry* of faithful pastors and teachers, *keep us steadfast in your truth*'.

St Barnabas the Apostle (11 June)

A new collect by the Liturgical Commission, based on St Paul's quotation of the saying of Jesus in Acts 20.35, 'It is more blessed to give than to receive.' It then illustrates Barnabas as a living witness to our Lord's injunction—cf. Acts 4.37, 11.24 and 15.37.

The Birth of St John the Baptist (24 June)

Another collect by Cranmer in 1549, summarizing in a succinct way the life and teaching of St John the Baptist. Apart from the 1662 substitution of 'repentance' for 'penance' it has been retained unaltered in successive Prayer Books. The Liturgical Commission has made one small change in ASB: in line 4 there has been a slight expansion, from preparing 'the way of thy Son', to preparing 'the way for the advent of your Son', which is more accurate.

St Peter the Apostle (29 June)

A new collect by the Liturgical Commission, based on St Peter's confession and our Lord's response in Matthew 16.16–18: 'You are the Christ, the Son of the living God ... On this rock I will build my Church'.

St Peter and St Paul, Apostles (29 June)

The Leonine Sacramentary contained a collect commemorating the martyrdom of St Peter and St Paul, and it continued to be used in the Gelasian and Gregorian Sacramentaries and in the Sarum Missal. Because the joint commemoration of the two saints was not observed in the Prayer Books, it did not appear in 1549.

Dr Massey Shepherd of the USA produced a new collect based on the original in the Leonine Sacramentary; and this has now been slightly revised by the Liturgical Commission, the main change being the replacement of 'by their martyrdom' by 'in their death as in their life'.

St Thomas the Apostle (3 July)

Another collect produced by Cranmer in 1549 and continued through successive Prayer Books with no significant change. A revised form of this collect appeared in the South African *Modern Collects*, 1972; and this has now been reproduced in ASB with one small change: in line 5 'word and sight' has been preferred to 'touch and sight'. The basis of the collect is John 20.24–9.

St Mary Magdalen (22 July)

The collect which Cranmer produced for St Mary Magdalen in 1549 was one of his less inspired efforts. It did not appear in 1552 and 1662; and when the feast was reintroduced in 1928, a new collect was introduced. This was considerably revised in the South African *Modern Collects*, 1972, and it has now undergone further revision by the Liturgical Commission. There are three significant changes:

1 Line 3: 'Witness to' is preferred to 'witness of'.
2 The rather clumsy 'Mercifully grant that by your grace we may be healed of our infirmities' has been replaced by the shorter and simpler 'Forgive us and heal us by your grace' in line 4.
3 Line 5: 'Risen life' is preferred to 'endless life'.

St James the Apostle (25 July)

Another collect by Cranmer in 1549 and used without change in successive Prayer Books. It is based on the call of St James in Matthew 4.21–2: 'He saw two other brothers, James the son of Zebedee and John his brother . . . and he called them. Immediately they left the boat and their father, and followed him.' The Liturgical Commission has now revised this:

1 Line 4: The phrase 'even to death' has been added—a reference to the apostle's martyrdom.
2 Line 5: 'Every selfish desire' has replaced 'all worldly and carnal affections'.

288

3 Line 6: 'Ready at all times to answer your call' has replaced 'evermore ready to follow thy holy commandments'.

The Transfiguration of our Lord (6 August)

The same as the collect for Lent 4. See p. 274.

St Bartholomew the Apostle (24 August)

This ancient collect first appeared in the Leonine Sacramentary and subsequently in the Gregorian Sacramentary as the collect for the feast of St John the Evangelist. It is in fact suitable for almost any apostle or evangelist. In the Sarum Missal it was used for St Bartholomew, and Cranmer followed suit, using the same petition, but producing a new preamble. 1662 then expanded the petition from 'to love that he believed, and to preach that he taught' to 'to love that word which he believed, and both to preach and receive the same'. The form in ASB is substantially that of 1662.

The Blessed Virgin Mary (8 September)

While this feast now falls on the commemoration of the Nativity of the blessed Virgin Mary, the collect has been adapted from the collect for the Falling Asleep of the BVM in the South African *Modern Collects*, 1972. The Liturgical Commission has made two changes:

1 Line 2: Inevitably a new preamble was required—'who chose the blessed Virgin Mary to be the mother of your only Son'.
2 Lines 3–5: The petition has been changed from 'Grant that we . . . may with her share the splendour of your eternal kingdom' to 'Grant that we . . . may share with her in the glory of your eternal kingdom'.

St Matthew the Apostle (21 September)

Another of Cranmer's collects in 1549, which has been retained in successive Prayer Books. The Liturgical Commission has made three changes:

1 Line 3: The phrase 'the receipt of custom' has been replaced by 'the selfish pursuit of gain'—accurately describing the activity of a tax-gatherer.
2 Line 5: 'Covetous desires and inordinate love of riches' has

been replaced by 'possessiveness and love of riches'.

3　Line 6: 'In the steps of' has been added in the interests of rhythm.

St Michael and All Angels (29 September)

An ancient collect, used regularly for this feast since the Gregorian Sacramentary with little change. 1549 added 'by thy appointment', a phrase which does not appear in the Latin. In the ASB text 'help' replaces 'succour'.

St Luke the Evangelist (18 October)

In 1549 Cranmer produced a new collect for the feast of St Luke. The Liturgical Commission has now produced another new collect, concentrating on two dominant features of St Luke's Gospel, love and healing power (lines 3 and 5).

St Simon and St Jude, Apostles (28 October)

Another of Cranmer's collects in 1549, clearly based on Ephesians 2.20–3, part of the New Testament reading for the day. It is interesting that the theme of unity, which is dominant in this collect, is also a dominating theme of St Jude's Epistle. Apart from 1662 replacing 'congregation' by 'Church', the collect has remained unchanged through successive Prayer Books.

All Saints' Day (1 November)

A further collect by Cranmer in 1549, based on Ephesians 4.11–13. Apart from two small changes in 1662, when 'holy saints' became 'blessed saints', and 'all virtues and godly living' became 'all virtuous and godly living', it has remained unchanged.

St Andrew the Apostle (30 November)

The only collect which emerged in 1552. Cranmer produced a new collect in 1549 based on the tradition of St Andrew's death by crucifixion. Probably owing to the Reformers' dislike of such ecclesiastical tradition, a new collect, based on the call of St Andrew, appeared in 1552 and has remained in use ever since. The Liturgical Commission has made three changes:

1　Line 4: 'And brought his brother with him' has replaced 'and followed him without delay', introducing the important idea of sharing the call with others.

2   Since 'readily' in line 3 implies 'without delay', the phrase 'to follow without delay' has been transferred to the petition in line 6, replacing 'to follow thy commandments'.

3   Line 7: A new line has been added—'to tell the good news of your kingdom'—which balances the reference to 'bringing his brother with him' in line 4.

St Stephen the First Martyr (26 December)

The collect for St Stephen in the Gregorian Sacramentary was first abbreviated by Cranmer in 1549 and then expanded by Bishop John Cosin in 1662, the result being a rather long and tortuous prayer. Both the 1549 and 1662 forms were addressed to Jesus Christ, harmonizing with the saint's dying prayer. In the Liturgical Commission's 1969 Report on Calendar and Lectionary, Canon E. C. Whitaker produced a shorter and simpler collect addressed to the Father, and this is the basis for the form in ASB.

St John the Evangelist (27 December)

The 1549 collect was originally the collect *super populum* for this day in the Leonine Sacramentary. 1662 considerably amplified the reference to light by adding to the final clause 'may so walk in the light of thy truth, that it may at length attain to the light of everlasting life'. The Liturgical Commission has now modified the entire prayer, basing it on John 8.12: 'I am the light of the world; he who follows me will not walk in darkness, but will have the light of life.'

The Holy Innocents (28 December)

A new collect by the Liturgical Commission, which, though based on Herod's ruthless action against innocent children (Matthew 2.16–18), is now extended to include all who suffer from cruelty, indifference and tyranny. It also prays that we ourselves should not be guilty of such dispositions.

Festival of the Dedication or Consecration of a Church

There was no provision for these occasions until 1928. A collect was then provided based on Psalm 93.5 and 1 Corinthians 3.16–17. In the Liturgical Commission's 1969 Report on Calendar and

Lectionary, the Rev. J. D. Wilkinson produced a new collect, in which the element of thanksgiving was more dominant. This is now the basis of the collect in ASB, to which the Liturgical Commission has added a new preamble.

(c) Lesser Festivals and Holy Days

Timothy and Titus (26 January)

This collect is based on the collect which appears in the South African *Liturgy 1975*. The Liturgical Commission has made two changes:

1 Line 4: 'To be his companions in the faith' replaces 'his true sons in the faith to be his companions'.

2 Lines 5–6: 'Grant that our fellowship in the Holy Spirit may bear witness to the name of Jesus' replaces 'Weld us together in the fellowship of the Spirit, that we may witness boldly to the name of Jesus'.

The Visit of the Blessed Virgin Mary to Elizabeth (31 May)

This collect in its original form was the work of the Rev. J. D. Wilkinson and appeared in the Liturgical Commission's 1969 Report on Calendar and Lectionary. It has subsequently been rewritten by the Liturgical Commission.

Holy Cross Day (14 September)

This is a slightly modified version of the collect for Holy Cross Day in 1928. The main change is in line 6, where 'suffer for his sake' replaces 'suffer shame and loss'. Cf. Matthew 16.24–5; John 3.14–15; Galatians 6.14.

Commemoration of the Faithful Departed (2 November)

This collect is substantially the same as that for Easter 3 and for a Funeral Eucharist. See p. 277.

Group Commemorations

This collect first appeared in the Liturgical Commission's 1969 Report on Calendar and Lectionary, where it had been adapted from an earlier collect produced by the Church in Wales. Three changes have been made in the 1969 draft:

1   Line 2: 'Your witnesses' replaces 'thine elect'.

2   Line 4: 'Make us thankful for their example' replaces 'following their example'.

3   Line 6: 'Faithful' replaces 'fruitful in good works'.

Of a Martyr or Martyrs

The preamble is borrowed from the 1928 collect for a Martyr. The rest of the collect is a new composition by the Liturgical Commission, based on 1 Peter 4.13–14: 'Rejoice in so far as you share Christ's sufferings ... If you are reproached for the name of Christ, you are blessed, because the spirit of glory and of God rests upon you.'

Of a Teacher of the Faith or Confessor

This is substantially the 1928 collect for a Doctor or Confessor. In line 6 'proclaim' replaces 'set forth'.

Of a Bishop

This is substantially the 1928 collect for a Bishop. In line 7 'give us grace' replaces 'grant us'.

Of an Abbot or Abbess

This is substantially the 1928 collect for an Abbot or Abbess. In line 5 'inflame us' replaces 'grant that we may be inflamed'.

Of Missionaries

This collect first appeared in the Liturgical Commission's 1969 Report on Calendar and Lectionary, and was written by the Rev. K. T. Street. The Liturgical Commission has slightly modernized it.

Of Any Saint

This collect is based on two collects in the South African *Modern Collects*, 1972. Lines 1–5 are from the collect for a Virgin other than a Martyr; lines 6–8 are from the collect for a Confessor.

The Ember Weeks

1   This collect first appeared in the Scottish Prayer Book of 1637,

where it was appointed to be said at Morning Prayer on those days when the Litany was not said. 1662 then included it in the Occasional Prayers and Thanksgivings, and as the collect at the Ordination of Priests. It has now been adapted by the Liturgical Commission, and is confined to those to be ordained deacons and priests.

2   A new prayer by the Liturgical Commission, which has some affinities with the 1928 prayer for the Increase of the Sacred Ministry. This again is confined to deacons and priests.

NB. It is unfortunate that both these prayers, as they appear in ASB, should specifically refer to deacons and priests. On page 21 of ASB Ember Days are defined as days when prayer is offered for 'all who serve the Church in its various ministries, both clerical and lay, and for all who are to be ordained or commissioned to those ministries.' The collects provided should therefore reflect this breadth and diversity of ministry.

The Rogation Days

1   The same as the collect for Easter 5. See p. 278.

2   A new collect composed by the Liturgical Commission, emphasizing the need for mutual dependence, and the will to provide for the needs of all people.

3   A new collect composed by the Liturgical Commission, but based on the first of the 1928 Rogationtide prayers, and the 1928 collect for Harvest Thanksgiving, which in its turn borrowed phrases from the second 1662 prayer for use in time of Dearth or Famine: 'to thy glory, the relief of those that are needy, and our own comfort'.

Harvest Thanksgiving

A revision of the 1928 collect for Harvest Thanksgiving, and again making use of the above phrases from the 1662 prayer for use in time of Dearth or Famine.

(d) Various Occasions

For the Unity of the Church

1   An old prayer, which first appeared in Germany in the eleventh century, and became part of the Ordinary of the

Roman Mass in the 1570 Missal. It was the prayer for peace, said immediately before the Pax. The original prayer was addressed to Christ, based on his promise in John 14.27, 'Peace I leave with you; my peace I give to you'. Apart from the fact that it is now addressed to the Father, it remains unchanged.

2 A new prayer by the Liturgical Commission, and addressed to the Trinity. It is another prayer which has been adapted from the CSI collect for Trinity Sunday.

3 Another new collect by the Liturgical Commission. It not only prays for the forgiveness of disunity, but for courage to face and accept unity.

For the Missionary Work of the Church

The same as the collect for Pentecost 12. See pp. 281–2.

For the Guidance of the Holy Spirit

1 The same as the first collect for Pentecost, except that the preamble has been slightly changed: 'Almighty God, at all times you teach' replaces 'Almighty God, who at this time taught'. See p. 279.

2 In the Gregorian Sacramentary this collect was appointed for Epiphany 1. It remained so in the Sarum Missal and in successive Prayer Books. It has remained unchanged.

For the Peace of the World

1 This collect was written by Dr Francis Paget, Bishop of Oxford 1902–11. It was included in the 1928 Occasional Prayers and Thanksgivings. It has remained unchanged.

2 The same as the collect for Pentecost 15. See p. 282.

In Time of Trouble

1 In the Gregorian Sacramentary, the Sarum Missal, and in successive Prayer Books, this was the collect for Epiphany 4. In 1662, however, it underwent significant revision. The 1549 form ran: 'that for man's frailness we cannot always stand uprightly; grant to us the health of body and soul, that all those things which we suffer for sin, by thy help we may well pass

and overcome'. The revised 1662 text ran: 'that by reason of the frailty of our nature we cannot always stand upright; grant us such strength and protection, as may support us in all dangers, and carry us through all temptations'. The 1662 text has been retained.

2   The same as the collect for Pentecost 13. See p. 282.

Thanksgiving for the Institution of Holy Baptism

The same as the collect for Epiphany 1. See p. 271.

Thanksgiving for the Institution of Holy Communion

The same as the first collect for Maundy Thursday. See p. 275.

At a Marriage

The same as the collect for the Marriage Service. See p. 381.

For the Sick

1   A new collect by the Liturgical Commission. The preamble is borrowed from the 1928 prayer for the Sick and Suffering, No. 29 in the Occasional Prayers and Thanksgivings.
2   Another new collect by the Liturgical Commission. This includes not only the sick, but those who minister to them.

For the Dying

A new collect by the Liturgical Commission, and based on the commendation in the Funeral Service.

At a Funeral

1   The same as the collect for the Funeral Service. See p. 399.
2   The same as the collect for the Funeral Eucharist. See p. 408.
3   The same as prayer No. 51 in the Additional Prayers for Funerals. See p. 408.

At a Funeral of a Child

The same as the collect for the Funeral Eucharist of a Child. See p. 408.

For the Appointment of a Bishop or an Incumbent

A revision by the Liturgical Commission of the 1928 Prayer during the Vacancy of a See or of a Parochial Charge, No. 11 of the Occasional Prayers and Thanksgivings. The substance of the prayer remains unchanged.

For an Enthronement or an Installation or an Induction

The same as the collect used at all Ordinations. See pp. 435–6.

For the Blessing of an Abbot or Abbess or the Installation of the Head of a Community

The same as the previous prayer for an Enthronement. See pp. 435–6.

For a Synod

A new collect by the Liturgical Commission, and based on the two collects for Pentecost. See p. 279.

For Those taking Vows

The same as the collect for Epiphany 2. See pp. 271–2.

For Vocations to Religious Communities

The same as the second collect for Good Friday. See p. 276.

For Social Responsibility

The same as the collect for Pentecost 11. See p. 281.

For Civic Occasions

A new collect by the Liturgical Commission based on Philippians 2.

Studies:
G. J. Cuming, *The Godly Order* (1983), ch. 3.
J. A. Jungmann, *The Mass of the Roman Rite* (1 vol. edn 1959), pp. 240–54.
G. G. Willis, *Further Essays in Early Roman Liturgy* (1968), ch. 2.

11

The Lectionary

A

HISTORY

1 The Jewish Background

Christianity inherited from Judaism the practice of the regular reading of Scripture in its worship. Although selected passages from the Law (the first five books of the Old Testament, or the Pentateuch as these are sometimes collectively named) had traditionally been read in connection with certain Temple festivals, it was in the synagogue that the systematic reading of Scripture developed. This was an attempt to fulfil the injunctions and exhortations contained in the Old Testament itself to read and meditate continually upon God's Law and to teach it to one's children (see, for example, Deut. 6.7; 11.19; Josh. 1.8). Among one particular group of Jews, the Essenes who lived a monastic style of life at Qumran, there was even an attempt to put this ideal of ceaseless meditation into practice in a more literal manner. Here, apparently, arrangements were made for a continuous expounding of the Law to take place within the community day and night, on some sort of rota basis, and for a corporate vigil lasting one-third of each night, during which the Law was read and studied.

In the synagogue the principal occasion for the reading of Scripture was the weekly Sabbath morning service, at which the books of the Law were read through on a continuous basis from week to week. The extract prescribed for the following Sabbath morning was also used at the Sabbath afternoon service and the services held on Monday and Thursday. The sequence of continuous reading (or *lectio continua* as it is usually called by scholars) was only interrupted at the major feast days of the year, when passages appropriate to the occasion were substituted. Claims have been made that there already existed in the first century a standard arrangement of the readings by which the whole Pentateuch was completed in exactly three years, or even in one year, but it seems more likely that a fixed lectionary system had not yet emerged, and that there was some diversity in practice and in the length of time it took to complete the books.

In addition to the readings of the Law at the Sabbath morning service, there had been added a reading from the prophetic literature (cf. Luke 4.16–30), but little is known about how this was organized. There may have been an independent cycle of continuous reading, or the individual extracts may have been arranged so as to complement the readings from the Law, or alternatively they may simply have been freely chosen by the reader or the ruler of the synagogue.

Whether or not the canonical psalms were regularly used in the synagogue services during the first century is far from clear. In the Temple liturgy some psalms were certainly used, on a selective basis, each day of the week having a proper psalm sung at the morning and evening sacrifice by the Levites, and appropriate psalms being prescribed for the various festivals. All these psalms were eventually taken over in the synagogue services, and gradually other psalms added to them, but it is not known when this began to happen. It has been suggested that there was even a triennial cycle for the Psalter at the Sabbath afternoon service, corresponding to that for the Law, but that seems unlikely, since it has left no trace at all upon the later synagogue liturgy where even in modern times only about half of the psalms are ever used. Thus it would appear that, with the exception of the feast of Purim, when the book of Esther was read, Old Testament Scriptures other than the Law and the Prophets were not generally included in the regular round of reading.

Studies:

L. Crockett, 'Luke 4.16–30 and the Jewish Lectionary Cycle' (*Journal of Jewish Studies* 17, 1966), pp. 13–46.

M. D. Goulder, *The Evangelists' Calendar.* 1978.

A. Guilding, *The Fourth Gospel and Jewish Worship.* 1960.

J. Heinemann, 'The Triennial Lectionary Cycle' (*Journal of Jewish Studies* 18, 1968), pp. 41–8.

L. Morris, *The New Testament and the Jewish Lectionaries.* 1964.

Charles Perrot, *La lecture de la Bible dans la synagogue.* Hildesheim 1973.

J. R. Porter, 'The Pentateuch and the Triennial Lectionary Cycle', in F. F. Bruce, (ed.), *Promise and Fulfilment* (1963), pp. 163–74.

2 Early Christian Practice

We have no explicit evidence in the New Testament for the existence of early Christian liturgical assemblies in which the Old Testament Scriptures were systematically read, but it is more than likely that the synagogue pattern was maintained at least among Jewish Christians in the first century, and probably also among Gentile Christians too. This presumption is supported by the fact that early Christian preaching and apologetic, as evidenced from the New Testament, drew strongly upon Old Testament texts, and especially the prophetic literature and the book of Psalms. Indeed many New Testament books probably have their roots in the exposition or sermon which customarily followed the readings in the synagogue service. St Paul gave instructions for his letters to be read aloud to the congregations to whom they were sent (Col. 4.16; 1 Thess. 5.27), and this was probably done at this point in the service—the Epistle certainly came to follow the Old Testament reading(s) in later Christian practice; and the collections of stories about Jesus (whether oral or written) which lie behind the Gospels were no doubt also told and retold in this setting. Attempts have been made by various scholars to demonstrate that certain New Testament books may have been composed precisely for public reading against the background of the supposed Jewish lectionaries of the period, though none of these theories has won widespread acceptance, especially in the light of uncertainties about the first-century synagogue lectionary arrangements (see, for example, the works by Goulder and Guilding cited above, and J. C. Kirby, *Ephesians: Baptism and Pentecost*, 1968).

Whatever may have been the situation in the first century, at least by the middle of the second century, according to the evidence of Justin Martyr at Rome, 'the memoirs of the apostles or the writings of the prophets are read for as long as time permits' (*First Apology*, 67) in the eucharistic service, and we have third-century evidence for the existence of regular services of the word and assemblies for instruction (see Tertullian, *De Cult. Fem.* 2.11; *Apostolic Tradition* 35, 39, 41; *Didascalia* 5.19.1). Justin's description lacks clarity and precision, but certainly implies that Christian writings of some kind might be read to the congregation as well as, or instead of, Old Testament Scriptures, and that there was generally no fixed lectionary. At this time consecutive sections of books of the Bible may have been read on succeeding Sundays, as in Jewish custom, with no attempt being made to relate to one another the passages from the two, three or more different books being used on any one occasion, or alternatively the readings may have been chosen by the preacher or presiding minister.

3 Later Developments

Clearer evidence of the way in which Scripture was read in Christian worship emerges from the fourth century onwards. It is not until the middle of the fifth century, however, that any written lectionaries for the major feasts of the year begin to emerge, and not until the seventh century that a complete eucharistic lectionary is found which covers all the Sundays of the year and other days when the Eucharist would be celebrated. It would appear from this evidence that *both* the consecutive reading of whole books of the Bible over an extended period *and also* the selection of particular extracts appropriate to individual occasions were practised.

With regard to the former, there are a number of collections of commentaries on whole books of the Bible by Christian authors from the third century onwards which were obviously first delivered as a consecutive series of sermons; and evidence from Jerusalem and Antioch in the fourth century tells of a regular period of daily instruction for both baptismal candidates and the faithful throughout the season of Lent (at Jerusalem lasting for three hours at a time), during which the bishop went through the whole Bible, beginning with Genesis. Traces of such *lectio continua* have also been detected underlying the provisions of later eucharistic lectionaries for other parts of the year, and it was also the normal manner in which the Scriptures were read in early Western monastic daily offices.

Selective reading at first seems to have been entirely at the presiding minister's discretion. Thus Augustine of Hippo at the beginning of the fifth century frequently refers to the exercise of his own choice with regard to the readings at the Eucharist. On the other hand, as the liturgical seasons and the saints' days began to develop in the fourth century, the custom became established of reading certain appropriate passages of Scripture on those occasions, and it was not expected that these would be changed from year to year. The readings for Easter and the fifty days following were probably the first to be fixed in this way, since they were the most ancient festivals in the Church's evolving calendar. Different geographical areas made their own selection as to what they considered appropriate for such occasions, and often differed significantly from one another, although there was no doubt some exercise of mutual influence, and there were some readings which were so obviously apposite for particular occasions that they tended to occur universally. Thus, for example, the book of Acts was read during the fifty days of Easter in both East and West, since that period was seen as the celebration of the 'age of the Church'—the eschatological anticipation of the Kingdom of Heaven to which the resurrection pointed.

Other factors besides mere appropriateness to the season might also influence the selection of specific readings for particular occasions. Thus, for example, the tendency found in the ancient Roman tradition (and preserved subsequently in the eucharistic lectionary of the Book of Common Prayer) to read on Sundays in Lent extracts from the Gospels which describe Jesus casting out demons can be attributed to the fact that it was the practice to exorcize those preparing for baptism at Easter on those days. Similarly, the proximity of a Sunday to an important saint's day could result in readings relevant to that occasion being assigned to it, as seems to have happened in the case of those for Trinity 5 in the Book of Common Prayer, again inherited from the ancient Roman tradition, which seems to have been influenced by the fact that the Sunday frequently fell close to 29 June, the feast of St Peter and St Paul.

The number of eucharistic lections used on any one occasion also varied from place to place. Sometimes there could be as many as four—one from the Law and one from the prophetic literature, following synagogue usage, to which were added one from the New Testament Epistles, the earliest Christian writings to appear, and finally one from the Gospels. In other places, however, there were only three—one from the Old Testament, one from the Epistles or Acts of the Apostles, and one from the Gospels. In many places there was a tendency to reduce the number of readings to two. In the Roman tradition, for example, it became customary to have Epistle and Gospel on Sundays, and Old Testament reading and Gospel on weekdays, whereas in the Byzantine tradition the two readings are always from the New Testament. Occasionally non-scriptural readings might be used at the Eucharist, usually on saints' days, when accounts of their life and death would be read, sometimes in place of the Old Testament lection. In the Western monastic daily offices readings from ancient Christian authors had a regular place alongside biblical readings.

It is often claimed that psalms were sung between the readings at the Eucharist from the earliest days of the Church, but the only evidence for this custom prior to the fourth century is a reference by Tertullian to a Montanist service (*De Anima* 9). Otherwise the singing of psalms seems originally to have belonged to Christian communal meals, and was gradually added to the hours of prayer, especially where they were observed corporately. In the fourth century, however, there is evidence from a number of places for the inclusion of a psalm in the eucharistic ministry of the word. Its position seems to have varied in different traditions: in some cases it came after the Old Testament reading(s), in others between Epistle and Gospel. It is not entirely clear whether it was originally included as an independent reading in its own right—Augustine, for example, once refers to it as a reading (*Serm.* 176)—or whether it was always regarded as a response to the reading which preceded it and therefore chosen to complement that. It certainly came to exercise the latter function: no attempt was made to include the whole Psalter in the course of the year, but psalms were included on the basis of their appropriateness to the reading or to the occasion in general.

Studies:

G. G. Willis, *St Augustine's Lectionary*. 1962.

For the early Roman lectionary system, see W. H. Frere, *Studies in Early Roman Liturgy, II. The Roman Gospel-Lectionary* (1934), and *Studies in Early Roman Liturgy, III. The Roman Epistle Lectionary* (1935).

For the Byzantine lectionary, see *The Year of Grace of the Lord: a Scriptural and Liturgical Commentary on the Calendar of the Orthodox Church, by a Monk of the Eastern Church* (1980).

4 *The Medieval West*

(a) *Eucharistic Lectionaries*

In the ancient Roman tradition, as in many other rites, there were liturgical assemblies every Sunday, Wednesday and Friday (see Chapter 4 above: The Calendar 1. The Week). When a fixed lectionary began to emerge, therefore, readings were generally assigned to these three occasions each week, as well as saints' days and festivals; only in the seasons of Lent and Easter were readings provided for every day of the week. With many local variations, this came to form the basis of the medieval Western calendar and lectionary. The enormous multiplication of festivals and saints' days in the course of the Middle Ages naturally led to a great increase in the provision of special readings, each of the more important occasions having its own lections assigned to it, and the less important saints' days having 'commons'—appropriate sets of readings not for each individual but for each category of saint (martyrs, bishops, abbots, etc.)—which could be used as required.

The result of all this was that by the end of the medieval period there were few days in the year which did not have their own readings, but this arrangement had evolved haphazardly over the centuries in response to the development of the calendar and to changing situations, and without anyone attempting to compile a comprehensive and balanced arrangement of biblical material. Some important New Testament passages were never read at all in the course of a year, while others were repeatedly frequently. Beneath the later selective readings remained traces of the older *lectio continua*, especially on the 'ordinary' Sundays of the year between Epiphany and Lent and between Pentecost and Advent (see, for example, the Epistles for Epiphany 3–5 in the Book of Common Prayer).

In addition to the biblical lections, each occasion was also provided with other propers—usually an introit, collect, gradual with alleluia or tract and sequence, offertory, secret, communion and post-communion. Of these the introit, gradual, offertory and communion were originally substantial portions of psalmody, the gradual psalm between the readings being the most ancient, and the others having been added to accompany lengthy liturgical actions—the entry procession, the collection and preparation of the bread and wine, and the communion of the people respectively. In the course of time, however, as the style of the eucharistic liturgy changed and these actions disappeared or occupied less time, so the psalmody shrank until it was usually no more than an antiphon, a single verse, the Gloria Patri, and the antiphon repeated. The alleluia attached to the gradual had formerly come between the last two readings in the days when the service normally had three biblical lessons, and the Tract was a portion of psalmody which replaced it during penitential seasons when the alleluia was inappropriate. The sequence began in the eighth century as a musical elaboration to the alleluia, to which in the course of time words were attached to form a hymnic element in the service. The collect, secret and post-communion were prayers used at different points in the service, sometimes linked in theme to the readings or the occasion, but sometimes being of a more general character.

(b) Office Lectionaries

The daily services of the 'cathedral' or non-monastic tradition originally had no regular scriptural readings included in them, and only used a small selection of psalms which generally did not change from day to day. This continues to be the case in many Eastern rites, which only have readings assigned for the festal form of the services, when they are selected for their appropriateness to the occasion, and use the whole Psalter only in those parts of the services originally derived from monastic usage. In the West, however, the *lectio continua* of biblical and non-biblical books had a regular place in the monastic forms of the daily offices, as did the recitation of the whole Psalter. In the course of the Middle Ages the monastic form came to be imposed on the whole Western church, but in this process the original pattern of *lectio continua* was heavily compromised by the proliferation of saints' days and other festivals. As in the case of the eucharistic lectionary, each of these tended to have selected 'proper' lections and psalms assigned to it, frequently including an account of the life of the saint of very questionable historical accuracy. Thus the preface to the first English Prayer Book of 1549 could with justification complain of the medieval provision that

> these many years passed, this godly and decent order of the ancient fathers hath been so altered, broken and neglected ... that commonly when any book of the Bible was begun, before three or four chapters were read out, all the rest were unread. And in this sort, the book of Isaiah was begun in Advent, and the book of Genesis in Septuagesima: but they were only begun, and never read through. After a like sort were other books of holy scripture used ... And furthermore, notwithstanding that the ancient fathers had divided the Psalms into seven portions, whereof every one was called a nocturn; now of late time a few of them have been daily said (and oft repeated) and the rest utterly omitted.

5 The Church of England

The 1549 Prayer Book largely retained the eucharistic readings for Sundays and major festivals which it inherited from the medieval Sarum usage. Such minor changes as were made consisted chiefly of the lengthening of some passages by the addition of a few verses to the beginning or the end, and of the occasional substitution of a New Testament reading for one from the Old Testament or Apocrypha. The collects which accompany the readings were also for the most part translations and adaptations of their medieval predecessors, but there were also some new compositions, especially among those for saints' days where the former versions had proved doctrinally unacceptable because they asked for the intercession or protection of the saint. Each occasion was also provided with a complete psalm as an introit, but all the other 'propers' of the medieval rites were abolished. The principle behind the selection of these psalms seems to have been to allocate ones which were thought appropriate to the particular occasion where possible, and then to fill in the rest with other short psalms in their numerical order.

For Morning and Evening Prayer, however, a completely new arrangement of psalms and readings was drawn up. The psalms were to be recited in numerical order once a month, and the Psalter was divided into sixty portions of roughly equal size for this purpose, one for each morning and evening, with the psalms appointed for the thirtieth day being repeated in those months which had thirty-one days. This cycle was broken by the intrusion of proper psalms on only four days in the whole year—Christmas, Easter, Ascension and Whitsunday. The Scriptures were also to be read through in order, one chapter from the Old Testament or the Apocrypha and one from the New Testament at each service, so that the Old Testament was completed (with a few omissions) once each year, the Gospels three times each year at Morning Prayer, and the Acts and Epistles three times at Evening Prayer (only two chapters of Revelation were ever read). The lectionary was based on the civil year and did not accommodate itself to the liturgical year at all, except by allocating the book of Isaiah to Advent, its traditional season, and by providing proper lessons for a small number of festivals. Of these only six days—Christmas, Circumcision, Epiphany, Easter, St John Baptist and All Saints— were given a full complement of such lessons for both Morning and Evening Prayer; on eighteen other days one or two proper readings were allocated, but fifteen Red Letter saints' days had none at all. The lectionary was so arranged that the continuous reading was resumed without any omissions after these interruptions.

In 1552 the introit psalms were entirely removed from the eucharistic lectionary, but apart from minor adjustments the

Collects, Epistles and Gospels remained unchanged through the subsequent revisions of the Prayer Book. Similarly, the system of psalmody for Morning and Evening Prayer was retained unaltered, except that Ash Wednesday and Good Friday were also provided with proper psalms in 1662. The lessons for Morning and Evening Prayer, however, have been revised several times in the course of the history of the Prayer Book. In 1559 a full set of proper lessons was appointed for all the major festivals of the year, and at the same time proper first lessons for all the Sundays of the year were introduced. Presumably it was felt that it was desirable for the people to hear the more edifying parts of the Old Testament when they attended church on Sundays and not merely whatever chapter happened to have been reached in the daily sequence. Since the whole of the New Testament was held in high esteem, it was apparently not thought necessary to make any special provision with regard to the second lessons. The Old Testament lessons consisted of selected chapters in their biblical order, and only very occasionally in the year does any attempt seem to have been made to ensure that the reading was appropriate to the season.

Minor adjustments to the lectionary were made in 1604 and in 1662, but the next major revision came in 1871. This retained the civil rather than the liturgical year as its basis for the weekday readings, but rearranged the distribution of the biblical material: many lessons were shortened, and chapter divisions disregarded when the sense of the passage required it; 42 chapters of the Old Testament were omitted, and 100 new ones added from 1 and 2 Chronicles and Ezekiel, previously omitted; 12 chapters from the New Testament were omitted and 28 new ones added, including material from Revelation; and the number of lessons from the Apocrypha was reduced from 132 to 44. The New Testament was now to be read through twice each year instead of three times, once in the morning and once in the evening. The proper lessons for Holy Days were also revised, but still no provision was made for proper New Testament lessons for Sunday services, although a second set of Old Testament lessons was appointed for each Sunday evening, to be used either as an alternative to the existing set or at a third service of the day, at which the minister might choose his own second lessons from the Gospels.

Another new lectionary was authorized in 1922. Here for the first time in the Church of England an attempt was made to match the disposition of the biblical material more closely with the progression of the liturgical year, and on the weekdays after Trinity passages from the Synoptic Gospels were arranged to form a composite life of Christ. Also for the first time proper second lessons were provided for all Sundays, alternative lessons for most Sundays, and lessons for the first Evensong of Holy Days. There was also an increase in the number of lessons drawn from the Apocrypha. This lectionary was subsequently incorporated in a slightly revised form in the proposed Prayer Book of 1927/8, and in that same revision some minor adjustments and additions were made to the eucharistic lectionary, mainly in the provision of alternative readings where the earlier lections were thought particularly unintelligible to a congregation (see, for example, Lent 4, Trinity 9), of 'commons' for most of the Black Letter saints' days, and of propers for other occasions in the year, as, for example, the weekdays of Lent, Harvest Festival, and Thanksgiving for the Institution of Holy Communion.

The 1922 lectionary met with some criticism, and in 1947 a new set of Sunday lessons appeared, arranged on a two-year cycle. This too was criticized for failing to do justice to the unfolding of salvation history in the course of the year, and a further lectionary was produced in 1955 which rearranged both Sunday and weekday readings, but retained the principle of a two-year cycle for Sundays. This was subjected to minor revision in 1961.

Two important documents which had a major impact on calendar and lectionary reform in the Church of England were published by the Joint Liturgical Group—*The Calendar and Lectionary* in 1967, and *The Daily Office* in 1968. The principal proposals of the former ultimately found acceptance not only in all the Protestant Churches in England but also in a number of provinces in the Anglican Communion. It saw the liturgical year as based on the three foci of Christmas, Easter and Pentecost, and hoped for the adoption of a fixed Easter. There would be nine Sundays before and six after Christmas, and nine Sundays before and six after Easter, involving the replacement of Advent by a longer pre-Christmas season, and the disappearance of Septuagesima, Sexagesima and Quinquagesima before Lent. The lectionary provided three readings—Old Testament, New Testament, and Gospel—for every Sunday of the year; and whilst paying due attention to the tradition of the Church, it nevertheless indicated a recognition of changing attitudes towards the understanding of Scripture. Earlier eucharistic lectionaries, based on a single year, had not provided an adequate presentation of the rich sweep of

Scripture, and particularly of the Old Testament. It therefore proposed a two-year cycle of readings, since there was considered to be sufficient material in the Bible to provide a good lectionary covering this period, bearing in mind that a second complete lectionary would also be required for the Daily Office.

For the first half of the liturgical year until Pentecost both calendar and lectionary were controlled by the progression of events in Christ's earthly life. Here the traditional four Sundays of Advent were manifestly inadequate to cope with the great themes of the Old Testament in preparation for his coming, and hence nine Sundays were suggested. After Pentecost the Church moved forward under the Holy Spirit: thus in the second part of the year the concern was with the People of God as it journeyed through time, and certain key passages in the Acts and Epistles were therefore of special significance. Indeed, throughout the year the 'controlling' lections were selected first—from the Old Testament before Christmas, from the Gospels from Christmas to Pentecost, and from the Acts and Epistles after Pentecost—and then the allied readings were chosen to support them. It was only then that they were given some order and sequence from which a progression of 'themes' emerged. This was very different from arbitrarily choosing a set of 'themes' and then looking for passages to fit them; the 'themes' simply indicated the thrust of the passages, and did not exercise rigid control. The passages spoke for themselves; and they could say different things to different people.

The Joint Liturgical Group's second publication, *The Daily Office*, supplemented the lectionary proposals by providing, first, a complete set of collects in traditional language; secondly, a regular course of psalmody on a thirteen-week cycle; and thirdly, a two-year lectionary for the office following the same calendrical pattern. Finally, in 1969 the Group published *An Additional Lectionary for use at a Second Sunday Service*, again based on the same principles. It was against the background of these documents, therefore, that work on the Anglican calendar and lectionary was begun. Under the Prayer Book (Alternative and Other Services) Measure of 1966 only *services* could be authorized for experimental use, and hence for the time being the only way in which new lectionaries could secure authorization was by appending them to particular forms of service. In 1967, therefore, the additional eucharistic lectionary material from the 1927/8 proposals—for the weekdays of Lent, Black Letter saints' days, and special occasions—was appended to Series 1 Holy Communion.

To this were added the Old Testament readings for Sundays and Red Letter days which had already appeared in the 1960 Indian Prayer Book, since these fitted with the 1662 material and provided a short-term improvement.

In 1969 the Liturgical Commission published its report, *The Calendar and Lessons for the Church's Year*, which accepted almost the whole of the Joint Liturgical Group's two-year eucharistic lectionary for Sundays, together with the collects and the lectionary for the second service. The Commission made certain amendments to it, and added material for saints' days. It also included a set of rules to provide guidance on the material to be used when Holy Days overlapped with one another. No such rules had existed in the 1662 book, and the 1927/8 rules had, of course, never been authorized. The lectionary was eventually appended to Holy Communion Series 3 and authorized in 1973, and the Table of Rules was also authorized in the same year under the Prayer Book (Further Provisions) Measure 1968. Meanwhile, the Joint Liturgical Group's lectionary and table of psalms from *The Daily Office* had been appended to Morning and Evening Prayer Series 2 Revised as an alternative to the existing arrangements, and they were authorized for use in November 1971. In 1975 a table of lessons for Holy Days was appended to Morning and Evening Prayer Series 3, and was authorized from November of that year. Finally, the Liturgical Commission produced a set of collects in contemporary language which were appended to the lectionary of Holy Communion Series 3 and were authorized for use from February 1977.

It is not surprising that this piecemeal authorization of calendar and lectionary material appearing in various documents revealed a number of anomalies. The Liturgical Commission therefore reviewed the whole field, and brought together all the material, except for the collects, in a comprehensive report, *The Calendar, Lectionary and Rules to order the Service* (GS 292), in 1976. This underwent a lengthy examination by a revision committee of the General Synod; and whilst many details were amended, the general principles underlying the previous work remained intact. It was authorized for use in October 1979 and subsequently incorporated in the Alternative Service Book. While the Joint Liturgical Group undoubtedly inspired a great deal of this extremely complicated process, the Church of England also owed a great debt to one member of the Liturgical Commission, Canon E. C. Whitaker, whose mastery of lectionary detail was quite remarkable. His patience and diligence in the long and exacting exercise resulted in the Commission describing GS 292 as 'Whitaker's Almanac'.

One element missing from GS 292 was a eucharistic lectionary for use on weekdays. The Liturgical Commission produced a set of proposals in 1976, but these met with opposition in the House of Bishops, where it was felt that the existing Roman Catholic lectionary should be adopted, largely on grounds of convenience and economy: it was already available in print, and its acceptance by the Church of England would be a gesture of ecumenical significance. On the other hand, the fact that it was geared to a different calendar was a disadvantage. After debate, a compromise was reached whereby the Liturgical Commission was asked to prepare a lectionary 'based on the Roman lectionary for those weekdays for which no separate provision is made'. Such a lectionary, so arranged that readings would be used on the same day as in the Roman Catholic Church, was finally approved in November 1979, and incorporated in ASB.

B

COMMENTARY

The Sunday Readings
(Tables 1A and B, pp. 983–1042; Table 3A, pp. 1049–60)

Introduction

There are some parishes or groups of parishes where the pattern of Sunday services must of necessity vary from week to week owing to a shortage of clergy. For example, it might only be possible to have a Eucharist once a fortnight or even once a month: on the other Sundays a reader takes Morning Prayer. The lectionaries for the Sunday Eucharist and the Sunday Office have been so planned, however, that where such a situation exists, it is still possible for worshippers to follow a coherent Ministry of the Word week by week. Seven readings are provided for every Sunday—three for the Eucharist and two each for Morning and Evening Prayer—all on a two-yearly basis except on a small number of occasions. The thrust or theme of these seven readings is generally the same; and with a few exceptions, the eucharistic readings for one year are the basis of the readings at Evening Prayer for the other year. If required, the eucharistic readings may also be used at Morning or

311

Evening Prayer, but not vice versa; since Office readings tend to be longer than those of the Eucharist, the use of such readings at the Eucharist might make the Eucharist unnecessarily long. Of the three eucharistic readings, the Gospel is mandatory; and if only two readings are used, the starred or controlling reading is to be preferred—the Old Testament reading on the nine Sundays before Christmas, and the New Testament reading on the Sundays after Pentecost. From Christmas to Pentecost there is an open choice between Old Testament and New Testament readings.

While the eucharistic lectionary, with small amendments, is that produced by the Joint Liturgical Group in 1967, it must not be thought that it is an entirely new composition. Many readings, particularly in the first half of the year, are traditional, coming not only from the 1549/1662 Prayer Books, but also from the pre-Reformation books. In the second half of the year many of the readings are also ancient, although not always allocated to the same Sundays. An effort has also been made in the Office lectionary to make the maximum use of the 1961 lectionary; although here, too, there has been a considerable reallocation of readings, owing partly to the fact that some of them have been borrowed for the Eucharist, and partly to the fact that the principle of course reading has been abandoned. To achieve a unity of theme between Old and New Testament readings and at the same time to pursue reading in course is simply not possible. Readings at Evening Prayer are generally taken care of, for they derive from the eucharistic readings of the other year. But at Morning Prayer an attempt has been made to rearrange the readings from the 1961 lectionary, together with other readings—less familiar, perhaps, but nevertheless valuable—so that each pair of readings cohere with each other and with the overall Sunday theme. It could be claimed that nearly all the 1961 lectionary has been included; but the context in which the readings are used is now new and more rewarding.

Six versions of the Bible were authorized for use under the Versions of the Bible Measure 1965: the Authorized Version of 1611, the Revised Version, the Revised Standard Version (the Common Bible), the New English Bible, the Jerusalem Bible, and the *Good News Bible* (Today's English Version). ASB has drawn on the last four of these versions in setting out the eucharistic readings for Sundays, Festivals and Greater Holy Days in full. Each version has its own particular merits, and while the choice cannot be entirely objective, an attempt has been made to comply with certain principles—accuracy of translation, simplicity, clarity, the requirements of reading aloud in public, and familiarity of language. There is, however, no obligation to use the text provided: any of the authorized versions of the Bible may be used. In the interests of intelligibility, small necessary adjustments are often made at the beginning of readings: 'He entered' becomes 'Jesus entered', while readings drawn from our Lord's discourses are prefixed by 'Jesus said' or 'Jesus said to his disciples'.

The Nine Sundays before Christmas

On the nine Sundays before Christmas the controlling Old Testament readings trace the story of the Creation, the Fall, and the Saving Purposes of God leading to the Incarnation. In the first period Genesis and Exodus predominate, successive Sundays illustrating the place of Abraham, Moses and Elijah in the divine dispensation. Then the prophetic witness takes over on Advent Sunday, retaining the traditional Advent theme of the coming of Christ, both at Christmas and at the end of time. Advent 2, which Cranmer's collect diverted into the function of 'Bible Sunday', retains its proper and related emphasis on the Old Testament witness to Christ. Then Advent 3 and 4 are concerned with two vital predecessors of Christ—John the Baptist and our Lord's Mother.

Christmas and Epiphany

With Christmas the Gospel becomes the controlling lesson, and from now until Pentecost it proceeds to set out the life and ministry of Jesus Christ in more or less chronological order. The problem of the Christmas–Epiphany period is the fitting of a great deal of material into a period which can vary considerably in length. It can only be resolved by dealing with some themes in alternate years. Christmas Day is provided with three sets of readings, ensuring adequate material for a midnight Eucharist. Christmas 1 then portrays our Lord's presentation in the Temple in both years. Christmas 2 attempts to cover two very different themes over the two years. In the first year it deals with our Lord's boyhood visit to the Temple—the only point at which it can really be fitted in; while in the second year an opportunity is provided for including the Epiphany itself in the Sunday material, by repeating the visit of the Wise Men but expanding it to include the flight into Egypt, so giving rise to the theme 'The Holy Family'.

The Sundays of Epiphany deal with different aspects of revelation—miracles, parables, the cleansing of the Temple. The most significant is Epiphany 1, which deals with the baptism of Jesus: this brings the Church of England in line with most other Churches in commemorating this important 'revelation' of Jesus—an event which was ignored in 1662.

The Nine Sundays before Easter

The three pre-Lent Sundays are devoted to crucial aspects of our Lord's ministry, seen under the titles 'Christ the Teacher, Christ the Healer, and Christ the Friend of Sinners'. The last of these titles forms a suitable introduction to the themes of Lent. In the Gospels baptism and temptations come together: but in the calendar, baptism is tied to Epiphany and temptations are tied to Lent. Any movement through our Lord's ministry must therefore be disturbed by the maintenance of the historical association in the calendar of the temptations with Lent. In deference to long tradition, therefore, but not in chronological order, Lent 1 deals with the temptations—the opening of the struggle of the King and his Kingdom against evil. This conflict then continues to be seen in the cleansing of the Temple and the casting out of devils (Lent 2), and Peter's confession and our Lord's announcement of the passion (Lent 3). Lent 4 provides a further prediction of the passion and the transfiguration—eminently suitable for mid-Lent—while in Lent 5 and Palm Sunday the cross comes increasingly clearly into view.

It should be noted that the Old Testament readings for the Sundays in Lent are remarkably similar to those of the ninth to the fifth Sundays before Christmas. Both deal with the creation and the fall and the working out of the pattern of redemption. At a very early date such readings were also used at the Easter vigil. They are singularly appropriate both before Christmas and before Easter. Before Christmas they provide a suitable background to our Lord's incarnation and ministry; before Easter they provide a suitable background to our Lord's redemptive work in the passion, death and resurrection.

Easter to Pentecost

The Gospel continues to be the controlling reading. In the first year it presents the resurrection appearances leading to the ascension. In the second year these are replaced by the concept of eternal life as presented in the great 'I am' passages in St John's Gospel: these point to the eternal Christ, and his abiding reality in the life of the Church and of the individual Christian. Easter 5 retains its traditional observance of Rogation Sunday under the theme 'Going to the Father'; while Easter 6 is a visible reminder that Ascentiontide is still within the great 'fifty days' of Easter. On this Sunday the theme of the ascension is repeated, so ensuring that Sunday worshippers do not miss the fact and the teaching of the day, even if they have missed the day itself.

Pentecost

The eucharistic readings for the season of Trinity in 1662 appear to be a random choice. The Epistles and Gospels apparently come from a pool of selected readings, which by as early as the seventh century had been arbitrarily attached to certain Sundays. This series existed in two forms, containing substantially the same passages but assigned to different weeks. One of these is reflected in 1662, the other is found in the old Roman missal. In neither case are the Epistles and Gospels co-ordinated: and there is just the trace in 1662 of a rudimentary progression through the Epistles, e.g. Romans (Trinity 6–8), 1 Corinthians (Trinity 9–11), Galatians (Trinity 13–15), Ephesians (Trinity 16–17, 19–21), Philippians (Trinity 22–3).

Now, in ASB, the season of Pentecost has sought to let Scripture speak for itself. The Epistle is the controlling reading, and throughout the season it is concerned with showing the various aspects of the life of the people of God as they move forward in the power of the Spirit on their pilgrimage between Pentecost and Parousia. At the same time it also seems right that our Lord's farewell discourse should also be heard by the Church in the season of Pentecost. In the first year, therefore, it is possible to provide passages from John 13–17 on eleven Sundays to supplement the controlling readings from Acts and Epistles. The last Sunday of Pentecost always concludes with 'Citizens in Heaven', a suitable finale to the Church's pilgrimage towards the ends of time.

A detailed treatment of all the readings in the New Lectionary, Sunday by Sunday, can be found in two works:

G. J. Cuming, (ed.), *The Ministry of the Word: a Handbook to the 1978 Lectionary*. 1979.
J. Gunstone, *Commentary on the New Lectionary*, 2 vols. 1973–4.

The Office Lectionary for Weekdays
(Tables 1A and 1B, pp. 983–1042)

The main purpose of the weekday readings at Morning and Evening Prayer is to ensure that virtually the whole of the Bible is read in the course of the year. Large tracts of the lectionary are based directly on the Lectionary of 1961, and some traditional readings at particular seasons are retained. So Isaiah and Thessalonians are read in Advent; Genesis and Exodus are read in the weeks before and after Easter; and 1 Peter is read at Eastertide. But where this lectionary differs from its predecessors is that all four courses of readings are now quite separate and distinct, and books from the Old Testament are no longer read through continuously both morning and evening. Tables 1A and 1B are so designed, that what is read at Morning Prayer in one year is read at Evening Prayer in the other. Total coverage of the material is therefore complete not only every year, but both morning and evening every two years. Even worshippers who only attend the shorter form of Evening Prayer with only one New Testament reading will nevertheless hear the whole New Testament over two years.

In the Old Testament it is inevitable that some books are not used in their entirety, e.g. Leviticus, Chronicles and Ezekiel; while duplicated material and long genealogies are omitted. As far as possible, when the historical books are read at one service, the Prophets and the other Old Testament books are read at the other. On occasions, however, exceptions have to be made. For example, in the weeks before and after Christmas, in order to maintain the traditional reading of Isaiah, it is necessary to have Isaiah 1–39 in the morning, and Isaiah 40–66 in the evening. In alternate years, therefore, the later Isaiah is read in the morning and the earlier Isaiah in the evening; but since the two parts of Isaiah are so different, this should present no serious problems. Again, since it is not possible to trace the whole course of Old Testament history from Genesis to the Exile and beyond in the course of one year, it is necessary after Easter to read Deuteronomy concurrently with passages from Exodus, Leviticus and Numbers; and this reading of Deuteronomy is so designed to begin just before the reading of the Decalogue in Exodus 20. Deuteronomy can therefore be seen as a kind of commentary on the Decalogue.

The New Testament lectionary is so planned that the Gospels are always read at one service, while the rest of the New Testament books are read at the other. The four Gospels are read in their entirety in the course of the year. St Matthew begins on the ninth Sunday before Christmas, not only because it is the first Gospel in the New Testament, but because its interest in prophecy makes it suitable reading at the beginning of the year. St John is read in Lent, leading conveniently to the traditional Johannine readings of Holy Week and Easter. St Luke begins on Easter 2, and this makes it possible to read St Luke and Acts as a continuous narrative, Acts taking over from the Gospel on the Monday after Pentecost XI.

At certain points in the year course reading is abandoned in favour of selected passages, notably in Holy Week, the weeks of Easter and Pentecost, and before and after Christmas. The weeks of Epiphany 5 and 6 and Pentecost 21 and 22 occur so irregularly that the readings during these periods either repeat what is given elsewhere or, in the case of the Old Testament, provide some less important passages. So, for example, in the week of Epiphany 6 the 'I am' passages of St John are matched by selected Old Testament passages from various books; and in the week of Pentecost 21 ceremonial passages from Leviticus are matched by selected passages from St Luke and Acts.

Well-known passages from the Apocrypha, nearly all used in the 1961 Lectionary, find a place in the lectionary; but in every case alternative readings are provided from the canonical books.

With independent lectionary systems for both Sundays and weekdays, it is inevitable that on occasions passages which are heard on a Sunday are also heard on the Saturday or Monday. Care has been taken, however, to avoid this whenever possible.

The Eucharistic Lectionary for Festivals and Greater Holy Days
(Table 3B, pp. 1061–4)

Cranmer took over most of his Red Letter day material in 1549 from the Sarum Missal; and this continues to be used in ASB, although with some amendments and additions. Old Testament readings have been added throughout, for which considerable use has been made of the material in the 1960 Indian Prayer Book. The most significant changes are as follows:

1   *The Naming of Jesus, or the Circumcision of Christ.* Since the Name of Jesus is now regarded as a more important theme than the Circumcision, the old Epistle from Romans 4.8–14, which concentrated on the Circumcision, has been replaced by Acts 4.8–12—St Peter's proclamation 'Neither is there any

other name under heaven . . . wherein we must be saved'.

2   *St Peter's Day.* Here there is a new Epistle. Acts 12.1–11, Peter's delivery from prison, is replaced by a passage from one of Peter's own Epistles—1 Peter 2.19–end, where he sets out the example of Jesus in facing suffering.

3   *St Philip and St James' Day.* The St James commemorated on this day is St James the Apostle. It was therefore rather misleading to have as the Epistle the opening verses of the Epistle of James, the Lord's brother. It has been replaced by Ephesians 1.3–14, a thanksgiving for the privilege of being a member of Christ.

The Eucharistic Lectionary for
(a) Lesser Festivals and Commemorations;
(b) Various Occasions
(Tables 3C and 3D, pp. 1065–70)

Much of this material is from 1928 but has been extended. While it is set out for use at Holy Communion, the material can equally well be used at non-eucharistic services.

Psalms at Morning and Evening Prayer

The provision of psalms at Morning and Evening Prayer on Sundays has been thought out afresh. Wherever possible, psalms have been chosen to fit the theme of the day, or the season. An effort has been made to make worshippers familiar with the most rewarding psalms, while avoiding the difficulty of a too frequent use of a very restricted number. Where psalms are repeated care is taken to keep the occurrences as far apart as possible. One hundred and seventeen psalms are included in the Sunday table.

An alternative to the monthly recitation of the psalter on weekdays has also been provided. This is based on a ten-week cycle, so arranged that every weekday in the ecclesiastical year has its own appointed psalms. The average amount of psalmody in each office is eighteen verses: the smallest number is seven, the largest is forty, and there are only three occasions when the number drops below ten. All the psalms are used in their normal order; and this inevitably means that some psalms have to be divided. This has been achieved, however, without damage to the sense. There are only sixteen occasions when psalms have had to be divided; and nine of these occur in Psalm 119. The cycle has also been arranged in such a way that no psalms are permanently fixed for morning or evening recitation. Over a period of twenty weeks, therefore, the entire psalter would be heard both morning and evening. There is, of course, the problem of certain psalms or portions of psalms being regarded as unsuitable for Christian worship. Much depends on the individual's approach to the psalms, and opinion is divided. Certain passages regarded as unsuitable have been placed in brackets; and these may be omitted. The omission, however, is completely optional.

Psalms at Holy Communion

Two psalms or portions of psalms are appointed for every occasion on which collects and readings are provided for Holy Communion. They may be used as introits, or between the readings. The selection is new, and does not follow the pattern of 1549 (see p. 306). In every case they have been chosen either as commentary on the readings or as appropriate to the season. They are provided in the hope that those worshippers whose attendance is confined to the Eucharist will receive a balanced diet of Scripture from the Old Testament as well as the New.

The Eucharistic Lectionary for Holy Week

Before the Reformation it was the custom to read the Passion according to St Matthew on Palm Sunday, St Mark on Tuesday, St Luke on Wednesday, and St John on Good Friday. 1549/1662 had a similar pattern, except that Mark was spread over Monday and Tuesday, and Luke was spread over Wednesday and Thursday. ASB follows the same principle of reading the passion narratives, but modifies the way in which it is done. St Mark is read on Palm Sunday; St Matthew is read over Monday, Tuesday and Wednesday in Year 1; St Luke over the same three days in Year 2; and St John continues on Good Friday. On Maundy Thursday John 13.1–15 is read.

St Mark is preferred to St Matthew on Palm Sunday for various reasons. It is a shorter, more compact passion narrative, and is now accepted as a profound piece of theological writing. Bearing in mind the fact that far more people will hear the passion narrative on Palm Sunday than on Monday, Tuesday and Wednesday, if a choice has to be made, then St Mark should take precedence. If there is more than one Eucharist on Palm Sunday, an alternative reading is provided from Matthew 21.1–13, the account of the triumphant entry into Jerusalem. On Good Friday the passion narrative from St John may be divided between Morning Prayer and Holy Communion.

The passion narrative from St Matthew is also read in alternate years in course at Morning Prayer on Sundays in Lent.

Special Observances

Special psalms and readings are appointed for Remembrance Sunday and Mothering Sunday. These are included with the eucharistic readings for the seventh Sunday before Christmas and for Lent 4 respectively. This material is intended for use at special services and should not be regarded as alternative readings for the Sunday Eucharist on these two days.

A collect, psalms and readings are also appointed for Harvest Thanksgiving and these appear in Table 3C (p. 1067). According to Rule 8 (p. 28) these may in normal circumstances replace the material of the Sunday Eucharist. The only occasions when they may not take precedence are on the Festivals of St Matthew, St Michael and All Angels, and St Luke.

A collect, psalms and readings for the Blessing of Oils are also provided for Maundy Thursday, appearing after the collect and readings for the day. The form of service for the Blessing of Oils is not in ASB.

Eucharistic Lectionary for Weekdays
(Table 4, pp. 1071–91)

For those churches where there is a daily Eucharist, or several weekday celebrations of the Eucharist, there are four approaches to the choice of a lectionary:

1 As in 1662, the propers for the previous Sunday may be used throughout the week, unless other provision is made, e.g. for a Festival. This would often entail using the same material on several successive days, which can be monotonous.

2 Morning or Evening Prayer can be combined with Holy Communion, and the Office readings in course can be used.

3 Use can be made of the material in Tables 3A, B, C and D. Indeed, by a judicious use of all four tables it is possible to provide different readings for almost every day.

4 If, however, a course of continuous daily reading is required independently of the Office, this is now provided in Table 4.

This material comes from the Roman Catholic weekday lectionary adapted for use with the ASB Calendar, but so arranged that it can still be read directly from a copy of the Roman missal. This is, in fact, the only satisfactory expedient. Some of the references would be difficult to follow in Bible or psalter, for the readings are composed of scattered verses: and although in the case of psalmody Note 5 (p. 1071) permits the use of other psalms or canticles, this is not a responsibility which every clergyman is eager to assume.

The lectionary begins on Advent Sunday instead of on the ninth Sunday before Christmas, and the two periods (a) 12 January to Ash Wednesday and (b) the whole season of Pentecost from Trinity Sunday, are designated 'Weeks of the Year'. This material may not supersede the material in Tables 1 and 3A and 3B. As with other ASB lectionary material, the material for Year 1 is used in years with an odd number, and the material for Year 2 is used in years with an even number. Two readings are provided for each day; the second is always from the Gospels, and the first is from the rest of the New Testament, the Old Testament or the Apocrypha. Except during the 'Weeks of the Year', when there is a two-year provision for the first reading, the provision is for one year. Week 34 must always be used in the week preceding Advent Sunday. No alternatives are provided for the readings from the Apocrypha, but it is suggested that Old Testament readings from Morning or Evening Prayer may be used instead. The important elements of the lectionary are as follows:

Advent

First Reading: For Advent 1–3, mainly from Isaiah, followed by individual Old Testament passages concerned with the Messiah.
Second Reading: With one exception, from Matthew and Luke: passages dealing with John the Baptist followed by the consecutive reading of Matthew 1 and Luke 1.

Christmas

First Reading: Consecutive reading of 1 John.
Second Reading: Passages from all four Gospels on the infancy and early ministry of our Lord.

Lent

First Reading: Individual Old Testament passages relating to

traditional Lenten themes.
Second Reading: Similar Gospel individual passages up to Lent 4, when selected passages from John 4 to 13 are read until Maundy Thursday.

Easter

First Reading: Consecutive readings from Acts.
Second Reading: Consecutive readings from John.

Weeks of the Year

First Reading: Consecutive readings from books of the Old Testament, Apocrypha, and New Testament on a two-year basis.
Second Reading: Consecutive readings from Mark, Matthew and Luke in that order on a one-year basis.

Admittedly it is an easy, inexpensive way of securing a weekday eucharistic lectionary: but the use of a Roman Catholic Missal is the only satisfactory method of approach. At some stage, however, the Church of England will have to ask itself the question, 'Is another lectionary really necessary, in view of the existing wealth of material available in the lectionary of the Daily Office and in Tables 3A, B, C and D?' If the answer is in the affirmative, the only adequate solution will be found in a system which integrates fully into the ASB Calendar and other lectionaries.

12

Initiation Services

A

HISTORY

General studies:
Michael Dujarier, *A History of the Catechumenate: The First Six Centuries.*
  New York 1979.
G. Kretschmar, 'Recent Research on Christian Initiation' (*SL* 12, 1977),
  pp. 87–106.
J. D. C. Fisher, *Confirmation Then and Now.* 1978.
G. W. H. Lampe, *The Seal of the Spirit.* 2nd edn, 1967.
L. L. Mitchell, *Baptismal Anointing.* 1966.
G. Wainwright, *Christian Initiation.* 1969.
—'The Rites and Ceremonies of Christian Initiation: Developments in the
  Past' (*SL* 10, 1974), pp. 2–24.
E. C. Whitaker, *The Baptismal Liturgy.* 2nd edn, 1981.

Collections of texts:
J. D. C. Fisher, *Christian Initiation: The Reformation Period.* 1970.
Peter J. Jagger, *Christian Initiation 1552–1969.* 1970.
E. C. Whitaker, *Documents of the Baptismal Liturgy.* 2nd edn, 1970.

1 *The Old Testament and Jewish Background*

Water has occupied a major place in the symbolism and ritual of
many religions, for it is naturally rich in associations. It can
express cleansing and purification, or refreshment and regeneration. It can be seen as bringing life, since water is necessary for all
life; but equally it can be seen as bringing death by drowning, and
in some religious myths water symbolizes the chaos before life
began, and in others death is a sea from across which no one
returns. In ancient Israelite practice water was used to cleanse from
impurity (see, for example, Lev. 15.5–13), and the prophets had
spoken of God's people being sprinkled with pure water to be
made clean in the messianic age (see, for example, Ezek. 36.25). In

the first century AD one Jewish group, the Essene community at Qumran, employed regular lustrations as a means of moral and ritual purification. Moreover, the initiation of converts from pagan backgrounds into Judaism included a ritual purification by baptism, in addition to the circumcision of male candidates. This process was preceded by instruction in the Law, and completed by the offering of sacrifice.

2 The New Testament

There were therefore plenty of precedents for the Christian adoption of baptism as the ritual of initiation of new converts into the messianic community. But the immediate precursor and inspiration appears to have been the practice of John the Baptist, who required submission to baptism as a sign of repentance. He in turn may have been influenced by the tradition of prophetic symbolism, by the Essene lustrations, by Jewish proselyte baptism, or by a combination of all three. The synoptic Gospels all record the baptism of Jesus himself by John (Matt. 3.16; Mark 1.10; Luke 3.21–2), when the Spirit is said to have descended upon him, and this obviously became a model for later Christian practice. It is not clear, however, whether Jesus himself instituted the practice of baptizing those who followed him, or whether this was something developed by the Church after the resurrection. The synoptic Gospels contain no account of Jesus baptizing anyone, but John 3.22 and 26 do speak of him doing so. In contradiction of this, John 4.2 states that he, unlike his disciples, did not baptize. Most New Testament scholars would doubt that the command in Matthew 28.19 to baptize 'in the name of the Father and of the Son and of the Holy Spirit' is an authentic saying of Jesus, and would consider it to have been put into his mouth by later Christians who were using this doctrinally developed formula in their initiation practice.

On the other hand, what is clear from elsewhere in the New Testament is that from early times it was the normal custom to initiate new converts into the Church through a process which included baptism, performed no doubt in a river, pool, or a domestic bath-house. The effects of this conversion experience are described in a variety of ways by different New Testament writers, including the forgiveness of sins, cleansing, illumination, new birth, incorporation into the death and resurrection of Christ, and reception of the Holy Spirit.

What else besides baptism was involved in the process of Christian initiation in the first century is not made very explicit in the New Testament. There may have been a preparatory period of instruction, but the Acts of the Apostles gives the impression that there was little, if any, delay between an individual's decision to become a Christian and the act of baptism itself, and it implies that the rite included a profession of faith in Jesus. Whether any other ceremonies formed a regular part of the ritual has been disputed. Some would see the reference to a post-baptismal imposition of hands in Acts 8.17f. and 19.5f., coupled with the reference to 'ablutions' and 'the laying on of hands' in Hebrews 6.2, as indicating what was the normal procedure in all acts of initiation, even though not always explicitly mentioned. Other scholars would suggest that the two instances in Acts are of exceptional situations and do not necessarily reflect the regular initiation practice of the Church, and would point to the fact that a post-baptismal imposition of hands was by no means a universal feature of initiation rites of the early centuries, a surprising omission if it were of apostolic origin. Similarly, some would believe that behind references in the New Testament to being 'anointed with the Holy Spirit' lies the liturgical practice of a literal anointing with oil in the initiation rite (see, for example, 1 John 2.20, 27), whereas others would see such references simply as a vivid metaphor. There is also uncertainty about whether or not children were baptized along with their parents in New Testament times: much depends upon how references to the baptism of 'households' (Acts 16.15, 31–4; 18.8; 1 Cor. 1.16) are understood.

Studies:

G. R. Beasley-Murray, *Baptism in the New Testament.* 1962.

W. F. Flemington, *The New Testament Doctrine of Baptism.* 1964.

R. Schnackenburg, *Baptism in the Thought of St Paul.* 1964.

For the question of the baptism of infants in the early Church, see K. Aland, *Did the Early Church Baptize Infants?* (1963); J. Jeremias, *Infant Baptism in the First Four Centuries* (1960), and *The Origins of Infant Baptism* (1963).

3 The Second and Third Centuries

A much clearer picture emerges from documents of the second and third centuries, but one which suggests considerable diversity of practice rather than a uniform procedure for initiation. Our earliest sources outside the New Testament—the *Didache* and the account given by Justin Martyr—provide only a very brief description. The former speaks of a triple pouring of water in the name of the Trinity, preceded by fasting, the latter adds the information that the rite involved the assent of the candidate and was followed by a celebration of the Eucharist.

Later sources furnish further details. Tertullian, writing in North Africa around 200, states that Easter and the fifty days of Pentecost following it was the normal period of the year for initiation to take place. The rite was presided over by the bishop, or by presbyters or deacons with his authority, and now included a prayer over the water by which it was 'endued with medicinal virtue'; this practice was probably introduced when the Church ceased to baptize in running or 'living' water and began to use domestic baths and pools instead. The order of the rest of the service seems to have been: a renunciation of the devil, accompanied by a laying on of hands; a threefold profession of faith by the candidate, in Father, Son and Holy Spirit, accompanied by a triple immersion in the water; an anointing with oil, symbolizing entry into the royal priesthood (cf. 1 Pet. 2.9); the making of the sign of the cross; and an imposition of hands accompanied by the invocation of the Holy Spirit. The newly baptized then received Holy Communion for the first time in the Eucharist which followed. We also learn from Tertullian that infants as well as adults were undergoing initiation, though he himself did not approve of the practice.

The *Apostolic Tradition* of Hippolytus, which is believed to have originated in Rome at about the same period, indicates that the process there was broadly similar. When candidates for initiation first presented themselves, they were examined as to their motives in seeking baptism. Those Christians who brought them had to testify to their suitability, and inquiry was made into their manner of life. They were then enrolled as 'catechumens' or learners for a period of three years, during which they underwent regular instruction. At the end of this time, their conduct was again examined in order to ascertain whether it truly corresponded to the faith they professed. If so, they then entered a period of final preparation, which included daily exorcism and a two-day fast before their baptism at Easter. After a night spent in vigil, they were baptized at cockcrow on Easter Day, the bishop first praying over the water, and the candidates making a final renunciation of Satan, accompanied by an anointing with 'the oil of exorcism'. As in Tertullian's account, the baptism itself involved a threefold profession of faith by the candidate, accompanied by a triple immersion in water. After coming up out of the water, the newly baptized were anointed with 'the oil of thanksgiving', and then dried themselves, put on their clothes, and joined the rest of the congregation. Then the bishop laid his hand on each one of them, praying for the gift of the Holy Spirit, and anointed them once more, this time on the head alone. The rite concluded with the kiss of peace, and the Eucharist followed. This document also witnesses to the fact that children were baptized along with adults.

The Syrian practice, on the other hand, was rather different. Our knowledge of the earliest period of this tradition is rather limited, and rests principally upon the evidence of the third-century *Didascalia* and certain apocryphal works, and has to be supplemented with the more plentiful fourth-century sources. Here the rites began with an act of renunciation, made by the candidate facing towards the west—the region of darkness—followed by an act of adherence, the equivalent of the Western profession of faith, made facing east, the direction of light. Then came a pre-baptismal anointing, which some scholars have considered was intended to be exorcistic, as in the West, but which seems rather to have originally been understood as signifying entry into the royal priesthood of Christ and identified with his messianic anointing with the Holy Spirit at his baptism in the Jordan. The immersion was accompanied by the indicative formula, 'I baptize you in the Name of the Father and of the Son and of the Holy Spirit'—the words found in Matthew's Gospel (28.19), which itself is thought to have originated in Syria. Unlike the West, there was no profession of faith at this point, since that had taken place earlier in the rite, and no post-baptismal ceremonies at all—anointing or laying on of hands with prayer—but the Eucharist followed directly upon the baptism.

Studies:

Geoffrey Wainwright, 'The Baptismal Eucharist before Nicaea' (*SL* 4, 1965), pp. 9–36.

G. Winkler, 'The Original Meaning of the Prebaptismal Anointing and its implications' (*Worship* 52, 1978), pp. 24–45.

4 *Later Developments*

The fourth century saw a number of very significant developments in the process of Christian initiation. Firstly, the catechu-menate began to decline. After the conversion of Constantine large numbers of people desired to join the Church, and the Church tended to welcome them as catechumens without the rigorous examination of the genuineness of their conversion and of their lifestyle which had earlier been customary. On the other hand, because it was thought that the remission of sins which baptism was believed to convey could only be obtained once, there arose a widespread tendency to delay receiving baptism itself as long as possible, so as to be more certain of gaining ultimate salvation. Thus the nominal catechumenate tended to grow longer and the 'real' catechumenate tended to shrink to what had previously been the period of final preparation, the six weeks or so before baptism at Easter, which developed into the season of Lent. Admission to the catechumenate was effected by a ritual which included the making of the sign of the cross on the candidate's forehead, and sometimes other ceremonial acts as well.

Because it could no longer be assumed that candidates for baptism had already undergone some sort of conversion exper-ience before their enrolment as catechumens, the style of the initiation rite itself began to change and it incorporated elements from pagan mystery religions, especially highly theatrical features designed to produce an intense and lasting psychological impres-sion on the candidates and change their life. The words 'awe-inspiring' and 'hair-raising' are often used by preachers of the period to describe the rites, and various striking pre- and post-baptismal ceremonies are mentioned, among them the clothing of the newly baptized in white garments in order to symbolize their purified status, and in parts of the East the giving of lighted candles to express their illumination through baptism. Moreover, the element of secrecy, which in earlier days had sometimes been a practical necessity because of sporadic persecution, was now used to add dramatic tension to the occasion, the candidates not being told what was to happen to them in advance, and only having the meaning of the various ceremonies explained to them after they had experienced them. Thus the emphasis shifted from the rite as an expression of a prior experience to the rite as a means of effecting that experience.

At this period can also be seen a tendency of the Eastern and Western traditions to adopt features from one another and so move towards a greater conformity of structure. Thus the East adopted a post-baptismal anointing, apparently in imitation of the

West, and the use of the indicative formula, 'I baptize you...' gradually spread to the Western Church, the threefold profession of faith now coming immediately before the act of baptism instead of during it. Having exported this formula, however, the East itself began to substitute in its own rites a passive form, 'N. is baptized in the name...', in order to express the conviction that baptism was the action of God rather than of any individual minister.

Later there came a transition from mainly adult to almost exclusively infant baptism. Exactly the same fear of failing to obtain salvation which at first had caused the tendency to defer baptism as long as possible led later to a desire to baptize babies as quickly as possible, especially in view of the high infant mortality rate, so that they should not risk dying unbaptized. Thus during the period in which the Church was involved in missionary expansion, both adults and their children underwent initiation together. Eventually, however, as Christendom became established, new adult candidates were rare and so only the children of Christian parents normally remained to be baptized. They continued to be admitted to the Church by a process which had originally been intended for adults, and thus were effectively treated as if they were adults who were unable to speak; thus they were admitted to a brief catechumenate in Lent, during which an element of solemn teaching of the Creed continued to be given to them, and sponsors or godparents answered the various questions in the rite of baptism on their behalf.

Studies:

T. M. Finn, *The Liturgy of Baptism in the Baptismal Instructions of St John Chrysostom.* Washington DC 1967.

H. M. Riley, *Christian Initiation.* Washington DC 1974.

E. J. Yarnold, *The Awe-Inspiring Rites of Initiation: Baptismal Homilies of the Fourth Century.* 1971.

—'Baptism and the Pagan Mysteries in the Fourth Century' (*Heythrop Journal* 13, 1972), pp. 247–67. For the later Byzantine tradition see Alexander Schmemann, *Of Water and the Spirit.* 1976.

5 The Medieval West

Apart from some further elaboration, the Eastern pattern has remained fundamentally unchanged down to the present day: babies still receive the full rite of initiation and become communicants straightaway. In the West, however, in the course of later centuries the process underwent further profound changes which drastically altered its appearance.

With the great increase in the number of Christians from the fourth century onwards and the enormous geographical expansion of the Church, something of a problem for Christian initiation was created by the large size of a bishop's diocese in most parts of the world, since it was now impossible for everyone to gather together for a single baptismal service at Easter, owing to the great distances and numbers of candidates involved. One solution to this problem would have been to create more bishoprics and so reduce the size of dioceses, but this was not generally done. The solution normally adopted, therefore, throughout the East and in most parts of the West, was for presbyters to deputize for the bishop and conduct the whole rite themselves, but using for the anointings oils previously blessed by the bishop.

Only at Rome and in southern Italy was this practice not followed. There dioceses in any case tended to be quite small and communication relatively easy, and so it was generally possible for a bishop to be present in most cases. Where it did become necessary for some reason to baptize in his absence, the custom was for presbyters to conduct the whole rite but to omit the particular post-baptismal ceremonies which the bishop had been accustomed to perform personally, the prayer for the Holy Spirit, accompanied by the laying on of hands, and the anointing of the head. The presbyter himself performed the other anointings in the rite, using oil blessed by the bishop. When the bishop was able to visit that church shortly afterwards, he would then perform the missing elements over the newly baptized, and thus supply what had been lacking. Because this delay in completing the rite could be kept very short, it was still possible to feel that the primitive unity of the initiation process and the bishop's part in it had been maintained.

In the course of time, however, the Roman usage was imposed upon the whole Western Church, and in different geographical contexts this solution did not work nearly so well. The delay between baptism and what came to be called 'confirmation' grew longer because of the rarity of episcopal visits. This was compounded by the negligence of parents in troubling to bring their offspring back to church on the occasion of an episcopal visit for a brief ceremony which did not seem to add anything vital—the child having already been admitted as a full communicant member of the Church and assured of eternal salvation at baptism. Because of uncertainty about the origin and theological significance of these detached ceremonies, parish priests too found it difficult to explain why it was important that Christians should be presented for them. In order to encourage the practice, various thirteenth-century Councils tried to fix age limits by which children should have been confirmed, and to threaten parents with penalties if they failed to ensure that this was done. Thus, to cite some English examples, Richard of Chichester in 1246 ordered parents to present their infants for confirmation by the age of one; the Council of Durham in 1249 set the age limit at five, and directed that parents who failed in this duty should be denied entry into the church until the omission had been rectified; and the Council of Exeter in 1287 prescribed three years as the limit, and ordered negligent parents to fast every Friday on bread and water until their children were confirmed.

Gradually, however, these *maximum* upper limits came to be widely thought of as the normal *minimum* ages for confirmation, and so by the end of the Middle Ages it generally came to be considered inappropriate for the rite to be administered until a child was at least seven years of age. This delay was encouraged by the growth of an interpretation of the rite which regarded it as bestowing an additional gift of grace which strengthened the Christian, arming and equipping him for the struggles and battles of life; clearly such a gift was better received not immediately after baptism but when most needed as the child grew up. This doctrine first emerged in a sermon quoted in a document known as the *False Decretals*, published about 850. Since it was wrongly attributed to a fourth-century pope, Melchiades, instead of to its real author, Faustus of Riez, a fifth-century bishop of no particular importance, it gained a wide currency in the centuries following, and was cited by a number of leading medieval theologians, including Thomas Aquinas. However, even at the end of the Middle Ages exceptions to this normal 'two-stage' pattern of initiation still remained: Queen Elizabeth I, for example, was baptized and confirmed three days after her birth.

The primitive practice of baptizing only at Easter and Pentecost, except in cases where there was imminent danger of death, continued to be prescribed by canon law in the West until the twelfth century. Nevertheless, because of the high risk of infant mortality, there was a growing tendency to encourage the baptism of babies as near as possible to the day of their birth. Indeed in

England as early as 693 it was enacted that infants must be baptized within thirty days of birth, the parents being fined thirty shillings if this were not done, and their property being confiscated if the child died unbaptized. By the thirteenth century, therefore, the practice of baptizing throughout the year was becoming widespread, and in the fourteenth century baptism within eight days of a child's birth tended to become the rule: the Synod of Avignon in 1337 even ordered baptism to take place within twenty-four hours of birth.

As a result of this, the period of the catechumenate disappeared from the process of Christian initiation, but the ceremonies which had accompanied it were not entirely dispensed with; they were simply telescoped into the introductory section of the baptismal rite itself. Thus, at the end of the Middle Ages the infant was admitted as a catechumen, with the sign of the cross, at the beginning of the service, and then followed in quick succession all the prayers, exorcistic anointings, and other ceremonies which had originally been spread over a period of six weeks in the earlier Roman rite, including the recitation of the Creed, the final vestige of the instruction of a catechumen, to which the Lord's Prayer and Ave Maria had subsequently been added. As a substitute for the catechumenate, the godparents were enjoined to teach the child these three formulas as he/she grew up. The whole of this preparatory section took place at the church door, the party moving inside to the font only for the baptismal rite proper. The renunciation, which had previously been one of the final elements of this sequence, had now been moved to a position immediately before the profession of faith in the baptismal rite, and cast in the form of a triple interrogation to make it parallel in structure to that formula.

For a long time children continued to be admitted to communion through their baptism, just as adults were, even after confirmation became separated from the initiatory rite. This has continued to be the case down to the present day in the Eastern Church, where, of course, the separation of what is there called 'chrismation' from baptism did not occur. In the twelfth century in the West, however, with the growth of the doctrine of 'realism' with regard to Christ's presence in the eucharistic elements, doubts began to be expressed about the propriety of giving bread to infants, because they would be unable to consume it with sufficient reverence, and so the practice developed of giving communion with wine alone, or just allowing very young children to suck the priest's finger after he had dipped it in the chalice. The subsequent withdrawal from all of the laity of communion from the chalice effectively, though unintentionally, excommunicated children, and it then became the general rule that they should not be admitted to communion until they reached 'years of discretion', although there were very different opinions as to when this should be considered to be: in some places seven was the age, in some ten, and in some fourteen, while in a few others the practice of infant communion lingered on until it was finally abolished by the Council of Trent in 1552. In England the Council of Lambeth in 1281 ruled that no one should be admitted to communion until after confirmation. The intention of this rule was not to prevent children from receiving communion but merely to encourage the neglected practice of confirmation.

Finally, one other significant change may be noted: the transition from public to private. Christian initiation had originally taken place in the context of the corporate worship of the Church, but for the sake of convenience and so that babies would not disturb the normal worship of the congregation, the rites in the West were eventually moved away from the main Sunday assembly, even though they still generally took place within the context of a Eucharist. Similarly, confirmation too, being a very brief ceremony, was often held more or less in private, even at the roadside as the bishop was passing.

Studies:

J. G. Davies, 'The Disintegration of the Christian Initiation Rite' (*Theology* 50, 1947), pp. 407–12.

J. D. C. Fisher, *Christian Initiation: Baptism in the Medieval West.* 1965.

6 The Reformation

Apart from the extreme radicals, the leaders of the Reformation did not question the practice of infant baptism, but proceeded to draw up revised and simplified rites. They dispensed with most of the ceremonies traditionally associated with Christian initiation, since they believed, with considerable justification, that these had either ceased to be understood altogether or had come to be interpreted in a superstitious sense in the popular mind. One version of the baptismal service, for example, produced by Martin Luther in 1526, began with the making of the sign of the cross on the infant's forehead, two prayers, an exorcism, the reading of

Mark 10.13–16 (the account of Jesus laying hands on children and blessing them, the Matthean version of which had become a part of the late medieval baptismal rite), and the laying on of hands accompanied by the saying of the Lord's Prayer. The baptismal party then moved to the font, where a triple renunciation and a triple profession of faith were made by the godparents in the name of the child. The child was baptized with the now traditional formula, 'I baptize you in the name...', and the service ended with the priest putting the white christening robe on the child while saying a prayer of blessing.

With their customary emphasis on the importance of edification, other Reformers tended to replace the symbolic actions with a wealth of didactic and hortatory words. For some, the idea of addressing the infant and the godparents making replies on his/her behalf presented difficulties, which they resolved by addressing the questions to the godparents themselves about their own faith. Thus, in the church order from Cologne commonly known as Hermann's *Consultation*, the section on baptism, which was the work of the Reformer Martin Bucer, contained a public 'catechism' of the parents and godparents which was to take place on the Saturday evening prior to the baptism. At this the minister was to read a very long statement to them, setting out what was held to be the true meaning of baptism, and then they were asked a long series of questions concerning their own faith and intentions. A further exhortation followed this, and afterwards came an exorcism of the child, the making of the sign of the cross, two prayers (drawn from Luther's rite), the reading of Mark 10.13–16, and an imposition of hands on the child, while the Lord's Prayer and Creed were recited. This service concluded with the singing of certain selected psalms and a prayer of thanksgiving and petition for the gift of the Holy Spirit. The baptism itself took place at the Eucharist the following morning, and the order of service began with another lengthy exhortation, the reading of Matthew 28.18–19, and a prayer. The children were then baptized and, after a hymn or psalm, the Eucharist continued.

With regard to confirmation, the Reformers were unanimous in rejecting the notion that it was in any sense a sacrament instituted by Christ, since there was no New Testament warrant for this, but many were happy to retain a rite in which those baptized in infancy might at an appropriate age and after due instruction be examined as to their beliefs, make a solemn profession of their faith, and receive a laying on of hands from the minister accompanied by a blessing or prayer for the strengthening power of the Holy Spirit. Some were even prepared to retain the name 'Confirmation' for this service, and some believed, mistakenly, that this had been the original function of the rite of confirmation in the early Church. Such services also generally constituted the rite of admission to full communicant status in the Church.

7 The Church of England

THE MAIN FEATURES OF THE MEDIEVAL AND PRAYER BOOK BAPTISMAL RITES

SARUM	1549	1552
(at church door)	(at church door)	(at the font)
	Exhortation	Exhortation
	Prayer	Prayer
Sign of cross	Sign of cross	
Prayers and exorcisms	Prayer	Prayer
	Exorcism	
Gospel (Mt. 19.13–15)	Gospel (Mk. 10.13–16)	Gospel (Mk. 10.13–16)
	Exhortation	Exhortation
Lord's Prayer	Lord's Prayer	
Hail Mary		
Creed	Creed	
Sign right hand	Prayer	Prayer
Procession to font	Procession to font	
(Blessing of font)	Exhortation	Exhortation
Triple renunciation	Triple renunciation	Renunciation
Anointing		
Triple profession	Triple profession	Profession of faith
Desire for baptism	Desire for baptism	Desire for baptism
	(Prayers over water)	Prayers
Triple immersion	Triple immersion	Immersion
Anointing	Vesting in white robe	Sign of cross
Vesting in white robe	Anointing	Lord's Prayer
Giving of candle		Prayer of thanksgiving
Charge to godparents	Charge to godparents	Charge to godparents

1549

As can be seen from the comparative table above, the first English Prayer Book contained a quite conservative revision of the baptismal rite, retaining a number of traditional medieval ceremonies, though it also made use of material from Reformed sources, especially the rites of Luther and Hermann's *Consultation* mentioned above. The first part was still to be carried out at the church door, like its medieval counterpart, but was to take place on a Sunday or other Holy Day at Morning or Evening Prayer, 'when the most number of people may come together', in order that they might both witness the baptism and also be reminded of their own baptismal commitment. Thus the intention was to restore baptism as a public service in normal circumstances, though provision was also made for a form of baptism for use in private houses in emergencies, after which the child was to be formally received into the Church.

The service of 'Public Baptism', as it was called, began with a brief exhortation to pray for the candidates, based on Hermann, followed by a free translation of one of the prayers from Luther's baptismal rite. There followed the making of the sign of the cross on each child's forehead and breast, with appropriate words (influenced by Hermann), and a further prayer and exorcism, drawn from the medieval rite. The minister then read Mark 10.13–16 (as in Luther's rite) and an exhortation, which drew attention to Christ's good will and desire to give the baptismal candidates the blessing of eternal life as evidenced by the Gospel reading, and invited the congregation in return to express their thanksgiving for this by saying the Lord's Prayer and their faith by reciting the Creed. After these two things had been done, the first part of the service ended with a further prayer for the candidates (once again drawn from Hermann) and the leading of them into church and to the font.

There the minister was to read an address to the godparents, which made it clear that the baptismal promises with regard to future belief and conduct were thought of as being made by the children through the godparents, who were their 'sureties'. Then followed a triple renunciation and a triple profession of faith (which used the form of the Apostles' Creed). Unlike other Reformed rites, a form of blessing of the baptismal water was retained, not for every baptism but whenever the water in the font was changed, once a month being recommended for this. Each child was baptized with a triple immersion (or pouring of water instead if the child were weak), using the traditional formula. Then came the ceremonies of vesting the child in a white robe and the anointing of the head, accompanied by appropriate formulas.

336

The service ended with a charge to the godparents (influenced by Hermann) concerning their responsibility for ensuring that the children were taught, as soon as they were able to understand, 'what a solemn vow, promise, and profession they have made by you', and were brought to confirmation after receiving instruction in the Christian faith.

The service of Confirmation in this book was similarly quite conservative in form. Its major innovation was the inclusion of an extensive catechism at the beginning, which the child was required to learn before being brought to the bishop, but the actual rite itself was substantially a translation of the medieval rite previously used, except that the anointing was omitted. After the prayer for the sevenfold gifts of the Spirit, the bishop was to make the sign of the cross on the forehead of each candidate, but without the use of oil, having prayed that God would 'confirm and strengthen them with the inward unction of the Holy Ghost' instead of with 'the chrism of salvation'. An explicit laying on of hands followed this, whereas in medieval practice this ancient gesture had tended to be subsumed into the making of the sign of the cross with oil. The rite ended with 'the Peace', a concluding prayer, not taken from the medieval rite but based on one in Hermann's Confirmation service, and the blessing. The final rubric reaffirmed the English medieval rule that 'there shall none be admitted to the Holy Communion, until such time as he be confirmed'.

1552

In the second Prayer Book changes were made in both the baptismal and the confirmation rites, not least as a consequence of the substantial criticism made of the earlier versions by Martin Bucer (text in Fisher, *Christian Initiation: The Reformation Period*, pp. 96–105, 244–50). Among his comments were that the first part of the Baptism service should take place in church so that all present might hear what was said; that all who came to baptism did not need to have the devil driven out of them by exorcism; that the blessing of the water, the anointing of the child, and the giving of the white robe, though ancient ceremonies, were no longer appropriate because of the superstitious opinions which people tended to have about them; that questions should not be addressed to uncomprehending infants but rather to the godparents, who should be asked to undertake to ensure that in due course the child would renounce Satan and profess belief in God.

Although this last point was not fully taken up, his other criticisms did have an effect on the 1552 revision.

Thus, the whole Baptism service was now to take place at the font. The exorcism, the blessing of the font, the putting on of the white robe, and the post-baptismal anointing were all deleted, and the only ceremonial acts which remained were the actual baptism itself and the signing with the cross, which was transferred from a pre-baptismal to a post-baptismal position. The Lord's Prayer and the Creed were also removed from their pre-baptismal position, a sensible amendment, since they interrupted the flow of the service. The Creed was omitted, since it occurred later in the service in the form of the profession of faith, while the Lord's Prayer was now placed after the act of baptism and the signing with the cross, and was followed by a prayer of thanksgiving, thus making the end of the service parallel in structure with Holy Communion, where the Lord's Prayer and thanksgiving prayer follow the reception of the sacrament. The triple renunciation and profession of faith were now run together, so that each was in the form of a single question and answer, and similarly only a single dipping in the water (or pouring) was prescribed.

Confirmation also underwent some significant changes. The opening rubrics to this revised version reveal that the word 'confirm' was now being used in a rather different sense, not that of the bishop 'confirming' the candidate with the Holy Spirit but in the Reformed sense of the candidate 'confirming' his or her faith: in place of the phrase which had spoken of the candidates having to 'ratify and confess' what their godparents had promised for them, the rubric now has the words 'ratify and confirm'. Similarly, the prayer for the sevenfold gifts of the Holy Spirit now asks God merely to 'strengthen them with the Holy Ghost the comforter and daily increase in them thy manifold gifts of grace', instead of asking him to 'send down from heaven ... upon them thy Holy Ghost the comforter with the manifold gifts of grace', a clear movement away from an understanding of the act as a sacramental outpouring to a view of it as prayer for the continuing activity of the Holy Spirit. The ceremonial acts of the signing with the cross and the Peace were also omitted, and a new prayer accompanied the laying on of hands:

> Defend, O Lord, this child with thy heavenly grace, that he may continue thine for ever, and daily increase in thy holy spirit more and more, until he come unto thy everlasting kingdom.

The Puritans would have wished to abolish Confirmation al-together, and were particularly unhappy with two features of the baptismal rite: firstly, the continued retention as an obligatory part of the service of a non-scriptural ceremonial act—the sign of the cross—and secondly, the baptismal questions still being addressed to an uncomprehending infant through the godparents, rather than a commitment to the Christian faith being made by the godparents in their own name. They were, however, unable to win any concessions either during the reign of Queen Elizabeth I or in the seventeenth century. Indeed in the canons of the Church of England drawn up in 1603 a special canon—No. 30—was inserted in order to explain and defend the use of the sign of the cross: it was a primitive feature of baptism, even though it had been abused in the Church of Rome, but it was not to be thought of as part of the substance of the sacrament itself. Moreover, in the 1662 book the baptismal interrogation was strengthened to make it even clearer that it was the candidate and not the godparents who was being bound by the promises: the phrase 'until he come of age to take it upon himself' was inserted in the preceding exhortation, and 'in the name of this child' was explicitly included in the first question. The service otherwise remained substantially unchanged at this revision, except for the addition of a promise of lifelong obedience to God's will at the end of the baptismal interrogation, and the amending of the prayer immediately before the act of baptism so as to reintroduce a petition for the blessing of the baptismal water, 'sanctify this water to the mystical washing away of sin'.

For the first time an order for Adult Baptism now appeared in the Prayer Book. This was not because it was expected that such a custom would spread but it was intended more as a temporary expedient: there were those who had not been baptized as infants during the period of the Civil War and Commonwealth owing to the widespread advocacy of believers' baptism and the neglect of infant baptism at that time, and such a rite was also needed 'for the natives in our plantations'. In its form it was essentially an adaptation of Infant Baptism, which was still seen as the norm.

Confirmation similarly remained substantially unchanged. The catechism was removed from the rite itself and placed earlier in the Prayer Book. It was replaced by the reading of a preface, which was drawn from the opening rubrics of the earlier version of the rite and explained the purpose of Confirmation as a ratification and confirmation of baptismal promises, and this was followed by an act of renewal of baptismal promises to be made by the candidates. The Lord's Prayer was inserted after the laying on of hands, again parallel to the structure of Baptism and Holy Communion. A new final collect was added before the blessing, and the rubric requiring Confirmation before admission to Holy Communion was amended to allow the exception of those 'ready and desirous to be confirmed'—a reflection of conditions under the Commonwealth when many had not been able to be confirmed because of the absence of bishops at that time.

1927/8

Very few changes of any substance in the Baptism service were included in the proposals for revision at this time. The opening rubrics included the directions that baptism was not normally to be deferred more than one month after a child's birth; that parents might themselves act as godparents for their own child, provided that there was at least one other sponsor; and that a deacon might baptize in the absence of a priest. In the rite itself minor changes were made in the language; the prayer after the Gospel was now to be said by all, as was already the common custom; and the phrase 'in the name of this child' was included in all the questions to be answered by the godparents, so as further to clarify their nature.

In the Confirmation service, however, there was a more substantial change. A new preface appeared, which claimed that confirmation was a following of the example of the Apostles in laying hands on those who had been baptized, as recorded in Acts 8, and that Scripture thus taught that 'a special gift of the Holy Spirit is bestowed through laying on of hands with prayer'. The renewal of the baptismal vows was cast in a more extended form than before, and consisted of a renunciation, an affirmation of faith, and a promise of lifelong obedience. Except for a longer final blessing, the remainder of the rite was unaltered.

Since 1928

By 1938 the desire for a change in the initiation practice of the Church of England was being expressed. A Joint Committee of the Convocation of Canterbury in a Report, *Administration of the Sacrament of Holy Baptism*, deplored the haphazard way in which infant baptism was administered and recommended a reform of discipline and a simpler alternative rite. Further reports from the Convocations—*Confirmation Today* (1944), *Baptism Today* (1949), and *Baptism and Confirmation Today* (1955)—not only endorsed the need for a new rite but also drew attention to the lively theological debate provoked by Dom Gregory Dix in 1946 in his essay, *The Theology of Confirmation in relation to Baptism*. He too deplored indiscriminate baptism and pleaded that one necessary reform was the reintegration of Baptism, Confirmation, and First Communion into a single rite. What provoked argument was his reiteration of the point made by Fr F. W. Puller and Canon A. J. Mason many years previously that initiation was incomplete until the indwelling Holy Spirit had been given in confirmation. The most weighty reply came from Professor Geoffrey Lampe in 1951 in *The Seal of the Spirit*, arguing that the fullness of initiation, including the gift of the Spirit, was conveyed in baptism: confirmation might convey certain gifts of grace associated with the Holy Spirit, but it was not an essential element of initiation. Meanwhile another commission appointed by the Archbishops produced yet another report in 1948, *The Theology of Christian Initiation*, which urged the reintegration of Baptism, Confirmation, and first Communion, but also supported the baptism of infants provided that it was not indiscriminate. On the vexed question of the relation of baptism to confirmation, it argued that both were initiatory. This mediating position was endorsed later in the same year by the Lambeth Conference.

It was against such a background that the Convocation of York produced a shorter rite of Infant Baptism in 1951, largely the work of Dr E. Milner-White, Dean of York. It had little to show for the eight years' work which had been put into it, for it was no more than a very modest revision of the proposed rite of 1927/8. It was used for a time on a limited basis in the Northern Province, but its very existence was destined to affect future events. The Convocation of Canterbury also put out a suggested rite of Adult Baptism and Confirmation in the report *Baptism and Confirmation Today*, but this too was little more than a conflation of the two orders of 1928 and never came into use. Much more radical were the proposals of the Liturgical Commission—its first essay in liturgical construction—in a report, *Baptism and Confirmation*, published in 1958. Here the Baptism, Confirmation, and first Communion of adults was set out as a reintegrated 'archetypal' rite, from which all the other rites were derived; the authority for baptizing was based on the baptism of Christ; and with regard to confirmation there was a preference for the 'Dix' rather than the 'Lampe' line.

Although there was no machinery for authorizing the use of the services drawn up by the Liturgical Commission, the Archbishops sent them to the Convocations for consideration. The reaction was highly critical, particularly in York. This was not surprising, for the Commission had rejected York's own rite as a basis for its proposals; but the two most serious objections expressed were with regard to the weight given to Christ's baptism and the emphasis placed on the gift of the Holy Spirit in confirmation. For the moment, therefore, the proposals were set aside. The strength of the second objection was again manifest in June 1966, when the 1928 initiation rites came before the Convocations and the House of Laity for authorization as Series 1 services under the Prayer Book (Alternative and Other Services) Measure. Baptism presented no problem, but Confirmation was rejected by the House of Laity for this very reason. Thus, temporarily, the only Confirmation service authorized for use was that of 1662.

In 1967 the Liturgical Commission produced its Series 2 proposals for Baptism and Confirmation, keeping the same structure as the 1958 rites, but simplifying the presentation and language and going a long way to meet the earlier criticisms. In particular, an attempt was made to accommodate differing views on the work of the Holy Spirit. This time success crowned their efforts, and the services came into use in 1968. The debate continued, however. In 1971 another commission, set up by the Archbishops and headed by the Bishop of Ely produced a report, *Christian Initiation: Birth and Growth in the Christian Society*; and this was followed in the next year by a report from the Doctrine Commission, *Baptism, Thanksgiving, and Blessing*. These documents focused attention on the possibility of alternative patterns of initiation, and on the need for a new service of Thanksgiving after Childbirth. After wide-ranging debate in the dioceses, the General Synod agreed in July 1976 that the latter should be prepared, but that no basic changes should be made in the former.

It was against this background that the Liturgical Commission published its Series 3 Initiation Services in August 1977. These were much more comprehensive than earlier proposals, including Thanksgiving for the Birth of a Child, Thanksgiving after Adoption, Prayers after the Death of a newly-born Child or a Stillbirth, the Renewal of Baptismal Vows, and Conditional and Emergency Baptism, as well as the various orders of Baptism and

Confirmation based on the 'archetypal' rite of integrated Baptism, Confirmation, and Holy Communion. These services, after revision by the General Synod, were finally authorized for use in February 1979 and in this form eventually appeared in the Alternative Service Book.

Studies:

Colin Buchanan, *Liturgy for Initiation: The Series 3 Services.* 1979.

J. B. M. Frederick, 'The Initiation Crisis in the Church of England' (*SL* 9, 1973), pp. 137–57.

B

COMMENTARY

THANKSGIVING
(i) FOR THE BIRTH OF A CHILD
(ii) AFTER ADOPTION

Studies:

C. H. B. Byworth and J. A. Simpson, *A Service of Thanksgiving and Blessing.* (Grove Booklets on Ministry and Worship, 5.)

G. J. Cuming, 'Churching of Women', in J. G. Davies, (ed.), *A Dictionary of Liturgy and Worship* (1972), p. 137.

Early History

According to Leviticus 12 a woman was considered ceremonially unclean for forty days after the birth of a male child, and for eighty days after the birth of a female child. At the end of these periods, she was then required to make a burnt offering and a sin offering at the door of the tent of meeting. She was then free to resume her normal life. Luke 2.22–4 provides some evidence for this practice when Mary came to be purified after the birth of Jesus. There is little evidence for the way in which the early Church regarded purification, but two references are of interest. The *Canons of Hippolytus* (336) laid down that mothers who were not yet purified should sit among the catechumens and not receive communion; while Bede (*Ecclesiastical History*, i.27) recorded that Pope Gregory, writing to Augustine of Canterbury, made the comment, 'If a woman within an hour of her delivery enters the church to give thanks, she is burdened by no weight of sin'. Purification and thanksgiving are clearly the principal features. They are evident in the medieval Roman form in the Sarum Manual 'Order for the Purification of Women after Childbirth before the Door of the Church'. The service was brief: the Lesser Litany, the Lord's Prayer, Psalms 121 and 128, the *preces* from the Marriage rite, and a collect of thanksgiving. The priest then sprinkled the woman, who was veiled, with holy water, led her into church ('churched'), and mass followed.

1549

The 1549 rite, under the title 'Order of the Purification of Women', followed the Sarum rite closely, although the woman was not sprinkled with holy water, nor was she led into church. The service was to be held 'nigh unto the quire door', and the woman was expected to offer the chrysom—or baby's baptismal robe—and other accustomed offerings. The baptism had already taken place, and the rite makes it clear that the mother was not expected to be present. In the service itself Psalm 128 was omitted, and if Holy Communion were to follow, the woman was free to communicate.

1552

1552 saw a change of emphasis. In the first place, the title of the service changed to 'The Thanksgiving of Women after Childbirth, commonly called the Churching of Women'. The woman therefore came to give thanks, rather than to be purified. Reference to the offering of the chrysom was omitted, and the service was to be held near the holy table, suggesting that Holy Communion was expected to follow.

1662

The 1552 title remained, and the service was now to be held 'in the customary place' or where the Ordinary directed. Because the Puritans objected to veils, the woman was now to be 'decently apparelled'. The psalm was also changed, 121 being replaced by 116.1–13, 16, which had reference to the woman and her intention to communicate–'I will receive the Cup of Salvation'. The absence of a blessing also suggested that Holy Communion would follow.

1928

The changes were minimal. The presence of the husband was encouraged, but was not compulsory; and two optional prayers and a blessing were included—the first prayer for the child's upbringing, the second prayer if the child had died.

Recent Developments

With the passage of time the service came under increasing criticism. The language of 1662/1928 was regarded as rather extreme, and the old concept of uncleanness was unwelcome. The need grew for some form of service which expressed genuine thanksgiving for the birth of a child. In 1965 the Liturgical Commission presented its proposals embodying three subjects:

1 Thanksgiving for the safe birth of a child and for the joy of creation.
2 Prayer for the parents.
3 Prayer to cover cases of a still-born child.

Unfortunately these initial efforts were rejected by the Convocations in 1966, being regarded as too brief and not sufficiently simple. For some time little was done; but in 1971 a new spur to fresh endeavour was provided by the publication of two reports. The Ely Report, *Christian Initiation: Birth and Growth in the Christian Society* (GS 30), pleaded for a new service of Thanksgiving for the Birth of a Child; while the Doctrine Commission's report, *Baptism, Thanksgiving, and Blessing* (GS 56), recommended that any new service should contain a prayer of blessing, and should be available to all who asked for it. In 1977 the Liturgical Commission published three forms with its Series 3 Initiation Services:

1 Thanksgiving for the Birth of a Child.
2 Thanksgiving after Adoption.
3 Prayers after the Death of a Newly-born Child or the Birth of a Still-born Child.

These were finally authorized for use in 1979, the first two appearing in ASB with the Initiation Services, and the third with the Funeral Services.

THANKSGIVING FOR THE BIRTH OF A CHILD

Notes 3 and 4 (p. 212) not only encourage the idea that the whole family should be present, but suggest that the Thanksgiving should take place during a public service—Holy Communion, or Morning or Evening Prayer—when other members of the Church can be present.

Section 1

A new prayer by the Liturgical Commission. This is to be said by the minister, expressing at the outset of the service joy and gratitude for the safe delivery of the child, for all who made it possible, and for the family's share in God's work of creation.

Section 2

A further new prayer in which the parents make their response and pray for wisdom and patience in the bringing up of the child.

Versicles and Responses
(section 3)

A series of versicles and responses which dwell on the wonder of God as loving creator. They are drawn from: Luke 1.46–7; Revelation 4.11; Revelation 15.36; Psalm 113.13; Psalm 115.13; Luke 1.50. As an alternative Psalm 100 may be used, or a hymn may be sung.

Gospel Reading
(section 4)

This reading is the passage from the 1662 service of Baptism. Its baptismal associations have long been questioned: but in the present context it is most relevant. The comment of Bishop I. T. Ramsey, Chairman of the Doctrine Commission in 1971, is worth quoting:

> In the first place Jesus showed a welcoming attitude towards children who had no claim on him, and whose parents, it seems, entered into no obligations. Second, he rebuked his disciples who thought this inappropriate. Third, he took the opportunity to explain what entry into the Kingdom meant and its preconditions, and finally he blessed them. (*Baptism, Thanksgiving, and Blessing*, GS 56, 1971.)

The Gift of the Gospels
(section 5)

An optional feature, introduced by the General Synod. An encouragement to the family to learn more of the good news of God's love, and to share in eternal life.

The Lord's Prayer
(section 6)

This is to be said by the whole congregation. See pp. 30–2.

Prayers
(sections 7–13)

The first prayer (section 7) is mandatory, the remainder are optional, provided at least one is said.

Section 7

A new prayer for the child and his/her growth in discipline and grace.

Section 9

A prayer for the home and the family. This prayer has affinities with the collect for Christmas 2, Year 1. See p. 271.

Sections 10–11

New prayers for the child and family, and for the husband and wife.

Sections 12–13

Prayers which are particularly suitable where the child is to be adopted; the second may also be used in cases where a child suffers from some deformity. It is No. 13 of the Concluding Prayers in Prayers for Various Occasions—see p. 143.

Section 14

A congregational prayer, which is similar to the prayer of welcome in the rites of Baptism and Confirmation. It is adapted from a prayer first used in the diocese of Southwark. It prays that the child may eventually be brought to baptism. See pp. 262–3.

Blessings
(section 15)

Two blessings of the whole congregation. These are the two provided in the Prayers for Various Occasions. See p. 144.

Additional Readings

If the service is held on its own, and not within the context of another service, the minister may supplement the existing material with hymns, a sermon, and additional readings, a selection of which is provided.

THANKSGIVING AFTER ADOPTION

For the first time the Church has provided an official rite to accompany the adoption of a child. The form is substantially the same as that for the Thanksgiving for the Birth of a Child. The changes are minimal, and are as follows:

Section 24

A new prayer for the natural parents of the child.

Section 25

A welcome of the child into the new family 'through : . . with . . . by . . . and in the love of God'.

Section 27

This prayer will be omitted if the child has already been baptized.

BAPTISM, CONFIRMATION AND HOLY COMMUNION

The basic rite of initiation in ASB is that of Baptism, Confirmation and Holy Communion. It was recommended in 1948 in the Theological Commission's report, *The Theology of Christian Initiation*, and the Liturgical Commission has consistently made it the core of its proposals in 1958, in Series 2 and in Series 3. It provides for a wide variety of needs, as the sub-title indicates (p.223). Today the number of adults who come to be baptized has increased significantly; and it is recognized that it is desirable that they should also be confirmed at the same time (Note 1, p. 225); nor is there any reason why people who have been baptized at some other time—perhaps in infancy—should not be confirmed with them. Then again it is not unusual for children and their parents to be baptized together: in such cases parents are baptized first and their children immediately afterwards; and if the children are not old enough to make the acts of decision and faith themselves, the parents can answer for them (Note 2, p. 225). Such parents hopefully will proceed to confirmation at the same service. Finally, this service provides an opportunity for parents who are already baptized and confirmed to bring their children to be baptized within the context of the worshipping Christian community. Considerable flexibility is allowed in its conduct, for churches vary in their internal arrangements. This is a matter which should be determined beforehand after consultation between the bishop and the parish priest.

The Preparation
(sections 1–4, 64–7)

The Preparation follows a pattern similar to that of Holy Communion Rite A, with its optional opening sentence—either of the day or season or the one provided—hymn or canticle. The Prayers of Penitence from Rite A may then follow. The collect, which is mandatory, is used at all Baptism and Confirmation services held within the context of the Eucharist. It replaces the Series 2 collect, which expressed a relationship between our Lord's baptism and Christian baptism not acceptable to some scholars and was concerned simply with those to be baptized. This new prayer is concerned not only with all candidates, but also with the Church assembled for the occasion, which is the true function of the collect.

The Ministry of the Word
(sections 5–9, 68–72)

A wide variety of readings is provided, all of which are set out in full on pages 261–74. To have set them out here would have obscured the structure of the rite. The Old Testament readings take into account the attention now paid to Old Testament typology—Noah and the Flood, the Crossing of the Red Sea, the Cleansing of Naaman. In the New Testament readings, the passage from Acts 8 used in the 1928 Confirmation rite, and in the Gospels the passage from Mark 10 used in 1549/1928 Baptism rites have both been omitted. The former had already proved contentious and not generally acceptable in the Series 1 discussions, while the latter is now generally recognized as not referring to baptism. If he so wishes, the bishop may choose readings other than those appointed.

The Decision
(sections 11–16)

Note 12 (p. 226) indicates that, with the bishop's permission, baptized and confirmed members of the congregation who wish to renew their baptismal vows (cf. p. 371) may do so before the Decision rather than at the end of the service. This provides adult candidates with an opportunity of seeing and hearing members of the Church expressing their commitment to the Christian faith before they themselves undertake this step and join this community. A further optional preliminary, provided in section 11, is for the bishop or a priest to state the duties of the parents and godparents, if children are to be baptized (sections 42–3, cf. pp. 365–6). The bishop then goes on to address all candidates for baptism and confirmation, together with parents and godparents. It is therefore necessary, as the rubric in section 12 indicates, that all these people must now 'stand before' him. Not only does this ensure that he can address them directly: it also ensures that they are visible to the congregation as they publicly make their Decision. After a short statement indicating to all concerned what it is they are expected to do—to affirm allegiance to Christ and to reject all that is evil—the bishop puts the three questions.

The Three Questions
(section 13)

The Decision corresponds to the ancient acts of renunciation, and as a necessary preliminary to baptism corresponds to Peter's exhortation in Acts 2.38, 'Repent and be baptized'. Repentance—metanoia—involves more than simply turning away from evil; it involves changing direction and turning towards something different. It is indeed 'repentance from misdeeds' (Rev. 2.22); but it is also 'repentance that leads to life' (Acts 11.18). The necessary first step is the turning to Christ; and until this is done, there can be no turning from evil. Without the former, there is no motive or inspiration to undertake the latter. The old acts of renunciation have therefore assumed a more positive attitude, and for this reason their name has now been changed to 'The Decision'. The wording of the first question, 'Do you turn to Christ?' comes from the act of penitence in the 1662 Holy Communion service, where the phrase occurs twice—in the absolution and in the preamble to the Comfortable Words. It had originally appeared in *The Order of the Communion* in 1548.

In the early centuries the acts of renunciation and the acts of faith were made at different times in the rites of initiation and indeed in different places. In the Roman rite of the seventh century, for example, the former were made on Easter Eve in the final Scrutiny, whereas the latter were made after the blessing of the font at the baptism itself. In Sarum they came together before the blessing of the font, and there they remained from 1549 to 1928. In 1958 the Liturgical Commission proposed leaving them together, but after the blessing of the font, so that the acts of faith and the baptism itself were in the closest possible proximity. Then in Series 2 they were separated, the decision, as the acts of renunciation had now become, coming before the blessing of the font, and the acts of faith coming after. Precedents for all these positions can be found in ancient rites; and ASB has continued with the Series 2 positions.

Where infants are concerned, it is important to be clear as to who is involved in the acts. It had long been the custom for the Church to address questions to children who did not understand them and for the sponsors to answer as the children's mouthpiece. This was the case in Sarum and it was continued in 1549 and 1552, despite the fact that it provoked criticism. The questions in Hermann clearly involved the godparents and not the child; and Bucer objected in *The Censura* and suggested that it should suffice for the godparents to 'give assurance' that an infant, when old enough, would renounce the devil and profess the Christian faith. 'From godparents it should be reckoned sufficient if they promise from their heart to give their best care to the matter.' (Whitaker, *Martin Bucer and the B.C.P.*, p. 96) It was also the Puritan view at the Savoy Conference: the questions should be put to the godparents 'in their own names'. Not only was this view rejected in 1662, but the bishops made their position even clearer by adding 'in the name of this child' to the first question. The sponsors were still the infant's mouthpiece. This situation was retained in 1928. In 1958, however, the Liturgical Commission proposed one small change: sponsors were no longer to reply 'in the name' of an infant, but 'on behalf of' an infant. The important

351

change came in Series 2: parents and sponsors were now asked to make the acts of decision and faith themselves, being at the same time reminded that it was their duty to bring up the infant to fight against evil and to follow Christ. The sponsors were in fact sureties for the infant, and they could only act in this capacity if they themselves were prepared to do these things. ASB now makes the situation absolutely clear: 'Parents and godparents must answer both for themselves and for these children.' (section 13) If sponsors cannot answer the questions sincerely with a good conscience, the problem is not a matter for liturgical reform: rather it is a matter of pastoral administration. In the case of a whole family being baptized together, if the children are not old enough to answer for themselves, the parents answer for themselves and for their children, making the responses in the plural, e.g. 'We turn to Christ' (Note 2, p. 225). The responses are also so framed that no one is left in the slightest doubt as to what is happening: sponsors and candidates clearly affirm—'I turn to Christ. I repent of my sins. I renounce evil.'

The Signing with the Cross
(section 14)

The signing with the sign of the cross was a feature of the pre-baptismal ceremonies in the early Church, not only at the renunciation but also at an earlier stage when the candidate was made a catechumen. It was so found in the Roman rite of the seventh century, and it remains clearly in Sarum. Here, when the infant was brought to the door of the church, at the very outset, he was signed with the sign of the cross on the brow. Later, immediately after the Renunciation, he was signed again, in oil blessed for the purpose on the breast and between the shoulder blades. It was a token of the divine help in the struggle to which the candidate was committed. As St Ambrose had aptly commented (c. 400), the candidate was 'anointed as Christ's athlete; as about to wrestle in the fight of this world'. The candidate was also signed and anointed with the oil of chrism immediately after baptism. Sarum therefore had three significant signings. 1549 reduced these to two: the first at the beginning, as in Sarum, when the priest also asked the name of the child, and then addressed the child by name; the second after the baptism with the oil of chrism. 1552, however, made radical changes: the first signing was dropped and there was no reference to the child's name until the baptism itself; the second signing then occurred immediately after baptism, but without any oil or other post-baptismal ceremonies. The baptism therefore came to be associated with the signing and the naming, and this continued in 1662 and 1928. A form of words also accompanied the signing in 1552—'We receive this child into the congregation of Christ's flock, and do sign him with the sign of the cross . . .'—which only strengthened the misconception that the baptism involved the water, the naming and the signing.

The Liturgical Commission attempted to clarify matters by making the signing one of the 'Ceremonies after Baptism', and by indicating that it should not take place until all the candidates had been been baptized. This was continued in Series 2. ASB, however, clearly associates the signing with the Decision before baptism, permits the use of oil (Note 3, p. 225), and allows the candidate to be addressed by name at this point (Note 5, p. 225). The option of having the signing as a post-baptismal ceremony still exists (section 21); but there is no doubt that neither naming or signing are now seen to be essential elements of the baptism itself, in spite of the fact that both the 1662 Catechism and the Revised Catechism stated that a child's name was given at his baptism. The signing is accompanied by a statement of its significance: it is a sign of lifelong commitment to fight against evil and to proclaim the faith of Christ crucified—an operation in which the whole Church is engaged. This is now indicated by the fact that the statement is no longer said by the priest alone, as it was from 1549 to 1928, but is now said by priest and congregation.

In Series 2 the Decision ended rather abruptly. A brief new prayer has therefore been added (section 15), asking for God's help in this undertaking. Provision is then made for the singing of Psalm 121 or some other suitable psalm or hymn, while the candidates, sponsors and ministers go to their appointed places for the Blessing of the Water, the Profession of Faith and the Baptism itself (section 16). Much depends on the arrangement of the church. If the font is in or near the sanctuary, little or no movement may be required; but if it is at the other end of the church, a procession is necessary. Those who are to be confirmed but not baptized may also need to move to some point other than the font where they can still be addressed by the bishop and make their profession of faith. A large degree of flexibility is permitted at this stage of the rite (Note 10, p. 226). But the one arrangement which should be avoided, despite its apparent convenience, is the transference of the Profession of Faith (sections 18, 53) to a position immediately after the Decision. This would simply return to the unfortunate pattern of 1662, which not only created the impression that the Decision and the Profession of Faith were a single unit, but also divorced the Profession of Faith from the baptism itself.

The Blessing of the Water
(sections 17, 52)

While the blessing of the water is not absolutely necessary—as is clear from Emergency Baptism (sections 106–11)—nevertheless it has a long tradition behind it and should not be regarded as an empty ceremony. In the seventh-century Gelasian Sacramentary and the seventh-century Roman *Ordo*, for example, there was a solemn procession to the font, where the bishop blessed the water in a lengthy prayer: he asked God by the Holy Spirit to give fecundity to the water and to purify it; he then recalled God's mighty acts involving water both in the Old Testament and the New; and finally he prayed that through the water the stain of sin might be erased, human nature might be restored to the divine image, and man might 'be reborn in a new infancy of true innocence'. The oil of chrism was then poured into the font in the form of a cross. Essentially the Sarum blessing of the water differed little from this, although there were some Gallican modifications. It was now in a eucharistic form, introduced by the Sursum corda, while there were added ceremonies—the plunging of a lighted taper into the font, a triple impregnation with oil and chrism, and the breathing of the priest upon the water. Furthermore, now that baptisms were more frequent, the blessing of the water was not required on every occasion: the water simply remained in the font until it was stale, and only when it was renewed was blessing necessary.

In 1549 there were radical changes. The blessing of the water was still an occasional ceremony, not used at every baptism; but it appeared as an appendix to the Private Baptism of Infants, with the direction that the water in the font should be changed at least once a month. Furthermore, the form was much shorter than that of Sarum and owed little to it. Cranmer took it from some Gallican source, whose origin is obscure. There is one opening prayer, containing a reference to our Lord's baptism in Jordan and the request 'Sanctify this fountain of baptism ... that by the power of thy word, all those that shall be baptized therein may be spiritually regenerated'. This was followed by eight short prayers, which have been found in a similar series of sixteen short prayers in the Mozarabic 'Benedictio Fontis'. The Mozarabic Missal, published by Ximenes in 1500, may easily have been known to Cranmer: on the other hand, he may also have been acquainted with some other Gallican source which has not yet been identified. The form ended with the Salutation and a collect for those about to be baptized, mainly from Sarum. All the ceremonies accompanying the blessing were removed, save for the sign of the cross at the words 'Sanctify this fountain of baptism'. Even more radical change took place in 1552, largely in deference to Bucer's criticisms. The nine prayers were reduced to four, and the first prayer with the crucial phrase 'Sanctify this fountain of baptism' was omitted. All that remained, therefore, was prayer for the candidates, which was said at the font immediately before the actual baptism on every occasion. 1662, however, restored the blessing of the water by inserting the phrase 'Sanctify this Water to the mystical washing away of sin' in the final collect—an expedient already adopted in the 1637 Scottish book, although in slightly different words. Further improvement then occurred in 1928 by separating the four short Mozarabic prayers from the collect by the heading 'The Blessing of the Water', and introducing the collect with the Sursum corda and the eucharistic formula 'It is very meet, right, and our bounden duty, that we should give thanks'.

The Liturgical Commission's 1958 proposals set a new pattern for the blessing of the water, by returning to a long prayer of thanksgiving which set out to expound the meaning of initiation within the context of our Lord's own baptism and redemptive activity before asking God to 'sanctify this water to the mystical washing away of sin'. This prayer immediately preceded the acts of renunciation and belief. Series 2 followed suit with a similar though slightly shorter prayer, although this was placed between the Decision (as it had now become) and the Profession of Faith. The prayer in Series 3 and ASB has remained in the same position, but now appears in a much more developed form, expressing succinctly the doctrine of baptism.

Set within the context of thanksgiving, it indicates some of the significant ways in which God has used and still uses water. In the natural order, it cleanses, and it brings refreshment and new life to a parched body or a dry land; but in addition to bringing new life, it can also bring death by drowning. In the Old Testament, for example, the children of Israel were rescued from slavery by the waters of the Red Sea; but at the same time those same waters brought death to their enemies. The themes of life and death are then illustrated further in the baptism, death and resurrection of Jesus Christ. The prayer then asks that God will bless and use the water, so that it may be the means whereby he cleanses the candidates, delivers them from sin, and brings them new life through the Holy Spirit. The water is the means appointed to convey God's salvation: 'Bless this water, that your servants who are washed in it may be made one with Christ in his death and resurrection'; it is efficacious for its specific sacramental purpose: it has not acquired some independent power of a magical and mechanical kind.

The Profession of Faith
(sections 18–19; 53–4)

In the early Western Church the profession of faith was closely associated with the actual immersion. In the *Apostolic Tradition* of Hippolytus, for example, as the candidate stood in the water he was asked three questions: 'Do you believe in God the Father—the Son—the Holy Spirit?' Each time, as he answered in the affirmative, he was immersed; and this was done separately for each candidate. The credal interrogations and the answers were the baptismal formula and nothing more was said. The profession of faith was the 'form' of the sacrament and the water was the 'matter'. Later it was found convenient to put the questions to all the candidates together before immersion; then they were immersed individually and a Syrian form of words was used over each one. This practice reached Rome by the eighth century and since then has been used continuously in the West. The formula at baptism has therefore become, 'I baptize you in the name etc'. This was the pattern normally used in 1549: since the blessing of the water was not performed on every occasion, the profession of faith was normally closely associated with the baptism. The only change was in the wording of the triple interrogation; this was now the entire Apostles' Creed, divided into three. In 1552, when the blessing of the water disappeared altogether, the Apostles' Creed took the form of a single interrogatory question, separated from the baptism itself by what were now the five prayers for the candidates. 1662 retained the pattern, but reintroduced the blessing of the water by adding the words 'Sanctify this water to the mystical washing away of sin' to the fifth prayer. 1928 further emphasized the break between the act of faith and the baptism itself by interposing a subheading 'The Blessing of the Water' together with the Sursum corda between the four short Mozarabic prayers and the fifth longer prayer.

The Liturgical Commission attempted to return to a more primitive pattern in its 1958 proposals by placing the acts of renunciation and faith after the blessing of the water and immediately before baptism; but the profession of faith now took the form of a single short question on the Trinity based on the words in the Prayer Book Catechism, followed by a promise to 'obey him in whom you have believed'. Series 2 further improved this by placing the Decision before the blessing of the water, and by making the single interrogation into three—one for each person of the Trinity—and each requiring the reply 'I believe and trust in him'. This form has now been continued in ASB and has been supplemented by a congregational affirmation of faith in the Trinity (section 19), an innovation borrowed from the 1969 Roman rite. While this is an undoubted improvement on 1662 and 1928, an opportunity to make it even better was lost at the Series 3 stage. In 1976–7 the Liturgical Commission proposed (GS 343) rephrasing the three questions so that the activities of the persons of the Trinity were expressed as continuing activities of a universal kind—a view which accords with Scripture: the Father was 'the maker of all', the Son 'the redeemer of the world', and the Holy Spirit 'the giver of life'. Unfortunately the General Synod preferred to retain the more familiar but also more restrictive vocabulary of the Catechism for the Father and the Son: the Father 'made the world', the Son 'redeemed mankind', and the Holy Spirit 'gives life to the people of God'.

As with the Decision, in the case of children not old enough to answer for themselves, it is the faith of parents and godparents which is involved. They have to answer both for themselves and for the children; and the faith is one in which they undertake to help the children live and grow.

The Baptism
(section 20)

St Paul's comparison of baptism with our Lord's death and resurrection would suggest total immersion—the disappearance of the old man beneath the waters and the rising of the new. But it is reasonably certain that from the third century onwards the normal practice was neither total immersion nor sprinkling, but the pouring of water over the candidate. In any case many fonts would preclude total immersion, certainly in the case of adults. It was also normal practice to dip or pour water over the candidate three times, symbolizing either the Trinity or our Lord's three days in the tomb (Whitaker, *DBL*, pp. 9, 115, 152). An exception was the Church in Spain, where a single dipping or pouring was preferred, in the interests of preserving the unity of the Godhead against heretical ideas (*DBL*, p. 115). Sarum directed that the child should be dipped in the water three times, once with the face to the north, once with the face to the south, and once with the face downwards. 1549 prescribed the same method except in cases where a child was weak; then it sufficed to pour water upon it. 1552 was much less precise: the priest was simply required to dip the child in the water, 'so it be discreetly and warily done'. Immersion seems to have been the norm, except in the case of sick or weakly children, and nothing was said about the number of times the dipping should be done. 1662 prescribed dipping, but rather less enthusiastically: it should only be undertaken if the godparents could certify 'that the child may well endure it'; otherwise the method was to be pouring. Adults were to be either dipped or poured, and again the number of times was not mentioned. Dipping or pouring have remained the options ever since, including ASB. Nor is there any specific direction as to the number of times the action should be undertaken. The 1958 proposals had directed that the water should be poured three times; but this proposal was dropped in Series 2, and in ASB Note 11 (p. 226) provides that, whereas a triple administration of water is a very ancient practice and is commended as testifying to the Trinitarian faith in which candidates are baptized, nevertheless a single administration is also lawful and valid. In every case the dipping or pouring is accompanied by the Western form, '*N*, I baptize you in the name of the Father, and of the Son, and of the Holy Spirit.'

The fact that the priest uses the candidate's name at this point is interesting, and has already been discussed (see pp. 352–3). The name simply establishes the identity of the candidate at the moment of baptism. The giving of the name is, and had been for centuries, quite independent of the act of baptism.

The Post-Baptismal Ceremonies
(sections 21–2)

At this point ASB has included two post-baptismal ceremonies, neither of which should be confused with the baptism itself. First, there is the signing with the sign of the cross on the forehead, if that has not already taken place; and this may be accompanied by the use of oil (Note 3, p. 225). Secondly, there is the optional giving of a lighted candle. There is no reason why either of these ceremonies should take place at the font; nor, in the case of infants, need they be in the priest's arms when he signs them.

Evidence for the anointing with oil immediately after baptism appears as early as the *Apostolic Tradition* of Hippolytus, and from the fourth century this was accompanied by the donning of the white robe. Sarum directed that immediately after baptism the priest was to anoint the infant on the head with the oil of chrism in the form of a cross; then it was clad in a white robe. By the Middle Ages the white robe had often become simply white bands tied around the forehead over the oil of chrism; but the charge remained, 'Receive this white robe and bear it stainless before the judgement-seat of Christ'. 1549 continued with both the anointing and the white robe; but 1552 once again broke with tradition. It omitted both the oil and the white robe, leaving only the sign of the cross and this was accompanied by a formula involving two separate and unrelated matters. It began with the statement, 'We receive this child into the congregation of Christ's flock'. Presumably the word 'receive' really meant 'welcome', for it was God who really received the infant, and prayers earlier in the rite had stated as much. It then went on to say that the sign of the cross was given 'in token that hereafter he shall not be ashamed to confess the faith of Christ crucified, and manfully to fight under his banner . . . and to continue Christ's faithful soldier and servant'. This was really a relic of the pre-baptismal signing, which has already been discussed (cf. pp. 352–4). Although approved by Bucer, this signing became a cause of bitter complaint on the part of the Puritans. Nevertheless, it was retained despite opposition; and indeed in 1603 Canon 30 had been framed to explain and justify its use. Both signing and formula remained in 1662 and 1928, being mistakenly held by many to be essential elements in the baptism itself.

The 1958 proposals attempted to put them in their true perspective by placing them under a new heading, 'The Ceremonies after Baptism', and by making it clear that the signing should not take place until all the candidates had been baptized and returned to their sponsors; furthermore, the opening statement about reception into Christ's flock was omitted. Series 2 and ASB have followed the same arrangement, and ASB has also restored the optional use of oil.

The giving of the lighted candle in the West is a medieval custom, first attested in an eleventh-century missal and included in Sarum with an exhortation to be like the Wise Virgins: 'Receive a lamp burning and without fault: guard thy baptism: keep the commandments, so that when the Lord comes to the wedding, thou mayest meet him together with the saints in the heavenly hall, that thou mayest have eternal life, and live for ever and ever. Amen.' This was not included in 1549, and it did not appear until the 1958 proposals, where it was included as an optional second post-baptismal ceremony. Both Series 2 and ASB have retained it, though with a shorter formula in which the congregation shares: it is now a symbol of the truth that the baptized person has passed from the kingdom of darkness to the kingdom of light, where he is expected to 'shine as a light in the world to the glory of God the Father'.

The Confirmation
(sections 23–36; 78–82)

After the versicles and responses, the traditional prelude to an episcopal blessing, the bishop prays for the sevenfold gifts of the Spirit, stretching his hands towards the candidates. The prayer is ancient, appearing in the Gelasian Sacramentary, and is based on Isaiah 11.2, where the sevenfold gifts rest upon the Messiah. In the Gelasian Sacramentary, as in Sarum, the central petition was 'Send down upon them the sevenfold Holy Ghost, the Comforter, from heaven'—a form from which 1549 differed very little: 'Send down from heaven the Holy Ghost, the Comforter, with the manifold gifts of grace'. But there was no doubt that these forms suggested that the Holy Spirit was bestowed. 1552 changed this, however, to 'Strengthen them with the Holy Ghost, the Comforter, and daily increase in them thy manifold gifts of grace'; and this change was retained in both 1662 and 1928. Here there was a change of ground, for it now appeared that in confirmation candidates were merely being strengthened with an increase of the Holy Spirit's gifts. In an integrated rite, with baptism and confirmation administered together, difficulties are less evident; but with a separate administration of rites problems are inevitable. Certainly the New Testament itself gives no clear guidance on the matter. The Archbishops' Theological Commission stated the problem fairly in 1948: '[The evidence] has features which seem to be conflicting, and it presents a "fluidity" in the accounts of initiation in the apostolic age' (*The Theology of Christian Initiation*, p. 11). Furthermore, 1662 could also be regarded as somewhat ambiguous: for while it would appear to support the view that initiation is complete in baptism, nevertheless weighty arguments have been produced to show that the evidence allowed a different interpretation. (See, for example, Canon A. J. Mason, *The Relation of Confirmation to Baptism*, 1891, pp. 427–31). Inevitably, recent prayers have attempted to make allowance for the uncertainty and are therefore patient of liberal interpretation. The 1958 proposals reverted to a simple form akin to Sarum: 'Send down from heaven upon them thy Holy Ghost the Comforter'; Series 2 was even briefer: 'Send forth upon them thy Holy Spirit'. ASB, however, has taken the petition directly from Isaiah 11.2 in the RSV version: 'Let your Holy Spirit rest upon them'. Such a version excludes neither view: the Holy Spirit is active in both baptism and confirmation.

This prayer, as the essential prayer of the rite, should be said by the bishop standing with his hands outstretched towards the candidates. Unfortunately this direction was missing in Sarum and it did not appear in any of the Prayer Books, thereby creating the mistaken impression in many people's minds that the essential prayer was the one which followed, during which the bishop laid his hand on the candidate's head.

In Sarum, once this prayer was said, the bishop proceeded to anoint each candidate on the forehead with oil and make the sign of the cross, with the words, 'I sign thee with the sign of the cross and I confirm thee with the chrism of salvation, in the name of the Father etc'. 1549 omitted the oil but continued with the sign of the cross and adapted the prayer, referring to the 'inward unction of the Holy Ghost'. 1552 went even further: the sign of the cross was abolished, the bishop laid his hand on each candidate's head, and a completely new prayer was said: 'Defend, O Lord, this thy child with thy heavenly grace'. Despite Cosin's criticism that this prayer was such that it could be said by any minister (*Works*, vol. v, p. 489), it was retained in 1662 and continued in 1928. To meet this criticism and to help solve the baptism–confirmation–Holy Spirit problem, the Liturgical Commission in 1958 first considered restoring the 1549 prayer, but finally decided on a new form 'Confirm, O Lord, thy servant with thy Holy Spirit'. The word 'confirm' could mean either to strengthen or to complete— and these two meanings did in fact indicate the two different ways of looking at confirmation; it was, furthermore, one of the verbs used in the 1549 form—'confirm and strengthen them with the inward unction of the Holy Ghost'. The verb 'confirm' ultimately found acceptance in Series 2, and has remained in ASB. The 1552 formula has not been rejected, however, for once the bishop has laid his hand on all the candidates, it is used as a prayer by the entire congregation (section 26).

From 1549 onwards, successive rites have directed that the bishop should lay his *hand* on each candidate's head, and the unvarying testimony of the Western Church has been that this should be his right hand. ASB also permits (Note 7, p. 226) the use of oil at this point, although no form of words is provided. Neither the notes nor the rubrics specify any particular method of administering the imposition of the hand, for much depends on the arrangement of the individual church. Candidates may kneel singly or in pairs before the bishop at the chancel steps, or they may kneel in a row at the altar rails while the bishop moves along the row; or if numbers are small they could even be confirmed at the font. What is important is the individual treatment of each candidate.

The Welcome
(sections 27–8, 58)

In the fourth century St John Chrysostom spoke of the delight with which the Church welcomed the newly baptized: 'As soon as they come forth from those sacred waters, all who are present embrace them, greet them, kiss them, rejoice with them, and congratulate them.' ASB now provides an opportunity for a similar, though less demonstrative, welcome to those who have just been made members of the Church. The congregational form, which is new, is adapted from a passage in the 1662 Catechism, which speaks of a baptized person being a member of Christ, a child of God, and an inheritor of the Kingdom of Heaven.

Section 28(82) provides for the renewal of baptismal vows by members of the congregation at this point. It is not envisaged that the entire congregation would take part in this renewal, but only those who may have a particular reason for so doing.

The Communion
(sections 29–31)

The Communion service—either Rite A or Rite B—now continues from the Peace. The Peace itself provides further opportunity for expressing a welcome to those who have just been baptized and/or confirmed.

BAPTISM AND CONFIRMATION WITHOUT HOLY COMMUNION

When Baptism and Confirmation are administered without Holy Communion, the service follows the same order as before as far as and including the Welcome (sections 1–28). One, two, or three readings may be used. After the Welcome the bishop may say one or more of the prayers provided in sections 32–9. The service then ends with the Lord's Prayer said by the congregation and the blessing (sections 40–1).

For Adults Who Have Now Been Baptized
(section 32)

A prayer of thanksgiving adapted from a prayer which first appeared in 1552 and has been used in successive Prayer Books. It seems probable that the Reformers may have been aware of a similar prayer in an Italian missal, written before 1100. It is important for its statement on regeneration: 'you have given your servants new birth'.

For Those Who Have Now Been Confirmed
(section 33)

A prayer for divine guidance and protection, based on a prayer in the 1549 Confirmation rite which Cranmer borrowed from Hermann. In Hermann it was a much longer prayer used before the laying-on of hands. In 1958 a reference to the candidates' life as communicants was added: 'strengthen them continually with the body and blood of your Son'.

For Children Who Have Been Baptized and Their Parents
(section 34)

The original form of this prayer appeared in Series 2, but it found its inspiration in the 1552 prayer in section 32 above. The final petition on parents was adapted from a prayer in the 1928 Baptism of Infants.

For All Christian People
(section 35)

A new prayer expressing first the thankful response of members of the congregation who have just witnessed the baptism of others, and secondly their desire to be faithful to their own baptism.

For the Church's Witness
(section 36)

Another new prayer which points to the mission of the Church 'to bear witness to Christ by lives built on faith and love' and to the place of the newly baptized and confirmed in that mission. It is desirable that services of initiation should look beyond the walls of the local church.

Congregational Prayers
(sections 37–9)

1 *Section 37:* A prayer for the healing of this world's ills. It is commonly ascribed to St Francis of Assisi, but this is most unlikely. Apparently it first appeared in print in France in 1913.
2 *Section 38:* A well-known prayer of dedication attributed to St Richard of Chichester.
3 *Section 39:* A new prayer produced by the Revision Committee of the General Synod in 1978.

The Conclusion
(sections 40–1)

The prayers are summed up by the Lord's Prayer recited by the congregation. No specific text is provided for the bishop's blessing. Each bishop is left free to use whatever form he thinks appropriate.

BAPTISM AND CONFIRMATION AT MORNING OR EVENING PRAYER

When Baptism and/or Confirmation takes place within the context of Morning or Evening Prayer, the service begins with the first part of either Office to the end of the second reading, after which a sermon may be preached. This is followed by sections 11–28 of the Baptism–Confirmation rite—or those parts of it which are required—up to and including the Welcome. The Office then resumes at the canticle after the second reading. After the third collect prayers from sections 32–9 of Baptism–Confirmation may be used. The propers provided in section 1, 4–9 of Baptism–Confirmation may also be used instead of those appointed for the day.

THE BAPTISM OF CHILDREN
(sections 42–63)

The Baptism of Children should normally be administered in the context of Holy Communion or of Morning or Evening Prayer, when the local church has assembled for worship. If this is not possible at least representatives of the congregation should be present, both to welcome the newly baptized and to be put in mind of their own baptism (Note 7, pp. 241–2). ASB clearly regards it as a public and not a private service. The choice of the word 'children' rather than 'infants' is deliberate. Infants who are not of an age to answer for themselves are certainly included; but this service may also be used for others who are not old enough to be regarded as adults but too old to be regarded as infants—old enough to participate intelligently in the service.

The Duties of Parents and Godparents
(sections 42–3)

The service begins with a statement by the priest on the duty of parents and godparents to give children the help and encouragement they need to grow up as committed, practising Christians.

This is, however, a responsibility which extends beyond parents and godparents to the 'family of the Church'; and the second paragraph reminds the congregation of the help and encouragement which they too can give. The statement ends by asking parents and godparents to declare their willingness to undertake this work.

The statement is an abbreviated and simplified version of the exhortation which appeared at the end of the 1549 Baptism service; and this in its turn owed something both to Hermann and to the charge of sponsors in the Sarum Manual. The latter required that children should be cared for until the normal age of confirmation at seven, and should be taught the Lord's Prayer, the Hail Mary and the Creed. In 1549 there was no mention of an age for confirmation, but children should be presented when they had learned the articles of the faith, i.e. the Creed, the Lord's Prayer and the Ten Commandments, and had been instructed in the Catechism. These requirements continued both in 1662 and 1928. The ASB statement is expressed in general terms and makes no mention of specific requirements, for these are now set out in Canon B.26.

After addressing parents and godparents, the priest addresses the candidates if they are old enough to understand, explaining briefly and simply, either in his own words or in the words of the text provided, the implications of baptism. Note 2 (p. 241) envisages such children joining their parents and godparents in making the responses.

The Ministry of the Word
(sections 44–6)

In Sarum the Ministry of the Word took the form of the Matthean account (19.13–15) of our Lord taking little children into his arms and blessing them. In line with Hermann, Cranmer took the same story from Mark (10.13–16) in 1549, and this was retained in successive rites until 1928. The 1958 proposals, however, rejected Mark 10, despite its long Anglican tradition, in preference for Galatians 4.4–7—the adoption of sons—and Matthew 28.18–20—our Lord's command to baptize all nations. Series 2 devised a form of homily with prayer, based on four short passages of Scripture: beginning with a reference to our Lord's baptism in Jordan, it continued with Matthew 28.18–19 and Acts 2.38—Peter's exhortation to repent and be baptized. The congregation then thanked God for their own baptism, after which the priest read Mark 10.14–16 and John 3.5–6—our Lord's statement to Nicodemus on the need for rebirth. This ended with another congregational prayer for the candidates.

ASB has now replaced this with a shorter homily, based on John 3.5–6, Matthew 28.18–19 and Acts 2.38, and ending with a single congregational prayer containing the two Series 2 ideas—thanksgiving for baptism and prayer for the candidates. Two points about this prayer (section 46) are worthy of mention: first, there is the recognition of the responsibility of the Church to help in the spiritual upbringing of the candidates—'that they may walk *with us* in the way of Christ'; secondly, there is the recognition that baptism is not an isolated event, but involves growth and development—the candidates should live a life in which they grow into their baptism.

This Ministry of the Word is omitted when the Baptism of Children is administered within the context of Holy Communion or Morning or Evening Prayer.

The Decision, the Baptism, and the Welcome (sections 47–58) are identical with those in the previous rite of Baptism–Confirmation (sections 11–22, 27). For commentary see pp. 350–60, 362–3.

The Prayers
(sections 59–63)

These prayers are mandatory when Baptism is administered by itself; they are omitted when Baptism is administered at Holy Communion; and they are optional when Baptism is administered at Morning or Evening Prayer:

1, 2 (Sections 59 and 60): These two prayers appear as a single prayer in section 34. The first is for the candidates, the second is for the parents; cf. p. 364.

3 (Section 61): The same as the prayer in section 35; cf. p. 364.

4 (Section 62): The Lord's Prayer; see section 40 (p. 364).

5 (Section 63): The grace from 2 Corinthians 13.14; cf. pp. 364–5.

THE BAPTISM OF CHILDREN AT HOLY COMMUNION

If the Baptism of Children takes place at Holy Communion, Rite A or Rite B may be used. The section numbers which follow refer to Rite A. The service begins with the Preparation and the Ministry of the Word as far as the sermon from Holy Communion (sections 1–18). Then follows the Baptism of Children as far as the Welcome (sections 42–58), except that sections 44–6 may be omitted. Holy Communion then continues from the Peace (section 30). Special sentences and a special preface are provided (p. 250), and if special readings are required, these may be taken from pages 261–74. Readings appointed for the day may also be used.

THE BAPTISM OF CHILDREN AT MORNING OR EVENING PRAYER

The structure of this combined service is similar to that of Baptism and Confirmation at Morning or Evening Prayer. The service begins with Morning or Evening Prayer to the end of the second reading. Then follows the Baptism of Children (sections 42–61), except that sections 44–6 (the Ministry of the Word) and 59–61 (the Prayers) are optional. The Office then continues from the second canticle. Prayers from sections 59–61 may be used after the third collect. If appropriate, the Office may be abbreviated, either by omitting the optional sections, or by using the shorter forms (pp. 73–87).

CONFIRMATION WITH HOLY COMMUNION

This combined service is similar in structure to that of Baptism and Confirmation with Holy Communion, and commentary on most of the service may be found there.

The Preparation
(sections 64–7)

Identical with sections 1–4. See p. 349.

The Ministry of the Word
(sections 68–74)

Identical in structure with sections 5–10 (pp. 349–50), but the choice of readings is slightly different. For the Old Testament reading Jeremiah 31.31–4 and Ezekiel 36.25a, 26–8 are appointed from the earlier service, together with Joshua 24.14–24—Joshua's final command to the children of Israel to be faithful. The New Testament readings all come from the earlier service: 1 Corinthians 12.12–13, Galatians 5.16–25 and 1 Peter 2.4–10. For the Gospel, two of the earlier readings—Matthew 16.24–7 and Mark 1.14–20—are appointed, together with Luke 24.45–end—Jesus' final commission to the disciples—and John 14.15–18—Jesus' promise of the Comforter.

The Renewal of Baptismal Vows
(sections 75–7)

The Decision (section 13) and the Declaration of Faith (sections 18–19) are now taken together. See pp. 350–2, 356–7. Candidates are informed at the outset that they are now to take the vows 'with your own mouth and from your own heart'.

The Confirmation
(sections 78–82)

This is identical with sections 23–6 (pp. 360–2); but it concludes with an option for other members of the congregation to renew their baptismal vows at this point (section 82), using sections 94–8.

The Communion
(sections 83–5)

The Communion continues from the Peace (Rite A, section 30) in the customary manner. A proper preface and post-communion sentence are provided (section 84).

CONFIRMATION WITHOUT HOLY COMMUNION

If Confirmation is administered by itself, the service follows the preceding order—sections 64 to 81; one, two, or three readings may be used. After section 81 the bishop continues with one or more prayers from sections 86–8:

Section 86: For those who have now been confirmed. See section 33, pp. 363–4.
Section 87: For all Christian people. See section 35, p. 364.
Section 88: For the Church's witness. See section 36, p. 364.

The congregation may then say one or more of the prayers in sections 89–91:

Section 89: See section 37, p. 364.
Section 90: See section 38, p. 364.
Section 91: See section 39, p. 364.

The service then ends with the Lord's Prayer said by everyone (section 92), and a blessing of his own choice by the bishop (section 93).

CONFIRMATION AT MORNING OR EVENING PRAYER

The structure of this combined service is again similar to that of Baptism and Confirmation at Morning or Evening Prayer. The service begins with Morning or Evening Prayer to the end of the second reading. Then follows the Confirmation (sections 75–81), and the Office continues from the second canticle. Prayers from sections 86–91 may be used after the third collect. If appropriate the Office may be abbreviated, either by omitting the optional sections, or by using the shorter forms (pp. 73–87).

THE RENEWAL OF BAPTISMAL VOWS ON VARIOUS OCCASIONS

In 1956 the Roman Catholic revised Rites of Holy Week provided for a renewal of baptismal vows at the Easter Vigil. This was, of course, by no means a complete innovation. On Christmas Day 1747 John Wesley had urged Methodists to renew their Covenant with God, and the first formal Covenant Service was held on 11 August 1775, since when it has been held regularly and has spread beyond Methodism, for example to the Church of South India.

The customary time for the renewal of the Covenant in Methodism is New Year.

ASB now provides for a renewal of baptismal vows, which may be held at Easter, New Year, or other suitable occasions. The order may be used at Holy Communion, at Morning or Evening Prayer, in conjunction with Baptism and/or Confirmation, or by itself. If used at Holy Communion, the renewal takes place after the sermon; and the Creed and the Prayers of Intercession and Penitence may be omitted. If used at Morning or Evening Prayer, it takes place again after the sermon, which precedes or follows the second reading, or at the end of the service. In either case propers from the Baptism–Confirmation Services may be used.

After a short charge, reminding those concerned of the meaning of baptism (sections 94–5), the minister asks the three questions of the Decision (section 96) and the three questions relating to faith (sections 97–8). For the commentary on these sections, see sections 13, 18–19 (pp. 350–2, 356–7). One or more of the following prayers may then be used:

Section 100: For all Christian people (see section 35, p. 364).
Section 101: For the Church's witness (see section 36, p. 364).
Sections 102–4: Three congregational prayers (see sections 37–9, p. 364).

CONDITIONAL BAPTISM
(section 105)

Baptism is a 'once-for-all' action and cannot be repeated. A person who lapses from the Christian faith and subsequently wishes to return cannot be rebaptized: a renewal of baptismal vows is what is then required. On the other hand, a person may not be sure that he was baptized as an infant or in his early years, and he can produce no evidence; or he may have doubts as to whether his baptism fulfilled the necessary conditions of a Christian baptism. The 1662 Order for the Private Baptism of Infants indicates the kind of questions which should be asked to determine the necessary conditions.

If there are any doubts, Conditional Baptism can be administered (section 105). The service of Baptism is used, and at the moment of baptism the minister inserts the words, 'N. if you have not already been baptized', before saying 'I baptize you in the name etc.'

EMERGENCY BAPTISM
(sections 106–11)

In the case of an infant who is likely to die, provision is made for baptism by a minister or by a lay person (section 107). This is a continuation of a practice accepted in the pre-Reformation Church and in successive Prayer Books. The minimum required by ASB, as in 1662, is the pouring of water over the infant with the words, 'I baptize you in the name, etc.', together with the Lord's Prayer and the blessing (section 108). Other prayers may be used if time and circumstances permit. A valuable pastoral note is provided in section 106, assuring parents who request such baptism that 'questions of ultimate salvation or of the provision of a Christian funeral for an infant who dies do not depend upon whether or not *he* had been baptized.' It is also made clear that baptism can be administered without a name provided the identity of the infant is clear and can be recorded (section 109). If the infant is fortunate enough to survive, *he* should subsequently come to church or be brought to church to take part in the full baptismal rite with the exception of the blessing of the water (section 17) and the actual baptism with water (section 20), both of which are omitted. The minister's address to the candidate (if old enough) before the profession of faith is also modified—he speaks of the faith into which 'you have been baptized' instead of 'you are to be baptized' (section 110), or his address to the parents and godparents is similarly modified (section 111).

13
The Marriage Service

A
HISTORY

Study:
Kenneth Stevenson, *Nuptial Blessing: A Study of Christian Marriage Rites.*
1982.

1 The Jewish Background

Some form of marriage appears to be a universal human institution, and nearly all societies have surrounded it with a quite complex series of ceremonies and customs, many of which have remained remarkably similar from culture to culture and age to age, in spite of other religious differences. In New Testament times Jewish marriage procedure was divided into two distinct stages. First came the ceremony of betrothal, and then, some time later, often as much as a year, the wedding itself, which in those days took place in the evening at the home of the bridegroom. The bride, wearing a long veil, and her companions went to the house in a procession accompanied by music and dancing. At the threshold of the house the marriage contract was written down, and then came the marriage feast, at the end of which special blessing-prayers were said by the bridegroom.

2 Early Christian Practice

We have very little evidence to indicate what the early Christians did with regard to marriage ceremonies, but it seems likely that at first, as in other respects, they followed substantially the Jewish model. Ignatius of Antioch, writing early in the second century, implies that the local bishop should be involved in some way, but it is not clear whether he means that the bishop should simply be consulted and asked for his consent to the marriage of members of his congregation, or, as seems less likely, that he himself should preside over the ceremony. Evidence from the end of the second century, however, appears to suggest that by this time, at least in some places, weddings were becoming more of a 'church' affair, presided over by ordained ministers and taking place before members of the local congregation. They may have included a special blessing of the couple and a celebration of the Eucharist. Western evidence from this period indicates that the preceding betrothal ceremony included a kiss, the joining of hands, the giving of a ring and possibly other gifts to the bride, and the covering of her head with a veil which she was expected to wear thereafter: all these customs were apparently derived from contemporary pagan practice.

3 Later Eastern Practice

The pagan custom of placing garland-crowns on the heads of the couple at a wedding had been criticized by the Western author Tertullian at the end of the second century, and he had argued that the bride should be veiled instead. However, by the fourth century crowning was a major feature of Eastern Christian marriage rites, and was defended by John Chrysostom on the grounds that crowns were symbols of victory over passion.

The oldest extant text of an Eastern rite, the eighth-century Byzantine rite, reveals that the two-stage process of betrothal and marriage had been retained. For the betrothal no explicit expression of consent is prescribed, but simply two prayers of blessing for the couple. For the marriage itself there are further prayers: first there is a litany with three special petitions for the couple; then comes a prayer of blessing, after which the couple are crowned and their hands are joined; and two further prayers of blessing follow.

From the tenth century onwards the two stages of the rite were usually celebrated on the same day, and often in a single service, and they began to become more elaborate. Further prayers were included, and the giving of a ring was added to the betrothal. Two rings (gold for the bride, silver for the groom) became usual from the eleventh century onwards, and in the twelfth century the couple began to be asked to express their willingness to marry one another at the very beginning of the rite. The central emphasis of the service, however, remains on the prayers of blessing for the couple, with their strongly positive attitude towards marriage as God's creation and their clear expression of the mutuality of the marriage-act, also brought out in the crowning of both bride and groom and the exchange of rings. As we shall see, this was not always true of Western practice. Although other Eastern traditions have rites which differ in many details from the Byzantine, their basic features and emphases remain fundamentally similar.

4 *The Medieval West*

When fixed liturgical texts appear at the beginning of the Middle Ages in the Roman tradition, they provide readings, psalms and prayers for a nuptial Eucharist, including a special blessing before the newly married couple receive communion. In this material, however, can be seen a tendency to concentrate on blessing the woman rather than the couple: the idea of a wedding as 'the bride's day' obviously has roots in ancient times, probably in pagan Roman tradition. Equally interesting is the choice of readings, which tend to convey a much less positive and joyful note than those of the East. Ephesians 5.22–33, with its image of Christ as the model for the bridegroom, is almost universally used in the East, but is entirely absent from early Western usage, and 1 Corinthians 6.15–20, with its warning to avoid fornication, is frequently found instead. Similarly, John 2.1–11, with its description of the marriage at Cana, is not as commonly used in the West as in the East, and its place tends to be taken by Matthew 19.1–6, with its reference to a man leaving his family and becoming one flesh with his wife. Other sources indicate that the primitive Western custom of a betrothal ceremony some time before the wedding continued to be practised, involving an expression of consent sealed by the giving to the bride of a ring and other gifts as tokens or pledges, and the evidence also suggests that the bride wore a veil for the wedding, but it is not clear whether this was put on at the service, or at the betrothal, or at some other time.

The non-Roman Western traditions, on the other hand, move more in the direction of mutuality. They tend to extend the blessing to the couple rather than restrict it to the bride, and to include the spreading of a veil or pall over the head of the bride and at least over the shoulders, if not the head, of the groom during this. In Spain an exchange of rings is found, as in the East, rather than just the giving of a ring to the bride. It is also in the Spanish tradition that we first encounter the ceremonial practice of the bride being 'given away'—handed over to the priest by her family, and then the priest himself joins the couple together by handing her over to the groom. This usually takes place towards the end of the service. In these traditions there emerges a blessing of the ring and other tokens in the betrothal ceremony, and they frequently add the blessing of the bedchamber to their liturgical provisions.

Later Western rites reveal a fusion of Roman material with local traditions, and tend as a consequence to be quite elaborate in their form. Thus they include prayers and blessings for the bride as well as for the couple, and stress such things as the remedy for human frailty and the avoidance of fornication as reasons for marriage. As in the East, betrothal and marriage eventually became united in a single service, and in the rites of Northern Europe from the twelfth century onwards all the ceremonial acts associated with both were grouped together at the beginning of the service, before the Eucharist, which included further prayers and blessings. This first part of the service often took place at the church door, and its order tended to be: the expression of consent; the giving away of the bride and her handing over by the priest to the groom; the joining of their hands; and the giving of the ring and other tokens (generally gold and silver), followed by prayers. The blessing of the ring might take place at the beginning or in association with its giving.

Although most of the service was in Latin, the giving of consent was usually in the vernacular, and its form varied greatly from one locality to another, with the gradual emergence in England and elsewhere of some positive form of marriage vow said by the couple themselves in addition to their response to an interrogative formula of consent. These vows usually accompanied the joining of hands, and the bride's version of both the consent-question and the vow often (but not always) began to include some expression of wifely obedience. There was a similar regional variation in the vernacular formula said by the groom at the giving of the ring. In 1215 the Fourth Lateran Council decreed that banns of marriage should be published on three Sundays before the wedding, and the final calling of the banns (in the vernacular) tended thereafter to be incorporated into the beginning of the service itself.

5 The Reformation

The marriage rite drawn up by Martin Luther was simple and straightforward. At the church door the priest asked the couple for their consent with a short question. They then gave each other a ring, without any blessing or other formula, and the priest joined their right hands, saying the words from Matthew 19.6, 'What God has joined together, let not man put asunder'—a formula which had already been used in this way in some European marriage rites from the end of the fifteenth century onwards. He then recited a formula declaring them to be married, and the procession moved into church to the altar, where he read a number of selected biblical passages, beginning with Genesis 2.18, 21–4. After this, he spread out his hands over them for a final prayer of blessing. There was no celebration of the Eucharist: in this respect, as in other features of his rite, Luther was simply adopting customs already known in sixteenth-century Germany. Later Lutheran rites tended to follow this same pattern, merely adding further prayers to the service, and a prefatory address to be read at the beginning.

Calvin directed that weddings were to take place during the public worship of the Church, before the sermon, but not on days when the Eucharist was to be celebrated. His order of service began with the reading of a substantial address explaining the origin and purpose of marriage. After this the minister asked whether there was any impediment to the marriage; he said a prayer for the couple; and put to each of them a lengthy question asking whether they consented to be married and would pledge themselves to one another. He then said another prayer for the gift of the Spirit to the couple; read Matthew 19.3–6; and declared that God had joined them together. A long prayer and a short blessing concluded the rite. There was no exchange of rings or joining of hands.

6 The Church of England

The marriage service in the 1549 Prayer Book was in two parts, the first taking place, not at the church door, but in the body of the church, and the second at the altar, and leading into the celebration of the Eucharist. The first part began in the Reformed manner with a long prefatory address explaining the reasons for marriage. Following medieval practice, this ended with a final opportunity for any impediment to be lodged, and the priest then asked the couple if they knew of any impediment. Next came the consent, expressed in response to a question put by the priest to each of them, composed of a combination of the forms in the medieval Sarum and Luther's marriage rites. The giving away of the bride followed, the priest asking 'who giveth this woman to be married to this man?' This was based on the medieval York usage, since the other English rites had no such question attached to the ceremony. The couple then joined hands and exchanged vows, the wording again closely following the traditional English forms. The ring 'and other tokens of spousage, as gold or silver', were placed by the groom on the priest's book, but not blessed, and were given to the bride with the traditional formula, 'With this ring I thee wed...' For no obvious reason the ring was to be placed on the left hand, and not the right, as had previously been the custom. Following this, the couple knelt and the priest said a prayer over them, a new composition but drawing to some extent upon traditional material. The priest joined their hands once more, reciting Matthew 19.6, a practice no doubt derived from Luther, and then declared them to be married, using a formula taken from the continental Reformer Hermann von Wied. The first part of the service ended with a blessing of the couple based on a medieval form.

The second half of the service began with a psalm (128 or 67), during which the priest and the couple moved to the altar for the prayers. These consisted of the Kyrie eleison, the Lord's Prayer, four versicles and responses, and four other prayers, which drew upon, but reworked, traditional medieval material. In the Euchar- ist which followed, there was to be either a sermon or the reading of a long exhortation concerning marriage, which quoted a variety of scriptural passages: this was again probably influenced by Luther.

Few changes were made to the rite in 1552, and none of any great significance. Perhaps the only alteration worth noting was the deletion of all reference to the giving of 'other tokens of spousage' by the groom to the bride along with this ring. The 1559 and 1604 Prayer Books similarly retained the service unchanged, in spite of strong Puritan opposition to the ceremony of the giving of the ring.

In the negotiations leading up to the 1662 Prayer Book, the High Church party would have desired the restoration of the 'tokens of spousage' and the laying of the priest's hand on the heads of the couple during the prayer which followed the giving of the ring. Neither of these proposals was adopted, however, and only minor changes in wording were made in the rite at this time, though the couple were directed to kneel down for the prayer after the giving of the ring. One significant alteration was made at the end of the service, but this was really only to bring the text into line with actual practice. It appears that for some considerable time wedding services had commonly dispensed with the celebration of the Eucharist. The long scriptural exhortation was now to follow directly after the final blessing, 'if there be no sermon', and the concluding rubric merely stated, 'It is convenient that the new married persons should receive the holy Communion at the time of their marriage, or at the first opportunity after their marriage.' Nevertheless, they were to continue to go up to the altar for the second part of the service.

In the proposed book of 1927/8 a number of changes were included, in addition to minor verbal amendments: the prefatory address was altered so as to remove the reference to 'carnal lusts' and to describe sexuality in more positive terms in its second reason given for marriage; the bride's promise to obey was deleted, so that the man and woman might be treated more equally; when the ring was given, the groom said, '... with my body I thee *honour*...', instead of 'worship', the desire for this change having existed among some since the seventeenth century; a passage of Scripture might be read in place of the final biblical exhortation; and when there was no celebration of the Eucharist, the service was to end with a further collect and short blessing of the congregation. For the first time a Collect, Epistle, and Gospel were provided for use at a nuptial Eucharist. This service was eventually authorized under the Alternative Services Measure 1965 virtually as it stood, though it did now include the option for the word 'obey' to be retained, and for the ring to be blessed.

The Liturgical Commission produced its proposals for a revised marriage service in 1975. By this time the whole process of liturgical revision was well advanced, and the service formed part of the contemporary language Series 3 rites. It was influenced by two recent reports, that of the Commission on the Christian Doctrine of Marriage, *Marriage, Divorce, and the Church* (1971), and that of the Church's Board of Social Responsibility, *Marriage and the Family in Britain Today* (1974). It was clearly recognized that any new marriage service must have a very different approach from that of 1662/1928. The earlier rites had assumed that the husband was head of the family and the wife was subordinate; and while this was a view still acceptable to many, others believed symmetry and not subordination to be the essence of a good Christian marriage. Some still desired the bride to 'obey' in the marriage vows, but others wanted the vows of both parties to be identical. At first the Liturgical Commission believed that these differences could be met simply by rubric, requiring the inclusion of 'obey' when desired by the couple; but after consideration by the General Synod two sets of vows were included, one expressing the traditional view and the other expressing the modern approach.

Some reservations were also felt about the ceremony of 'giving away'. Why should it be necessary if a couple faced their marriage as two equal partners? Then again, the traditional reasons for marriage as expressed in the preface to the Prayer Book service had in recent decades been criticized for expressing a wrong order of priorities. In 1662, and in 1928, the creation and nurture of children had been given precedence, the acceptance and enjoyment of sex had come second, and the mutual society, help and comfort of the partners had come last. It was now felt that the order should be completely reversed, and the mutual society, help and comfort of the couple was of prime importance—a view which in fact Martin Bucer had expressed in his *Censura* as long ago as 1551: 'I should prefer that what is placed third among the causes for marriage might be in the first place, because it is first' (Whitaker, *Martin Bucer and the Book of Common Prayer*, pp. 120–2). In addition to giving expression to these new emphases, the new service also made one important modification in structure. Traditionally the marriage rite had always preceded the Eucharist; but an opportunity was now provided to celebrate the rite within the Eucharist, if the parties so desired. The rite was finally authorized for experimental use as from 1 November 1977, and subsequently incorporated into the Alternative Service Book.

B
COMMENTARY

Introduction
(sections 1–5)

The first five sections are optional and allow the service to begin in one of three different ways:

1   All five sections may be omitted, and the service may begin in the traditional manner with section 6 (the Preface). In this case the collect and readings come later.

2   All five sections may be used, if the marriage rite is set within the context of Holy Communion.

3   All five sections may be used, whether Holy Communion is to follow or not.

In 1549, 1552 and 1559 it was assumed that the Wedding Service would be followed by Holy Communion. In 1549 it normally took place 'in the body of the church' on a Sunday after Morning Prayer and before the Eucharist; and in the canons of 1603, Canon 62 laid down that weddings must take place 'in time of Divine Service'. A modification was made in 1662, however, owing to Presbyterian objections that some couples would be unfit or unprepared for communion, that it should not be mandatory to communicate when coming to be wed. 1662 therefore stated: 'It is convenient' [not compulsory] 'that the newly-married persons should receive the holy Communion at the time of their Marriage, or at the first opportunity after their Marriage.' When Wheatly published his commentary on the Prayer Book in 1710, he reported that the practice (i.e. of communicating at the time of marriage) was by universal consent laid aside and discontinued (p. 479).

Section 1

No reference is made to the service taking place 'in the body of the church': the couple simply 'stand before the priest'. This allows for the wide variety of arrangements which now exist in the interior of churches. Note 3 (p. 285) should also be observed in conjunction with this section: seating accommodation should be provided for the couple, in order to avoid undue strain and discomfort during the readings and the sermon.

Section 3

The collect is a modern version of the collect for the marriage Eucharist in 1928. It conforms to the pattern of the other collects in the ASB Occasional Offices, in praying for all who are present at the service.

THE MARRIAGE

The Preface
(section 6)

Cranmer used a variety of sources in compiling the Preface in 1549: the Sarum and York Manuals, the *King's Book*, Luther's Marriage Rite, and Hermann's *Consultation*. With only a few minor verbal changes this was retained in 1662; and 1928, while toning down the language, did not change the content. The Preface in ASB, however, is new both in language and content. It begins by reminding the congregation that they are present, not only to witness the marriage of the couple, but also to pray for them and to share their joy. It then goes on to point out that marriage is a gift of God, involves lifelong commitment, and has a hallmark of self-giving love. The three purposes of marriage are then stated in an order which is the reverse of that in 1662. Mutual help and comfort is now the primary purpose; indeed it is the one certain lifelong need. The second and third purposes—sexual intercourse and children—are not necessarily appropriate in every marriage, and in later years may have declining significance. An attempt is made to express a more positive approach to sexuality, as something joyful and spiritually creative rather than as a grudging concession for the avoidance of fornication. Finally, on the question of children, by avoiding the specific word 'procreation' and by using more general terminology, couples who have a family by adoption—equally a gift of God—are included.

The Charges
(sections 7–8)

The two charges are the equivalent of a fourth reading of banns. The charge to the congregation (section 7) was until 1928 the final sentence of the Preface; but in view of the fact that it is addressed to them and not to the couple, it has been made a separate section of the service. The charge to the couple (section 8) is still based on the text in the York Manual. The legal reasons against marriage are: the existence of a previous legal marriage; a relationship within the prohibited degrees; and the lack of consent by parents or guardians in the case of minors. Until 1928 an interrupter was required to deposit a substantial sum, which was forfeit if the objection could not be proved. ASB makes no reference to the consequences involved in an objection, for these are not liturgical, but legal matters.

The Declarations of Consent
(sections 9–10)

What was traditionally known as 'the Espousals' began at this point. In 1549 the questions were a combination of the forms in the Sarum Manual and Luther's Marriage Rite. Until and including 1662 the question to the bride included the word 'obey'; but this was dropped in 1928 and the questions to both parties became identical. In ASB the traditional language has been retained to a considerable degree, but some changes have been made. Luther's phrase 'according to God's law in the holy estate of matrimony', together with 'in sickness and in health' have been omitted to avoid repetition. Both are contained in the vows which follow; and in any case the content of the questions is all-embracing—a lifelong commitment to honour, comfort, protect, forsake all others, and to be faithful.

The Giving Away
(section 11)

The Sarum Manual provided for the giving of the woman by her father or a friend, but without any form of words. York provided both ceremony and words: the priest asked, 'Who gives me this wife?', indicating that the father was giving the woman to the priest, representing God, who then gave her to the man, as God gave Eve to Adam. In 1549 Cranmer opted for the York pattern, but changed the wording to a less explicit form—'Who giveth this woman to be married to this man?' This form remained in use down to 1928. ASB has retained the ceremony but made it optional and has omitted the form of words. It recognizes that some people still accept the ceremony, not only as a sign of willingness on the part of the bride's parents to accept the new relationship, but also as a symbol of their past care and support. Others dislike it, however, because it is indicative of an inequality of status and a relic of outworn ideas of the bride being a chattel handed over by the father. An optional ceremony without words allows for both points of view.

The Vows
(sections 11–12)

Here the traditional 'Nuptials' begin. In pre-Reformation times a considerable period could elapse between these and the 'Espousals', which were really a formal recognition of the engagement. The making of the vows and the taking of the other's right hand by each party are traditional elements of a legal conveyance: the contracting parties are named, the legal term 'to have and to hold' is used, the limits are stated—'from this day forward . . . till death us do part'—and the whole contract is subject to ecclesiastical law—'according to God's holy law'. In 1549 Cranmer based the vows on the Sarum form, but made some changes. In Sarum the woman promised to be 'bonere and buxum in bedde and at te borde', indicating her willingness to be 'bonnaire'—gentle—and 'boughsome'—obedient; at the same time both parties 'plighted their troth', that is, they pledged their fidelity or allegiance. Cranmer omitted the woman's undertaking to be 'bonere and buxum' and required the woman to 'give' rather than 'plight' her troth. 1662 made one further change: 'till death us depart' became 'till death us do part' at the request of the Puritans who argued that 'depart' was being used improperly. It was 1928, however, which made the significant change. The bride was no longer required to 'obey' and the vows of both parties became identical.

ASB recognizes that certain words and phrases have sunk deeply into English life, so as much of the traditional wording as possible is retained in this crucial part of the rite. Furthermore, the rubric indicates that the couple marry each other and are themselves the ministers of the sacrament: they are to face each other and they are not required to make their vows 'after the Minister' as in 1662/1928; the only people involved in the sight of God are themselves, and the priest and the congregation are the witnesses. Note 6 (p. 285) does recognize, however, that some couples may be rather nervous and tense at this moment and may need some prompting by the priest. The important question is the requirement to 'obey'. Some couples, firmly believing in the equality of status, wish to follow the 1928 line by not including it in the bride's vows. For them Form A is provided, in which the vows of both parties are identical. Other couples, however, still wish the bride to 'obey'. It must be said that nowhere in Scripture, and in particular in Ephesians 5.22, Colossians 3.18, and 1 Peter 3.1–5, is equality in marriage urged. These passages use the Greek verb *hupotasso* to express the related function of husband and wife, and this is translated by such English verbs as 'be submissive to', 'be subject to', or 'accept the authority of'. The best single word to express these ideas still seems to be 'obey'. However, if the idea of complementarity is to be fully expressed, the 'obeying' by the woman needs to be matched by some reciprocal action on the part of the man. The New Testament suggests a number of things a man should do: he should 'pay honour', 'love', 'please', 'nourish', and 'cherish' (1 Cor. 7.33; Eph. 5.28–33; 1 Pet. 3.7). After considering a number of alternatives—'honour', 'adore', 'respect', 'worship'—the General Synod finally accepted 'worship'. The bride therefore promises to 'obey' her husband, and the bridegroom promises to 'worship' his wife. These phrases were therefore incorporated into Form B of the vows; and before the service the couple inform the priest which form of the vows they propose to use.

The Blessing and Giving of Rings
(sections 13–16)

It was an ancient Roman custom for the man to give a ring to the woman as a sign of betrothal; and by the ninth century this action was duplicated by the giving of a ring at the time of marriage. In fact the giving of this second ring with the formula 'With this ring I thee wed' could be regarded as a sealing of the wedding contract.

In the Sarum rite, when the couple had plighted their troths, the bridegroom laid the ring together with gold and silver, representing the ancient bride-price, on a dish or book. The priest then blessed the ring and handed it back to the bridegroom who recited this formula: 'With this ring I thee wed, and this gold and silver I thee give: and with my body I thee worship, and with all my worldly chattels I thee endow; in the name of the Father, and of the Son, and of the Holy Ghost; Amen.' While he recited the Trinitarian invocation, he placed the ring first on the thumb and then on successive fingers of the bride's right hand until he reached the fourth finger, where he left it. The rubric continued, 'because in that finger there is a certain vein, which runs from thence as far as the heart; and inward affection, which ought always to be fresh between them, is signified by the true ring (*sonoritate*) of the silver'. Cranmer used both the Sarum words and ceremony in 1549 but modified them. The bridegroom still laid the ring and 'other tokens of spousage' on the priest's book; but in deference to the Reformers' distaste for the blessing of inanimate objects, it was no longer blessed. Instead the priest handed it back to the bridegroom, who placed it immediately on the fourth finger, not of the right hand, but of the left, while reciting the same formula. In 1552, despite Bucer's approval of 'the tokens of spousage', these were changed to 'the accustomed duty to the Priest and Clerk', while the reference to the giving of gold and silver was omitted from the bridegroom's formula. 1662 made one further small change: on the suggestion of Bishop Cosin, the bridegroom was required to hold the ring on the bride's fourth finger while he recited the formula. Apparently one further change was omitted, either by accident or by a last-minute change of mind. The Puritans had objected to the phrase 'I thee worship'; and it was agreed that 'I thee honour' should be substituted. For some reason the change did not take place, and it was left to 1928 to make the change: 'with my body I thee honour, and all my worldly goods with thee I share'. The bridegroom was also relieved of his requirement to give the priest and the clerk their accustomed duty.

In ASB the priest simply 'receives the ring(s)', either from the bridegroom or the best man; and provision is now made—as in Sarum—for him to bless it. The form of blessing, however, tries to meet the objections still felt about the blessing of inanimate objects by praying that the ring may, by God's blessing, be to the couple a symbol of unending love and a reminder of the covenant they have made. Provision is also made for both parties to give and receive rings, and the words which both bride and bridegroom use are identical in each case. If only the bridegroom gives a ring, the bride still uses the same formula, except that the word 'receive' replaces 'give'. The formula is now significantly different from the traditional formula. The latter—'with this ring I thee wed'—suggested that the marriage itself was effected by the giving and receiving of a ring, whereas in fact the essential element was the exchange of vows and the ring was simply a token and a pledge of this covenant. The new formula therefore begins with a simple statement of fact: 'I give you this ring as a sign of our marriage.' It then goes on to express the depth of commitment— the giving of the entire self and the sharing of all resources of every kind; and all this is done 'within the love of God'. This is another significant change, due primarily to the Archdeacon of Durham, the Venerable Michael Perry, and much more expressive than the customary 'In the name of the Father, etc.' The self-giving love in marriage is now set within the greater mystery of the self-giving interpenetrating divine love which exists within the Holy Trinity.

The Declaration, the Joining of Hands and the Blessing
(sections 17–19)

There was no declaration and joining of hands in the Sarum rite. They were an innovation in 1549, borrowed from Hermann, who in turn was simply following Luther and even earlier German rites. A declaration and joining of hands was in fact medieval German practice. Cranmer took Hermann's order and expanded it. He began with a prayer for the couple, borrowing phrases from Sarum including the form for the blessing of the ring; he followed with the joining of hands, then the declaration—taken from Hermann—and ended with the Sarum blessing of the couple. With minor changes this remained until 1928.

ASB simplifies the order and clarifies the meaning. The prayer for the couple is postponed until later in the service: the declaration of marriage therefore immediately follows the marriage itself, which is logical. The joining of hands now follows rather than precedes the declaration, thereby setting the seal on what has taken place. Moreover, the priest makes it crystal clear in the declaration that the couple are the ministers of the sacrament: his function as the Church's representative is 'to proclaim' their marriage and to bless them. The verb 'proclaim' is preferred to the earlier 'pronounce', which today is normally associated with legal sentences. In view of the fact that the declaration was originally imported from Germany, it is an interesting possibility that the phrase 'the giving and receiving' of a ring may well reflect the German custom whereby each of the couple gave and received a ring. The priest then joins the right hands of the couple and makes the declaration from Matthew 19.6/Mark 10.9: 'That which God has joined together, let not man divide.' This corrects a mistranslation which existed in 1549/1662. The Greek text is 'that which', not 'those whom'—a fact which Hermann clearly realized—'Was Gott zusammen füget, soll kein mensch scheiden.' The underlying idea is that God creates a bond rather than joins the persons. The blessing, prepared at the instigation of the Revision Committee of the General Synod, is a combination of the first blessing of the couple in 1662, and the final blessing at the end of the 1662 rite, both of which are based on Sarum.

The Acclamations and the Registration
(sections 20–1)

The blessing of the couple may be followed by acclamations. If so desired, they may be sung as anthems while the registration of the marriage takes place. These acclamations—an innovation in ASB—are based on the seven blessings of the bride and bridegroom in Jewish marriage rites, which help to make them such joyful occasions.

Provision is now made for the registration to take place publicly as part of the service, if the couple so desire. It is an important element in the service, and some people feel that the disappearance of the couple and their families into a vestry at the end of the service creates something of an anticlimax.

The Reading and the Sermon
(section 22)

In 1549 and 1552, as in Sarum, where it was assumed that the Eucharist would follow, the Epistle and Gospel, together with a sermon or the homily, were part of the rite; but 1662, where no Eucharist was assumed, made no provision for a Scripture reading, although a sermon or the homily were mandatory. 1928 restored the Epistle and Gospel if there was to be a Eucharist; and if no Eucharist were celebrated, there had to be either a sermon, or the 1662 homily, or a Scripture reading. ASB insists on at least one Scripture reading, whether there is a Eucharist or not; but the sermon is optional. No homily is provided.

The Psalms
(section 23)

The intention at this point in the Sarum rite, as in 1549/1662, was for the clergy to proceed to the altar, followed by the couple who knelt at the steps, with the bridal party behind them. Sarum provided for the use of Psalm 128, with its emphasis on the gift of children, during this procession. In 1549 Cranmer still provided Psalm 128, but also included Psalm 67, with no reference to children, as an alternative. 1662 continued with these two psalms, and 1928 added Psalm 37.3–7 as a further general alternative. ASB still provides three psalms, but has substituted Psalm 121 for the portion of Psalm 37; it also permits a suitable hymn as a further alternative.

The Prayers
(sections 24–30)

These prayers are mandatory, except that a choice may be made between nos. 26 and 27. Obviously no. 26, a prayer for the gift of children, will not be suitable in every case.

No. 24
A new prayer by the Liturgical Commission, for the gift and guidance of the Holy Spirit, based on the 1662 final blessing.

No. 26
A new prayer by the Liturgical Commission, for the gift of children, based on the 1662 prayer for children.

No. 27
A prayer for the married life of the new couple, taken from the CSI Marriage Rite.

No. 28
Other prayers may be included at this point, either prayers from sections 31–8, or extempore prayer, or prayers produced by the couple themselves.

No. 30
The blessing of both the married couple and the congregation is that of Trinity Sunday from Rite A in ASB. The Nuptial Mass in the Sarum rite was that of the Trinity.

Additional Prayers
(sections 31–8)

These additional prayers are all optional.

No. 31
A prayer for the couple, based on a prayer in the Marriage Service of the new American Prayer Book.

No. 32
A new prayer for the couple by the Liturgical Commission, and inspired by the 1928 blessing of the couple.

No. 33
A new prayer by the Liturgical Commission for God's blessing on the sexual relationship of the couple.

No. 34
An adaptation of a prayer in the Marriage Service of the new

American Prayer Book, for the witness of the couple in contemporary life.

No. 35
A modern replacement by the Liturgical Commission of the long 1549/1662 prayer 'O God, who by thy mighty power hast made all things out of nothing'. Some of the phraseology is borrowed from a similar prayer in the new Roman Catholic Marriage Rite.

No. 36
A new prayer by the Liturgical Commission, asking that the marriage may contribute to the couple's growth in the Christian life. It ends with lines attributed to St Richard of Chichester.

No. 37
A new prayer by the Liturgical Commission, which may be used as a brief alternative to nos. 31–4.

No. 38
A prayer for the home and family life of the couple, based on the new Mothers' Union Prayer.

THE MARRIAGE SERVICE WITH HOLY COMMUNION
(section 39)

In the interests of clarity, directions are provided for the use of the Marriage Service with Holy Communion. Either of two orders may be used, propers are provided, and Rite A or Rite B may be used for the Eucharist.

First Order

The Marriage Rite is set within the context of Holy Communion: it follows the Ministry of the Word and the Sermon, and it includes all the elements up to and including the Registration (sections 4–21). The Eucharist then follows, beginning at the Peace, and the post-communion prayers may include any of the Additional Prayers from the Marriage Service (sections 31–8).

Second Order

This is the more traditional form. The Marriage Service starts at the Preface (section 6) and continues to the Registration (section

21). The collect and the Ministry of the Word and sermon then follow (sections 1–5), after which the Eucharist continues from the Peace, as in the First Order.

The Propers
(section 40)

An indication is given of the use made of these propers in other rites before ASB:

Genesis 1.26–8, 31a	S. Africa; America; Rev. Rom.
Ephesians 3.14–end	1928; S. Africa; America
Ephesians 5.21–33	1662 Homily; America; Rev. Rom.
Romans 12.1, 2, 9–13	Rev. Rom.
1 Corinthians 13	CSI; America
Colossians 3.12–17	America; Rev. Rom.
1 John 4.7–12	America; Rev. Rom.
Matthew 7.21, 24–7	America
John 15.9–12	1928; S. Africa; America: Rev. Rom.
Mark 10.6–9	America; Rev. Rom.
John 2.1–11	Rev. Rom.

14

Funeral Services

A

HISTORY

Studies:

Geoffrey Rowell, *The Liturgy of Christian Burial*. 1977.

Richard Rutherford, *The Death of a Christian: The Rite of Funerals*. New York 1980: centred round current Roman Catholic rites, but contains much historical information, theology and practical advice.

1 Early Christian Practice

Our knowledge of early Christian funeral practices is very scanty indeed. The Church inherited from Judaism the practice of burial as the normal means of disposal of the dead, and, as one might expect, there seem to have been special prayers to accompany this act. Third-century evidence suggests that spices were used to prepare the body for burial, as indeed is recorded in the case of the burial of Jesus himself (Mark 16.1; Luke 23.56—24.1; John 19.39–40), and that the Eucharist was offered on the day of the funeral and also on the anniversary of the death. Fourth-century evidence speaks of the singing of psalms and hymns at funerals (John Chrysostom mentions in particular Psalms 22, 23 and 116), and Christians were instructed to eschew all sumptuous funeral pomp, rich grave-clothes, and lavish trappings: a simple shroud for the body and the giving of alms as a memorial were all that were necessary. Attempts were also made to persuade them not to wear the dark mourning garments of pagans but instead white garments expressive of Christian hope, and not to indulge in the common practices of wailing, rending of garments, and spreading of ashes, which implied a lack of faith in the resurrection. The Church, however, eventually lost this battle.

2 Later Eastern Rites

Eastern burial rites, though differing greatly from one another in details, all have a broadly similar outline pattern. Firstly, there is an introductory section consisting of prayers and responses, and often also of psalmody, which is usually said in the house of the deceased. Then there follows a funeral procession to church, during which psalms or other chants are recited. At the church (or sometimes at the tomb, if the procession goes directly there) there is a service of prayers, hymns and psalms, generally with two passages of Scripture read as Epistle and Gospel. There may be a ritual farewell, as for example the last kiss—an ancient custom derived from pagan practice—or this may take place instead when the procession reaches the grave. The procession from the church to the place of burial is accompanied by further psalms, anthems or responses; and the burial itself is usually a simple act of committal, with short prayers of commendation and the sprinkling of earth on the body.

3 The Medieval West

In the developed rites of the West a similar outline pattern can be discerned. Psalms and prayers are said after death, while the body is washed and prepared for burial; further psalms and antiphons are used in the procession to church; in the church a special office of the dead, consisting of psalms and readings, is prescribed, and a Mass is celebrated for the soul of the departed; after this there is a procession to the grave, with further psalms; and prayers are said at the burial. These rites lay very great stress on the note of judgement and fear in place of the earlier emphasis on entry into the joy of paradise.

4 The Reformation

In this, as in other areas of liturgy, the Reformers greatly simplified the medieval practices, and in particular purged them of all prayers for the departed and all reference to any possible intermediate state of purgatory after death, since they held that the fate of the deceased was determined and final at the moment of death and could not be affected by any prayers or the offering of a Mass made for them by others. Indeed, because of what they regarded as the superstitious attitude towards death prevalent in the medieval Church, the extreme Reformers refused to allow any rites at all to accompany the act of burial, viewing it merely as a utilitarian necessity. Even the Reformed tradition provided only a minimal religious observance. John Knox's Genevan Service

Book of 1556, for example, directed that 'the corpse is reverently brought to the grave, accompanied with the congregation without any further ceremonies, which being buried the minister goeth to the church, if it be not far off, and maketh some comfortable exhortation to the people, touching death and resurrection.'

The Lutheran tradition, however, retained rather more of the older practices, and provided for psalms and hymns, or sometimes readings, to be used at the graveside, or on the way to it, and after the burial either a simple preaching of the true Christian hope of resurrection, or a more extensive service in church, with readings, hymns and prayers—but for the living and not for the departed.

5 The Church of England

The 1549 Prayer Book was more conservative still. Its burial rite comprised four elements:

(a) a procession to the church, or directly to the grave, accompanied by the saying or singing of appropriate scriptural sentences;

(b) the burial itself, with more sentences for use at the grave while the body was prepared for burial, and then words of committal, accompanied by the casting of earth on the body, and prayers commending the deceased to God;

(c) a short office for the dead to be said in church, either before or after the burial, consisting of three psalms (116, 139 and 146), a reading (1 Cor. 15.20–58), Kyries, Lord's Prayer, versicles and responses, and a concluding prayer, which made petition for the departed;

(d) the celebration of the Eucharist, for which a psalm (42), collect, Epistle (1 Thess. 4.13–18), and Gospel (John 6.37–40) were provided.

In the 1552 Prayer Book considerable changes were made, mainly by extensive deletion. The procession was retained, as were the sentences while the body was prepared for burial, but there then followed simply the words of committal (still with the casting of earth), the reading from 1 Corinthians, Kyries, Lord's Prayer, the concluding prayer from the office for the dead, and the collect from the Eucharist; everything else was now omitted. Moreover, alterations were made in the wording of the act of committal and the two final prayers so that there was no longer any commendation of the soul of the deceased to God, but simply the committal of the body to the ground, nor any direct petition for the departed.

In the 1662 order further changes were made. A new rubric at the beginning stated that 'the Office ensuing is not to be used for any that die unbaptized, or excommunicate, or have laid violent hands upon themselves.' Two psalms (39 and 90) were provided after the procession, with the rubric that one or both of them should be used when 'they are come into the church'. The reading from 1 Corinthians was to follow. The rest of the service took place at the grave as before, with some minor changes in wording and the addition of 'the grace of our Lord Jesus Christ' etc. at the end.

The 1927/28 service returned more to the pattern of the 1549 rite, since prayer for the departed and requiem celebrations of the Eucharist had now become more widely accepted, not least as a consequence of the experiences of the First World War, when they seemed to provide an answer to pastoral need. Additional sentences were provided for use in the procession, and provision also made for the use of any of the traditional penitential psalms (6, 32, 38, 51, 102, 130, 143). In the service in church Psalms 23 and 130 were included as possible alternatives to Psalms 39 and 90, and rubrics permitted the use of the response 'Rest eternal grant unto them, O Lord: and let light perpetual shine upon them' in place of the Gloria Patri at the end of the psalms, and the use of the anthem, 'O Saviour of the world, who by thy cross and precious Blood hast redeemed us; Save us and help us, we humbly beseech thee, O Lord' before or after any of the psalms. Alternative readings to 1 Corinthians were also provided (2 Cor. 4.16—5.10; Rev. 7.9–17; Rev. 21.1–7).

At the grave Psalm 103.13–17 could be used in place of the sentences while the body was prepared for burial, and an alternative form of committal, based on the prayer of commendation in the 1549 rite, was provided. A new final sentence was added to this part of the service, and the ancient versicles and responses from the 1549 service were restored as an optional feature of the prayers which followed. Three new prayers were also included for optional use, one asking for light and peace for the departed, one for those who mourn, and one asking for the strengthening of faith in the communion of saints; and other appropriate prayers from elsewhere in the Prayer Book could also be added. Rubrics at the end permitted the prayers to be said in church with the psalms and reading, and the burial to precede this part of the service if

desired. Provision was also made for a celebration of the Eucharist, using the collect from the prayers, 1 Thessalonians 4.13–18 or
2 Corinthians 4.16—5.4 for the Epistle, and John 6.37–41 or John
5.24–9 for the Gospel. Finally, a special order of service was
included for the burial of a child, which followed the outline of the
normal service but offered more appropriate sentences and
prayers, and prescribed Psalm 23 and Mark 10.13–16 for use in
church.

Although never legally approved, the 1928 rite was widely used
in the years which followed, and was included in the Series 1
provisions in 1966. There was some unease among Evangelicals
because of the inclusion of specific prayer for the departed in this
order, but it managed to secure a substantial majority for its
authorization. Meanwhile, the Liturgical Commission had completed their work on a new rite in 1964, and it was subsequently
published with the rest of the Series 2 services in 1965. Its long
introduction, in addition to discussing the thorny problem of
prayer for the departed, dealt with the question, 'What ought we
to be doing at a burial service?' The reply is sufficiently important
to merit quotation:

> Having faced the question afresh in the light of theological and pastoral
> considerations, the Commission puts forward the following fivefold
> answer:
>
> (a) To secure the reverent disposal of the corpse.
> (b) To commend the deceased to the care of our heavenly Father.
> (c) To proclaim the glory of our risen life in Christ here and hereafter.
> (d) To remind us of the awful certainty of our own coming death and
>   judgement.
> (e) To make plain the eternal unity of Christian people, living and
>   departed, in the risen and ascended Christ.
>
> It would perhaps be natural to add a sixth point, namely the
> consolation of the mourners; but the Commission believes that this
> object should be attained by means of the objects already included in
> its answer.
>
> In giving effect to this answer in liturgical form, the Commission has
> set before itself the following practical aims:
>
> (a) That one burial service should suffice for all baptized persons
>   (including suicides); but an exception has had to be made in the
>   case of burying children.
> (b) That the rite should not assume that the soul of the deceased

is, at the time of the burial of the body, in any particular place or state.

(c) That as much as possible of the existing material should be used, even though some parts must be simplified or used in a different way.

(d) That the congregation should be given a more active part than at present.

(e) That as little as possible of the service should be required to take place out of doors.

(f) That the orders of service provided should, the committal of the body being omitted, be suitable for use as memorial services (The Church of England Liturgical Commission, *Alternative Services. Second Series*, 1965, pp. 105–6).

This quotation sets out admirably not only the principles underlying the Series 2 services but also those of Series 3 which ultimately appeared in the Alternative Service Book. Unfortunately, despite being passed by the Convocations in October 1966, the Series 2 services failed to secure acceptance in the House of Laity, the prayers for the departed proving to be the stumbling block. Attempts at amendment were unsuccessful, and eventually at the end of 1968 the whole matter was referred back to the Liturgical Commission. It was hoped that a fresh start might be made, although little help was given to the Commission as to the meaning of a 'fresh start'. Indeed, in January 1969 the two Archbishops informed their Convocations that they had asked the Liturgical Commission to draft a new Burial Service, 'it being left to the Commission to determine the width or the narrowness of the word "new".'

In this unenviable position help was given by the Doctrine Commission, which produced its report, *Prayer and the Departed*, in January 1971. This expressed the hope that, despite different views on this vexed question, sufficiently broad areas of agreement existed for certain forms of prayer to find general acceptance. It then set out five forms of prayer for Christian and non-Christian dead, which had been accepted by the entire Commission and represented an important advance in being unitive. When the General Synod discussed the report in November 1972, it passed a resolution which, though at odds with the Doctrine Commission's attempts to find a *modus vivendi*, nevertheless marked a significant step forward. This stated that, while the Synod recognized that some members of the Church of England would not wish to use prayers for the departed, there were others who valued them and wished them to be included in services, provided that they were optional.

Armed with this advice, the Liturgical Commission set about the task of drafting the Series 3 services, and eventually published its proposals in 1973 (GS 147). The principles already stated were adhered to; the general structure of the proposed Series 2 services was left unaltered; and a good deal of familiar material was retained; but the general effect of the services was rather different: 'We hope that ... the remains of medieval gloom have finally given way to a more authentically Christian note of confidence and hope' (GS 147, p. 6). The title had also changed: they were 'Funeral Services', not 'Burial Services'; for it was recognized that less than 50 per cent of funerals now included burial. Cremation, and even burial at sea, as well as interment were therefore provided for. This time there was little controversy. The General Synod considered the proposals in 1974 and, after some amendment of detail by a Revision Committee, they were authorized for use in January 1975, and subsequently incorporated in the Alternative Service Book.

B
COMMENTARY

The Service in Church

Note 2 (p. 306) makes it clear that the phrase 'in Church' does not preclude the possibility of the service being held elsewhere. It can also be held at the graveside, at a crematorium, at sea, or even in a house (see also notes 4–5, p. 306). It can also be a Funeral Service or a Memorial Service. Nor is anything said about the service being held for unbaptized or excommunicate persons who have died: that is a matter belonging to canon law rather than to liturgy.

The Sentences
(sections 1–2)

The service begins with the Sentences, only the first of which (John 11.25–6) is mandatory. John 11.25–6 was used in the Sarum burial rite, and Cranmer took it with Job 19.25–7 as the first two of three anthems to be said or sung during the procession from the churchyard gate to the church or grave. Cranmer's third anthem—from 1 Timothy 6.7 and Job 1.21—was new, and had not appeared in the medieval rite. These three sentences persisted through successive Prayer Books to 1928, which added another six. Of the 1928 provision, ASB has omitted Job 19.25–7, and retained Deuteronomy 33.27, Matthew 5.4, and Romans 8.38–9. Job 19.25–7 was omitted, despite its long associations with the rite, because it is wrong to take this particular verse out of context, and because modern authorized translations are not suitable for use at funerals. ASB also added four new sentences—Lamentations 3.22–3, John 3.16, 1 Corinthians 2.9 and 1 Thessalonians 4.14, 18. The mandatory sentence—John 11.25–6—with its reference to 'true faith' and 'sure hope', establishes at the outset the positive note of confidence which the service tries to convey.

The Collect
(section 3)

The collect, which comes from the 1928 Burial Service, has affinities with the Apostles' Creed and again echoes the opening sentence from John 11.25–6. The prayer is mandatory and is said by the whole congregation, who ask for a strengthening of faith and hope at the time of bereavement.

The Psalms
(section 4)

Four psalms are appointed—23, 90 (portions), 121, 130—of which one or more is used. References to the use of 23 (a psalm of confidence) at funerals are as early as St John Chrysostom (fourth to fifth century); but it did not appear in English funeral rites until 1928. Psalm 90 is a lament, dealing with man's transience: it was appointed in 1662 together with Psalm 39; these had been used in funeral rites compiled by Robert Sanderson and Jeremy Taylor during the Commonwealth, when the Prayer Book was banned. Psalm 121 is new in ASB; but as a psalm described as a 'farewell liturgy', in which someone departing on a journey is blessed, it is eminently suitable for funerals. Psalm 130, one of the traditional penitential psalms, with its expression of trust in God, was introduced in 1928.

ASB also provides four further passages of psalmody as alternatives: 27, one of the psalms from the medieval *Dirige*, or Mattins of the Dead; 42.1–7, from the 1549 burial Eucharist; 118.14–21,

399

28–9, a psalm of thanksgiving, probably used at the Feast of Tabernacles; 139.1–11, 17–18, one of the 1549 burial psalms.

The Readings
(section 5)

Three main readings are provided which are set out in full. One or more of these must be read. John 14.1–6 is a new passage, in which Jesus speaks of going to prepare a place for his disciples in his Father's house. It is also used in the new American Prayer Book and in the Revised Roman rite. The passage from 1 Corinthians 15 has been traditionally read at funerals. It was used in Sarum, in German Church Orders, and in successive Prayer Books from 1549 to 1928. In ASB only selected verses are used, producing a much shorter reading, but leaving the argument intact. The third reading is 1 Thessalonians 4.13–18, which 1549 took from Sarum as the Epistle at the funeral Eucharist: 1552 and 1662 had no funeral eucharistic propers, but it reappeared in 1928 as the Epistle.

Ten alternative readings are provided by reference only, the most notable being John 6.35–40, which in 1549 and 1928 was the Gospel for the funeral Eucharist, and in Sarum had been the Gospel for Tuesday Masses for the Dead.

A Sermon
(section 6)

Provision is made for a sermon: but it is not mandatory.

Verses from the Te Deum, or a Hymn
(section 7)

An innovation in ASB is the saying or singing of the second part of Te Deum by the congregation as a response to the Ministry of the Word. This section, addressed to Christ, is particularly appropriate with its references to our Lord overcoming the sting of death, and its prayer that he will bring us with the saints to everlasting glory. For further comment on the Te Deum, see pp. 109–11. If desired, an appropriate hymn may be sung instead.

The Prayers
(sections 8–13)

The prayers are introduced by the Lesser Litany and the Lord's Prayer.

The rubric (section 9) then permits other prayers to be used at this point, and it is so worded that the choice is not restricted to those in sections 50–60. Sufficient freedom is therefore provided to meet all the requirements of conscience. This rubric was inserted in this form to implement the resolution of the General Synod in November 1972 after the debate on the Doctrine Commission's Report *Prayer and the Departed*. See pp. 397–8.

Section 10

A prayer for those who are still alive—principally the mourners—with three petitions: that they may (*a*) use their time on earth aright; (*b*) be brought to repentance; and (*c*) be given strength to follow Christ. This prayer is mandatory. It is a new composition, first appearing in the Series 3 Funeral service.

Section 12

A significant feature in the proposed Series 2 Funeral Service was the clear distinction made between the commendation of the deceased person to God, and the committal of the remains to their last resting place. This distinction is continued in ASB, although in a slightly different form. In 1662 the commendation of the soul was combined with the committal of the body. Now, in ASB, the whole person is commended to the mercy of God, thereby providing an admirable climax to the service in church. It expresses the willingness of those who love the deceased person to let that person go.

Section 13

The concluding prayer is one of the 'irenic' forms proposed by the Doctrine Commission in *Prayer and the Departed*. Their own comment merits quotation:

> If we interpret prayer for the departed as implying a present lack on their part (and not all members of the Commission accept this interpretation), the only thing we can say for certain that they do lack, in terms of biblical eschatology, is the resurrection at God's climax of history, the *parousia*. The New Testament does not give us an individualistic idea of perfection. This involves the whole Church, and it will not be available for any until it is available for all. That is why the early Christians prayed *Maranatha*, 'O, our Lord, come!' (1 Cor.

401

16.22; Rev. 22.20; *Didache*). They looked forward to the *parousia*, and so may we, as the time when God's will would be done in heaven and on earth alike, when Paradise Lost would be Paradise Regained. The Commission therefore suggests the following as a form of words which could be used *ex animo* by Anglicans of all theological persuasions, although some will still deem it more expedient not to use intercession at all in respect of the departed. It only asks for such things as we are scripturally persuaded are in accordance with God's will and have not already been granted. (*Prayer and the Departed*, 1971, pp. 55–6.)

The Committal
(sections 14–19)

In 1662 the Committal preceded the prayers. In ASB there is a greater degree of flexibility. It may take place in the 1662 position; or it may follow the prayers; or in the case of a cremation, it may precede the service in church (see Note 6, p. 306). There is much to be said for having the Committal after the prayers, especially if it is to take place elsewhere.

Section 14

The Committal may begin with an optional sentence from Revelation 14.13. In the Sarum rite, this sentence was part of the Epistle in the Mass for the Dead, and it was also used as an antiphon in the Office for the Dead. Cranmer used it in 1549 to follow the Committal, and it appeared in this position in successive Prayer Books until 1928. In view of the fact that the present rite ends with other sentences of Scripture, it seemed more appropriate to use Revelation 14.13 as an introductory sentence.

Sections 15–16

The sentence is followed either by verses from Psalm 103 or by the anthem 'Man born of a woman'.

Psalm 103, vv. 8, 13–17

In these verses the transitoriness of man is set against the enduring love and mercy of God. They first appeared as an alternative to the traditional anthem in 1928.

Man Born of a Woman

Tradition ascribes this anthem to Notker, a monk of St Gall in Switzerland (d. 912) and the originator of sequences: but the evidence is by no means conclusive. He is said to have been inspired by the sight of a bridge being constructed over a mountain gorge at Martinstobel, through which the river Goldach goes from St Gall to the Lake of Constance: the anthem expressed his realization of the danger which confronted the builders. The opening verse, from Job 14.1–2, was a lesson at Mattins of the Dead; but the whole anthem was an antiphon to the Nunc Dimittis in the Sarum office of Compline in the third and fourth weeks of Lent. In its original form it was a series of verses each followed by a response reminiscent of the Trisagion, and the response still appears twice in 1662. The anthem was very popular in medieval Germany, being used not only on occasions of mourning but also before battles and on days of trouble or disaster. Luther composed a metrical version of it, which was equally popular; and this was translated by Coverdale in his *Ghostly Psalms*—a translation which appears to have affected the version used in 1549. The phrase 'Suffer us not at our last hour', for example, was a piece of Luther via Coverdale which did not appear in the medieval antiphon.

The use of this anthem while the corpse was 'made ready to be laid into the earth' reflects the medieval custom of interment without the coffin. Furthermore, until 1662 the burial of the body in the grave normally preceded the rest of the service. This rather gloomy anthem was therefore heard at the outset, and the subsequent prayers presented the mourners with the more confident note of the resurrection. It would also be argued that the statement 'in the midst of life we are in death', while perhaps reflecting Notker's reaction to the extreme danger to which the bridge-builders were exposed, is hardly in accord with New Testament teaching, which is rather 'in the midst of death we are in life'. The anthem is, however, of long standing and has been retained in ASB.

Section 17

The words of the Committal have been subject to considerable development. The medieval Sarum form was simply, 'I commend thy soul to God the Father almighty, earth to earth, ashes to ashes, dust to dust, in the name of the Father...' Cranmer made two additions in 1549: the phrase 'and thy body to the ground' was inserted before 'earth to earth', and the passage from Philippians 3.21, 'in sure and certain hope', was appended after 'dust to dust'. 1552 then deleted the reference to commending the soul and prefixed the remaining committal with the opening words of the second funeral sermon in Hermann's *Consultation*: 'Forasmuch as it hath pleased Almighty God of his great mercy, to take unto himself the soul of our dear brother here departed, we therefore commit...' The commending of the soul was therefore replaced by a statement recognizing that God had already received it. This was the form which was retained in 1662. 1928, however, provided an alternative, which began with a form closer to 1549, commending the soul and committing the body. ASB has now produced a form which also has close affinities with the 1549 form, but with one important modification. In view of the fact that the commendation of the whole person has taken place at the end of the service in church (section 12), the whole person is again referred to, but with an alternative verb: 'We have entrusted our *brother* to God's merciful keeping, and we now commit *his* body...' Any kind of dichotomy between body and soul is therefore avoided.

Alternative forms of wording are provided for cremation and burial at sea (see Note 5, p. 306); and no directions are given for casting earth upon the coffin in the case of burials, although there is no reason why this should not be done. This custom, retained in successive Prayer Books, was a relic of the medieval ceremony of hallowing the grave.

Sections 18–19

The service concludes with two sentences of Scripture—Psalm 16.11 and Jude 24–5. The former provides a parallel to the medieval antiphon, but less forbidding in tone. The latter is an ascription of praise, ending the service on a note of hope and confidence.

Section 13, at the conclusion of the service in church, may also be used as an alternative ending (see pp. 401–2).

THE FUNERAL OF A CHILD

This service follows the same pattern as the service for an adult; but the propers and other material indicated below are appropriate to children. It is kept as short and as simple as possible, in view of the fact that the mourners will be under considerable stress. No special form for a child existed before 1928.

Section 20

The introductory sentence is Revelation 7.17 but others may be added from the former order for adults (sections 1–2). The opening collect is omitted.

Section 21

Only one psalm is provided.

Section 22

Either or both of the Scripture readings are used. In Mark 10.13–16, the emphasis is on the deceased child—Jesus' acceptance and blessing of children; in Ephesians 3.14–19, the emphasis is on the mourners—Paul's prayer that his readers may be strengthened by God and brought to know his love. The sermon and the section of the Te Deum are omitted.

Sections 23–4

Following the Lesser Litany and the Lord's Prayer comes a new prayer for faith in time of darkness and for strength. It is adapted from a proposed prayer in the unauthorized Series 2 service.

Sections 25–8

These sections are identical with sections 9–13 in the adult service. See pp. 400–2.

Sections 29–32

An abbreviated form of committal from the service for adults. See pp. 402–4. Psalm 103 is obviously more appropriate than 'Man born of a woman has but a short time to live.'

405

*Prayers after
the Birth of a still-born Child or
the Death of a newly-born Child*

Until 1928 no provision at all was made for such occasions; and even in 1928 the provision was meagre—a single prayer at the end of the Order for the Churching of Women. Initially new provision was made in the Series 3 Initiation services, as an appendix to the Thanksgiving for the Birth of a Child; but subsequently it was felt more appropriate to include this material with the Funeral Services. These prayers are not really for liturgical use. The rubric in section 33 merely indicates occasions when these prayers may be found pastorally appropriate.

Sections 34–5

Two new prayers by the Liturgical Commission. The first is for mourners, the second for the mother.

Section 36

A prayer for the parents, adapted from the 1928 prayer for the mother.

Section 37

A prayer for the parents, adapted from the Intercession for those who suffer in Holy Communion Rite A.

Section 38

A prayer taken from the Order for the Burial of a Child, section 24. See p. 405.

Section 39

A new prayer by the Liturgical Commission, commending the child to the love of God.

Sections 40–1

A catena of verses from the psalms—46.1, 73.26, 38.21, 42.6 and 42.7. A selection of psalm passages, mostly from the Funeral Services, is provided as an alternative.

A Form which may be used at the Interment of the Ashes
(sections 42–5)

This short service, which is in effect an abbreviated form of Committal, is held at the grave, or the vault, or wherever the ashes are to be laid permanently. It begins with a sentence (section 2), which is followed by the form of committal (section 43), a brief prayer for the bliss of all believers (section 44) and the Grace (section 45).

A Service which may be used before a Funeral
(section 46)

Because a request is often made for a body to rest in church overnight before a funeral, a short form of service is provided for the arrival of the body. Alternatively it could be used at home before the body is taken to church. All the material comes from the Funeral Services, and obviously this form can be adapted. Care should be taken, however, that there is no undue duplication of material which is to be used in the Funeral Service itself.

The Funeral Service with Holy Communion
(sections 47–9)

1549 followed Sarum in providing for a Eucharist at a Funeral. The provision was omitted in 1552 and 1662 but restored in 1928. ASB now makes provision for a Funeral to be held within a service of Holy Communion without any unnecessary duplication of material. Either Rite A or Rite B of Holy Communion may be used: the section numbers below refer to Rite A:

1	The Ministry of the Word, from Sentence to Sermon	Funeral service, sections 1–6
	(Propers may also be taken from the Funeral Service sections 48–9, 51–3)	
2	Prayers	Holy Communion, sections 20–1; or Funeral Service, sections 50–60
3	Penitence and the Peace (optional)	Holy Communion, sections 25–31
4	Holy Communion, from the Preparation of the Gifts to the Giving of the Bread and Cup	Holy Communion, sections 32–47
5	Prayers	Funeral Service, sections 9–10, 12–13
6	After Communion	Holy Communion, sections 50–5
7	The Committal—normally taken separately	Funeral Service, sections 14–19

1   Propers are also provided for:

The Funeral of a Child combined with Holy Communion (section 48). The collect is a new composition by the Liturgical Commission, based on the two final prayers in the 1928 Order for the Burial of a Child.

2   A Eucharist which is not combined with a Funeral (section 49). The collect is substantially the same as those for Easter 3 and the Commemoration of the Faithful Departed.

Additional Prayers
(sections 50–60)

A selection of eleven additional prayers which are for public or private use and are not intended to be exhaustive. Many of these are familiar or have been adapted from familiar prayers.

Section 50

A new prayer, giving thanks for the life of the departed.

Section 51

An amended form of a prayer in the Series 2 proposed services. It originally appeared in the 1954 South African Prayer Book.

Section 52

A prayer originally suggested in a Memorandum from the Archbishops in May 1968.

Section 53

An amended form of another prayer in the Series 2 proposed services. It was based on a petition in the old Roman canon.

Section 54

The adaptation of a 1928 Commemoration of the Departed. 1928 was in its turn a modification of a prayer by Bishop John Wordsworth of Salisbury. He is thought to have based it on a form in W. E. Scudamore's *Words to take with us.*

Section 55

Another amended prayer from the Series 2 proposed services for mourners.

Section 56

A new prayer by the Liturgical Commission, but so devised as to include the well-known phrase 'those whom we love but see no longer'.

Section 57

A prayer for mourners, based on the Second Beatitude—Matthew 5.4. It has been attributed to Bishop Charles Lewis Slattery of Massachusetts. In the American 1928 Prayer Book it was included in the Burial Service of a Child. It was also in our own 1928 book.

Section 58

A 1928 prayer which has been included, presumably for mourners. Dean Milner-White claimed it to be Elizabethan. Newman appears to have quoted it in Sermon 20 in his *Sermons on Subjects of the Day*.

Section 59

This prayer has been drawn from the Intercessions in Holy Communion Series 3.

Section 60

A short litany, proposed by the General Synod Revision Committee, and drafted by the Rev. R. J. Avent.

15

The Ordinal

A

HISTORY

General studies:
Bernard Cooke, *Ministry to Word and Sacraments*. Philadelphia 1976.
Nathan Mitchell, *Mission and Ministry: History and Theology in the Sacrament of Order*. Wilmington, Delaware, 1982.

1 The Old Testament and Jewish Background

Evidence for the earliest period of Israel's history suggests that originally there was no separate class of 'priests' or cultic ministers, but instead the head of the family or leader of the tribe had the responsibility for ministering before the Lord and offering sacrifice on behalf of his people. Thus, for example, we read of Noah (Gen. 8.20), Abraham (Gen. 22.1–19), and Jacob (Gen. 31.54) doing just that. Similarly, the earliest traditions concerning the Exodus from Egypt portray Moses as leader of the people mediating between God and the emerging nation and transmitting the divine commandments to them.

After the settlement in Canaan, however, a recognizable class of paid, professional cultic officials began to emerge, whose main functions seem to have been to discern the divine will, chiefly by casting lots, and to tend the family or tribal sanctuary (see, for example, Judges 17.5—18.6). Gradually this occupation came to be the special prerogative of the tribe of Levi, who had no land of their own and so needed to be employed by others. Nevertheless, even at this stage, although the Levites may have looked after the many sanctuaries scattered throughout the land, individual Israelites could still offer the sacrifices themselves, in accordance with the ancient tradition. Similarly, after the establishment of the monarchy, the king continued to preside over sacrifices offered on behalf of the nation and to bless the people (see, for example,

2 Sam. 6.17–18), and thus performed functions which were later to be thought of as exclusively priestly.

It was natural that the cultic officials attached to the royal Temple at Jerusalem should enjoy a particular prestige over those at rural shrines, whose ministry began to decline as the centralized monarchy and its cult increasingly acted for the whole nation, and, under King Solomon, Zadok and his descendants managed to find favour and secure this privileged position. Attempts were constantly made to close down the old rural sanctuaries and to concentrate all cultic worship at the one Temple in Jerusalem, and though this was never entirely successful, it led to the unemployed Levites from elsewhere having to accept a subsidiary and fairly menial role in the Jerusalem Temple duties, while the primary priestly functions were retained by the Zadokites. By now, therefore, genealogical lineage determined entry to the two ranks of cultic ministers, the priests and the Levites: it was an hereditary 'closed shop', which came to have the exclusive right of offering sacrifice, the older custom of individuals performing this ministry themselves eventually disappearing.

After Jerusalem fell to the Babylonians in 587 BC, the Israelite monarchy came to an end, the worship of the Temple ceased, and many of its officials were sent into exile. After it was restored, the priests tended increasingly to be regarded as the leaders of the people, in the absence of a monarchy, and the office of high priest emerged as a quasi-royal figure, the focus of both civil and religious leadership. At first this appointment was for life, but later in the Herodian period (37 BC to AD 70) it was reduced to a limited term. Because the number of those who had a right to be priests and Levites was so large at this time, it had ceased to be a full-time occupation for all but a very few. The rest were divided into twenty-four clans or courses, each consisting of an average of 300 priests and 400 Levites. These courses came up to Jerusalem to perform one week of service in the Temple in turn, and lived at home in their towns and villages for the rest of the year.

Originally there appears to have been no form of ritual admission to office or ordination for Temple ministers, but later the practice was for candidates to be examined as to their credentials and then, after a purificatory bath, solemnly invested with the robes of office before taking part in special sacrifices. The ritual of anointing seems to have belonged exclusively to the coronation of the king in pre-exilic times, and only in the post-exilic period was it taken over into the consecration of the high

411

priest and then subsequently extended to the ordination of all priests. This practice only lasted for a while, however, and by the New Testament period it had once again fallen into disuse.

Outside the Temple cult the exercise of liturgical functions was not restricted to permanent, ordained officials in New Testament times. In domestic practice the ancient tradition of the right and duty of the head of the household to act on behalf of his family remained: he it was who presided over communal meals and recited the blessings over the food and drink in the name of all. Similarly, the synagogues, which came into existence sometime during or after the exile in Babylon, were essentially a lay movement: anyone might be invited to participate in the services by leading the prayers, reading the Scriptures, or delivering a sermon or exposition. Apart from the privilege of pronouncing the Aaronic blessing (Num. 6.24–6), itself a practice derived from the Temple liturgy, the priests had no special place in the synagogue services, and although the supervision of the worship was in the hands of an appointed officer, the ruler of the synagogue (cf. Luke 8.41, 49; 13.14; Acts 13.15), he too had no special prerogatives beyond the responsibility for keeping order and inviting members of the congregation to fulfil the various liturgical roles. Even the rabbis, respected though they may have been for their learning, did not have an exclusive claim to an authoritative teaching ministry.

It has often been suggested that there was an established pattern of rabbinic ordination in first-century Judaism, involving the laying on of hands, which provided a model for subsequent Christian practice. More recent research, however, has cast great doubts on such assertions, as lacking any really firm evidence. Indeed Lawrence Hoffman has claimed that the term 'rabbi' itself did not come into use until after the destruction of the Temple in AD 70, and that, although subsequently individual rabbis did appoint their disciples as rabbis themselves, nevertheless, if there ever was any liturgical ceremony associated with this act, we do not know anything about it.

Studies:
Aelred Cody, *A History of Old Testament Priesthood.* Rome 1969.
Lawrence Hoffman, 'Jewish Ordination on the Eve of Christianity' (*SL* 13, 1979), pp. 11–41.
Joachim Jeremias, *Jerusalem in the Time of Jesus.* 1969.
Roland de Vaux, *Ancient Israel.* 1961.

2 *The New Testament*

The epistles of St Paul presuppose that all Christians, and not just a select few, are involved in ministry, but that their ministries are not identical: there are varieties of gifts and ministries, and everything is to be done in accordance with the particular gifts which each individual has received from God through the Holy Spirit (I Cor. 12.4ff.). Thus, for example, many different people play a part in the community's worship (I Cor. 14.26–33).

A similar impression is given by other parts of the New Testament. In I Peter 2.5, for example, the Church is thought of as a priesthood, an image derived from the Old Testament, from Exodus 19.6, where God tells Moses that the people of Israel will be 'a kingdom of priests'. It is here intended to express the relationship between the Church and the world, just as in Exodus it had been used to express the relationship between Israel and the other nations; as a priest is to minister to his people, so is the Church to minister to the world. Whatever some leaders of the Reformation may have thought, it is not trying to say anything about the liturgical functions of individual Christians *within* the Church, nor is it necessarily denying the possibility of certain ministries being restricted to specific officers, any more than its use in the Old Testament had ruled out the existence of a definite order of priests within Israel.

The fact that the New Testament stresses the involvement of all Christians in ministry has caused some to doubt the existence of any permanent leaders in the earliest Christian communities. Although this fails to do justice to the New Testament data, it does offer a valuable warning against assuming too readily either that there was a fully developed formal structure of appointment or ordination of community leaders from the very beginning, or that the same pattern of leadership existed in every place. The evidence suggests on the contrary that there was considerable diversity and pluriformity with regard to types and models of leadership in the different Christian communities of the first century, and that explicit and formal appointment or ordination tended more often to be a later development, after the first generation of believers had died, than a feature of the earliest groups of converts, where authority and power tended to be more implicit and informal. In some instances it would appear that the first converts or founders of a local Christian congregation naturally assumed responsibility for it, in others that those who displayed outstanding gifts, especially of teaching or prophesying/ preaching, took charge.

A formal title was not always given to those occupying this position, and so, for example, Paul has to speak vaguely of 'those who labour among you and are over you in the Lord' (1 Thess. 5.12). On the other hand, specific names were given to certain groups of people who seemingly had some authoritative role within the early Church, among which the most notable are:

(a) 'The Twelve': this group appears to go back to the lifetime of Jesus and to have been intended as a symbolic representation of the twelve patriarchs and tribes of Israel, the nucleus and focus of the eschatological community. By the time that most of the New Testament literature was written, however, the Twelve seem already to belong to the past; in Acts they tend to fade from the scene, and no successors are ever appointed to their office, with the sole exception of the addition of Matthias to replace the faithless Judas at the beginning. This is probably because, even after they died, they were still thought of as remaining in the number of those who 'in the new world ... will sit on twelve thrones judging the twelve tribes of Israel' (Matt. 19.28).

(b) 'The Seven' (Acts 6.1–6): There is no foundation in the New Testament or in other early Christian literature for seeing these as the first deacons: it is not until the third century that such an identification is made. It would appear rather that their role was to provide a leadership group for the Greek-speaking Jewish Christians parallel to that of the Twelve for the Aramaic-speaking element, and, like the latter, they seem to have belonged entirely to the first generation of the Church and to have had no successors to their office.

(c) 'Apostles': this group includes the Twelve, but extends beyond them, although how far beyond does vary from author to author in the New Testament. Luke, for example, defines an apostle in such a way as virtually to exclude all but the Twelve (Acts 1.21–5), and many scholars would doubt whether Paul extended the concept of apostolate much beyond the Twelve, himself, James the brother of the Lord, and Barnabas. Other scholars, however, would argue on the basis of such texts as Romans 16.7; 2 Corinthians 8.23; 11.13; Philippians 2.25; 1 Thessalonians 2.6 that as far as Paul was concerned the circle of apostles was much wider and may even have included at least one woman. In so far as it is possible to define what an apostle was or did at all, it seems to have been involvement in the founding and building up of the first Christian communities, though not normally remaining to act as their resident leader.

(d) 'Prophets': these are often associated with apostles. In the lists of ministries in both 1 Corinthians 12.28 and Ephesians 4.11 they are mentioned second, after apostles, and in Ephesians 2.20 apostles and prophets are described as the foundation upon which the Church is built.

(e) 'Teachers': these are mentioned third in the list of offices in 1 Corinthians 12.28, and they and the prophets are said to have functioned as leaders of the local Christian community in Acts 13.1.

(f) 'Elders': these are described as forming part of the leadership of the Jerusalem church in Acts 11.30; 15.2ff.; 16.4; 21.18. Outside Jerusalem Acts 14.23 tells of Paul and Barnabas appointing 'presbyters in every church' in Lyconia and Phrygia, and presbyters are also found at Ephesus (Acts 20.17). Some would judge these references to be historically reliable, but others would doubt whether any churches with which Paul was involved would have had such a structure, and suspect that Luke may be reading back into that situation the leadership patterns of his own later community. Certainly, in the New Testament letters which are generally considered to be genuinely by Paul, there is no mention of such an office, and it does not fit in particularly well with the models of ministry which he describes. What is clear is that at a somewhat later stage, among the second and third generations of Christians, many Christian communities did come to have groups of what are called in Greek *presbyteroi* (elders) or alternatively *episcopoi* (bishops) as their leaders, assisted by *diakonoi* (deacons). These are mentioned in a number of New Testament books generally considered to have been written around the end of the first century, among them 1 Timothy, Titus, 1 Peter. Similarly, the *Didache* witnesses to a situation where the leadership of prophets and teachers seems to be giving way to that of bishops and deacons (15.1).

Did New Testament churches know of anything corresponding to formal appointment or ordination? There is little to suggest such a practice among the earliest writings, and it is probable that

415

leaders tended to emerge quite naturally in the first Christian communities. However, there are signs that with the growth of leadership by groups of presbyter/bishops and deacons came the development of a more formal appointment procedure. Presumably as the original founders and leaders of a community died, it would not always be obvious who should succeed them, especially if the possible candidates were not so unmistakably endowed with appropriate gifts as the former leaders had been, and some agreed means became necessary therefore by which leaders might be chosen and installed.

Although we are far from having a firm or complete picture of the nature of such a procedure, there are at least hints of what it might have contained, chiefly in the Pastoral Epistles (see especially 1 Tim. 1.18; 4.14; 5.22; 2 Tim. 1.6) and in the Acts of the Apostles, where, as has been suggested above, the descriptions of commissioning and appointment probably reflect to some extent what was done in the author's own community at the time of writing (Acts 1.23–6; 6.5–6; 13.1–3; 14.23). Sometimes at least election by the whole community may have been involved; at other times prophetic nomination or the casting of lots may have been used to determine God's choice of minister. For the act of appointment was seen not just as the action of the community but as the outworking of the election by God through the Holy Spirit, and, at least according to the Pastoral Epistles, the spiritual endowment necessary for the ministry was mediated to the candidate through it. Prayer seems to have been a central feature, which is hardly surprising, and sometimes the laying on of hands is spoken of, though the absence of explicit reference to this in other instances may not necessarily mean that it was not used, but simply that it was not considered sufficiently significant to demand mention, as being just the customary gesture accompanying solemn prayer and indicating its object.

Studies:

Paul F. Bradshaw, *Liturgical Presidency in the Early Church*. 1983.

Raymond Brown, *Priest and Bishop*. New York 1970.

Edward J. Kilmartin, 'Ministry and Ordination in Early Christianity against a Jewish background' (*SL* 13, 1979), pp. 42–69.

Douglas Powell, 'Ordo Presbyterii' (*JTS* 26, 1975), pp. 290–328.

Edward Schillebeeckx, *Ministry: a Case for Change* (1981; revised edn: *The Church with a Human Face*, 1985).

3 Ministry in the Second and Third Centuries

In the course of the second century a number of developments can be observed. Firstly, the community leadership of prophets and teachers declined steadily and eventually came to be supplanted everywhere by that of formally appointed presbyters and deacons. This process seems to have been encouraged by the necessity to be able to distinguish between true and false teachers—the 'pedigree' of a formally appointed minister being easier to trace and verify than that of a 'charismatic', especially if the latter were itinerant.

The second development was related to the first and was the gradual emergence of a separate office of bishop, as leader of a local presbyterate or group of elders. This provided a further focus for unity and touchstone for orthodoxy, making it possible to determine more easily which groups of Christians were heretical and which not, for 'where the bishop is, there is the church' (Cyprian, *Ep.* 66.8). Nevertheless, even after the emergence of the episcopate, the whole presbyterate seems to have retained to a considerable extent its earlier collective responsibility for the general oversight of the life and worship of the local Christian community, and the bishop presided as head of this corporate body. It was only in the course of the third century that the bishop began to assume a more independent role and presbyters came to be more clearly his subordinates, and the collegiality of the body of bishops started to assume greater importance than the collegiality of the bishop with his presbyterate. At the same period the term 'priest' (in Latin *sacerdos*) began to be applied for the first time to the ministry of the bishop, and to some extent to the corporate presbyterate, in so far as they were seen as sharing in his ministry.

Thirdly, virtually all ministerial and liturgical functions became increasingly restricted either to the ordained ministers themselves or to other lesser officials appointed by the bishop—'minor orders' as they would later be called. Thus, for example, the bishop himself became the exclusive president of all liturgical acts and chief minister of the word, prophets and teachers gradually being excluded from these roles, and even the liturgical *action* of reading the Scriptures in church, originally open to anyone to exercise, was turned into the permanent *office* of a reader. In the course of the third century even these different offices, to which a person would originally have been appointed for a lifelong ministry, began to be seen instead as a pyramidical structure through which one might pass from the lower orders to the higher.

4 *The Apostolic Tradition of Hippolytus*

Although references to ministries are quite plentiful at this period, references to a ritual of ordination are almost non-existent. The sources speak of the existence of an appointment or election, but fail to describe how it was done. For this reason, the *Apostolic Tradition* of Hippolytus has assumed crucial importance, in providing the only full account of ordination procedure prior to the fourth century. Even here, however, one needs to exercise extreme caution in using this information, since it is by no means certain that all churches in the third century would necessarily have followed a similar practice, and some scholars would even suspect that the text of this part of the document may well have been 'touched up' by later hands so as to make it correspond more closely with what had become the standard practice in the fourth century. It gives directions and prayers for the ordination of bishop, presbyter and deacon, all of which are apparently intended to follow a broadly similar pattern, though detailed instructions are only given in the case of the bishop. One of the most striking features which emerges is the close relationship between the ordained ministry and the local Christian community. Not only are the ministers drawn from the community themselves, but the act of ordination is the action of the whole community.

Firstly, all the people participate in the election of the candidate, though not necessarily in the initial nomination. This should not be thought of as pointing to some notion of the ideal of democracy in early Christianity, nor, at this stage, to a principle that a congregation should choose its own ministers. As the prayers themselves make clear, ordination was seen both as an action of God and an action of the Church: it was God who appointed the ministers, and the Church discerned and mediated that appointment through its election. There was thus no dichotomy between actions 'from below' and 'from above'. The Church's discernment might even override an individual's own lack of a sense of vocation, as happened later, for example, in the case of both Ambrose and Augustine of Hippo, and it contrasts with more modern views that an 'internal call' must always be primary.

Then the community assembles on a Sunday, the regular day for corporate worship, and prays that God will bestow the necessary gifts on the man whom he has chosen, firstly in silence and then through the prayer spoken by the bishop while hands are laid upon the ordinand. This imposition of hands seems to have been understood not as signifying the transmission of grace or power from ordainer to ordinand, but rather as indicating the one for whom prayer was made and expressing his incorporation into the particular ministerial order, while the bestowal of the Holy Spirit was effected by a fresh outpouring at each ordination in response to the prayer of the Church. Almost certainly the ordination of presbyters and of the first bishops would have been presided over by the collective presbyterate, with one of their number saying the prayer, and perhaps vestiges of this remain in the continued participation of other presbyters along with the bishop in the laying on of hands at the ordination of a presbyter. Other bishops would have begun to attend the ordination of a bishop in order to witness the proceedings and verify that the candidate was genuinely the choice of the whole community and not someone intruded by a particular faction; but it was inevitable that in the course of time they would come to replace the resident presbyterate in the presidency of the rite and in performing the laying on of hands. In the case of the ordination of a deacon the bishop alone lays his hand on the candidate.

While the ordination procedure stresses the relationship of the ordained ministry to the community, the content of the prayers lays emphasis on the relationship of the ministry to the tradition, and the nature of the offices is here defined by the use of typology drawn from the Old Testament. This is not simply incidental: it witnesses to a belief in the fundamental continuity of God's work through history, the promise of the new covenant in the old and the fulfilment of the old in the new. It does not mean that the Old Testament offices were seen as the historical origin of the orders of the Christian ministry, but that the Christian realities were there foretold, and it provides an analogy by which they may be understood even though they cannot be precisely defined. Moreover, in two of the three prayers the Old Testament typology is explicitly fused with, and hence modified by, an image drawn from the New Testament. Thus the bishop's office is understood to succeed both to that of the high priest and also to that of the apostles, and the model for the diaconate seems to be the ministry of the Levite and the service of Christ himself. The presbyter's office is, interestingly, defined not by means of a cultic reference but by use of the analogy of the seventy elders appointed by Moses to govern the people (Num. 11.16ff.), suggesting that community leadership rather than liturgical function was seen as primary to the role. The same typology may also lie behind the account of the mission of the seventy in Luke 10.1ff.

The prayer provided for each order of ministers asks God to bestow the particular gifts of the Holy Spirit thought requisite for the effective fulfilment of that office. Thus that for a bishop asks God to 'pour forth that power which is from you, of the princely Spirit which you granted through your beloved Son Jesus Christ to your holy apostles'; that for a presbyter 'the Spirit of grace and counsel of the presbyterate, that he may help and govern your people with a pure heart'; and that for a deacon 'the holy Spirit of grace and caring and diligence'.

The ordination of a bishop culminates in a celebration of the Eucharist in which the newly ordained presides, thus fulfilling the liturgical function of the order to which he has just been admitted and giving symbolic expression to his new place within the community. A similar procedure was probably also followed in the case of presbyters and deacons.

In addition to the orders of bishop, presbyter and deacon, the *Apostolic Tradition* also refers to other ministries within the Church to which some sort of formal appointment was made: subdeacons and widows were simply nominated to their office without any further ceremony, while a reader was appointed by the bishop handing him the book from which he would read, the same gesture which the ruler of the Jewish synagogue had used when inviting someone to read the Scriptures at a service. On the other hand, there is no formal appointment for virgins—they simply choose that form of life for themselves—nor for those who claim to have the gift of healing: it is said that the facts themselves will reveal the truth of such a claim.

Studies:

Paul F. Bradshaw, 'Ordination', in G. J. Cuming, (ed.), *Essays on Hippolytus* (1978), pp. 33–8.

E. C. Ratcliff, '*Apostolic Tradition:* questions concerning the appointment of the Bishop' (*SP* 8, 1966), pp. 266–70; reprinted in A. H. Couratin and D. Tripp, eds, *E. C. Ratcliff: Liturgical Studies* (1976), pp. 156–60.

E. Segelberg, 'The Ordination Prayers in Hippolytus' (*SP* 13, 1975), pp. 397–408.

5 Later Developments

(a) Election

In the *Apostolic Tradition* of Hippolytus ordination had comprised two main elements, the manifestation of God's choice of minister through the election by the Church, and the prayer of the Church for the bestowal of the gifts needed to fulfil that ministry. Although the Church continued to believe that it was God who chose and made men ministers, election came to be thought of as no more than a preliminary to the 'real' act of ordination, the ritual of prayer and laying on of hands, which consequently was thought of as the means by which the gift of the office itself was bestowed on the candidate. Election, therefore, became relatively unimportant and even dispensable. In particular, the link between the whole community and the choice of a minister tended to be pared down until all that remained was a very tenuous thread. Frequently deacons, and later presbyters too, were not elected at all but appointed directly by the bishop, acting alone. In some places only the presbyters voted in the election of a bishop; in others the bishops from neighbouring churches, or even the secular ruler, had a powerful voice in the selection. Even where others retained a part in the process, it was eventually reduced to a purely nominal act, lacking any real power or influence on the outcome.

Nevertheless, vestiges of the former situation remained in the rites themselves. Thus in the East and also in the Gallican tradition in the West, a candidate for ordination to any of the orders was presented to the people, who declared their acceptance of him by responding with the acclamation, 'He is worthy'. The Roman custom was slightly different. Here the ordination of presbyters and deacons took place at one of the four Ember seasons in the year. The candidates, chosen by the Pope, were presented to the people at the Wednesday and Friday Eucharists during the week (the only weekdays on which the Eucharist was regularly celebrated in the ancient Roman tradition) in order to give opportunity for objections to be raised; and they were then ordained on the Saturday. On the other hand, candidates for the episcopate were elected in their provinces and then came to Rome for examination and approval by the Pope prior to their ordination by him.

Whatever the reality of the situation, however, ordination formularies continued to make reference to the process of election, and also to the belief that the choice of the candidates was the work of God. Thus all Eastern rites retain a formula, apparently dating at least from the fourth century, which gives expression to this. It is now associated with the imposition of hands, but no doubt originally constituted an introduction to the ordination ceremony, declaring the result of the election and inviting the prayers of the people. It occurs with varying wording in the different Eastern traditions, but its substance is as follows:

> The divine grace which heals what is infirm and supplies what is lacking chooses the subdeacon/deacon/priest N. to be deacon/priest/ bishop of ... Let us pray therefore that the grace of the Holy Spirit may come upon him.

(b) The Prayers

These continue to ask for the bestowal of the requisite graces and powers to fulfil the particular office to which a man is being admitted, but they display a tendency to enumerate these in greater detail, and sometimes ask for the bestowal of the office itself. There is also a growth in the use of 'priestly' vocabulary and imagery, first in relation to bishops and later in relation to presbyters. On the other hand, the prayers reveal an interesting and diverse development in the use of typology. Eastern and Gallican texts show a greater interest in elaborating New Testament images and allusions, whereas the Roman prayers give a more prominent place to the Old Testament. Thus, whereas other prayers for the diaconate from the fourth century onwards link that office with Stephen and his companions (Acts 6), the Roman tradition elaborates the reference to the Levites. Similarly, the Roman prayer for presbyters combines the typology of the seventy elders appointed by Moses to *govern* the people, used in the *Apostolic Tradition*, with that of the sons of Aaron, who exercised a *priestly* ministry. The number of prayers said over each ordinand also tends to multiply in all later rites, especially so in some Eastern traditions, partly as a result of the confluence of earlier variant traditions and partly out of an innate love of elaboration.

(c) The Development of Symbolism

The earliest symbolic addition to the pattern described in the *Apostolic Tradition* is found in the fourth-century Syrian *Apostolic Constitutions*, where in the ordination of a bishop the book of the Gospels is held open over the candidate's head at the point in the service where one would have expected the laying on of hands, which is not explicitly mentioned at all. This ceremony continues to be a feature of Eastern rites, but as an addition to the imposition of hands, and it was also found in Gaul in the fifth century, and from there made its way into the Western tradition. A variety of theories have been offered to explain its significance: it may have been intended to express the bestowal of the power of the gospel (or even the yoke of the gospel, as some rites prescribe that the book should be laid on the neck of the candidate—or is this a later rationalization of a practice the original meaning of which had been forgotten?); or to symbolize the descent of the Spirit; or the book may have been understood as representing Christ himself and hence ordination as his act; or it may even have been a legacy of an ancient practice of attempting to discern the divine choice of candidate by reference to the passage at which the book fell open, a version of the casting of lots of Acts 1.26.

Practices with regard to the imposition of hands varied. Although it came to be a universal rule that at least three bishops had to be present at the ordination of a bishop, all three do not always lay hands on the candidate. In the East only the bishop reciting the prayers does this, while the other two hold the book of the Gospels over the candidate (in *Apostolic Constitutions* it was held by deacons). Similarly, in the ordination of a presbyter in the East only the bishop lays his hand on the candidate: the presbyters merely stand by. In both cases Rome apparently followed a similar practice at one time, and only in the Gallican rites were the prescriptions found in *Apostolic Tradition* retained, whereby all bishops laid hands on a candidate for the episcopate and all presbyters joined in the imposition of hands on a new presbyter. Whether the other practices are simply ancient variants or for some reason a deliberate suppression of a former universal custom is not known.

As rites developed, they all began to add to the central action of prayer accompanied by the laying on of hands both the solemn vesting of the ordinand with the robes of his office and the handing over to him of instruments which he would use in his new ministry—the former probably being an imitation of Old Testament ordination practice, the latter perhaps copied from the custom of appointing a reader by handing to him the book from which he was to read. These ceremonies differed in their precise details in different traditions. At least from the fourth century bishops were also solemnly enthroned at the conclusion of their ordination, though in the West this developed into a separate rite when bishops ceased to be ordained in their own cathedrals.

A further variation which is manifested in later rites is the precise point in the eucharistic celebration at which the ordination is to take place. For example, the Byzantine arrangement (which seems to be related to what is understood to be the principal liturgical function of the order being conferred) came to be for the deacon to be ordained after the Eucharistic Prayer and before communion so that he might assist in its administration, the presbyter before the Eucharistic Prayer so that he might be involved in its recitation, and the bishop at the beginning of the whole rite so that he might preside over the entire celebration. In the Roman tradition, on the other hand, all three orders were conferred after the Epistle, and a newly ordained deacon would read the Gospel. A change also took place in the order in which the texts of the rites were arranged in the liturgical books: the older tradition was to place them in descending order (bishop, presbyter, deacon), but later the ascending order (deacon, presbyter, bishop) was adopted.

(d) Minor Orders

We have seen that the *Apostolic Tradition* included instructions for the appointment of subdeacons, widows and readers. Although later documents mention a variety of other offices, the Eastern tradition in general recognizes only subdeacons and readers (sometimes also called 'cantors' or 'psalmists') as minor orders, but ordains them, like the other orders, by prayer and the imposition of hands, a practice found as early as the fourth century. They also receive appropriate symbols of their office. The ancient Roman rites, on the other hand, provided for a ccremonial appointment for only acolytes and subdeacons, and this was very simple: the acolyte was handed a linen bag, the receptable then used to carry the consecrated bread, and the subdeacon received an empty chalice. The Gallican tradition, however, included a formal handing over of the symbols of office, accompanied by a bidding and solemn blessing, for all five minor orders known in the West, subdeacons, acolytes, readers, exorcists and doorkeepers.

Texts:
H. B. Porter, *The Ordination Prayers of the Ancient Western Churches.* 1967.

Studies:
P.-M. Gy, 'Ancient Ordination Prayers' (*SL* 13, 1979), pp. 70–93.
H.-M. Legrand, 'Theology and the Election of Bishops in the Early Church' (*Concilium* 2.7, 1972), pp. 31–42.

6 The Medieval West

The later Western ordination rites emerged out of a fusion of the earlier Roman and Gallican traditions. The Roman rites had provided in the case of each of the three orders: a bidding, inviting the people to pray for the candidate; the litany, which expressed their intercession and replaced the silent prayer of the people in the *Apostolic Tradition*; a collect summing up their prayer; and the ordination prayer itself, which at a later stage gained an opening dialogue and thanksgiving modelled on the Eucharistic Prayer. The Gallican rites were somewhat simpler: after the presentation of the candidates to the people and their declaration of assent, there was a bidding inviting them to pray, and then, presumably after a period of silent prayer, the ordination prayer itself followed. At a later stage, apparently under the influence of the Old Testament practice of anointing priests, the curious practice developed of anointing the hands of newly ordained presbyters with oil, and later still the heads of bishops began to be anointed.

When these two traditions later became fused, all the texts were retained, with the result that a candidate was ordained twice over, as it were, the Gallican material following the Roman material in the rites. These rites were subsequently elaborated with a wealth of secondary ceremonial, including solemn vesting and the handing over of instruments of office. The various Pontificals, which contained the ordination services, differ in many minor details from one another, but the following table illustrates the main features of a typical late-medieval arrangement, the elements derived from the old Roman tradition being indicated by the use of capital letters, and those from the Gallican tradition by the use of italics. Because by this time presbyters were usually designated 'priests', that term will be used for them hereafter.

It will be seen from the table that the examination of a candidate for the episcopate, which had previously been a preliminary to the rite, has now come to be incorporated within it, and similarly in case of priests and deacons the (nominal) opportunity for the people to object to candidates, which had been conducted on the preceding Wednesday and Friday in the Roman tradition, has now

BISHOP	PRIESTS AND DEACONS
Presentation	Presentation
Examination	Opportunity for objections
BIDDING	
LITANY WITH SPECIAL SUFFRAGE	LITANY WITH SPECIAL SUFFRAGES
Imposition of hands by all bishops with imposition of Gospel book	*Imposition of hands on deacons by bishop alone*
COLLECT	BIDDING, COLLECT, AND
ORDINATION PRAYER	ORDINATION PRAYER FOR DEACONS
Unction of head	Delivery of stole and Gospel book to deacons
Ordination prayer	*Bidding and Ordination prayer for deacons*
Delivery of gloves, staff, ring, mitre, Gospel book	Vesting of deacons in dalmatics
	GOSPEL READ BY A DEACON
	Imposition of hands on priests by bishop and priests
	BIDDING, COLLECT, AND
	ORDINATION PRAYER FOR PRIESTS
	Vesting of priests with stole and chasuble
	Bidding and Ordination prayer for priests
	Unction of hands of priests
	Delivery of paten and chalice to priests

(Although, for the sake of clarity, the first ordination prayer in the rite for the episcopate has been shown as of Roman origin and the second Gallican, the two are really one prayer, broken in the middle by the anointing. This prayer was the original Roman ordination prayer with the Gallican interpolated into the middle of it.)

become a part of the service itself. It will also be observed that in this service the litany has become detached from the bidding and collect which originally began and ended it and been placed near the beginning of the rite. The reason for this was probably the desire to avoid having to go through it twice, once for deacons and once for priests. Moreover, in all three cases the imposition of hands has become detached from the ordination prayers. This seems to have happened because, owing to the large number of candidates for ordination at any one time, it was impractical to repeat the prayers for each one. Thus a silent imposition of hands on each candidate was introduced before the prayers were said collectively while hands were extended over them all. Although the problem of numerous candidates did not usually arise in the case of the episcopate, the alteration was also made here, presumably in order to bring it into line with the other orders. In the course of time it was felt desirable to enrich this silent imposition of hands with some formula similar to those accompanying other actions in the rites. Many Pontificals adopted the words *Accipe Spiritum Sanctum*, 'Receive the Holy Spirit', while others included here, or elsewhere in the rite, the hymn *Veni Creator*.

The complexity of these late medieval rites provided a source of dispute for theologians of the period, who did not have the advantage of knowing the earlier history of the liturgy. Faced with the variety of prayers, ceremonial actions and formulae, different scholars arrived at different conclusions as to which should be accounted as the central and essential elements by which the grace and power of each order were conferred upon the ordinand. Thus, for example, some considered that it was the imposition of hands and whatever formula now accompanied this; some that anointing should be included; while others looked to the handing over of the instruments of office with the accompanying words.

7 *The Reformation*

The leaders of the Reformation rejected the medieval theology and practice of ordination. They considered both the hierarchical structure of the ministry and the concept of a sacrificial priesthood to be contrary to the teaching of the New Testament. Martin Luther believed that, through the priesthood of all believers, all Christians were able to minister in the congregation, but 'since we are all priests alike, no man may put himself forward, or take upon himself without our consent and election, to do that which we have all alike power to do'. Other Reformed churches, on the other hand, including later Lutheran churches, took a somewhat higher view of the ordained ministry, and believed that a separate order of ministers of word and sacrament was of divine institution. Not surprisingly, all the minor orders of ministry were swept away, as having no scriptural foundation. Some retained an office of bishop or superintendent, but saw it as merely a particular function and not as constituting a separate order of ministry. Some retained the office of deacon, but generally made it concerned not with liturgical matters but with the care of the needy, since they saw this as its scriptural purpose. Many rejected the term ordination itself, as being non-scriptural and tainted with medieval misconceptions, and preferred to speak instead of 'the election of ministers', but others, mainly Anglicans and Lutherans, did continue to use the word, and a few were even prepared to continue to call ordination a sacrament, because it was a rite instituted by Christ, though they did not consider that it conferred grace or an indelible character on the recipients, as the medieval theologians had taught.

The Reformers abandoned the complex ceremonies of medieval ordination practice, and turned to the evidence of the New Testament for the essentials of ordination. They believed that it taught that the process should involve: preparation through fasting and prayer by the whole Church; some form of election of the candidate by the congregation; and solemn prayer for him. Most, though not all, also included an imposition of hands. To these New Testament essentials, the Reformers added two other major features. The first was a thorough examination of the orthodoxy, moral standards, and authenticity of the vocation of each ordinand, culminating in a public declaration of his faith and intentions within the ordination service itself, usually in the form of a series of set questions and answers, for which there was already precedent in the case of the ordination of a bishop. This they believed to be necessary to counteract the lax standards of the Middle Ages and ensure that only pure Reformed doctrine would be preached. The second feature was that ordinations were to take place within the regular Sunday worship of the Church and usually in the congregation in which the man was to minister, so that the people might be involved in the whole process, and were to include a substantial element of preaching on the duties of both minister and congregation.

Luther, for example, produced an ordination rite which became the basis for the services in most Lutheran churches. It included: prayer by the congregation for the candidate; an address by the presiding minister on the qualities and duties required of a minister; a series of questions to the candidate; and an imposition of hands performed by the presiding minister and other ministers, during which the presiding minister was to say the Lord's Prayer and 'if he desires or time permits' an ordination prayer proper. Although Luther espoused the principle that the candidate should have been elected by the congregation, practice did not always accord with theory on this point.

Calvin, on the other hand, prescribed a thorough-going process of election. When a new minister was required, a suitable candidate was to be nominated and examined by the other ministers. If he satisfied them, the approval of the people was then to be sought. A period of time was allowed during which inquiries could be made about the candidate and any objections lodged. If nothing was discovered against him, he was then formally elected by the people and set apart with prayer by the other ministers, Calvin omitting the imposition of hands because of what he regarded as superstitious beliefs that it was the means by which grace and power were conferred on the candidate.

Texts:

B. J. Kidd, *Documents illustrative of the Continental Reformation* (1911), pp. 330–4.

U. S. Leupold, (ed.), *Luther's Works* 53 (Philadelphia 1965), pp. 122–6.

W. D. Maxwell, *The Liturgical Portions of the Genevan Service Book* (2nd edn, 1965), pp. 165–74.

E. E. Yelverton, *An Archbishop of the Reformation* (1958), pp. 83–94, 131–41.

G. W. Sprott, *The Book of Common Order of the Church of Scotland* (1901), pp. 13–30.

—*Scottish Liturgies of the Reign of James VI* (2nd edn, 1901), pp. 111–31.

Studies:

J. L. Ainslie, *The Doctrines of Ministerial Order in the Reformed Churches of the Sixteenth and Seventeenth Centuries*. 1940.

J. J. von Allmen, 'Ministry and Ordination according to Reformed Theology' (*SJT* 25, 1972), pp. 75–88.

B. A. Gerrish, 'Priesthood and Ministry in the Theology of Luther' (*Church History* 34, 1965), pp. 404–22.

G. Hok, 'Luther's Doctrine of the Ministry' (*SJT* 7, 1954), pp. 16–40.

Duncan Shaw, 'The Inauguration of Ministers in Scotland: 1560–1620' (*Records of the Scottish Church History Society* 16, 1966), pp. 35–62.

Bryan D. Spinks, 'Luther's Other Major Liturgical Reforms: 2. The Ordination of Ministers of the Word' (*Liturgical Review* 9.1, 1979), pp. 20–32.

8 The Church of England

1550

The first Prayer Book of 1549 did not contain any ordination services, but they were published separately shortly afterwards, in March 1550. They made no provision for the minor orders but retained the ministries of bishop, priest and deacon, concerning which the preface to the services claimed that 'from the Apostles' time there hath been these orders of ministers in Christ's Church'. The primary source for these services was apparently a rite which had been drawn up by the German Reformer, Martin Bucer, who came to England in 1549. He had directed that, since there were three orders of ministers in the Church, changes should be made in the rite so that when a bishop was ordained it should be carried out 'more solemnly and at greater length' and when a deacon was ordained it should be simplified. As can be seen from the table on p. 431, this was what was done in the Anglican services. Additional elements which have been adapted from traditional medieval practice are indicated by capital letters.

The preface to the services required the candidates first to be examined and shown to have the qualities necessary for the ministry, but, unlike other Reformed rites, made no mention of the need for election, nor was there any reference to the ordination having to take place before the congregation among whom the man was to minister. Hence all that exists is the traditional nominal opportunity for objections in the rites for deacons and priests. The preface went on to say that ordinands were then to be admitted to their office 'by public prayer with imposition of hands'. However, the central petition for the candidates in Bucer's prayer before the laying on of hands has been entirely deleted in the Anglican rite for priests, turning it into a prayer for the congregation instead, and no such prayer at all is included in the service for deacons, though there is one based to some extent on medieval forms in the rite for bishops. It would seem, therefore, that the essential 'public prayer' of ordination was held to be the litany with its special suffrage and concluding collect, preceding the ordination proper, which was still regarded as the act of the bestowal of the powers of the office on the candidate.

Not surprisingly, therefore, the imposition of hands itself is not accompanied by prayer, but by an appropriate imperative formula, as tended to be the case in the medieval rites, and the traditional involvement of priests in laying hands on a new priest and all bishops present in laying hands on a new bishop is also retained. John 20.22–3 was incorporated into the formula used for the ordination of a priest, as it already had been in some of the later medieval rites, and another New Testament phrase from

THE FIRST ANGLICAN ORDINAL

BUCER	DEACONS	PRIESTS	BISHOPS
Sermon	Sermon	Sermon	
Veni sancte spiritus		(see below)	(see below)
Introit: Pss. 40, 132 or 135		Introit: Pss. 40, 132 or 135	Introit: Pss. 40, 132 or 135
		Eucharist begins	Eucharist begins
Epistle: Acts 20.17–35; 1 Tim. 3; Eph. 4.1–16; or Tit. 1.5–9; Ps. 67		Epistle: Acts 20.17–35 or 1 Tim. 3	Epistle: 1 Tim. 3.1–7
Gospel: Mt. 28.18–20; Jn. 10.1–16; 20.19–23; or 21.15–17		Gospel: Mt. 28.18–20; Jn. 10.1–16; or 20.19–23	Gospel: Jn. 21.15–17 or 10.1–16
		'Come Holy Ghost'	Creed
	PRESENTATION	PRESENTATION	PRESENTATION
Final inquiry for objections	Shorter Final Inquiry	Final Inquiry	Reading of King's mandate for consecration.
			Oath of Royal Supremacy
			OATH OF OBEDIENCE TO ARCHBISHOP
			Bidding
	LITANY and Collect	LITANY and Collect	LITANY and Collect
	Eucharist begins		
	Epistle: 1 Tim. 3.8–13 or Acts 6.2–7		
	Oath of Royal Supremacy	Oath of Royal Supremacy	
Exhortation to candidates		Exhortation to candidates	ADDRESS TO ELECT
Examination and concluding prayer	Examination	Examination and concluding prayer	Examination and concluding prayer
Silent prayer		Silent prayer	'Come Holy Ghost'
Prayer		Prayer	Similar Prayer
Imposition of hands by ministers with blessing	Imposition of hands by BISHOP with special formula	Imposition of hands by BISHOP and PRIESTS with special formula	Imposition of hands by BISHOPS with special formula
	DELIVERY OF NEW TESTAMENT	DELIVERY OF BIBLE, CHALICE, AND BREAD	IMPOSITION OF BIBLE DELIVERY OF STAFF
	GOSPEL OF THE DAY		
Creed		Creed	
Eucharist	Eucharist	Eucharist	Eucharist
Prayer	Special Collect	Special Collect	Special Collect
Blessing	Blessing	Blessing	Blessing

2 Timothy 1.6–7 formed the basis of the formula for a bishop, but in the case of a deacon the bishop simply said, 'Take thou authority to execute the office of a Deacon', etc, presumably because no appropriate New Testament verse could be found. The

newly ordained continue to receive appropriate symbols of office, as they had done in the Middle Ages, but slight differences in these suggest a subtle shift of emphasis: a deacon receives the whole New Testament and not just the book of the Gospels, a priest receives a Bible as well as a chalice and bread, and a bishop is given only the pastoral staff and no other insignia of his office; moreover, a Bible is laid on his neck by the presiding bishop after the imposition of hands, instead of a Gospel Book being laid on his neck by two bishops during it.

1552

The 1550 rites had directed that candidates for the diaconate and priesthood should be vested in 'a plain alb', and candidates for the episcopate in a 'surplice and cope'. In response to protests from extreme Protestants that this was perpetuating the medieval concept of ministry, all directions about vesture were now omitted, and significant changes made in the delivery of the symbols of office: priests were no longer given the chalice and bread but only the Bible, and bishops similarly no longer received the pastoral staff, but simply the Bible, instead of having it laid on their necks. A number of other minor alterations were also made at this revision, and the ordination services were henceforward always bound up in a single volume with the Prayer Book, though retaining their own title page.

1662

No significant changes were made when the Prayer Book was revised in 1559 and in 1604, in spite of vociferous complaints from those who wanted a form of ordination much closer to that of the Calvinist churches. In the 1662 revision most of the important alterations then made were intended to exclude an identification with the ministry of the Reformed churches: the preface was amended to make episcopal ordination essential for admission to the ministry of the Church of England; changes were made in the readings prescribed in the services to make it clear that bishops and priests were regarded as differing in order and not simply in degree; and additions were made to the formulas at the imposition of hands on priests and bishops which explicitly named the orders being conferred—though this was probably also intended to counter Roman Catholic criticism that the ordination services were unsatisfactory because they had lacked this feature.

1927/8

Some small changes were made at this time, the most important being an improvement in the element of prayer in the rites. A bidding, a period of silent prayer, and an ordination prayer (cast in 'eucharistic' form) were inserted immediately before the imposition of hands in the rite for deacons; the prayers before the imposition of hands in the other two rites were also cast in eucharistic form; and a brief petition for the candidates was restored to the prayer in the rite for priests. The litany was to be optional, and a period of silent prayer was to replace it when it was not used in the rite for bishops.

Since 1928

The 1662 services continued to be used in the Church of England, and, with minor modifications in the rest of the Anglican Communion, though some provinces did adopt similar features to those proposed in the unsuccessful English revision. The most important advance in the revision of ordination services, however, came in the rites adopted in the Church of South India in 1958. These included a preface which affirmed that there were three essential elements in ordination: election by the people (of which the presentation of the candidates in the service represented the last step); prayer; and the imposition of 'apostolic hands'. All three rites, for bishops, presbyters and deacons, followed a common structure and were set within the context of a Eucharist. The presentation of the candidates was followed by a reading of the authorization of the diocese for the ordination, and the assent of the congregation to it. After the Ministry of the Word, the presiding bishop read a short statement on the nature of ordination, and put a series of questions to the candidates. Then came a period of silent prayer by the congregation, the singing of the hymn 'Come Holy Ghost', and the ordination prayer, during which hands were laid on the candidates, as in the practice of the early Church. The rites ended with the giving of a Bible to each of the newly ordained (and the pastoral staff to a newly ordained bishop), the exchange of the right hand of fellowship, and a declaration that the candidates had been duly ordained. A novel expedient was employed when there was more than one candidate to be ordained to an order: instead of the whole ordination prayer being repeated over each one, the prayer was said collectively over all, and when the central petition for the candidates was reached, that alone was repeated for each ordinand while hands were laid on him, and then the concluding portion of the prayer was said.

These services were very favourably received by liturgical scholars throughout the world, and subsequently provided the pattern for those in the Church of North India and Pakistan, in the new American Book of Common Prayer, in the 1968 proposed Ordinal of the unsuccessful Anglican–Methodist scheme of union in England, and through that for those in the *Methodist Service Book* of 1975, though in each case the model was freely adapted. The Liturgical Commission of the Church of England did not produce a Series 1 or Series 2 form of ordination, but began work directly on proposals for a series 3 Ordinal in the light of these earlier texts. This was published in 1977, and its debt to the services of the Church of South India and the Anglican–Methodist Ordinal was very evident; but there were also notable differences. For example, an Old Testament reading was included, as was a statement of the 'office and work' of each order before the Declaration. But perhaps the most significant alteration was the restoration of the Litany, in accordance with the Anglican tradition of its being part of the essential 'public prayer' which should accompany the imposition of hands. The General Synod accepted the underlying principles and the general structure of the new rites, and only minor details were revised. Authorization was given in 1978, and the services finally appeared in this form in the Alternative Service Book.

Studies:

Paul F. Bradshaw, *The Anglican Ordinal*. 1971.

E. P. Echlin, *The Story of Anglican Ministry*. 1974.

T. S. Garrett, 'The Ordinal of the Church of South India' (*SJT* 12, 1959), pp. 400–13.

—*Worship in the Church of South India* (2nd edn, 1965), ch. 9.

E. C. Ratcliff, 'The Ordinal of the Church of South India' (*Theology* 63, 1960), pp. 7–15; reprinted in A. H. Couratin and D. Tripp, (eds), *E. C. Ratcliff: Liturgical Studies* (1976), pp. 173–82.

E. C. Whitaker, *Martin Bucer and the Book of Common Prayer* (1974), pp. 175–83.

B
COMMENTARY

Since a great deal of the material and the section numbers for the respective services for bishops, priests and deacons are identical, there is no need to provide separate commentaries for each order.

The Title

1549 and 1552 'ordained' deacons and priests, and 'consecrated' bishops. 1662 'made' deacons, 'ordained' priests, and 'consecrated' bishops. CSI reverted to the 1550 verbs; but the Anglican–Methodist Ordinal made one modification, speaking of 'the ordination or consecration' of bishops. This nomenclature has been retained in ASB, making it clear that all three groups of ministers are in orders; but out of respect for tradition 'consecration' is retained for bishops. The new Roman Pontifical uses 'ordain' throughout.

The title 'presbyter' has also been included for the second order. CSI used this as the sole title: but again the Anglican–Methodist Ordinal made the modification—'presbyters also called priests'. ASB has simply inverted the titles—'priests called presbyters'. The term 'presbyter' is in fact the oldest of the titles for the second order, and there is no doctrinal significance in the use of either title. What they both mean is evident in the Ordinal itself. In an ecumenical context, however, 'presbyter' can be a reconciling term.

The Preparation
(sections 1–3)

Ordinations take place within the context of the service of Holy Communion, and any authorized form of the latter may be used (Note 5, p. 338). The preparation follows the same order as Holy Communion Rites A and B with one small exception—there is no opening sentence of Scripture: it was considered by the General Synod to be unnecessary in this particular case. The collect (section 3) is the same for all three orders. It is an adaptation of the second collect for Good Friday, originally one of the solemn Good Friday prayers from the Gelasian Sacramentary (see p. 276), and was produced by the Revision Committee of the General Synod.

In common with other opening collects in ASB, it includes all those present at the service and not simply the candidates.

The Ministry of the Word
(sections 4–10)

The readings, which have few affinities with those of 1662, have been chosen to indicate appropriate aspects of the various ministries. The archbishop or bishop is still free to choose alternative readings, if he so wishes (Note 6, p. 338).

The Old Testament Reading
(section 4)

1 *Deacons*

Isaiah 6.1–8. The call of Isaiah. This is also used at the combined service for deacons and priests.

2 *Priests*

Isaiah 61.1–3a. The priest is presented as an evangelist and a conveyor of comfort; *or* Malachi 2.5–7. The priest is presented as a teacher and a messenger of the Lord.

3 *Bishops*

Numbers 27.15–20, 22–3. Joshua is commissioned by Moses to be leader of the children of Israel by the laying on of hands. It emphasizes the authority of the bishop as leader.

For 'This is the word of the Lord', see p. 33.

The Psalm
(section 5)

1 *Deacons*

Psalm 119.33–8. A prayer for God's help and guidance.

2 *Priests*

Psalm 145.1–7, 21. The psalmist declares his intention of singing God's praises and proclaiming his mighty deeds. This is also used at the combined service for deacons and priests.

3 *Bishops*

Psalm 119.165–74. A prayer for God's help and guidance.

The New Testament Reading
(section 6)

1 *Deacons*

Romans 12.1–12. This reading was taken from the Anglican–Methodist Ordinal. St Paul's appeal to all the brethren, with their diversity of gifts, to be united in offering themselves to God as a living sacrifice. This is also used at the combined service for deacons and priests.

2 *Priests*

2 Corinthians 5.14–19. St Paul appeals to his readers to follow the example of Jesus Christ and exercise a ministry of reconciliation.

3 *Bishops*

2 Corinthians 4.1–10. St Paul reveals the problem of being a faithful apostle: nevertheless 'we proclaim Christ Jesus as Lord, and ourselves as your servants, for Jesus' sake.'

The Gospel
(section 8)

1 *Deacons*

Mark 10.35–45. This reading was taken from the Anglican–Methodist Ordinal. Our Lord's statement to his disciples on the importance of service.

There has been a long tradition for one of the deacons to read the Gospel in the West. The tradition was maintained in 1662. To have retained the custom in ASB would have involved a considerable restructuring of one service: and this was considered unwise. A uniformity of structure was also retained in CSI, the Anglican–Methodist Ordinal, and in the new Roman Pontifical. In fact, the Gospel can still be read by a deacon, although he would now have to be chosen from candidates for the priesthood.

2 *Priests*

John 20.19–23. A well-known passage which was used in 1662 as one of the Gospels at the Consecration of Bishops. Jesus gives his disciples the power to forgive and retain sins. This is also used at the combined service for deacons and priests.

3 Bishops

John 21.15–17. Another passage used in 1662 as one of the Gospels at the Consecration of Bishops. It was also appointed in the Anglican–Methodist Ordinal. Jesus' charge to Peter to feed his sheep.

The Sermon
(section 9)

In 1550 the rites for Deacons and Priests began with a sermon or homily 'declaring the duty and office of such as come to be admitted Deacons/Priests; how necessary that Order is in the Church of Christ, and also how the people ought to esteem them in their office.' Here Cranmer was following Bucer, and the practice was continued in 1552 and 1662. The medieval Pontificals had normally connected the sermon with declarations of canonical impediments, moral prohibitions, and the dangers of simony. In ASB, however, the sermon is no longer restricted to the earlier necessities, particularly in view of the change in the patterns of vetting and training ordinands, and of the fact that the Declarations contain sufficient on these matters.

The Creed
(section 10)

While this follows the normal pattern of Holy Communion Rites A and B, the recitation of the Creed is optional. For Commentary, see pp. 197–9.

The Presentation
(sections 11–12)

In the West the archdeacon has traditionally had a close association with ordinands. As early as the ninth century he was required by canon law to examine them: while in *Ordo Romanus VIII* he was involved in the vesting of deacons prior to their ordination to the priesthood. In Sarum as well as in 1550 and successive Ordinals it was customary for the archdeacon to present candidates, although 1550/1662 made provision for a deputy or substitute. A similar provision is made in ASB. A new element, which first appeared in the Anglican–Methodist Ordinal, is for the archdeacon to indicate publicly the candidate's name and the place in which he was appointed to serve: he is called to serve 'in the Church of God', but he is also called to a particular assignment within that Church. The archdeacon is no longer asked whether he has examined the candidates and found them worthy of ordination. In present circumstances this has already been done. The bishop therefore informs the congregation of this fact and asks of them two things: their assent to the ordination and their promise to uphold the newly ordained in their ministry. The congregation is closely involved in what is being done. Unlike Sarum and 1550/1662, ASB makes no provision for objections to be raised against any of the candidates: under present procedures this is no longer considered necessary.

In the combined service for deacons and priests (sections 11–12, 14–15) candidates for the diaconate are presented first and a charge is then read to them by the bishop before the candidates for the priesthood are presented. This avoids unnecessary and too frequent movement from one order to the other. Care should be taken that all the candidates are visible to the congregation throughout.

The presentation of bishops is similar in structure to that of deacons and priests, but it is made by two fellow-bishops and is followed immediately by the reading of the Royal Mandate for the ordination by the Provincial Registrar, a declaration of assent by the bishop-elect to the historic formularies of the Church of England, and a promise to use only authorized forms of service. This has replaced the Sarum 1550/1662 Oath of Obedience to the Archbishop.

The Declaration: The Address
(section 13)

The bishop addresses the congregation setting out the office and work of each order.

Deacons

In 1662 this address came in the course of the questions; but it is more logical to state the facts before the questions related to them are asked. It is similar in content to the 1550/1662 address, and also to that in the Anglican–Methodist Ordinal: indeed many of the phrases are lifted directly out of the latter. (This in its turn borrowed heavily from CSI.) The office and work of a deacon is essentially pastoral, and its keynote is service: he is 'called to serve the Church of God' and to assist the priest 'under whom he serves'. His duties are a little less restricted than they were in 1662. There he could only baptize in the absence of the priest and preach 'if he be admitted thereto by the Bishop'. In ASB he may baptize 'when required to do so', while his only restriction in preaching is that it must be done 'in the place to which he is licensed'.

Priests

The address in 1550/1662 was essentially a translation from Bucer's *De ordinatione legitima*. An abbreviated and slightly simplified version of this appeared in the Anglican–Methodist Ordinal, and ASB has again borrowed heavily from the latter. Once again the keynote is that of service and the priest's pastoral duties are seen in the context of the Good Shepherd. The general tone is rather less sombre than that of the original; and a new note is struck in the recognition that a priest needs the active co-operation of his congregation in a task of evangelism which is not limited to the parish: he is to be seen 'joining with them in a common witness to the world'.

Bishops

In 1550/1662 there was no address on the duties of a bishop. ASB has again drawn heavily on the charge in the Anglican–Methodist Ordinal, but the two introductory sentences are new. The first emphasizes the bishop's role as leader not only in serving and caring for the people of God, but also in working with them in the oversight of the Church—another recognition of the active role of laity as well as clergy. The second emphasizes his role as a guardian of the faith, unity and discipline of the Church—a responsibility which he shares with his fellow-bishops. It is therefore a collegiate responsibility. But in addition to all this he has pastoral responsibilities to clergy as well as to laity, and wide evangelistic responsibilities, being required to promote the mission of the Church 'throughout the world'.

The Declaration: the Questions
(section 14)

Before the Reformation only bishops were normally examined

during the service: although there were precedents for the public examination of deacons and priests in some medieval pontificals. Cranmer, however, followed Bucer in applying the examination to all three orders. Strictly speaking it is not an 'examination'. The candidates are in fact making a public declaration of their belief in their vocation and of their acceptance of its duties. In 1550 the ordination of priests took eight of its nine questions from Bucer's *De ordinatione legitima*. Four of these together with three others (one of which was based on the Sarum admonition to deacons) formed the examination of deacons; while the examination of bishops was a combination of material from the Sarum examination and Bucer. The examination of bishops and priests concluded with the same prayer taken from Bucer; in the case of deacons there was no concluding prayer.

In ASB deacons and priests answer precisely the same questions. At combined services, therefore, all candidates can answer together. There are eight questions, most of which come from 1550/1662 via the Anglican–Methodist Ordinal:

1   An acceptance of God's calling.
2   An acceptance of Scripture, leaving room for a variety of attitudes on verbal inspiration.
3   An acceptance of the traditional doctrine of the Church of England.
4   An undertaking to be obedient to those in authority.
5   An undertaking to engage in prayer and study, not only as a means of self-improvement, but as a defence in controversy. This final point was a new addition in ASB.
6   An undertaking to fashion one's own life and that of one's household according to the way of Christ. In 1550/1662 this question used the word 'families'; in ASB the word 'household' has been substituted to avoid infringing contemporary susceptibilities. Wives and children today are no longer content to be moulded by the male of the family into a set pattern.
7   An undertaking to be truly ecumenical—a new commitment in ASB.
8   An undertaking to be an evangelist.

The questions to bishops are substantially the same, with two variations. Instead of 'respecting' authority, bishops are asked to 'exercise' it; and the final question on witness and evangelism is differently phrased, with a requirement that bishops are to 'lead' their people in evangelism.

The question in all three services ends with a modernized version of the 1550/1662 prayer, that the candidates may receive God's help to be faithful to the declarations they have just made. At this stage 1662 indicated that in the case of bishops-elect they should now 'put on the rest of the Episcopal habit': but no such instruction was given to deacons and priests—they were all required at the outset to be 'decently habited'. ASB has included a note (Note 7, p. 338) that 'where it is agreed that those to be ordained are to be clothed in their customary vesture, it is appropriate that this should take place after the Declaration'. Certainly it is the custom for bishops-elect to vest in scarf and chimere at this point; it also allows deacons and priests to vest in dalmatics and chasubles respectively, provided the bishop is willing.

The Prayers
(sections 15–17)

In ASB the Prayers preceding Ordination have three elements: Silent Prayer, *Veni Creator*, and the Litany. The rubric enjoining prayer places particular emphasis on 'The Prayers of the People' by printing them in capital letters. This is the ancient element of 'Public Prayer' referred to in the Preface to the 1662 Ordinal, which with the Imposition of Hands was thought to constitute the form and the matter of ordination.

Silent Prayer (section 15)

In the *Apostolic Tradition* of Hippolytus—the earliest extant description of the ordination of a bishop—a period of silence was kept prior to the ordination prayer. During this silence hands were laid on the candidate and all prayed that he might receive the gift of the Holy Spirit. The medieval Pontificals continued this practice of silent prayer with an imposition of hands for all three orders; while Bucer prescribed silent prayer before ordination, although with no imposition of hands (Whitaker, *Martin Bucer*, p. 181). Cranmer followed Bucer by including a rubric enjoining silent prayer before the *Veni Creator* in 1550, but confined it simply to the ordination of priests—a rather unusual restriction. This solitary demand for silent prayer—the only one of its kind in the Prayer Book—remained in both 1552 and 1662. The Anglican–Methodist Ordinal included it in all three orders, and ASB has done the same.

Veni Creator (section 16)

The hymn *Veni Creator* has been attributed—though not with absolute certainty—to Rabanus Maurus (*c.* 776–856), Abbot of Fulda and Archbishop of Mainz. In medieval breviaries it was used as the Office Hymn for Terce at Pentecost; and it was also used in the Missal as part of the priest's preparation for Mass. It had found its way into ordination rites by the eleventh century, being found first in the Pontifical of Soissons. In Sarum it was used for bishops and priests, but not for deacons. Bucer used a similar hymn at ordinations—*Veni Sancte Spiritus*—after the sermon and before the examination. In 1550 Cranmer put *Veni Creator* in the Bucerian position before the examination in the ordination of priests, but after the examination and before the ordination prayer in the consecration of bishops. Like Sarum, he omitted it in the case of deacons. 1662 made the situation more uniform by putting it before the ordination prayer in both rites.

Cranmer's attempt at translation was singularly unsuccessful and in 1662 it was replaced by John Cosin's translation from his *Collection of Private Devotions*, together with a rather lengthy alternative which was a revision of the translation in *Archbishop Parker's Psalter*. In the course of time the latter tended to disappear and Cosin's version became the Anglican norm. Other versions of the hymn are, of course, well known. The old Methodist Ordinal used a version by Dryden, while the Anglican–Methodist Ordinal provided the Bridges version from the *Yattendon Hymnal* as an alternative to Cosin. ASB provides the Cosin version only and places it between the silent prayer and the Litany in the rites for bishops and priests.

The Litany (section 17)

The inclusion of the Litany in ordination rites is of long standing and evidence for it exists in the Gregorian Sacramentary. In 1550 Cranmer followed Sarum in placing the Litany after the presentation in the rites for priests and deacons, while in the rite for bishops it came before the examination. These positions were retained in 1662. The Anglican–Methodist Ordinal omitted the Litany, but it was restored in ASB, coming as the final piece of 'public prayer' immediately before the imposition of hands in all three rites. Unlike Cranmer, who used the entire Litany, including the Supplication in time of War, ASB employs an abbreviated version, only those sections being included which are relevant to the occasion. It therefore contains Part 1 (the Invocations), Part 2 (four of the five Deprecations only), Part 3 (the Intercessions for the Church, together with a special petition for those who are to be ordained), and Part 6 (the Conclusion). The Conclusion takes the place of the act of penitence in the Eucharist, and the final prayer, which must be said by the archbishop or bishop, asks not only that the prayers may be heard, but that sins may be forgiven.

The Ordination
(sections 18–19)

The CSI Ordinal marked a return to more primitive custom. In the case of all three orders, the imposition of hands took place during a long prayer, the central petition of which asked for the gift of the Holy Spirit. This central petition was then repeated over each candidate while hands were laid on him. Clearly this was a petition, addressed to God, and not a formula addressed to the candidate, which it was in 1662. The weakness of 1662 was that the formula drew attention away from the prayer. CSI had rectified this and at the same time produced three fine prayers, which drew from Professor Ratcliff the remark that they would 'bear favourable comparison with any of their historic equivalents' (*Theology*, January 1960, vol. lxiii, no. 475, pp. 12–13). It was not surprising, therefore, that the Anglican–Methodist Ordinal not only followed the CSI procedure, but also borrowed heavily in the prayers for all three orders. In its turn ASB has followed the Anglican–Methodist Ordinal for both procedure and texts.

The rubric in ASB (section 18) directs the candidates to kneel before the bishop. In the case of a combined service for priests and deacons, the deacons are ordained first. Since only the bishop is involved in the laying on of hands in the case of deacons, it is possible for deacons to kneel in a row, and the bishop to pass from one candidate to another. In the case of priests and bishops, however, they must kneel singly before the ordaining bishop in order to allow other priests and bishops to gather round and assist in the laying on of hands for their respective orders. But in all cases the ordaining bishop should 'stretch out his hands' towards those to be ordained.

The prayers for all three orders have a similar structure, consisting of (1) Address, Praise and Thanksgiving, (2) Petition for the Holy Spirit, (3) Prayer for Grace necessary to the particular Order.

1 Address, Praise and Thanksgiving

Although the prayers do not begin in the same way as a Western eucharistic preface with the Sursum corda (and there is no historical or liturgical reason why they should), their opening paragraphs are in terms of praise and thanksgiving: 'We praise and glorify you ... and now we give you thanks'. In the case of deacons, it is for the gift of Jesus Christ, who took upon himself the form of a servant. In the case of priests and bishops (which are identical), it is for the royal priesthood of God's people, with Jesus as their great high priest, pouring out his gifts of ministry for the building up of his Body, the Church.

2 Petition for the Holy Spirit

The same petition for 'sending down the Holy Spirit' is said separately over each candidate as hands are laid on. Medieval Pontificals and even Cranmer had used such phrases as 'Receive/ Take the Holy Spirit', which are open to the criticism that the ordaining bishop himself has the Holy Spirit to impart. Asking God to send the Holy Spirit helps to avoid this difficulty, and the position is made even clearer by the phrase in the preceding paragraph of the prayer which speaks of 'your servants, whom we ordain in your name'. The petitions end with a reference to the particular ministry to which the candidate is being ordained—to the office and work of a deacon, or a priest, or a bishop. This leads naturally into the final paragraph of the prayer.

3 Prayer for Grace necessary to the Order

The final petition is for God to give the candidates what is needful for their particular ministries. In the case of deacons, service and teaching are the keynotes; in the case of priests, offering spiritual sacrifices, pronouncing absolution, and proclaiming the gospel; in the case of bishops, ruling and leading, guarding the faith, and being an ambassador for Christ.

The Giving of the Bible
(section 20)

By the late Middle Ages various ceremonies had been attached to ordination. The deacon was given a stole—in some places a dalmatic—together with a book of the Gospels; the priest had a stole put over his shoulders and was given a chasuble, together with a paten and a chalice; and the bishop was given a staff, a ring, and a mitre. Indeed for many people the 'handing of the instruments' was the matter of the sacrament of ordination. Cranmer considerably modified these ceremonies in 1550. The deacon was still given his New Testament, the priest was given his Bible in one hand and 'the Chalice or Cup with the bread' in the other; and the bishop had a Bible laid upon his neck and was given a pastoral staff. But the ceremonies of vesting and anointing disappeared, being replaced by solemn prayers for each order, which were to be said immediately before the close of the Eucharist. Then in 1552 the priest lost his chalice and paten, and the bishop lost his pastoral staff, although in his case the words used with the staff were retained and combined with the words used with the Bible. 1662 retained the 1552 procedure. A relic of the traditional vesting has returned in recent years, however. It is now customary for deacons to be vested after ordination with a stole over the left shoulder and tied under the right arm, and priests after ordination to be vested with a stole over both shoulders.

In the CSI Ordinal all three orders were given a Bible and in addition the bishop was given a staff. The Anglican–Methodist Ordinal simply gave a Bible to all three orders. ASB in accordance with Prayer Book tradition, gives a New Testament to deacons and a Bible to priests and bishops. In the case of deacons it is given 'as a sign of the authority given you this day to speak God's word to his people.' In the case of priests it is given 'as a sign of the authority which God has given you this day to preach the gospel of Christ and to minister his Holy Sacraments.' Both of these are very much in line with 1662. 1662 has also been followed in the case of bishops, where there is no mention of authority: rather 'the words of eternal life' are given as a guide in the work of pastor and evangelist. Note 8 (p. 338) permits a bishop to receive a pastoral staff, and a priest a chalice and paten after the delivery of the Bible. No form of words is provided; but the existing words at the delivery of the Bible significantly are appropriate in both cases to the delivery of these symbols of office.

The Communion
(sections 21–2)

The Communion Service resumes at the Peace. A proper preface, a post-communion sentence and a proper blessing are provided.

There are also proper post-communion collects for each order: these are relics of the final solemn prayers for each order which replaced the medieval second imposition of hands and blessing. The ASB prayers are new translations of the prayers in the new Roman Pontifical. Note 4 (p. 338) also provides for the various new ministers to take an active part in the Eucharist. Precisely what they may do is not indicated: the note merely says that they may 'exercise their new ministry in the course of the service' at the invitation of the presiding bishop. It is therefore for the presiding minister to decide what they shall do.

16

The Liturgical Psalter

A

HISTORY

The canonical psalms were composed over a period of about eight hundred years, the oldest ones probably dating from around 1000 BC, and the whole collection being completed by 200 BC. Most of them cannot be dated with any precision and might have been written at almost any time between these dates. King David was traditionally attributed with the authorship of many of them, but the majority of scholars today would seriously question the reliability of this tradition. Many psalms appear to have been intended for liturgical use in the Temple cult, often for special occasions such as the coronation of a king (Ps. 2), a royal marriage (Ps. 45), or a pilgrimage to Jerusalem (Ps. 122), though others may have been written as individual prayers. Eventually some psalms came to be used in synagogue worship, but at what date is uncertain.

The Book of Psalms was very highly valued by the first Christians: they saw it as *the* prophetic book *par excellence* of the Old Testament, believing it to have been written by David under the influence of the Holy Spirit (see, for example, Mark 12.36) and to have been referring to the Messiah who was to come. They therefore interpreted the psalms christologically, and understood them as speaking about Christ, or as addressed to Christ, or as the words of Christ himself. They seem to have used them in the ministry of the word (see, for example, Luke 24.44; *Didascalia* 5.19.1) and at their communal meals (Clement, *Strom.* 7.7; Tertullian, *Apol.* 39; Cyprian, *Ep.* 1.16; *Apostolic Tradition* 25), and also to have incorporated them into their prayer-forms (Acts 4.25–6). Psalmody later came to have a major place in the Daily Office, and to be used at various points in the Eucharist and in other services.

Since the main language of the developing Church as it spread westwards was Greek, many early Christians used the Greek translation of the psalms known as the Septuagint, which had been made by the Jews about 200 BC. Later in the West Latin translations began to appear. Of these only two were widely used for liturgical purposes. The older of the two is known as the Roman Psalter, and may have been the work of the fourth-century scholar Jerome, though some modern scholars would dispute this. The other, known as the Gallican Psalter because it achieved a wide currency in Gaul, is certainly his work. Although he later made a new and more accurate translation directly from the original Hebrew instead of from the Greek, this never won popularity, and churches went on using one of the other two versions with which they had already become familiar. Thus the text of the psalms used in England in the Middle Ages was a descendant of the Gallican Psalter. Anglo-Saxon and English translations of this were made, though for the purpose of private prayer rather than for liturgical use.

At the time of the Reformation, however, vernacular versions of the psalms began to be used in worship throughout Europe. Generally metrical in form, they constituted the means by which the laity might be given an active and vocal part in the liturgy. Thus Luther himself wrote metrical renderings of the psalms and set them to music, often using popular folk-song tunes. Metrical psalms and hymns also appeared in the services of the Reformed tradition, the number gradually increasing as more were translated in this way until in some places, as for example Scotland, the whole Psalter was rendered into metre. The Marian exiles returning home in Queen Elizabeth's reign introduced metrical psalms into England, where they were widely used, and some have remained as firm favourites in Anglican hymnbooks down to the present day (e.g. 'All people that on earth do dwell').

Prior to this in England translations of the psalms had already been made as part of English versions of the Bible. The first of these to be given authority was the Great Bible of 1539, translated by Miles Coverdale. The Psalter in this was a revision of Coverdale's earlier translation of 1535. Coverdale was not a Hebraist and so made his translation from the Latin and from other Reformation versions. The 1540 edition of the Great Bible contained a few small corrections to the Psalter, and it was this version which was used with the first Prayer Book of 1549 and bound up with the 1662 revision. Thus, although much loved by subsequent generations of Anglicans for its beauty, the

Prayer Book Psalter is in effect an English translation of a Latin translation of a Greek translation of the original Hebrew, and consequently not the most accurate rendering of the Psalms.

By the end of the nineteenth century, therefore, there was some feeling that the time had come for a new translation to be made, and in 1913 official action was taken: a committee of Convocation was appointed to revise those passages of the psalter 'in which the language is specially obscure or misleading', and it produced a report in 1916 which suggested a very small number of changes. It was widely criticized for being insufficiently thorough, and the only result of its work which found its way into the proposed 1927/8 Prayer Book was the permission to omit certain psalms or portions of psalms which were enclosed within brackets, most of these being passages suggested for omission by the committee as unedifying. Subsequently there were a number of unofficial attempts at revising the Psalter, but the next official move was not made until 1958 when a commission was appointed to 'remove obscurities and various errors of translation' in the text of the Psalter, whilst retaining 'the general character in style and rhythm of Coverdale's version'. The final report of this commission appeared in 1963, and was authorized for permissive use as *The Revised Psalter*.

In 1970 the Liturgical Commission invited one of its members, David Frost, to begin work on a liturgical Psalter suitable for use in the services in modern English then in the process of preparation by the Commission. At first it was hoped that it could be done merely by a modest revision of Coverdale's version. However, as work proceeded, it became clear that a fresh translation from the original Hebrew was really necessary, since modern study of the Hebrew language and of the textual problems of the Old Testament had made possible the recovery of the meaning of many words and phrases previously regarded as totally obscure. A translation of a sample selection of psalms was made by David Frost and Andrew Macintosh and published in 1973 under the title, *Twenty-Five Psalms from a Modern Liturgical Psalter*. Meanwhile, in 1972, a panel of eight Hebrew and biblical scholars had been convened to co-operate with Dr Frost in the work of translation, and the whole project was completed in 1977 and published as *The Psalms: a new translation for worship*.

Although the aim of the panel was to produce a new rendering of the original, they did not seek novelty for its own sake, and felt free to incorporate many phrases from earlier translations. They similarly retained as far as possible the images and idioms of the Hebrew, and did not avoid slight archaisms appropriate to poetry. On the other hand, because they were producing a version primarily intended for public recitation and singing, they did not feel themselves bound at every point to the strict letter of the Hebrew text, though translating the meaning of the whole as far as they were able. On occasion, to give singers sufficient syllables to sing, they added one or two words to a half-verse, but always as justifiable expansions of the meaning of the original. Where a Hebrew phrase would have been obscure if translated baldly, they sometimes added an explanatory word, or offered a paraphrase or a double translation to convey the full meaning. Where the translation seemed to require it, verses were renumbered and redivided, though the parallelism of Hebrew poetry was preserved, as were most of the divisions into half-lines indicated by Jewish tradition. As in the 1928 Psalter, some verses were bracketed in order to allow them to be omitted by those who thought them unsuitable for Christian worship.

The following notes are intended to indicate how improved knowledge of the meaning of Hebrew words and of the history of the text of the Hebrew Bible enabled the sense of some previously obscure passages to be restored in the Liturgical Psalter. They are drawn from a more comprehensive collection of notes on the text of this translation of the Psalter compiled by Andrew Macintosh in 1977.

For more detailed treatment of the Psalms as an Old Testament text, readers are advised to consult such works as H. Gunkel, *The Psalms* (Philadelphia 1967); S. Mowinckel, *The Psalms in Israel's Worship* (Oxford 1962); J. Rogerson and J. McKay, *The Psalms* (3 vols, 1977); A. Weiser, *The Psalms—a commentary* (1962).

B

COMMENTARY

SPECIAL ABBREVIATIONS FOR THIS SECTION

C	Miles Coverdale's version of the Psalms in the Book of Common Prayer.
H	Denotes 'Hebrew' or 'Hebrew text'. For the latter, see *Biblia Hebraica*, ed. R. Kittel, 3rd edn or *Biblia Hebraica Stuttgartensia*, ed. H. Bardtke.
LXX	The Septuagint (Greek) version of the OT.
Symm.	Symmachus A minor Greek version of the OT.
Targum	The Aramaic translation of the OT.
Pesh. or Peshitta	The Syriac translation of the OT.
Jer. or Jerome	The Latin translation of the Psalms made by Jerome from the Hebrew OT (called I.H. *Iuxta Hebraeos*).
Vulg. or Vulgate	The Latin translation of the Greek (LXX) version of the Psalms.
MS(S)	Manuscript(s)
>	Denotes 'whence' or 'becoming'
<	Denotes 'deriving from'

I   GENERAL NOTE ON *nephesh*

The word *nephesh* has a wide range of meanings, though in C it is consistently translated 'soul'.

In places it has a physical sense and denotes 'the throat' or 'neck' (see, e.g., Pss. 69.1; 105.18). Elsewhere it denotes the inner personality or the self and is often rendered in this translation simply by 'I' or 'me' (<'my soul') or 'they', 'them' (<'their soul'). When it is said, e.g., that the wicked 'band together against the *nephesh* of the righteous' (Ps. 94.24), 'life' seems to be an appropriate translation of the term and it has been adopted in such passages.

The translators chose to avoid rendering *nephesh* consistently by 'soul' on the grounds that it is in some places wrong, and also because it might suggest the later theological ideas of the soul (as opposed to the body).

There are a few places, however, where 'soul' has been retained; here it was judged to express the meaning best in English and without the danger of its being misunderstood (e.g. Ps. 55.20).

2 GENERAL NOTE ON *emeth*

The H noun is derived from a root meaning 'reliable, faithful, sure'. Used in connection with persons, it denotes reliability and trustworthiness. C's translation 'truth' was judged misleading, for it suggests philosophical ideas which are not part of the H word.

PSALM 2

VERSE 10 *govern yourselves in fear and trembling*: C's 'rejoice unto him with reverence' (lit. 'rejoice with trembling') is unlikely to be correct. Similarly, C's 'Kiss the Son'. Rabbinic commentators of the tenth and eleventh centuries suggest a tradition that the H word usually translated 'rejoice' could also carry the meaning 'display fear' and that the H word usually translated 'kiss' could also mean 'be properly governed, ordered'. (Cf. RV note at Gen. 41.40.) The evidence of comparative philology now substantiates these meanings which fit the context admirably. The translations 'kiss his feet with trembling' (so e.g. RP, RSV), 'kiss the king' (NEB) are based upon conjectural emendations. The consonants interpreted 'son' (implausible in itself because that word is Aramaic rather than Hebrew) are likely to be a corrupt dittograph.

PSALM 4

VERSE 3 *his wonderful kindness*: The translation is based upon a small correction to H by comparison with Ps. 31.23, cf. NEB. The traditional text appears to mean 'The Lord has separated for himself a pious one' (cf. C and RP) which does not fit the context as well.

PSALM 6

VERSE 7 *eyes*: This is what the text means (cf. RV, RP and NEB); not 'beauty' (C).

PSALM 7

VERSE 8 *take your seat*: A small correction to H (cf. NEB) which otherwise appears to mean 'on high, return' (>C 'lift thyself again' cf. RP).

sit in judgement: A small correction to H which otherwise seems to mean 'The Lord will judge...' RP emends the text in a different (and less satisfactory) way. NEB treats the H phrase as a relative clause, but the translators thought an imperative was more natural in the context. The meaning 'sit' is partly derived from 'sit in judgement' immediately before.

PSALM 8

VERSE 2 *is yet recounted*: The H word is clearly attested with this meaning (cf. Judg. 5.11). The traditional pointing appears to understand the consonants as an imperative, which gives no sense. C's 'thou hast set' is highly dubious. A change of pointing (but not of consonants) gives the passive meaning, cf. NEB; RP emends the consonantal text.

babes and sucklings: this is taken with the 'majesty recounted above the heavens' rather than with the following phrase, which contributes to a separate stanza or verse. (Contrast C, RP and NEB.)

VERSE 6 *god*: The H word means 'gods', 'god' or 'God'. Early Jewish tradition interpreted the word as 'angels' (so C and RP). The meaning of the psalm is that man is the chief creature of God's creation, only a little less than divine.

PSALM 9

VERSE 6 *strongholds*: The H word usually means 'desolations' (C 'destructions'). However, there is evidence in other Semitic languages to suggest that here the word means 'strongholds', cf. NEB and Job 3.14. RP's translation is dubious and there is no evidence in its favour.

VERSE 17 *death*: Lit. 'Sheol', i.e. the abode of the dead. Cf. Greek 'Hades'—not hell in the sense of the place of torment.

PSALM 10

VERSE 3 *He spurns*: So probably, in accordance with Jewish tradition, H's 'He blesses' (>C 'speaketh good of') is understood, cf. RP. 'He blesses' of H is itself likely to be a euphemism which avoids the unseemly words 'curse God' (even when such action is predicated of the wicked), cf. Job 1.5 and 2.5, 9. C's 'speaketh good of the covetous whom God abhorreth' is an ingenious interpretation of H, but it fails to understand the word 'He blesses'. (NEB's translation depends upon an emendation of H.)

PSALM 12

VERSE 6 *crucible . . . gold*: 'crucible' is the likely meaning of the word in question (left untranslated in C). The change of one letter in another word gives the meaning 'gold' rather than 'to the earth' which is obscure if not corrupt, cf. RP and NEB.

PSALM 14

VERSES 5–7 of C's version are not in H. They derive ultimately from other parts of the OT *via* Romans 3.13–18 where they are collected and whence they found their way into the LXX (Greek) version of Psalm 14. It is because this version lay behind the Latin (Vulgate) psalms known to C, that the verses are present in C.

VERSE 7 *turns again the fortunes*: The H phrase is now understood in this way, cf. RP and NEB. The translation 'turn the captivity' (so C) is a later Jewish interpretation of the H phrase which is quite unsuitable in some contexts. (The ancient versions in a number of places in the OT support the meaning given here.)

PSALM 15

VERSE 5 *to his neighbour*: A slight change is made to H on the authority of one of the ancient versions (LXX). As it stands, H appears to mean 'to do evil' which does not make sense. C has given a double translation of the word. 'To his own hindrance' (so also RP and NEB) is a doubtful interpretation of 'to do evil'.

PSALM 16

VERSE 3 *As for those who are held holy*: The text probably refers to holy (gods), i.e. idols (cf. NEB), rather than to holy (people), whence C's 'saints'. RP emends the text.

PSALM 18

The tenses of the psalm have been understood to have a past reference, i.e. to a past deliverance of God for which the psalmist gives thanks.

VERSE 9 *from his nostrils*: The literal meaning of the H word, cf. RP and NEB. Contrast C's 'out in his presence'.

VERSE 46 *aliens humbled themselves before me*: Lit. 'the sons of the foreigner (>C 'strange children') shall be obsequious before me'. The H verb can mean 'to lie' (C 'dissemble') and 'to be obsequious'. The latter meaning is more likely here, cf. RP and NEB.

PSALM 22

VERSE 9 *brought me to lie at peace*: The H word is, on philological grounds, likely to retain here its originally physical meaning 'to make to lie flat' (cf. Jer. 12.5). The word generally has the connotation of security, and that is here conveyed by the words 'at peace'. C's 'my hope' is derived from the LXX and 'when I hanged yet' is probably supplied *ad sensum*.

VERSE 16 *are withered*: A variant MS reading is attested which, on philological grounds, is likely to have the meaning 'be shrunken, shortened'. The reference is therefore probably to diseased rather than to tortured limbs. H, unaltered, has 'like the lion' which in the context gives no sense. C's 'they pierced' is probably derived from the Vulgate (if not from the LXX). There is a Hebrew verb near in form to the word 'like a lion' but it is attested with the meaning 'to dig' and not with the meaning 'to pierce'. NEB's 'they have hacked off' is based upon a comparison with a very dubious Akkadian verb. RP's attempt to preserve the meaning 'pierce' by appeal to the same philological theory that lies behind the NEB is even more dubious. For reasons of metre as well as of sense, the words *my hands and my feet are withered* are transferred to the beginning of this verse. In H they occur after the words 'hem me in' (here verse 17).

VERSE 30 *How can those who sleep in the earth do him homage*: A conjectural restoration of the text gives this meaning, cf. RP and NEB. H, unaltered, seems to mean 'they have eaten and have done homage, all the fat of the earth' which is nonsensical (cf. C).

PSALM 23

VERSE 2 *make me lie down*: Such is the meaning of the H word, cf. RP and NEB. C's 'he shall feed me' is wrong.
still waters: The H expression denotes 'waters of quietness', 'waters of rest', which may be simply descriptive, adjectival. It is not necessary to spell out the metaphorical possibilities. Cf. C's 'waters of comfort' and NEB's 'waters of peace'.

VERSE 3 *refresh*: The H word means 'to restore, refresh'. C's 'convert' is wrong in this context.

VERSE 4 *shadow of death*: The greatly loved translation has been retained here. For this phrase, see further on Psalm 107.10.

PSALM 24

VERSE 4 *idols*: The H word means, lit. 'emptiness, vanity' (cf. C's 'vanity'); but here it is likely specifically to denote 'idols'.
Nor sworn his oath to a lie: <H lit. 'has not sworn with reference to deceit', cf. C's 'nor sworn to deceive his neighbour' and RP 'nor sworn to his neighbour deceitfully' which are somewhat free.

VERSE 6 *of such a kind as this*: The H word is well attested with the meanings 'class of people' as well as 'generation'. It is the former meaning that is appropriate here. RP and NEB on another theory understand the word to mean 'fortune, lot' which is less likely.
God of Jacob: The LXX has 'God of Jacob' and this is probably what is intended by the psalmist. H has simply 'Jacob'.

PSALM 26

VERSE 9 *Do not sweep me away*: Such is the meaning of H. Cf. and contrast C's 'O shut not up', which is impossible.
me: See general note on *nephesh*.

PSALM 27

VERSE 5 *to seek his will in his temple*: Such is the likely meaning of H. C's 'visit his temple' is dubious. The H verb denotes (lit.) 'to inquire'.

PSALM 29

VERSE 1 *sons of heaven*: The H expression means lit. 'sons of God(s)'. C's 'ye mighty' (itself a free paraphrase) and 'rams' (dubious in the context) are a double translation of H. which goes back to the LXX. RP paraphrases 'O ye hosts of heaven'; NEB has simply 'You Gods'.

VERSE 8 *rends the terebinth trees*: The verb was thought to carry this meaning and the noun (repointed) means terebinths. A reference to God's destruction of forest and woodland is here more likely than to his bringing about the premature birth of animals. C has 'maketh the hinds to bring forth young' and continues 'and discovereth the thick bushes' (cf. here *strips bare the forests*). RP and NEB seek by (somewhat dubious) philological considerations to turn 'discovereth the thick bushes' into another reference to premature birth in the animal world. The resulting sense is little short of ludicrous.

PSALM 31

VERSE 5 *you will redeem me*: The translation of the H tenses in the

Psalms is very uncertain. The translators took the view that since this psalm opens with a prayer for deliverance, a future reference for *you will redeem* was more likely than a past reference (so C 'thou hast redeemed me').

VERSE 33 *a city besieged*: H lit., a 'city of siege'. Cf. C's strong city'. RP's (so also NEB) 'time of trouble' is achieved by emending the text, which is unnecessary.

PSALM 32

VERSE 10 *forward course*: Cf. NEB. The H word was understood to have here this meaning on the basis of philological evidence and on the authority of some medieval Jewish commentators. There is no philological evidence to support the translation 'mouth' (so C and RP), which is likely to represent a guess.

PSALM 35

VERSE 12 *I am as one bereaved of his children*: H means (lit.) '(there is) bereavement-of-children for me'. Cf. and contrast C 'to the great discomfort of my soul'. For 'soul' (C) and 'I' in the present translation, see general note on *nephesh*.

PSALM 37

VERSE I *Do not vie with*: Cf. NEB. Such is the meaning of the H words rather than 'fret not thyself because of' (so C and RP).

PSALM 38

VERSE 17 *I am ready to fall*: Cf. RP and NEB. H means (lit.) 'I am ready for stumbling'. C's 'I am set in the plague' is dubious. The word translated 'stumbling' can mean also 'limping' but not 'plague'.

PSALM 39

VERSE 2 *but found no comfort*: The H preposition has a privative sense, 'without achieving any good' (>here found no comfort). C's (so RP) 'I kept silence from good (words)' is less likely. NEB changes the pointing unnecessarily.

PSALM 40

VERSE 2 *pit of roaring waters*: The H word in question means 'roaring' and is used in connection with raging water. RP's 'miry pit' (so NEB) is achieved by emendation. C's 'horrible pit' is dubious as a translation of H. The word 'waters' is here supplied in order to make the meaning clear.

VERSE 8 *my ears you have marked for obedience*: H means (lit.) 'you have bored ears for me', cf. Exodus 21.6 for this institution which signified willingness on the part of a slave to continue in the service of his master.

PSALM 41

VERSE 3 *if illness lays him low, you will overthrow it*: H means (lit.) 'all his lying in his sickness thou wilt overthrow'. The H word corresponding to 'lying' can also mean 'bed'. But C's 'make thou all his bed in his sickness' gives a dubious sense to the verb even if it avoids the comical 'overthrow his bed in his sickness'. NEB emends and RP is dubious.

VERSE 8 *a deadly thing has got hold of him*: H means (lit.) 'a thing of belial (i.e. destruction or the like) has got hold of him', cf. RP (though it should not be assumed that the same etymological view of 'belial' was here adopted). NEB interprets the phrase as a 'spell'. C's 'let the sentence of guiltiness proceed against him' is dubious.

PSALM 42

VERSE 2 *when shall I come and see his face*: This is the likely meaning of the consonantal text. The traditional Jewish pointing attempted to impose a passive meaning upon the word corresponding to 'see' for reverential reasons. Hence C's 'when shall I come to appear (i.e. to be seen) before the presence of God'.

VERSE 8 *from Mizar among the hills of Hermon*: Cf. RP and NEB (lit.) 'and the Hermons (or Hermon) from the hill of Mizar'. C translated the proper noun (Mizar) of the unidentified peak of Hermon, 'and the little hill of Hermon!'.

PSALM 45

VERSE 3 *tread down your foes and triumph*: The H words corresponding to this phrase are transferred from their place (in H) at the beginning of the following verse. The sense *tread down* is achieved by a change of pointing and by omitting the H conjunction 'and'. For the former of these changes there is support in the LXX. *your foes* is supplied in English *ad sensum*. H unaltered seems to mean 'and your honour, prosper' (>C (so RP) 'Good luck have thou with thine honour') for which it is difficult to find a coherent translation. NEB emends the consonants of H substantially and translates 'your limbs resplendent in royal armour'.

VERSE 6 *your throne is the throne of God*: H may imply that the king's throne is like the throne of God (so RP and NEB) or that the king is addressed by the title *Elohim*. This word usually means 'God' but may possibly be used here as an honorific title for the king. The present translation is designed to allow for both main possibilities.

PSALM 47

VERSE 10 *For the mighty ones of the earth are become the servants of God*: H (lit.) means 'For to God (belong) the mighty ones of the earth, he is highly exalted'.
mighty ones: the word is now recognized sometimes to mean 'rulers', 'mighty ones' and sometimes 'shield'; cf. RP and NEB. C's 'for God which is very high exalted, doth defend the earth, as it were with a shield' is, however, very dubious.

PSALM 48

VERSE 3 *where godhead truly dwells*: The H phrase means lit. 'the furthest parts of the North' (>C cf. RP 'on the north-side lieth') which is a reference to the mythical home of the gods in the far north. The poet, equating mount Zion with this place, means that mount Zion is the true home of God (so here *where godhead truly dwells*).

PSALM 49

VERSE 11 *The tomb is their home for ever*: with the authority of three of the ancient versions the order of two consonants is inverted to give this sense, cf. RP and NEB. H unaltered means (lit.) 'In them their houses for ever' whence C's dubious 'they think that their houses shall continue for ever'.

VERSE 14 *They are driven*: The H word means (lit.) 'They have been appointed (to Sheol)'.
death is their shepherd: Cf. RP and NEB. The H word (translated here in accordance with the simile of the verse) 'is their shepherd' is capable of the sense 'to feed' (>C 'death gnaweth upon them'), but this gives here a less likely sense *they slip down easily into the tomb*; cf. RP. The sense is achieved by restoring the text (a) by repointing the verb (>lit. 'they go down'); (b) by combining the consonants of two words in H as received

and by consequent repointing (>lit. 'with ease'); (c) by inverting the order of two consonants of a further word with consequent repointing (>'to the tomb'). The verse is a very difficult one and there are a number of possible solutions. The restoration proposed here is effected with the minimum of textual alteration and gives a reasonable sense in the context.

PSALM 50

VERSE 10 *the cattle upon the mountains*: The H phrase was taken to mean (lit.) 'the cattle upon the cattle-hills'. The second H word translated 'cattle' can also mean 'thousand' hence C's and RP's 'a thousand hills'. NEB understands the word as 'thousand' but refers it to the 'cattle' rather than to the 'hills'. It is unlikely, however, that H would use numerals in this way.

VERSE 13 *a sacrifice of thanksgiving*: The H word can mean 'thanksgiving' or 'sacrifice of thanksgiving'. The latter meaning is intended here. Cf. C's 'to offer unto God thanksgiving'.

PSALM 51

VERSE 4 *in your judging*: The H word means that God does the judging rather than that he is judged, cf. RP and NEB; contrast C's 'when thou art judged'.

PSALM 52

VERSE 4 *and every deceit of the tongue*: The H phrase, lit. 'tongue of deceit', is more likely to be a second object to 'you love' than a vocative, cf. NEB. Contrast C and RP, 'O thou false (RP deceitful) tongue'.

PSALM 55

VERSE 19 *and groan aloud*: A fairly literal rendering of H, cf. RP and NEB. C's 'and that instantly' is impossible.

VERSE 23 *they do not keep their word*: On philological grounds the H phrase is thought to mean (lit.) 'they have no covenant/oath' (>*they do not keep their word*), cf. NEB 'they have no respect for an oath'. The principal noun in the phrase must be distinguished from another well-known word having the meaning 'change' (cf. Arabic *hlf*) by which C's 'they will not turn' is presumably explained.

Psalm 58

VERSE 7 *let them be trodden down*, let them wither like grass: H is emended to give this meaning. The emendation required for RP and NEB's translation is more far-reaching and therefore less attractive. Unaltered H is virtually untranslatable and C's 'when they shoot their arrows let them be rooted out' is highly dubious.

VERSE 8 *miscarriage*: Such, rather than 'snail' (so C) is now thought to be the meaning of the H word, cf. RP and NEB.
that has not seen: The H word is emended by changing one letter. Unaltered it seems to imply a 3 m. pl. subject; cf. C's (unlikely) 'let them not see'.

VERSE 9 *let them be cut down like*: By emendation one word of H is made a verb 'let them be cut down' and the adverb 'like', cf. RP and NEB. C's 'or ever your pots be made hot with thorns' is highly dubious if indeed it is intelligible.
like brambles: This sense is achieved by emending one H word. Unaltered the word seems to mean 'like a living (thing)'; (>C's 'as a thing that is raw').
angrily: H lit. (after emending the initial letter) 'in anger' (unaltered 'like anger').
a man: Supplied in English *ad sensum*.
sweeps aside: The literal meaning of the H verb, cf. RP and NEB. C's 'vex' is dubious. C's treatment of this (very difficult) verse is dubious ('let indignation vex him, as a thing that is raw').

Psalm 59

VERSES 3–5 The order of the phrases in English is not that of H and has been adopted in the interests of clarity.

VERSE 7 *They return*: A literal rendering of the H word. C's 'they go to and fro' is dubious as is RP's (so presumably NEB's) understanding of the philology of the word.

Psalm 60

VERSE 3 *steeped*: There are two H homonyms, the one meaning 'to (cause to) see'; the other 'to (cause to) be saturated with'. The latter verb is intended here, cf. RP and NEB and contrast C's 'thou hast shewed'.
bitter draught: H lit. 'something hard', cf. RP and NEB and contrast C's 'heavy things'.
to make them stagger: A literal rendering of the H expression. C's is wrong.

PSALM 65

VERSE 2 *To you shall all flesh come to confess their sins*: Two words from the following verse in H are taken with this verse and the pointing (but not the consonants) of the H verb is emended to give the literal sense 'to you all flesh shall bring words of sins', cf. RP and NEB. H, as pointed, has 'to you all flesh shall come' [next verse] 'words of sins'. C has 'unto thee shall all flesh come' (verse ends).
against us: A variant reading is adopted (with the support of the LXX) to give this sense. The other reading is 'against me'.

VERSE 10 *you level the ridges between*: A literal rendering of H, cf. RP and NEB. C's 'sendest rain into the little valleys thereof' is dubious.

VERSE 11 *the tracks where you have passed drip with fatness*: A difficult H phrase which seems to mean lit. 'thy tracks drip with fatness', cf. RP's 'thy paths overflow with plenty'. NEB's 'the palm trees drip with sweet juice' is dubious.

VERSE 13 *meadows*: So H, cf. NEB. C's 'folds' is not accurate and RP's 'mountains' is achieved by emendation.
are clothed: A literal rendering of H. C's 'shall be full' is less striking.

PSALM 68

VERSE 4 *through the deserts*: A literal rendering of H. C's 'upon the heavens' (cf. also RP) is dubious. C's 'as it were upon an horse' is not to be found in H.

VERSES 11–13 The next few verses are amongst the most difficult in the Hebrew Bible. An attempt has been made to make sense of H without changing the received text; considerable progress in understanding the verses is achieved by recognizing in them reported speech.

VERSE 13 The words of this verse are taken to be descriptive of the spoil, cf. NEB. C and RP introduce words which are not in H. C 'ye shall be as the wings of a dove'; RP 'Israel is like a dove'.

VERSE 15 *The mountain of Bashan is a mighty mountain*: A fairly literal rendering of H, cf. RP. The H expression 'mountain of God' is here an intensive one and does not mean that the mountain is God's. C's 'as the hill of Basan, so is God's hill' is dubious.

VERSE 17 *thousands upon thousands*: H lit. 'a repetition of thousands'. C's 'thousands of angels' is dubious.
the Lord came from Sinai into his holy place: The division of consonants into

463

words is changed (with consequent restoration of one letter and change to the pointing) and gives this meaning, cf. RP and NEB. H unaltered is unintelligible. C has 'the Lord is among them, as in the holy place of Sinai' which is dubious.

PSALM 72

VERSE 17 *Let its ears grow fat like the grain of Lebanon*: The H verb is emended by the omission of two letters to allow it to be predicated of 'its ears' (<lit. 'its fruit'). H, then, means lit. 'Let its fruit flourish like Lebanon', cf. RP and NEB. C's '[his fruit] shall shake' is dubious.
its sheaves thicken: The H noun is emended to give the sense *its sheaves*, cf. RP and NEB. The verb 'thicken' is supplied in English *ad sensum*. H unaltered has 'from a city' which in the context is hardly capable of translation (>C 'shall be green in the city like grass').

PSALM 73

VERSE 6 *put* on . . . *as a necklace*: A fairly literal translation of H, cf. RP and NEB. C's 'they are so holden with' is dubious.
clothe themselves . . . as in a garment: A fairly literal rendering of H, cf. RP and NEB. C's '[are] overwhelmed with' is dubious.

PSALM 76

VERSE 4 *the eternal hills*: H is emended on the authority of one of the ancient versions (LXX), cf. RP. It is assumed that H's (unaltered) 'prey' (>C 'the robbers') arose because a scribe mistook the H word meaning 'eternal' for a homonym meaning 'prey' and then substituted a more common word for 'prey' to strengthen his interpretation.

VERSE 5 *valiant*: Such is the meaning of the H expression (cf. RP and NEB) rather than C's 'proud'.
were dumbfounded: The H verb is thought, on philological grounds, to have this meaning, cf. NEB. C's 'were robbed' (cf. RP's 'were made spoil') is less likely.

VERSE 10 *you crushed*: The pointing of H (but not the consonants) is emended to give this sense. Unaltered it seems to mean 'the wrath of man shall praise you', cf. C 'the fierceness of man shall turn to thy praise'.

PSALM 77

VERSE 2 *I stretch out my hands*: By comparison with Ps. 143.6, H is emended by the addition of the H word for 'I spread out', cf. RP (though there is no notice of emendation) and NEB *my hands*: the pointing (but not the consonants) of the H word is emended. C's 'my sore ran' is dubious.

VERSE 10   *lost its strength*: H is emended by the omission of two vowel letters (with subsequent change of pointing) to give the literal sense 'become weak, sick', cf. RP and NEB. H unaltered has 'I have pierced'. C appears to confuse H (unaltered) with the verb 'to be weak, sick'.

VERSE 18   *in the whirlwind*: A literal translation of H, cf. RP and NEB. C's 'round about' is a mistranslation.

PSALM 81

VERSE 7   *secret place of my thunder*: A fairly literal rendering of H, cf. RP and NEB. C's 'what time as the storm fell upon thee' is dubious.
cringe before him: Cf. RP and NEB and contrast C's 'been found liars'. See on Ps. 18.46.

PSALM 82

VERSE 1   *council of heaven*: H lit. 'council of God'. The reference is to God's heavenly court. C's 'princes' goes back to an old Jewish interpretation of the phrase, viz. that God is the judge of human rulers.

PSALM 83

VERSE 13   *thistledown*: Such rather than 'wheel' (so C) is the likely meaning of the H word, cf. RP and NEB.

PSALM 84

VERSE 5   *The highways to Zion*: H means lit. 'in their hearts are the highways'. 'To Zion' is added in English *ad sensum*, cf. RP and NEB.

VERSE 6   *dryness*: H (lit.) means 'balsam trees' which grow in very dry land. *Dryness* here seeks to convey the essential meaning of H, cf. RP and NEB. C's 'misery' is dubious.
finds there a spring from which to drink: H means lit. 'they make it a spring' >*find a spring from which to drink*, cf. RP and NEB. C 'use it for a well'.
till the autumn rain shall clothe it with blessings: A fairly literal rendering of H, cf. RP. C understands the word translated 'blessings' as 'pools' which implies a different pointing of H, NEB, too, understands the word as 'pools' but also emends H fairly substantially.

VERSE 10   *stand at the threshold*: A fairly literal rendering of the H word, cf. NEB. C's (cf. RP's) 'door keeper' implies an official function rather than that the psalmist is merely lingering at the threshold of the temple.

VERSE 11   *rampart*: The H word, usually rendered 'sun' (cf. C's 'light'), here means 'a pinnacle, battlement', cf. NEB. RP's 'defence' is somewhat colourless as a translation.

PSALM 88

VERSE 5   *I lie among the dead*: The H word is emended by the omission of one letter (also *sin* for *shin*). By reference to an Arabic cognate the word is then given the meaning 'to lie, be prostrate', cf. NEB. Unaltered H seems to mean 'free', cf. C's 'free among the dead' which makes no sense. RP emends more radically to allow 'I am become like unto the dead' which is not necessary.

PSALM 89

VERSE 6   *sons of heaven*: H has lit. 'sons of gods'. C and RP have 'among the gods'. NEB 'in the courts of heaven'. Cf. on Psalm 29.1.

VERSE 10   *Rahab like a carcase*: A fairly literal rendering of H, cf. NEB (footnote). C's '[Egypt] and destroyed it' is dubious. Rahab, which in places means Egypt (cf. Ps. 87.6) here refers to the primeval chaos-monster, cf. Isa. 51.9.

VERSE 17   *our heads*: H. lit. 'horns'. The image is of a wild animal whose horns are exalted when it is fit and healthy.

VERSE 18   *our king belongs to the Lord*: The H word often translated 'shield' also in places (as here) can mean 'ruler, king'. H means lit. 'to the Lord is our king'. RP and NEB interpret the preposition 'to' as an emphatic particle which, though possible, seemed to the panel less likely in the context. For the psalm goes on to refer to David as (human) king. C has 'the Lord is our defence'!
he that rules over us to: H lit. 'our king'. As king has already been used in this verse, we have adopted a synonymous expression here. For the preposition 'to' see on the phrase above.

PSALM 90

VERSE 5   *cut short*: Two H homonyms are now recognized: the one means 'to flood, sweep away' (>C and RP 'scattered'); the other means 'cause to cease, stop' (>here *cut short*).
dream: The word usually translated 'sleep' (so C) can also mean 'dream',

cf. Jer., RP and NEB.

of the morning: The order of two H words is inverted to give this meaning, cf. RP.

VERSE 9   *sigh*: This is what H means, cf. RP and NEB. C's 'tale that is told' derives from Jerome's *quasi sermonem loquens*, a free paraphrase of the H word which can mean 'mediation' as well as 'sigh'.

PSALM 91

VERSE 2   *He will say*: A change of the pointing (but not of the consonants) gives this sense, cf. RP and NEB. H (as pointed) 'I will say' (so C). The change is supported by two of the ancient versions (LXX and Jer.).

VERSE 3   *curse*: A change of the pointing (but not of the consonants) gives this meaning as opposed to H (as pointed) 'pestilence' (so C). This alternative tradition is an old one (it is present in the LXX) and better fits the context of a psalm which invokes God's protection against curses and spells.

VERSE 16   *fill him*: The H words 'fill' and 'cause to see' (>C 'shew') are sometimes impossible to distinguish. 'Fill' is the more likely here, cf. RP and NEB.

PSALM 92

VERSE 14   *sturdy and laden* with branches: The H words denote the sturdy and luxurious growth of trees rather than healthy and well-fed human beings, cf. RP and NEB and contrast C's 'fat and well-liking'.

PSALM 93

VERSE 4   *Poundings*: The reference is to waves crashing down, cf. English 'breakers'.

VERSE 5   *than the mighty . . . sea*: Cf. RP and NEB. C's 'mighty and rage horribly' is highly dubious as a translation of H.

PSALM 95

VERSE 4   *depths*: such is the likely meaning of the H word (cf. RP) rather than 'corners' (so C) which goes back to the LXX and probably a corrupt H. NEB has 'farthest places'.

peaks: So H, cf. RP. C's 'strength' is very dubious.

VERSE 7 *his people and the sheep of his pasture*: So one H manuscript (supported by Pesh.) cf. Pss. 79.13 and 100.2. The word 'his hand' is probably a corrupt addition to H. RP's and NEB's emendation of H (>'ye shall know his power') is unnecessary and fails to note that the H MS referred to above does not have the word 'his power' (<lit. 'his hand').

VERSE 8 *Meribah and Massah*: are the place-names mentioned in the story of the wanderings of the Israelites in the desert (see Exod. 17.7; Num. 20.13; Deut. 33.8; Deut. 6.16 and 9.22). In English translation it is necessary to decide whether to reproduce the names of the places (which is primary) or to try to bring out the meanings of the place-names (i.e. 'Strife' and 'Testing'). The translators preferred the former alternative.

VERSE 10 *loathed*: Such is the meaning of the H word, cf. RP. C's 'grieved with' is less satisfactory.

PSALM 99

VERSE 4 *The Mighty One is king*: A slight change of pointing (but not of the consonantal text) gives this meaning. C's 'the King's power loveth judgement' reflects accurately H as it stands, but it makes little sense. This translation avoids the rearrangement of the H verse division undertaken by RP and NEB.

PSALM 100

VERSE 2 *we are his*: So many H manuscripts, cf. RP and NEB. This reading reflects an ancient tradition and is preferable to 'not we ourselves' which, although also an old reading, is erroneous and constitutes an absurd statement of the obvious.

PSALM 103

VERSE 5 *being*: It was thought probable on philological grounds that the H word (which has long been a puzzle to scholars) bears some such meaning, and it is supported by the tenth-century Rabbinic authority Saadya. 'Desire' (LXX and Vulgate) and 'mouth' (C and AV) are likely to be guesses for they cannot be supported by the evidence of philology. RP's 'all thy life long' represents a conjectural emendation. NEB's 'prime of life' rests on philological considerations less likely to be correct than those upon which *being* rests.

PSALM 104

VERSE 7 *The deep covered it as with a mantle*: Some doubt attaches to H's 'thou hast covered it' (so C and RP); for why should God be said to cover the earth with water only (v. 8) to uncover it again? Furthermore, there is some variation in the way the word is treated in the ancient versions. A change of two consonants (and consequent repointing) makes the 'deep' the subject of the verb, cf. NEB. The next verse then adverts to God's 'rebuke' of the deep.

PSALM 105

VERSE 18 *neck*: lit. 'throat' (see general note on *nephesh* 'soul'). H means lit. 'his throat came into iron', cf. RP and NEB. C's 'the iron entered into his soul' is impossible because *nephesh* is the subject of the verb.

VERSE 31 *gnats*: Such is the meaning of the H word rather than C's 'lice', cf. RP. NEB has 'maggots'.

PSALM 106

VERSE 21 *Glory of God*: H has 'their glory' which represents a correction to the text made by the scribes in ancient times in order to avoid the unseemly statement that God's glory had been diminished. The original meaning as intended by the psalmist has been restored, cf. RP, NEB.

PSALM 107

VERSE 10 *deadly shadow*: The expression 'shadow of death' (so C) in H is an intensive and is comparable to modern English 'a deadly dull sermon'. But the expression may retain some suggestions of death and this is allowed for in the translation. See also Ps. 23.4.

PSALM 108

VERSE 7 *holy places*: The H abstract noun has this concrete meaning here, cf. RP and NEB. Contrast C's 'holiness'.

PSALM 110

VERSE 3 *Noble are you from the day of your birth*: A change of pointing (but not of the consonants) of three H words gives this sense (lit. 'with you is nobility from the day of your birth'), cf. NEB. RP's solution is similar but less satisfactory. It is scarcely possible to translate H (as pointed), cf. C's dubious 'In the day of thy power shall the people offer free will offerings with an holy worship'.

radiant: a change has been made to the accentuation (but not of the consonants). The resulting noun is assumed to have here the related meanings 'dawn' and 'radiance'. H then means (lit.) 'radiance to you'. >*Radiant are you*. The same meaning is posited by the NEB but it is achieved by inverting the order of two consonants and thereafter on grounds of comparative philology. RP also emends the text but with a less satisfactory meaning. H (unaltered) seems to mean 'from dawn' which, with the preposition 'from', gives little sense; cf. C's 'of the morning'.

VERSE 6 *Glorious in majesty*: A slight change to the consonants of one word and to the pointing of another gives, lit. 'full of majesty' >*glorious in majesty*, cf. NEB. H has lit. 'he will fill the corpses' (>C's and RP's dubious 'he will fill the places with the dead bodies').

wide land: H has a singular noun 'large land'. Cf. and contrast C's 'divers countries'.

PSALM 113

VERSES 5, 6 The H. order of the phrases has been rearranged in English so that the meaning is expressed more clearly.

PSALM 118

VERSE 27 *guide the festal throng*: No change is made to H. It is very doubtful whether the H word, here rendered *festal throng*, could mean 'sacrificial animal' (cf. C's 'sacrifice') and equally doubtful is the idea that such an animal should be tied to the horns of an altar. H was taken to mean (lit.) 'bind the pilgrimage with ropes'. The phrase is recognized to constitute one of the major problems of the Psalter, and a number of possible interpretations have been proposed. (NEB's treatment is similar to the present one, though it adopts a variant reading from a Dead Sea scroll fragment.)

PSALM 119

VERSE 48 *worship you with outstretched hands*: Three words from H are deleted (in C 'thy commandments which I have loved'), for with them the verse is too long; and nowhere else in the psalm are there two words for the law in the same verse. Two consonants are added to the word translated 'unto' in C to allow the translation [*worship*] *you*, cf. RP.

VERSE 61 *the snares ... encompassed me*: H lit. 'the ropes of the wicked surround me', cf. RP. C's 'congregations . . . have robbed me' (cf. NEB) is less likely to be correct.

VERSE 113   *double minded*: Cf. RP and NEB. The H word, which occurs only here in the sense of moral imperfection, denotes what is divided. C's 'that imagine evil things' is dubious.

PSALM 120

VERSE 1   *That he may answer*: a slight change of the pointing (but not of the consonants) gives this preferable sense. H (as pointed) 'and he answered' (so C, RP and NEB). But the rest of the psalm suggests that God's answer has not yet come.
what will he do . . . what more will he do: Cf. RP and NEB. A common H idiom which C has failed to understand.

PSALM 122

VERSE 3   *where pilgrims gather in unity*: Cf. NEB. The word 'pilgrims' is added in English *ad sensum*. H taken to mean (lit.) 'where there is a gathering in unity'. C's 'that is at unity in itself' is dubious, as is RP's 'where houses stand close together' which in any case does not fit verse 4 as well.

PSALM 126

VERSES 1, 5   *turn(ed) again the fortunes*: See note on 14.7.
restored to life: The H word here means lit. 'healthy, strong', cf. Job. 39.4, and Isa. 38.16. RP and NEB. C's 'dream' arises because a homonym in H has this meaning.

PSALM 127

VERSE 3   *honour*: The H word is, on philological grounds, likely to have this meaning here. C's 'sleep' is unlikely in the context and there are very considerable objections to RP's interpretation of the phrase as sexual union ('he blesseth . . . in their beds'); NEB regarded the word as unintelligible, but since then our understanding of the problem has improved.

PSALM 128

VERSE 3   *within your house*: H lit. 'in the sides of your house'. It is the wife who is referred to, not the vine, cf. RP and NEB. C has 'vine: upon the walls of thine house', which is dubious.

PSALM 130

VERSE 6   *more than watchmen*: So lit. H. C's 'before the morning watch' is wrong.

PSALM 132

VERSE 5   *Ja-ar*: A proper name which should not be translated, cf. RP and NEB. Contrast C's 'in the wood'.

PSALM 133

VERSE 3   *like the dew*: (2nd line). The words are supplied in English *ad sensum*. H does not mean that the dew of Hermon falls on Zion.

PSALM 137

VERSE 5   *forget its mastery*: The meaning of the H word is uncertain and the translation is based on the context here and in Psalm 102.4.

PSALM 139

VERSE 2   *you discern*: Such is probably the meaning of the H verb here (cf. NEB) rather than C's (cf. RP's) 'thou art about'.

VERSE 8   *spread out my wings towards the morning*: A more likely interpretation of the H phrase (cf. NEB) than C's (cf. RP's) 'take the wings of the morning'.

VERSE 10   *will enclose me*: A reading from the Dead Sea scrolls is here adopted to give this more likely meaning, cf. NEB. H, unaltered, has 'and the day around me turn to night'. >C's 'then shall my night be turned to day'.

VERSE 12   *knit me together*: A fairly literal rendering of H, cf. NEB and contrast C's 'thou hast covered me'. RP has 'fashioned me'.

VERSE 20   *exalt themselves*: A reading from the Dead Sea scrolls (with support from Symm. and Jerome) is adopted to give this meaning, cf. NEB. H as received is obscure. C (cf. RP) has 'take thy name in vain' which is dubious.

PSALM 141

VERSES 7, 8   These verses are extremely difficult.

VERSE 7   *They shall be cast down by that Mighty One who is their judge*: lit. 'They shall be cast down at the hands of the Rock who is their judge'. C's

'Let their judges be overthrown in stony places' (cf. RP) is dubious.

VERSE 8   *As when a farmer breaks the ground*: One H word is emended on the authority of two of the ancient versions (Symm. and Jerome, cf. LXX and Pesh.) so that the phrase means lit. 'Like a cleaver (sc. ploughman) who breaks up on the land', cf. RP. Unaltered H has two participles. C 'as when one breaketh and heweth wood'. 'Wood' is supplied by C and is not present in H. NEB's solution to the problem is different and involves more substantial changes to the pointing.
their bones: The H word is emended with the authority of one of the ancient versions (LXX), cf. RP and NEB. Unaltered H has 'our bones' (so C).

PSALM 142

VERSE 4   *I look . . . and see*: A variant reading from the Dead Sea scrolls is adopted here.

PSALM 144

VERSE 15   *no miscarriage or untimely birth*: A fairly literal rendering of H, cf. RP and NEB. C's 'no decay; no leading into captivity' is dubious and misleading.

PSALM 145

VERSE 16   *Your bounteous gift*: The H phrase is ambiguous having the literal force 'what pleases'. It could mean 'with what pleases them' (i.e. what they want). NEB 'what they desire' or 'what pleases you' here your *bounteous gift*.

PSALM 147

VERSE 3   *binds up their wounds*: A literal rendering of H, cf. RP and NEB. Contrast C's 'giveth medicine to heal their sickness'.

PSALM 150

VERSE 1   *in his sanctuary*: The H abstract noun (C 'holiness') here denotes (God's) *sanctuary*, cf. RP and NEB.

INDEX OF
READINGS AND PSALMS
IN THE
ALTERNATIVE SERVICE BOOK

The numbers in italic refer to the page in the the Alternative Service Book on which the passage can be found. Excluded from the index are Tables 1 & 2— Psalms and Readings for Morning and Evening Prayer (pp. 983–1048)—and Table 4—A Daily Eucharistic Lectionary (pp. 1071–91).

GENERAL INDEX